Systematic and Engaging
Early Literacy

Systematic and Engaging Early Literacy

Instruction and Intervention

Barbara Culatta
Kendra M. Hall-Kenyon
Sharon Black

PLURAL
PUBLISHING
INC.
SAN DIEGO
OXFORD
MELBOURNE

KH

PLURAL PUBLISHING
INC.

5521 Ruffin Road
San Diego, CA 92123

e-mail: info@pluralpublishing.com
Web site: http://www.pluralpublishing.com

FSC
www.fsc.org
MIX
Paper from
responsible sources
FSC® C011935

Culatta, Barbara author.
   Systematic and engaging early literacy : instruction and intervention /
Barbara Culatta, Kendra Hall-Kenyon and Sharon Black.
      pages cm
   Includes bibliographical references and index.
   ISBN-13: 978-1-59756-345-1 (alk. paper)
   ISBN-10: 1-59756-345-5 (alk. paper)
   1. Language arts (Early childhood) 2. Literacy programs. I. Hall-
Kenyon, Kendra, author. II. Black, Sharon (Sharon J.), author. III. Title.
   LB1139.5.L35C85 2013+
   372.6—dc23
                                    2012032255

10/6/14

Contents

Contributors

Gary Eldon Bingham, PhD
Assistant Professor
Department of Early Childhood Education
Georgia State University
Atlanta, Georgia
Chapter 4 and 10

Sharon Black
Associate Teaching Professor
Dean's Office
McKay School of Education
Brigham Young University
Provo, Utah
Chapters 1, 3, 4, 6, 8, 9, 11

Barbara Culatta, PhD
Professor
Communication Disorders
Brigham Young University
Provo, Utah
Chapters 4, 5, 6, 8, 9, 12, 13, 14

Kendra M. Hall-Kenyon, PhD
Associate Professor
Early Childhood Education
McKay School of Education
Brigham Young University
Provo, Utah
Chapters 5, 6, 7, 8, 9, 12, 14

Byran Korth, PhD
Assistant Professor
Early Childhood Education
McKay School of Education
Brigham Young University
Provo, Utah
Chapter 10

Esther Marshall
Doctoral Student
Educational Inquiry, Measurement, and Evaluation
McKay School of Education
Brigham Young University
Provo, Utah
Chapter 10

Brenda L. Sabey
Professor and Dean
School of Education
Dixie State College
225 South 700 East
St. George, Utah
Chapter 7

Ann C. Sharp
Assistant Professor
School of Education
Utah Valley University
800 West University Parkway
Orem, Utah
Chapter 7

Carol Westby, PhD, CCC-SLP
Adjunct Professor
Brigham Young University
Provo, Utah
Consultant
Bilingual Multicultural Services
Albuquerque, New Mexico
Chapter 2

John Wilkinson
Visiting Professor of Elementary Education, Brigham Young
   University
Instructional Design and Assessment for Elementary Education
   Teacher Candidates
Collaborative Communities of Inquiry
Provo, Utah
Chapter 13

Chapter 1

Laying Foundations: Principles and Practices to Guide Early Literacy Programs

Sharon Black

Introduction

During recent years a barrage of studies, reports, and new national policies have dealt with literacy (Christie, Enz, & Vukelich, 2007), ranging from the accountability-focused No Child Left Behind to the prescriptive common core. In response, various educators and organizations have produced innumerable systems, programs, methods, strategies, textbooks, manuals, software, game kits, book sets, Web sites, and so forth, trying to help children become literate. Success with these resources has varied (Figure 1–1).

However, according to the National Center for Education Statistics (2011) the percentage of fourth graders reading at both basic and proficient levels has gone up only two points between 2002 and 2011 (32% to 34% and 24% to 26%, respectively). The percentage of eighth graders on the basic level was one percentage point lower in 2011 than in 2002 (43% to 42%), and the percentage on the proficient level was the same in 2011 as in 2002 (30%).

Figure 1–1. From experimenting with letters to enjoying a book in the class reading corner, classroom literacy is a complex and multifaceted challenge.

Needs

Perhaps the reason no one has been able to simply solve the literacy problem is that literacy is not a simple process, children are not simple beings, and there is no simple answer. Learning to read is a multidimensional process; each child's literacy behaviors are individualized and varied; and each child needs different forms and levels of support (Council of Chief State School Officers [hereafter referred to as InTASC], 2011; NAEYC, 2009).

Programs

A program may be skillfully systematized and efficiently executed, but it won't be effective for children who are too bored or distracted to listen. Or it may focus on entertainment and engagement to the extent that it gives inadequate, spotty, or disconnected coverage to skills and concepts that children really need to know. Those who design a program must consider first the characteristics and needs of the children who will participate in it. A program needs to be systematic so that necessary skills and concepts are covered with explicit instruction and presented so that they can be easily understood. But at the same time it must be engaging enough that children will participate and learn.

Children

Not all children learn in exactly the same ways. They have different learning strengths and preferences that make literacy experiences accessible and meaningful to them (Gallas, 1994; InTASC, 2011). Some of them have language difficulties, which may include specific impairments, basic delays, language-poor backgrounds, or a number of other barriers requiring extra scaffolding and support. Others have different learning strengths, and they need to associate literacy knowledge and skills with a wider variety of experiences, from which all children benefit.

Children come to school with different experiences concerning uses of and attitudes toward literacy. Most have developed their own ways of understanding literacy (Au, 2000), as families and communities read and write in different contexts for different purposes. Family traditions may involve singing together, reading or telling stories, or communicating with extended family by letters or email. But literacy is also integral to cultural practices such as festivals, rituals, religious events, and even birthday celebrations (Barratt-Pugh, 2000). Hall and Robinson (2000) used the phrase "firmly grounded in children's and family's own life-worlds" (p. 85). And those life-worlds differ.

All children need to know that their home/community knowledge of literacy connects with school and with their efforts to learn to read (Au, 2000; IRA & NAEYC, 2008). A "mismatch between the literacy culture of the home and that of the school" (McGee & Richgels, 2000, p. 316) can result in a literacy learning gap. A literacy program must be systematic enough that all children are able to understand and process the knowledge and skills, and engaging enough that every child finds in the school community a place where his or her own knowledge and experience are accepted and encouraged.

Dimensions and Perspectives of This Book

This book approaches literacy programming as a multidimensional blend of systemization and motivation. Lessons are purposefully sequenced and structured; pedagogy is research based. Both content and methodology are purposefully chosen. But at the same time instruction must be engaging for the children: attracting and holding their attention; helping them think imaginatively and creatively; engaging them in talk that encourages them to express themselves and reinforces their thinking and their individuality.

This book approaches children as learners with a multiplicity of characteristics, backgrounds, and needs. A wide variety of lesson approaches are described and exemplified, allowing children to participate, learn, and shine according to their individuality. The teacher and the speech-language pathologist (SLP) are considered as co-participants in literacy learning.

Table 1–1. Principles and Practices to Be Developed in This Book

	Purpose	*Application*
Systematic and explicit instruction	Lessons follow a logical developmental sequence; they are explicitly presented so content is easy for children to understand.	Teachers and SLPs plan lessons with a purpose behind what is taught and how it is taught. Children also are able to understand what they will learn, why it is important, and what they are expected to be able to do.
Frequent exposure	Children receive frequent exposure to literacy targets.	Although children learn at different speeds, every child should receive sufficient and varied opportunities to learn.
Meaningful experiences	Teaching is meaningful to children, individually and as a group.	Lessons, activities, and themes are tied to students' interests and personal experiences.
Engaging lessons and activities	Teaching captures and holds children's interest.	Widely varied, creative, age-appropriate, child-centered instruction and materials keep students active and personally involved.
Interactive instructional conversation	Teachers and SLPs plan and structure purposeful "talk" during lessons and activities.	Teachers and SLPs constantly hone relationships, assess needs, individualize instruction, respond to children's contributions, and motivate children as they explore, learn, laugh, create, and play together.

This introductory chapter overviews five principles for classroom practice by which teachers and SLPs can present systematic instruction through meaningful, engaging strategies and activities. These principles are explained in the introductory chapter to provide a context for considering and understanding the more specific techniques and strategies presented in succeeding sections. Table 1–1 previews these principles and shows their relationships. Chapter 2 gives more theoretical background on the principles and applies them to dynamic systems theory. The following chapters, which are organized by components and aspects of literacy instruction, assume these principles as they describe instructional strategies and give specific lesson examples.

Systematic and *engaging* are broad descriptors. Both include a wide variety of instructional techniques and opportunities for teachers and SLPs to be creative as well as sensitive in planning lessons and activities for children.

Systematic Instruction

An effective literacy approach is systematic. Certain knowledge and skills are needed, and they build upon and synthesize with each other. Many authors have commented that most children require *systematic and explicit* instruction in skill areas. This section looks at a basic systematic approach, then examine the frequently related term—*explicit*—which indicates a teaching approach by which systematic instruction can be delivered with the necessary clarity and specificity.

Systematic, Developmentally Appropriate Programming

The National Association for the Education of young children emphasized this need in a joint position statement with the International Reading Association (NAEYC & IRA, 2009).

Children do not become literate automatically; careful planning and instruction are essential. Adults—parents and teachers—must give young children the experiences they need, including exposure to books; rich conversations; experiences in drawing, pretend play, and other symbolic activities; and instruction in recognizing letters and making connections between letters and sounds. At all times, experiences should be challenging yet achievable, creating interest, engagement, and responsiveness. (p. 1; emphasis in original)

Thus curriculum must be carefully considered and purposefully planned; relationships must be easy to grasp; and the sequence must be logical. Though rich variety is stressed, the variety is purposefully selected according to systematic planning.

NAYEC and the IRA collaborated on a document that recommends that teachers use a "continuum of reading and writing development [that] is generally accepted and useful" (IRA & NAEYC, 2008, n.p.). They stressed that children go through such developmental sequences at different rates and according to different patterns. These organizations noted that although code instruction is systematic, teachers must be alert to the interaction and interplay between children's development and their learning, making sure that teaching strategies and activities are developmentally appropriate for the children they teach (as individuals as well as age groups).

The literacy program that shares the name of this book, *Systematic and Engaging Early Literacy*, has a Web site that includes systematic curricula for preschool, kindergarten, and first grade, along with a wide variety of engaging lessons and activities attached to it: http://education.byu.edu/seel.

Explicit Teaching Methodology

Explicit teaching segments are purposefully structured and sequenced by the adults who direct them (Kaderavek, 2011, p. 317). They need not be lengthy (sometimes only 15 minutes), but they are focused and specific. Phonological awareness, vocabulary, oral language, decoding, and letter knowledge are among the skills that are effectively taught through explicit (often direct) instructional practices, systematically sequenced. Basic components are consistent across these lessons, although variety within those components is encouraged.

Explicit Introduction

Students have a stronger sense of purpose if they understand the nature and sequence of the lesson presentation and any activities that will be involved with it. Such an "advance organizer" enables them to process the lesson more efficiently (Eby & Kujawa, 1994). If the children will be reacting to stories, creating products, or acting on objects, these things are introduced as well (Figure 1–2).

After introducing the lesson, the teacher models examples and demonstrates their use. This may be as simple as showing pictures of items that begin with a target letter. Games, songs, brainstorming, or hands-on activities can be involved as well. SLPs can prepare children for these sessions by pre-teaching vocabulary and introducing concepts with examples, thus helping children with language deficits to anticipate (and even practice) ways they can participate in the lesson. Examples of specific lessons are found throughout this book, particularly in Chapters 5 (phonological awareness), 6 (phonics), and 7 (developmental spelling), as explicit teaching must be consistent and prominent with these skill areas.

Figure 1–2. A teacher presents a story to introduce sounds in an explicit lesson.

Purposeful Guided Practice

The modeling is generally followed by guided practice, with tasks that challenge the children but can be achieved with appropriate adult support (McGee & Richgels, 2000; see also NAEYC, 2008), consistent with developmentally appropriate practice. Practice is often provided in smaller groups or at stations so that sequences and activities can be adapted to a variety of children's needs. The core standards of the Interstate Teacher Assessment and Support Consortium (InTASC, 2011) affirm the importance of learning opportunities structured in terms of a variety of student backgrounds and learning styles. Standard 1 is stated as follows:

> The teacher understands how learners grow and develop, recognizing that patterns of learning and development vary individually within and across the cognitive, linguistic, social, emotional, and physical areas, and designs and implements developmentally appropriate and challenging learning experiences. (p. 10)

Stories, games, manipulatives (e.g., letter tiles or blocks), crafts, songs, puppets, dramatic play, and associated movement are just a few of many types of practice activities that may be involved.

During this type of guided practice, the teacher keeps up a continual stream of interactive conversation with the children—confirming and reinforcing, commenting on the children's responses and ideas, carefully pronouncing words that illustrate the target skill or concept. Under the surface of seemingly playful chatter, she asks questions to assess understanding, monitors participation, and provides the repetition and the review that researchers find essential in learning new skills (Gunther, Estes, & Schwab, 2003).

During full group and small group sessions, SLPs monitor the children's responses and provide scaffolding for those whose language skills may not be adequate for full participation. Small group activity sessions can be conducted by a paraprofessional, parent, volunteer, or another classroom helper in order to allow for smaller groups and more variety. SLPs should be careful not to "hover over" students with special needs (Murawski & Dieker, 2008).

Composition of groups should vary (sometimes homogeneous, sometimes mixed) and the same adult shouldn't lead the lowest of the homogeneous groups every time, to avoid children becoming labeled because they are always assigned to the specialist (Murawski & Dieker, 2008). Teachers and other classroom participants may rely on SLPs to show them how to make learning activities accessible for students who have difficulty participating because of language problems (Palincsar, Collins, Marano, & Magnusson, 2000), also recommending extension activities as appropriate (Ehren, 2000).

Frequent Exposure

Children must be exposed to a literacy target (e.g., letter, sound, alliteration, rhyme, word family, or short vowel words) frequently enough that they quickly recognize it; they need to actively practice using it; and they must review it until they achieve automaticity — the "use or lose" concept of memory (Gunter et al., 2003, p. 299). In addition to guided practice in small group sessions and at stations, exposure to literacy targets can be embedded in contexts and routines that occur throughout the day, with variety to keep children interested and involved. In fact, many "non-instructional" classroom contexts (e.g., transitions, cleanup time, beginning and end of day) provide excellent opportunities for additional exposure and practice. In describing the ideal kindergarten classroom, the National Association for the Education of Young Children (NAEYC, 2008) specified, "Children learn . . . the alphabet in the context of their everyday experiences. Exploring the natural world of plants and animals, cooking, taking attendance, and serving snack are all meaningful activities to children" (n.p.).

In many classrooms time is wasted as students arrive, take off and hang up their outerwear, and eventually take their seats, gather on the rug, select a station, or otherwise begin with the first major happening of the day. A little target practice can be slipped in if children are greeted by an interesting or unusual object or an intriguing picture or poster that quickly catches their attention and reminds them of letters or sounds they have been learning. As children have a little more practice with letters and sounds, some teachers provide an opportunity to write a letter or a word on a chart, or they may post an easy-to-read note with a personal message for the students. Such techniques help to get minds off the playground and onto literacy. If *S* is a targeted letter children might transition between classroom locations in "*S*-ways"—skip, slip, slide slither, stomp, strut, sneak, etc. Such a review is quick, but memorable. Snack items can sometimes be chosen to include target sounds (crackers, cookies, carrots, etc., for /*k*/), or snack activities might rhyme (munch, crunch, bunch, lunch).

The nature as well as frequency of exposure must depend on the needs and learning styles of the children. During most activities the children are able to use the literacy target several times and to see, hear, and say it—often to write it as well. SLPs can make important contributions by helping teachers to be aware of the individual and group strengths of children who have difficulty and by guiding their colleagues in arranging opportunities for these students to communicate as part of regular school routines and activities (Giangreco, 2000; see also Bauer, Iyer, Boon, & Fore, 2010). Specific activities for practicing literacy targets throughout the day are highlighted in many parts of this book, particularly in Chapters 3 through 7, which focus on areas of skill development. Chapter 14 demonstrates how repeated practice can fit in with planned lessons and units.

Meaningful Experiences

Instructional experiences should be structured so that each child is able to understand information and master skills. But each child must also be able to find individual meaning in the learning experience, engage personally in the lessons and activities, and have opportunities to interact in meaningful ways with instructors and peers.

Children enjoy a game or activity and temporarily grasp at a skill that helps them succeed at it. However, skills that are not meaningful in terms of their own lives and interests may take little root and lack the strength needed to develop comprehension—the most significant goal of literacy. A strong literacy program for preschool and early elementary grades must place the explicitly taught and frequently reinforced skills in meaningful contexts and teach the students literacy components that will help them make their own meaning from what they read and hear.

Personal Knowledge and Interests

Kindergarten children come to school with a five-year storehouse of knowledge and experiences, which most of them like to recall, examine, and share. When teachers can link lessons to items in that storehouse, students become more attentive and more personally involved. Preexisting knowledge provides associations that make new knowledge easier to remember, retrieve and apply. Merely brainstorming things they have or do in their homes that begin with *P* makes the /*p*/ sound part of their intimate lives as they share experiences with their classmates. In modeling examples, the SLP and teacher need to remember, of course, that /*p*/ is the first sound in *piñata* and *poi* as well as in *princess*.

In order to individualize meaning, teachers must know their students well. Children's writing advocate Donald Graves (1985) recommended drawing three columns on a sheet of paper: the first listing the names of the children in the class; the second noting something that each child is interested in, knows about, or does well; the third adding a check mark when the child's specialty area has been confirmed. Whether the list is compiled on paper or an electronic chart, teachers and SLPs can consider items on such a list in planning lessons/reviews/activities. This information should also be incorporated into student-teacher conversations. If the class includes students with specific language impairment who may have difficulty sustaining attention (Kaderavek, 2011), SLPs will find this information on student interests of particular value. Some children are especially interested in dinosaurs; others are more concerned with playing soccer. Thus Camarata and Nelson (2006), who use conversational techniques in working with students with language difficulties, have recommended that conversations be "tailored to the child's own interests [as well as] language level" (p. 256).

Family and Community Experiences

As Barton (2001) explained, "School learning needs to be located within the broader context of learning in the home and the community" (p. 23). It has been suggested that gaining literacy should be considered as an apprenticeship experience (Resnick, 2001). Thus teachers and SLPs would do well to remember the many ways children can observe and participate daily in literacy experiences with their families: for example, receiving and writing letters, making shopping lists, following instructions, reading menus, receiving notes from parents, siblings, or friends. Some see fewer literacy *activities* in the home, but do experience literacy more subtly through reading street signs, billboards, or product labels (see Barratt-Pugh, 2000). Some have experienced language communication via text messages, iPads, or computers. Extending such common activities brings home to school, endowing school activities with home meaning. Simulations and dramatic play can be meaningful classroom activities: a thank you letter, an invitation to a party, a schedule for the day, a menu for snack, a game of restaurant or store.

Literacy experiences can be incorporated as part of play or become the theme of play (McGee & Richgels, 2000; Neuman & Roskos, 1990). For example, "eating out" might be a brief drive-through for fast food as part of a busy day activity or a well-developed simulation in which students make signs, write up formal menus, write down orders, and write up checks (McGee & Richgels, 2000). Simple props and costumes can bring extra excitement to dramatic portrayal.

To help diverse children recognize themselves as part of the schoolroom literacy community, teachers and SLPs can deliberately embed literacy experiences in topics that children recognize as "culturally relevant" and "culturally affirming" (McGee & Richgels, 2000, p. 136; see also InTASC, 2011, p. 13). For example, they may use stories featuring characters from cultural groups represented in class. Many design games around cultural holidays or festivals or invite parents to come to the classroom to share cultural food or describe customs.

Gradually, students learn to use their new language and reasoning skills, as well as their new knowledge, in a number of different contexts (Verhoeven, 2001). Regardless of nature, method, strategy, or source, *meaning* must be considered in literacy teaching. When children find personal interest and meaning in their literacy experiences, engagement in the instruction occurs as a natural outcome.

Engaging Lessons and Activities

In studying classrooms of young children, Walsh, Sproule, McGiness, & Trew (2011) found that "teachers who created the highest quality learning experiences" seemed to be expert at "breaking down dichotomies between informal and formal learning, and between play and work" (p. 109). They found that such teachers could make almost any topic playful and engaging for their students. Pellegrini and Galda (2000) affirmed, "Play is an important part of children's schooling. It is a vital part of young children's lives and offers many opportunities to make classroom learning fun and relatively easy" (p. 58). In subsequent chapters in this book, playful and engaging lessons are described which range from pretending a trip on a slippery ship to learn words in the *-ip* family (Chapter 14) to performing a zany dance to practice the sound of */f/* (Chapter 11), from comparing a frog's feet to swim fins to better understand an expository text (Chapter 9) to acting out a story about a lost bear to examine narrative structure (Chapter 8). As children enjoy participation, active engagement allows them to associate literacy with success and fun (Morrow, 2001; Neuman, 2006).

Cognitive Benefits

But the benefits of engagement go beyond merely having a good time. In her book *Enthusiastic and Engaged Learners* (2008, p. 15), Marilou Hyson defined *engagement* as the active component of positive learning. She explained that engagement "includes attention, persistence, flexibility, self-regulation" (see also Ponitz, Rimm-Kaufman, Grimm, & Curby, 2009). If children are interested and involved in a lesson or activity, these behavioral factors more easily and naturally emerge. Attention is necessary for understanding and applying a story, responding effectively in a game, or completing a craft activity—and persistence is often involved for effective game/activity participation. Flexibility and creativity are of course vital for teachers and SLPs to produce engaging lessons and activities, and these crucial capacities should be developed in students who actively participate. Young readers who are engaged gain the motivation to read, and they want to do it for both enjoyment and information (Morrow, 2001); thus they are more likely to "reach their full potential as literacy learners" (Marinak & Gambrell, 2008, p. 9). Children who fully engage in literacy lessons are learning behaviors of successful students, which can be developed to serve them well as they progress through school (Ponitz et al., 2009, p. 116).

Real-Life Associations

Children are engaged when they are able "to connect literacy with real people and real lives" (Gallego & Hollingsworth, 2000, p. 8). Guthrie, Wigfield, and colleagues found that hands-on activities were particularly effective in increasing student engagement; their experiment included the addition of hands-on science in reading expository information (Guthrie, Wigfield, Humenick, Perencevich, Taboada, & Barbosa, 2008). (For specific lessons of this nature, see Chapter 9 on teaching expository texts.) From this form of active engagement students learn to think as they are provided with opportunities to build conceptual knowledge and language skills in conjunction with experiences provided, along with opportunities to connect this new learning to what they already know (Neuman, 2006).

The engagement that Guthrie et al. (2008) referred to as "situational interest" can be stimulated by other forms of hands-on or personal participation experiences as well, particularly through involvement in dramatic play, story enactments, and other imaginative activities in which characters and happenings are involved. In this book, the chapters on skill development (3–7) include many ways of using creative characters, activities, and scenarios to engage children imaginatively with remembering and practicing skills. Chapter 8 includes suggestions for enacting stories, and dramatic play is involved in both print knowledge (Chapter 3) and arts integration (Chapter 11) (Figure 1–3).

Particularly as children become personally involved with stories, engagement integrates cognitive with motivational factors (Verhoeven & Snow, 2001), whether they see themselves in *Ella the Elegant Elephant* (D'Amico & D'Amico, (2004) as she is nervous over her first day of school or enjoy dancing like a group of prairie dogs who have a "frenzy" with fuzz picked from a green tennis ball (Stevens & Crummel, 2005; see Chapter 11). Additional

Figure 1–3. Children learn and remember when they are fully engaged and able to find joy in the learning experience.

---

instructional factors found by researchers and observers to increase engagement include opportunities for choices (Davis, 2010; Gutherie et al., 2008), opportunities to collaborate with peers (Davis, 2010; Morrow, 2000, 2001), and access to a variety of activities and materials (NAEYC, 2008).

Perhaps most significant, Verhoeven and Snow (2001) have cautioned that the critical factor of engagement can occur "only if joy is part of the experience" (p. 4). Teachers and SLPs must design lessons and activities that combine learning with joy.

Interactive Instructional Conversation

An engaging classroom is "a dynamic learning environment" in which every participant both teaches and learns, and teachers and SLPs recognize "each child as a unique 'knower'" (Fallon & Allen, 1994, p. 551). To achieve this environment, social support and social context are significant (Verhoeven & Snow, 2002), and the teacher purposefully establishes and maintains these necessities. One of her most important strategies for doing this is the use of "classroom talk," considered by Hodgkinson and Mercer (2008) to be "the most important educational tool for guiding the development of understanding and jointly constructing knowledge" (p. 11).

Environment for Interaction

A purposeful and engaging classroom is not a quiet classroom. As linguists and educators continually affirm, children learn language by being immersed in language. Both conscious and subconscious processes are involved. A focused but playful literacy classroom has a characteristic sound. It is not dominated by a lecturing adult voice or by child voices aimlessly chattering. A careful listener would notice that an adult voice and multiple child voices interchange and blend in what can eventually be recognized as a pattern. The adult voice leads and guides as necessary, sometimes making a brief "presentation" to instruct, then inviting "exploration" in which students are invited to express their reactions, feelings, and ideas (Barnes, 2008).

Sometimes this is referred to as *interactive instruction*. As Barnes (2008) asserted, "Learning is never truly passive" (p. 2). If an experience is to leave a lasting imprint on a student, he or she must be an active participant in that experience and be encouraged and guided to find insights as part of the process (Intrator, 2001, p. 26). Teachers and SLPs work from the assumption that each student has something to say that extends beyond the answers that might exist in the adult's mind (Center for Research on Education, Diversity, and Excellence, 2002). Interactive instruction invites and enhances such insights. The adult elicits students' comments, listens and reacts to their input, and extends (without evaluating) their ideas as appropriate (Figure 1–4).

Invitations for and Responses to Students' Comments

The teacher or SLP elicits students' comments by asking questions, making remarks that invite response, structuring a situation to attract responses (e.g., pictures, hands-on observation), or inviting comments on a text read, among many options. She encourages students to talk so they can "[try] out new ways of thinking and understanding some aspect of the world: to see how far a new idea will take them" (Barnes, 2008, p. 4). Whether the discussion is centered on various uses of print they have noticed in the community, how they can relate to characters in a story, or how they can apply

Figure 1–4. Teacher and children engage in continual interactive conversation.

what they have just read about caring for turtles, the adult tries to use questions or conversation starters for which there is no *one* right answer so that children can explore their own thinking. "How would you feel if . . . ?" and "What would you do if . . . ?" and "Have you ever seen . . . ?" or "Have you ever done (or felt, or wondered) . . . ?" or "How do you think _____ felt?" or "What do you think will happen next?" can be good ways to begin.

Instructional conversation is vital to student interest and engagement, as it allows the SLP or teacher to encourage, recognize, and reinforce the thinking of all students. To encourage participation and keep the exchange reciprocal, the adult must acknowledge and often elaborate students' contributions. Sometimes positive body language is all that is necessary (eye contact, a thoughtful nod). Verbal acknowledgment must be sincere and specific (beyond "good job") and should be delivered in a respectful tone of voice that signals acceptance (Rosenfield, Hardy, Crace, & Wilder, 1990). Some teachers acknowledge and reinforce children's contributions by writing them on the board or on a chart in very simple terms—possibly even a key word, depending on the age and on the reading and language level of the group.

Perhaps the ultimate tribute to a student's comment is for the teacher or SLP to elaborate it or extend it, or to encourage the student to do so. An adult can validate a child's response by incorporating it into an additional question, a strategy sometimes called *uptake* (see Hardman, 2008) (e.g., "I'm glad you say you would want to help. What do you think you might do to help?") Or she might elaborate with more information. When a teacher or SLP focuses the group's attention on a student's contribution, more discussion is likely to follow, and all will gain a better understanding of the subject (Staton,1988). Teachers and SLPs often pass the conversation to give peers a turn (Barton, 1991; Green, Weade, & Graham, 1988). As positive feedback is given, more students contribute to the conversation and thus the thinking becomes more complex (Ketch, 2005). Children learn as they explain things to peers and as they listen to peers' thinking and ideas (Morrow, 2000).

For children who have difficulties with language, the SLP can prime prior knowledge before a discussion and support information retrieval as the exploration continues (Westby, 1997). If a student's use of language during discussion is inaccurate or inadequate, the SLP (or an adequately primed teacher) can recognize the affect and reflect back the student's feeling (Bretherton, Fritz, Zahn-Waxler, & Ridgeway, 1986). ("Jon was scared when he thought he'd seen a ghost. I'd be scared too. Wouldn't you?")

The adult's skillful use of instructional conversation maintains engagement and enables learning. On the surface this conversation seems casual and spontaneous; beneath the surface it is carefully orchestrated. Dialogue during literacy instruction can be used (1) to teach both language and reasoning processes, (2) to involve children in using and practicing a target skill or concept, (3) to assess the skills and needs of the individual children and provide appropriate explanations or scaffolding, and (4) to encourage children to extend and explore their ideas. Instructional conversation often asks; it does not always tell. It listens and affirms; it does not always correct. It respects; it never demeans.

Conclusion

This book works from the position that early childhood and early elementary classrooms should be purposeful, structured, accepting, creative, joyful places. If teachers and SLPs work together as a mutually supportive, collaborative, interactive team (see Hadden & Pianta, 2006), focused on meeting the needs and enhancing the development of all children, such goals can become reality. SLPs can participate in full-class instruction (ASHA, 2001; Justice, McGinty, Guo, , & Moore, 2009) and/or provide small group opportunities (Ritzman et al., 2006) or individual instruction. The coming chapters assume this teacher/SLP/class group/individual child relationship and suggest ways various participation plans and patterns can be used.

As in this chapter, specific suggestions are interspersed in most chapters on various teaching topics. They describe important aspects of early literacy programs, frequently applying to them the principles and practices referred to in this chapter: systematic instruction, frequent exposure to literacy targets, meaningful experiences, engaging lessons and activities, and interactive instructional conversation. The chapters also acknowledge that literacy is a multifaceted area of study and that children have a wide variety of backgrounds and needs (see NAEYC/IRA, 2008). Thus ideas, methodologies, strategies, and even assumptions are based on research and illustrated with multiple classroom applications and incidents.

As mentioned earlier, in the course of discussing and exemplifying principles and methodologies many of the chapters refer to a program with the same title as this book: Systematic and Engaging Early Literacy (SEEL). Book content is not limited to this program, but because the program is based on the same underlying principles (described throughout this chapter) and because studies of the program have validated its effectiveness with many of them, SEEL examples and experiences are mentioned in many places. The SEEL Web site (http://education.byu.edu/seel) includes systematically organized curricula for preschool, kindergarten, and first grade levels. Its database consists of explicit and engaging lessons and motivating activities to support all elements in these curricula.

The chapters in this book are previewed in the chart designated as Table 1–2. The following chapter relates some of the principles from this chapter more specifically to SEEL through the lens of dynamic systems theory. Subsequent chapters go into depth on important aspects of the literacy experience.

Table 1–2. Chapters and Brief Summaries

No.	Title	General Content
2	Dynamic Systems Theory Applied to Language and Literacy Learning	Chapter 2 discusses the development of dynamic systems theory, explains its contributions, and applies it to the Systematic and Engaging Early Literacy (SEEL) project that is compatible with and mentioned frequently throughout this book.
3	Learning What Print Means: Print Awareness in School, Home, and Community	This chapter focuses on teaching print awareness, print concepts, and preliminary print skills. Included are both importance and specific strategies for (1) creating a print-rich environment, (2) teaching meaning and characteristics of print, and (3) using strategies for receptive and expressive experiences.
4	Exploring Squiggles on Paper: Teaching and Practicing Letter Knowledge Skills	Chapter 4 continues the skill sequence by addressing the importance of children acquiring letter names and sounds, along with strategies for helping them do so. After examining the role of letter knowledge in developing literacy, the authors suggest learning methods, ranging from studying letters in names to using letters to symbolize objects, meanings, and events.
5	Recognizing and Manipulating Sounds: Phonological and Phonemic Awareness	The nature and development of phonological and phonemic awareness are discussed, along with related skills that intersect and interact with these factors. Instructional strategies are presented to help children make meaning as well as provide them with systematic and explicit phonological and phonemic awareness instruction.
6	Putting Letters and Sounds Together: Phonics and Decoding Strategies	Phonics is the focus for this chapter, with emphasis on its place as one of many aspects of a literacy program. The nature and advantages of both synthetic and analytic approaches to teaching phonics are mentioned, and advantages and methods for combining them in teaching both reading and writing are described.

Table 1–2. *continued*

No.	Title	General Content
7	Using Sounds and Letters to Form Words: Developmental Spelling	The authors describe the stages of spelling development, important principles that comprise the foundation of spelling instruction, and instructional concepts related to the developmental stages that should be addressed when creating spelling instruction for young children.
8	Bringing Stories to Life: Approaches to Understanding and Enjoying Narratives	This chapter explores the potential of appealing stories to develop and refine a variety of literacy skills as children listen to, discuss, analyze, tell, retell, enact, re-enact, and perform them. The authors explore the nature of the demands story comprehension places on children, including structural analysis and visual representation.
9	Learning About the World: Exploring and Comprehending Expository Texts	This chapter treats the importance and feasibility of using expository texts with preschool through early elementary grade children. Useful strategies for teaching comprehension based on both content and organizational aspects of these texts are included.
10	Working with Parents: Ways to Involve Parents in Early Literacy at Home and at School	The importance of parents' involvement with their children's literacy development is emphasized, with suggestions for ways teachers and SLPs can encourage parents' support. The authors suggest components of a literacy-rich home environment and beneficial book-sharing practices, then discuss parents' participation in the classroom.
11	Enriching Language and Literacy: Integrating Visual Arts, Music, Dance, and Drama	This chapter suggests ways of integrating arts with literacy instruction and experiences. The author examines ways participation in the arts can develop cognitive skills and abilities that are instrumental in literacy development. Suggestions are made to help children make meaning and express themselves in visual arts, music, dance, and drama.

continues

Table 1–2. *continued*

No.	Title	General Content
12	Assessing Students' Needs and Progress: Use of Data to Adjust Instruction	The authors discuss necessary considerations involved with administering early literacy assessments, along with specific procedures for gaining information about children's performance both in developing skills and in making meaning from their literacy experiences.
13	Learning and Improving Together: Collaborative Professional Development	Chapter 13 is concerned with ways teachers, SLPs, and others work in collaborative groups to increase their effectiveness in literacy instruction. The benefits of professional learning systems are discussed, along with specific research-based information on making these systems effective. Suggestions and examples are included for creating positive learning environments, utilizing research-based curriculum and instruction, and implementing specific professional development structures.
14	Applying Systematic and Engaging Practices: Planning Units and Lesson Activities	In this final chapter, the literacy components in the book are brought together to illustrate how a teacher or SLP can plan systematic and engaging units and lessons for classroom implementation. It includes a brief discussion of key considerations in planning instruction for young children, illustrated by a sample unit plan and instructions for specific lesson activities.

References

American Speech-Language-Hearing Association (ASHA). (2001). Knowledge and skills needed by speech-language pathologists with respect to reading and writing in children and adolescents. *ASHA Desk Reference, 3,* 355–386.

Au, K. H. (2000). Literacy instruction for young children of diverse backgrounds. In D.S. Strickland & L.M. Morrow (Eds.), *Beginning reading and writing* (pp. 35–45). New York, NY: Teachers College Press.

Barnes, D. (2008). Exploratory talk for learning. In N. Mercer & S. Hodgkinson (Eds.), *Exploring talk in school* (pp. 1–15). Thousand Oaks, CA: Sage.

Barratt-Pugh, C. (2000). The socio-cultural context of literacy learning. In C. Barratt-Pugh & M. Rohl (Eds.), *Literacy learning in the early years* (pp. 1–26). Buckingham, UK: Open University Press.

Barton, D. (2001). Literacy in everyday contexts. In L. Verhoeven & C. E. Snow (Eds.), *Literacy and motivation: Reading engagement in individuals and groups* (pp. 23–37). Mahwah, NJ: Lawrence Erlbaum Associates.

Bauer, K. L., Iyer, S. N., Boon, R. T., & Fore, C., III. (2010). 20 Ways for classroom teachers to collaborate with speech-language pathologists. *Intervention in School and Clinic, 45*(5), 333–337. doi:10.1177/1053451208328833

Bretherton, I., Fritz, J., Zahn-Waxler, C., & Ridgeway, D. (1986). Learning to talk about emotions: A functionalist perspective. *Child Development, 57*(3), 529–548.

Camarata, S. M., & Nelson, K. E. ((2006). Conversational recast intervention with preschool and older children. In R. J. McCauley & M. E. Fey (Eds.), *Treatment of language disorders in children* (pp. 237–264). Baltimore, MD: Paul H. Brookes.

Center for Research on Education, Diversity & Excellence. (2002). *Teaching through conversation*. Retrieved from http://www.crede.org/standards/5inst_con.shtml

Christie, J. F., Enz, B. J., & Vukelich, C. (2007). *Teaching language and literacy: Preschool through the elementary grades* (3rd ed.). Boston, MA: Pearson.

Council of Chief State School Officers. (2011). *Interstate Teacher Assessment and Support Consortium (InTASC) model core teaching standards: A resource for state dialogue*. Washington, DC: Author. (Referred to in text as InTASC)

Davis, L. (2010). Toward a lifetime of literacy: The effect of student-centered and skills-based reading instruction on the experiences of children. *Literacy Teaching and Learning, 15*(1,2), 53–79.

Eby, J. W., & Kujawa, E. (1994). *Reflective planning, teaching, and evaluation: K–12*. New York, NY: Macmillan.

Ehren, B. J. (2000, July). Maintaining a therapeutic focus and sharing responsibility for student success: Keys to in-classroom speech-language services. *Language, Speech, and Hearing Services in Schools, 31*, 219–229.

Fallon, I., & Allen, J. (1994). Where the deer and the cantaloupe play. *Reading Teacher, 47*(7), 546–551.

Gallas, K. (1994). *The languages of learning*. New York, NY: Teachers College Press.

Gallego, M. A., & Hollingsworth, S. (Eds.). (2000). *What counts as literacy: Challenging the school standard*. New York, NY: Teachers College Press.

Giangreco, M. F. (2000, July). Related services research for students with low-incidence disabilities: Implications for speech-language pathologists in inclusive classrooms. *Language, Speech, and Hearing Services in Schools, 31*, 230–239.

Graves, D. H. (1985). *Writing: Teachers and children at work.* Portsmouth, NH: Heinemann.

Green, J. L., Weade, R., & Graham, K. (1988). Lesson construction and student participation: A sociolinguistic analysis. In J. L. Green & J. P. Harker (Eds.), *Multiple perspective analysis of classroom discourse* (pp. 11–47). Norwood, NJ.: Ablex.

Gunter, M. A., Estes, T. H., & Schwab, J. (2003). *Instruction: A models approach* (4th ed.). New York, NY: Pearson Education.

Guthrie, J., Wigfield, A., Humenick, N., Perencevich, K., Taboada, A., & Barbosa, P. (2006). Influences of stimulating tasks on reading motivation and comprehension. *Journal of Educational Research, 99*(4), 232–245, 256.

Hadden, D. S., & Pianta, R. B. (2006). Clinical consultation with teachers for improved preschool literacy instruction. In L. M. Justice (Series Ed.), *Emergent and early literacy series: Clinical approaches to emergent literacy intervention* (pp. 99–124). San Diego, CA: Plural.

Hall, N., & Robinson, A. (2000). Play and literacy learning. In C. Barratt-Pugh & M. Rohl (Eds.), *Literacy learning in the early years* (pp. 81–104). Buckingham, UK: Open University Press.

Hardman, F. (2008). Teachers' use of feedback in whole-class and group-based talk. In N. Mercer & S. Hodgkinson (Eds.), *Exploring talk in school* (pp. 131–150). Thousand Oaks, CA: Sage.

Hodgkinson, S., & Mercer, N. (2008). *Exploring talk in schools.* Thousand Oaks, CA: Sage.

Hyson, M. (2008). *Enthusiastic and engaged learners: Approaches to learning in the early childhood classroom.* New York, NY: Teachers College Press.

International Reading Association (IRA) & National Association for the Education of Young Children (NAEYC). (2008). Learning to read and write: Developmentally appropriate practices for young children. Retrieved from www.education.com/reference/article/Ref_Learning_Read_Write/

Intrator, S. (2001, August). Teaching the media child in the digital swarm. *Arts Education Policy Review, 102*(6), 25–27.

Justice, L. M., McGinty, M. A., Guo, Y., & Moore, D. (2009). Implementation of responsiveness to intervention in early education settings. *Seminars in Speech and Language, 30*(2), 59–74.

Kaderavek, J. N. (2011). *Language disorders in children: Fundamental concepts of assessment and intervention.* Boston, MA: Allyn & Bacon.

Ketch, A. (2005). Conversation: The comprehension connection. *Reading Teacher, 59*(1), 8–13.

Marinak, B.A., & Gambrell, L.B. (2008). Intrinsic motivation and rewards: What sustains young children's engagement with text? *Literacy Research and Instruction, 47*, 9–26. doi:10.1080/19388070070174946

McGee, L. M., & Richgels, D. J. (2000). *Literacy's beginnings* (3rd ed.). Boston, MA: Allyn & Bacon.

Morrow, L.M. (2000). Organizing and managing a language arts block. In D. S. Strickland & L. M. Morrow (Eds.), *Beginning reading and writing* (pp. 83–98). New York, NY: Teachers College Press.

Morrow, L. M. (2001). *Literacy development in the early years* (4th ed.). Boston, MA: Allyn & Bacon.

Murawski, W. W., & Dieker, L. (2008). 50 ways to keep your co-teacher: Strategies for before, during, and after co-teaching. *Teaching Exceptional Children, 40*(4), 40–48.

National Center for Education Statistics. (2012). *The condition of education*. Retrieved from http://nces.ed.gov/programs/coe/figures/figure-rd 2-2.asp

NAEYC. (2008). Top 10 signs of a good kindergarten classroom. Retrieved from http://www.education.com/reference/article/Ref_Top_10_Signs _Good/

NAEYC & IRA. (2009). Where we stand on learning to read and write. Retrieved from www.naeyc.org/files/ . . . WWSSLearningToReadand WriteEnglish.pdf

Neuman, S. B. (2006). N is for nonsensical. *Educational Leadership, 64*(2), 28–32.

Neuman, S. B., & Roskos, K. (1990). Play, print, and purpose: Enriching play environments for literacy development. *Reading Teacher, 44*(3), 214–221.

Palincsar, A. S., Collins, K. M., Marano, N. L., & Magnusson, S. J. (2000, July). Investigating the engagement and learning of students with earning disabilities in guided inquiry science teaching. *Language, Speech, and Hearing Services in Schools, 31*, 240–251.

Pellegrini, A. D., & Galda, L. (2000). Children's pretend play and literacy. In D. S. Strickland & L. M. Morrow (Eds.), *Beginning reading and writing* (pp. 58–65). New York, NY: Teachers College Press.

Ponitz, C. C., Rimm-Kaufman, S. E., Grimm, K. J., & Curby, T. W. (2009). Kindergarten classroom quality, behavioral engagement, and reading achievement. *School Psychology Review, 38*(1), 102–120.

Resnick, L. B. (2000). Literacy in school and out. In M. A. Gallego & S. Hollingsworth (Eds.), *What counts as literacy: Challenging the school standard* (pp. 27–41). New York, NY: Teachers College Press.

Ritzman, M. J., Sanger, D., & Coufal, K. L. (2006). A case study of a collaborative speech-language pathologist. *Communication Disorders Quarterly, 27*(4), 221–231.

Rosenfeld, L., Hardy, C., Crace, R., & Wilder, L. (1990). Active listening. *Soccer Journal, 4*, 45–49.

Staton, J. (1988) *Dialogue journal communication: Classroom, linguistic, social, and cognitive views.* Norwood, NJ: Ablex.

Verhoeven, L. (2001). Prevention of reading difficulties. In L. Verhoeven & C. E. Snow (Eds.), *Literacy and motivation: Reading engagement in individuals and groups* (pp. 123–134). Mahwah, NJ: Lawrence Erlbaum Associates.

Verhoeven, L., & Snow, C. E. (2001). Literacy and motivation: Bridging cognitive and sociocultural viewpoints. In L. Verhoeven & C. E. Snow (Eds.), *Literacy and motivation: Reading engagement in individuals and groups* (pp. 1–20). Mahwah, NJ: Lawrence Erlbaum Associates.

Walsh, G., Sproule, L., McGuinness, & Trew, K. (2011). Playful structure: A novel image of early years pedagogy for primary school classrooms. *Early Years, 31*(2), 107–119.

Westby, C. E. (1997). There's more to passing than knowing the answers. *Language, Speech, and Hearing Services in Schools, 28*, 274–287.

Children's Books

D'Amico, C., & D'Amico, S. (2004). *Ella the elegant elephant.* New York, NY: Arthur A. Levine Books/Scholastic.

Stevens, J., & Crummel, S. S. (2005). *The great fuzz frenzy.* China: Harcourt.

Chapter 2

Dynamic Systems Theory Applied to Language and Literacy Learning

Carol Westby

*Without play, a child's ability to develop
and function effectively in the world is at best
impaired and at worst as good as impossible.*
(Hubbuck, 2009, p. 127)

Theories of Language/Literacy Learning

In the first chapter Black discusses the underlying principles that are developed throughout this book, on which the project Systematic and Engaging Early Literacy (SEEL)[1] is also based:

---

[1]The Systematic and Engaging Early Literacy (SEEL) project is an initiative developed by Barbara Culatta and Kendra Hall-Kenyon, now implemented in preschool and kindergarten classrooms. It is based on the principles and practices developed throughout this book. Some of the examples in many of the chapters have been adapted from lessons implemented in this program, accessible from the SEEL website at http://education.byu.edu/seel

- ◆ Instruction activities are engaging and playful.
- ◆ Instruction activities are meaningful to the children.
- ◆ Instructional exchanges are reciprocal between teachers and children; they engage in conversations.
- ◆ Skills are taught explicitly.
- ◆ Children have intense exposure to targets.

Why are these principles important if children are to develop fluent reading and comprehension of what they read or listen to? Why is playful practice a primary foundation for the systematic and engaging activities?

During the first decade of the 21st century, federal mandates under the No Child Left Behind Act (NCLB) resulted in changes to the ways reading was taught to school-age children. The *Report of the National Reading Panel* (2002) listed components essential for reading proficiency (phonemic awareness, phonics, fluency, vocabulary, and comprehension). In efforts to meet the literacy goals of NCLB, educators increased the frequency and intensity of teacher-directed activities, focusing particularly on phonological/ phonemic awareness and fluent decoding. In elementary schools the efforts to meet literacy goals of NCLB sometimes resulted in actions like eliminating recess (so there would be more time on task) and in preschools and kindergartens, reducing the size of play areas and replacing playful activities with more structured, teacher-directed activities targeting alphabetic knowledge and phonological awareness (Golinkoff, Hirsh-Pasek, & Singer, 2006; Pellegrini, 2008).

Clearly children need to be fluent decoders if they are to comprehend what they read. If children's decoding is too slow and labored, so much of their working memory is occupied by decoding that they do not have sufficient resources left to comprehend what they read. The assumption of those implementing the phonologically based reading programs appeared to be that if children read fluently, they would have available the resources they needed to comprehend. Researchers, however, acknowledge that reading requires two related but separate capabilities: (1) having a broad knowledge of a language, and (2) understanding the mapping between language and print, which relies on phonological awareness and alphabet knowledge (Hoover & Gough, 1990).

Fluent decoding does not ensure comprehension. Many educational practices in kindergarten through 3rd grade, however, have focused on development of the mapping between language and print almost to the exclusion of attention to comprehension. Although phonological awareness/phonemic awareness skills and alphabet knowledge/print awareness are important for emergent literacy, they are insufficient by themselves for ensuring the development of text comprehension, which is the ultimate goal of literacy. Despite the emphasis placed on skill development in recent years, a study reviewing the effects of Reading First, *Reading First Impact Study: Interim Report* (2008), indicated that "the program did not increase the percentages of students in grades one, two, or three whose reading comprehension scores were at or above grade level" (p. 6). Whitehurst, director of the Institute of Education Sciences, the Education Department's research arm, suggested that it was possible that "in implementing Reading First, there is a greater emphasis on decoding skills and not enough emphasis, or maybe not correctly structured emphasis, on reading comprehension." He further suggested that the program's approach might be effective in helping students learn building-block skills but that it did not take children far enough along to have a significant impact on comprehension (Glod, 2008). Although the reading methods employed in Reading First projects were all to be evidence based, they did not result in better oral language and comprehension—which were the desired ultimate outcomes.

Reading instruction during the first two-thirds of the 20th century involved some combination of phonics and a look-say approach. The 1970s brought an even stronger emphasis on phonics and skills development. In the last 20 years of the 20th century, the whole language approach to literacy instruction spread across the country. The focus of this approach was on making meaning in reading and expressing meaning in writing. Reading and writing were to be done for real purposes. Any phonics instruction that occurred was to be done in the context of reading. Students were encouraged to use four cuing systems to guess what the words were:

◆ Graphophonemic, the shapes of the letters and the sounds that they evoke
◆ Semantic, the word you would expect to occur based on the meaning of the sentence so far

◆ Syntactic, the part of speech or word that would make sense based on the grammar of the language
◆ Pragmatic, the function of the text

The whole language movement was in part a reaction to a trend in much of the 20th century that focused on the mastery of reading and writing skills, leaving little time in the school day for reading for pleasure or writing on topics of one's choice. Little explicit teaching of any language concepts occurred in whole language lessons. Children were to learn by constructing knowledge as they were exposed to interesting texts to read. The assumption was that children would learn to read as they had learned to talk: without direct, explicit teaching of any aspect of language or reading. By the end of the 20th century, serious concerns were being raised about the effectiveness of the whole language approach. The *Report of the National Reading Panel* (2000) put the nail in the coffin of the whole language movement. Review of reading research demonstrated the value of explicit instruction in phonological awareness, phonics, and fluent decoding to reading achievement. The report, however, also documented the need for explicit vocabulary and text comprehension instruction.

A back-to-the-basics movement triggered by critiques of the whole language philosophy and concerns of reading performance of U.S. children and institutionalized by federally funded Reading First programs focused on decoding skills. Although there was nothing in these reforms that mandated the suspension of comprehension instruction, the reforms resulted in a subtle repositioning that emphasized teaching decoding skills and gave little attention to teaching comprehension (Pearson, 2010). Several factors are moving us to a more inclusive approach to the teaching of reading: the work of the Rand Study group (Snow, 2003), which outlined an agenda for work on reading comprehension; the Carnegie Report *Reading Next* (Biancarosa & Snow, 2006), which focused attention on the difficulties of older struggling readers; the limited outcomes of the Reading First programs, which had given attention primarily to teaching decoding; and the need to address multimodal literacies (e.g., reading on the Internet) (Afflerbach & Cho, 2010).

An effective literacy program must address the need for both fluent decoding skills and comprehension in meaningful ways. Both the traditional phonics approach and the whole language approach were primarily philosophical approaches to the teaching of reading. They failed to consider what is known about how children best learn. Systematic and Engaging Early Literacy provides an integrative literacy program that addresses the need to teach both decoding and comprehension and that is based on what is currently known about how children learn.

In a culture where written language is prominent and readily available, basic literacy is a natural extension of an individual's linguistic development (Fillion & Brause, 1987). Of course reading requires some skills unique to the written modality (alphabetic/orthographic knowledge), but written language is not simply oral language in a written form. Written language involves more abstract and/or complex vocabulary, syntactic patterns, and discourse organizations. When we teach reading, we are teaching more than orthographic knowledge; we are teaching language. State educational systems require the use of evidence-based programs and practices (EBP) when teaching reading. EBP should involve the integration of (a) clinical expertise/expert opinion, (b) external scientific evidence, and (c) client/patient/caregiver desire to provide high quality services reflecting the interests, values, needs, and choices of the individuals we serve. Language/literacy instruction should be based on a theory of language learning. Our understanding of how children learn language has changed over the last 60 years. In the last four decades of the 20th century, four major theories of language development were proposed: behaviorist, nativist, interactionist, and emergentist.

- ◆ The *behaviorist theory,* proposed by B. F. Skinner (1957), suggested that children imitate what they see and hear and that children learn through operant conditioning via imitation and reinforcement. This perspective underlies the applied behavior analysis approach (ABA) frequently used to teach skills to children with autism and underlies many approaches to the teaching of discrete phonics skills.
- ◆ The *nativist theory*, proposed by Noam Chomsky (1965), argues that language is a unique human accomplishment. All children have an innate language acquisition device (LAD) that allows them to understand the rules of whatever language they are listening to. The whole language approach to literacy assumed these same principles held for literacy learning: Children would acquire literacy simply by being exposed to it.

◆ The *interactionist perspective* is a combination of both the nativist and behaviorist theories (McWhinney, 1999). It consists of two components. The first aspect, the information-processing theories, based on a connectionist model, show that the brain is excellent at detecting patterns. The second aspect of the interactionist perspective is the social-interactionist theories. These theories suggest that there is a native desire to understand others as well as being understood by others. A frequent theme is that language *emerges* from usage in social contexts, using learning mechanisms that are a part of a general cognitive learning apparatus (which is what is innate).

◆ The *interactionist perspective* has become associated with *emergentist* theories. Two current emergentist theories of language acquisition, connectionism and dynamic systems theory, attempt to account for the interaction of biological constraints that the child brings to the language learning with environmental factors. Both of these theories maintain that language *emerges* as a consequence of interactions between children and adults across multiple domains (language, cognitive, motor, and sensory) (Evans, 2008). It is hypothesized that neural networks develop as a result of input from these interactions. As these neural networks become elaborated, they detect regularities in input. It is through these networks that children's knowledge of the regularities of a language system emerges: the syntactic regularities, vocabulary usage, types of language functions (e.g., requesting, commanding, reasoning, predicting, inferencing, projecting into thoughts and feelings of others, arguing), pragmatic rules for social interaction, discourse organization, and orthographic patterns. Roskos and Christie (2011) propose that the dynamic systems approach provides a framework for understanding the complex relationships between play and literacy.

According to emergent theories, neither nature nor nurture alone is sufficient to trigger language learning; both of these influences must work together in order to allow children to acquire a language. The findings of many empirical studies support the predictions of these theories, suggesting that language acquisition is a more complex process than many believe. Interactionists argue that language learning is influenced by the desire of children to communicate with others. Children are born with a powerful brain that matures slowly and predisposes them to acquire new understandings that they are motivated to share with others (Tomasello, 2003). Emergentist theory has a communication focus—it goes beyond verbal utterances. It also encompasses nonverbal actions that reflect an understanding of meaning. Such nonverbal social behaviors often have the same effect as words to accomplish the ends that verbal language does. For example, a look or tone of voice can extract a reaction that is the same as when language alone is used. This theory is also associated with Vygotsky's model of collaborative learning (Vygotsky, 1978). Collaborative learning is the idea that conversations with adults or peers help children both cognitively and linguistically.

Developers of the Systematic and Engaging Early Literacy (SEEL) project assume an emergent perspective on language development. A dynamic systems approach to learning, as proposed by Nelson and colleagues (2004, 2008), provides the rationale for SEEL practices. Nelson and colleagues used the term "a dynamic tricky mix" to explain how language emerges in both neurotypical children and children with language impairments. A complexity of factors influences children's language/literacy learning. The approach is considered a tricky mix, because there is no one mix that is ideal for every child. These factors interact in different ways in different children. Intervention with children involves keeping track of the complexity of factors influencing children's language/literacy performance and providing ways of boosting children's depth of engagement so that their learning emerges. Nelson and colleagues propose that it is possible to dramatically accelerate a child's language/literacy learning when one considers a convergence of conditions that promote learning.

Components of a Dynamic Systems Approach

A dynamic tricky mix approach considers the multiple complex conditions that need to converge at or above threshold levels to support learning at the highest rates. When all the components contribute to learning, children develop a deep enjoyment and absorption in the activity of learning. Nelson proposed the LEARN acronym as a way of organizing these components. The SEEL curriculum exemplifies the LEARN components. The LEARN framework has five conditions: **L**aunching conditions, **E**nhancing conditions, **A**djustment conditions, **R**eadiness conditions, and **N**etwork conditions. According to Nelson's concept of a dynamic tricky mix, to promote development educators need to ensure that they address these components in their teaching.

Launching Conditions

Children become more involved in tasks and better remember tasks if they are motivated to participate and challenged appropriately (Guthrie & Humenick, 2004). They are more motivated to be involved when educational activities are purposeful and meaningful to them and they become more engaged with the activities. SEEL employs engaging, playful activities, rather than drill or worksheet activities, to promote phonological awareness, print awareness, alphabet knowledge, orthographic patterns, and discourse comprehension. When activities are positive and interactive, the literacy learning process motivates literacy learning, transmits positive attitudes about reading and writing, and assists in skill development (Guthrie & Knowles, 2001; McKenna, 2001; Verhoeven & Snow, 2001).

Why is play so important as a launching condition? Play is seen as a basic biological behavior (Brown, 2009). Animal research has shown that active play stimulates brain-derived neurotropic factor (which stimulates nerve growth) in the amygdala (where emotions get processed) and the dorsolateral prefrontal cortext (where executive decisions are processed) (Gordon et al., 2003; Panksepp et al., 2003). Furthermore, the amount of play has been correlated to the development of the brain's frontal cortex, which is the important brain region responsible for much of what we call *cognition*: discriminating relevant from irrelevant information, monitoring and organizing our own thoughts and feelings, and planning for the future (Byers & Walker, 1995). Play activity helps sculpt the brain. Learning and memory seem to be fixed more strongly and last longer when learned in play. Lester and Russell (2008) argue that the main contribution of play to learning is to help children understand the links between motivation, emotion, and reward, allowing them to coordinate their feelings, thoughts, and behavior and to experience the feeling of learning. Neuman and Roskos (1992) reported that words embedded in playful contexts are learned better and faster. This may be because there is a linking of the activity with the emotional memory of the activity and a metawareness (executive function) of the activity. Memory that links the emotional experience of an event with the what, when, and how of the event is termed *episodic memory* (Tulving, 1993). This type of memory makes it possible for children to have conscious recollection of personal happenings and events from their personal past and mental projection of anticipated events into their future. Episodic memory enables children to better recall the experience and to transfer the learning to other situations. Episodic memory enables children to make predictions and inferences (which are essential for text comprehension).

Systematic and Engaging Early Literacy (SEEL) teachers have commented that the playful activities designed to teaching phonological/phonemic awareness, alphabetic/orthographic knowledge, and comprehension "hook" the children so that they excitedly become engaged in the activities. Drill and worksheet can develop semantic memory (for words and concepts) and procedural memory (scriptal memories for how activities are to be done), but they are unlikely to promote episodic or autobiographical memory. Teachers have reported that children remember the SEEL activities from day to day and week to week. For example, a first grade girl who had been in a kindergarten using the SEEL curriculum came to the kindergarten open house with her younger brother. When she entered the room, she turned to her brother and said, "You'll have so much fun here. You'll learn all about -*ack*." When the teacher questioned her about what she meant, she reminded the teacher. "We learned about Jack and his black backpack. We made snacks and put the snacks in the backpack." Not only did she remember many of the playful activities from kindergarten, she also remembered the purpose of the activities—the letter-sound patterns they were learning.

Enhancing Conditions

These conditions are of two types: (1) the interaction strategies that adults use to facilitate students' learning and (2) the metacognitive strategies that students use to guide their own learning. Learning is also enhanced in SEEL by the explicit, intense instruction provided by teachers. Teachers explain to children what they are learning, why they are learning, and how they are to display their learning in phonological/phonemic awareness skills, alphabetic/orthographic knowledge, and comprehension. They give children multiple experiences with each skill or concept. It is not a matter of repeating the same activity multiple times, but of experiencing a variety of different activities emphasizing a pattern or concept.

Learning is also enhanced by the conversations and scaffolding teachers employ in their lessons. Language is socially constructed and dependent on the scaffolding support of others that promotes shared meaning (Vygotsky, 1978). Social interactions enhance learning, particularly when in this process children develop self-regulation and begin to be able to guide and monitor their own learning. Within the context of engaging, playful activities, the SEEL curriculum involves teachers in carefully scaffolding their interactions with children in the phonological/phonemic awareness, alphabetic/orthographic knowledge, and comprehension components of the program. When implementing SEEL activities, teachers use instructional conversation (IC) to support students' development of academic language (Saunders & Goldenberg, 1999). ICs are theme-based discussion lessons geared toward creating opportunities for students' conceptual and linguistic development. According to Cazden (1988), instructional conversation is "talk in which ideas are explored rather than answers to teachers' test questions provided and evaluated" (p. 54). Goldenberg provides five critical features of this type of teacher-student interaction:

- ◆ It is interesting and engaging.
- ◆ It is about an idea or a concept that has meaning and relevance for students.
- ◆ It has a thematic focus that, while it may shift as the discussion evolves, remains discernible throughout.
- ◆ There is a high level of participation, without undue domination by any one individual, particularly the teacher.

◆ Students engage in extended discussions—conversations —with the teacher and among themselves.

Many researchers acknowledge the importance of mediated social interactions with adults for literacy learning (Hiebert & Martin, 2001; Moll, 1992; Morrow & Gambrell, 2001). Skills taught in teacher-directed instruction should also be facilitated in interactive contexts, engaging children and activating their attention (Dahl, Scharer, Lawson, & Grogran, 1999; Lyon, 1999; Verhoeven, 2001). As teachers and students engage in ICs, they are learning a literate language style. Teachers use language structures and functions as follows:

◆ To clearly describe the children's activities and the activities of characters in books. Children learn to use language to vividly report their activities and the products they produce and to report events of a story they have heard. Such reporting language can form a basis for the development of language children can use to regulate their own behavior.

◆ To explain reasons for the activities in which children participate and the reasons for characters' behaviors in books. Children learn to use language to reason about and evaluate their own behavior and the behavior of characters in stories.

◆ To refer to thoughts and feelings of the child and of the characters in stories. Modeling of this type of language is critical for the development of both interpersonal theory of mind (thinking about what someone else or a character in a story is thinking or feeling) and intrapersonal theory of mind (which involves reflecting on one's own thoughts and feelings). If children are to comprehend stories, they must be able to understand the perspective of the characters. And if they are to develop self-regulation of their own behavior, they must be able to reflect on what they know and do not know, how they feel about activities or events, and how they respond to these activities and events. Development of both types of theory of mind is highly dependent on children being around adults who model the language of the two types of theory of mind (Lucariello, 2004).

◆ To predict "what will happen if . . . " in activities and stories. Children must be able to predict consequences of their own

behaviors and the consequences of the behaviors of characters in stories. Such prediction is dependent on the use of
episodic memory (mentioned in the Launch Conditions section). One cannot predict if one cannot connect the present
situation with other experiences, and such connections are
dependent on episodic memory, which is dependent on an
emotional base. When modeling predictive language, teachers must link the present experience to past experiences
and knowledge, and then suggest logical relationships to
future situations. Predictions cannot be just wild guesses.

Through these ICs children are learning to use language to report,
predict, reason, and take the perspectives of others. These language
interactions guide them in learning to "read between the lines"—to
make inferences that are especially critical for text comprehension
(Snow, 2002).

Enhancements to learning come not only from the teachers but
also from the children. Learning of new language/literacy skills is
enhanced by children's developing metacognitive awareness. The
enhancing strategies employed by the teachers using SEEL focus
children's attention and encourage planfulness and plan monitoring. The playful nature of the activities engages children so they
attend to the task, and creative aspects of the activities involve the
children in planning how they will do the activities, monitoring the
outcomes of their activities, and reflecting on their play afterwards.
Children who engage in mature, planful role-taking play in educational programs exhibit significantly better executive function skills
than children in traditional skills-based educational programs. The
better children do on executive function tasks, the better they self-
regulate their behaviors, and the better they perform on academic
measures (Diamond, Barnett, Thomas, & Munro, 2007).

Adjusting Conditions

Adjusting conditions are of two types: (1) the adjustments teachers
make to lessons based upon their observation and evaluation of
children's response to activities, and (2) the adjustments children
make as a result of their attitudes about the task and their capa-

bility to do the task. Teachers are aware that children are not all at the same developmental levels. Some children come to school with more knowledge and skills than others, and some children require more opportunities to learn new concepts or skills. Consequently, teachers identify the degree of support and practice that individual children require. For many children in general education classrooms, the activities presented in whole class and small group sessions are sufficient. For children who require additional playful experiences to develop the skills or concepts, the multiple activities can be provided so that children are not simply redoing the same tasks they did in the general education class in large and small group activities.

Children themselves make adjustments to how they approach learning activities. Children with both high and low ability who desire to the learn material for the sake of learning or because they enjoy the learning activities are likely to persist as tasks become more challenging. In contrast, children who focus on a final product or evaluation of performance (especially if they are of lower ability) are less likely to persist as tasks become challenging (Elliot & Dweck, 1988). Stipek and colleagues (1998) compared 4- to 6-year-old children enrolled in direct-instruction classrooms with those enrolled in more developmentally appropriate child-centered programs that incorporated play. Teachers in the direct-instruction classrooms employed a didactic approach to teaching basic literacy skills using commercially prepared materials (worksheets) that were not embedded in personally meaningful activities or connected to the children's daily experiences. Teachers evaluated and rewarded correctness of responses. Children in the child-centered programs spent less time in direct academic instruction, and teachers were less likely to evaluate correctness of specific responses. Children in the didactic classes did perform better on assessments of number and alphabet skills than the children in the child-centered classrooms. However, compared with children in developmentally appropriate classrooms, children from direct instruction classrooms rated their own abilities significantly lower, had lower expectations for success on academic tasks, showed more dependency on adults for permission and approval, showed less pride in their accomplishments, claimed to worry more about school, and were less likely to choose challenging tasks. Once children begin to perceive themselves as relatively less able to profit from classroom instruction than their peers, those perceptions have long-term effects on children's self-esteem and feelings about school (Ackerman, Izard, Kobak, Brown, & Smith, 2007). SEEL employs the best of a direct teaching approach and a child centered approach. It teaches early phonological awareness/phonics skills explicitly (the children are told what they are learning and why), but the instruction is done in child-friendly ways that promote the joy of learning to develop mastery, rather than learning to receive a positive teacher evaluation.

In interviews, teachers using Systematic and Engaging Early Literacy have reported that even children identified for special education (Tier 3 in response to intervention programs) have remained engaged throughout the year by the playful activities. They noted that children participating in the SEEL program have not shown the frustration with literacy activities focusing on alphabetic/orthographic knowledge that they observed in children in previous years when they did not use a SEEL approach. One teacher attributed this to the fact that children saw a purpose for learning (to participate in the activities) that children who were taught the skills discretely (i.e., as isolated tasks to learn the letters and sounds) did not perceive.

Readiness Conditions

The term *readiness* is used more broadly than it has been used in traditional literacy programs. In these contexts, reading readiness referred to the readiness to profit from beginning reading instruction or the point at which a person is ready to learn to read and the time during which a person transitions from being a non-reader into a reader. In Systematic and Engaging Early Literacy the concept of readiness conditions refers to the children's temperamental characteristics and the language/literacy, cognitive, social-emotional, and self-regulation skills they bring with them into the program. Raver (2002) reports that children who are socially competent and who can self-regulate and communicate are more ready for school and are more successful in school. By identifying the readiness conditions for each child, teachers know what they need to teach, and they monitor children's development over the course of the program so that they can adapt the program as needed for individual children.

Network Conditions

Knowledge is best remembered and used when it is consolidated or linked to/networked with other knowledge. This is essential for developing the neural networks essential for representational thought. All SEEL activities involve theme-based, playful experiences rather than isolated skill-based drills or lessons. Hence networking of knowledge is facilitated. SEEL activities involve integration of visual, auditory, tactile/kinesthetic, and motor skills. For example, children play with words rhyming with -*uck*. They listen to a story, *One Duck Stuck* (Root, 2001), of a duck who gets stuck in the muck. As the teacher reads the story, she encourages the children to describe how the duck became stuck in the muck and explain how the duck was finally able to get out of the muck. They discuss how the duck might have felt while she was stuck and how she felt when she got out of the muck. They compare this story with *Duck in the Truck* (Alborough, 2000). The children make muck (with pudding; ground, moistened Oreos; or water and dirt). They feel the muck and get items stuck in muck; they pluck paper ducks with -*uck* words on them from the muck, noting the initial letters and reading the words; they stick their hands in the muck and proclaim, "Yuck, I'm stuck in muck." They report their experiences of getting things stuck in muck. They explain why things can get stuck in muck, but not water. They re-enact the stories of *One Duck Stuck* and *Duck in the Truck*. They sing a song about duck behaviors. Throughout the day (and week), teachers highlight other examples of -*uck* and vocabulary and concepts from the story. Such experiences are multisensory; they integrate visual, auditory, tactile (and potentially taste and smell) experiences, thus promoting neural networking. Playful practice promotes neural networking because in the process of playing and re-enacting stories children are using all of their senses. They are using language in meaningful contexts, and in so doing they are developing an understanding of the relationships among people, objects, and events that are reflected in narrative and expository texts and are developing the complex oral language skills necessary to convey these relationships.

Play-Literacy Relationships

Foundations for Comprehension

If children are to become proficient readers, they must develop fluent skills in decoding print. But fluent decoding is not sufficient to be a good reader. Children must also comprehend what they read or what is read to them. To comprehend, students must develop a literate language style that requires specific vocabulary and syntactic patterns. They must also recognize the structures of narrative and expository texts and understand the types of content in these texts. To do this, children must build mental models of texts (Perfetti, 1997; Yuill & Oakhill, 1991).

Multiple levels of mental representation are necessary for developing these mental models. At the microstructure level, mental modeling requires understanding of the words and syntax of the text, and the words and syntax of written texts are more abstract and complex than the words and syntax of oral texts—more decontextualized (Zwiers, 2008). At the macrostructure level, persons must understand the temporal and cause-effect relationships that exist among people, objects, and events, and they must possess a theory of mind (ToM). ToM has both intrapersonal and interpersonal components (Lucariello, 2004). *Intrapersonal ToM* involves children's ability to reflect on their own understanding, thoughts, and feelings. Intrapersonal ToM is essential if children are to monitor and self-regulate their own behavior and learning. Using intrapersonal ToM, children reflect on their attitudes toward activities, determine if they understand or do not understand, and decide what they might do when they do not understand. *Interpersonal ToM* involves the realization that others have thoughts, feelings, and beliefs. Interpersonal ToM is essential for children to project into the thoughts and feelings of others (such as characters in stories), and to use this knowledge to reason about persons' behaviors. Children must then use working memory to integrate the microstructure and macrostructure elements of their models with information and experiences they pull from their long-term memory to develop a complete mental model for a discourse. Children's mental models enable them to inference—to "read between the lines of a discourse." Without the ability to make inferences, discourse comprehension is limited to literal understanding.

What can be done to promote children's mental modeling? Mental modeling is not unique to processing written text. It is essential for comprehension of all extended discourse. Mental modeling underlies all pretend play. Pretend play provides children with both a way to show their mental representation of the world and a way to develop a mental representation for objects, events, and relationships in the world (Lifter & Bloom, 1998). It is this understanding of the temporal and cause-effect relationships in the world that children must bring to the task of mental modeling of texts. Mental modeling requires theory of mind because one must be aware that one is thinking. The very act of pretend play is a manifestation of ToM because it requires children to distinguish what happens in the world from what occurs in the mind. As children engage in play with others, they must be able to attend to and interpret the intentions of one another as they play. This requires that they be able to observe affect and use language and social experiences to interpret the significance of that affect (Garfield, Peterson, & Perry, 2000). In the process they are developing higher levels of theory of mind. In play they are learning to make a variety of inferences that they will also need in texts. Play serves as more than a launcher that motivates children to learn. It contributes to children learning cognitive, linguistic, and social-emotional skills that are essential for both social and academic success.

Children are engaged in play throughout the majority of SEEL activities. Even when they are focusing on phonological/phonics skills, they are playing. As they learn about the letter *Bb*, they pretend to take a trip on the big *B* bus or a baby *B* bus. The ride is sometimes bumpy and bouncy. They beep the horn as they back up. They go to a bakery to buy bagels. In another example, instruction can relate to events that occur in the story *Lost!* (McPhail, 1993). Children engage in story enactment. They are learning words in the *-ap* family (*map, nap, lap, cap*) as they re-enact the story, but they are also learning the structure and content (theme and relationships) of the story. In this story a large brown bear falls asleep inside a snack truck and awakes to find itself lost in the big city. During story enactment, a child pretends to be a lost bear. Another child helps the bear search for its home. Their quest takes them around the city, and they end their day in the library where they find a map to get the bear back home. After a long ride on an outbound bus, boy and bear find themselves in the woods. As the grateful bear disappears into the woods, the boy realizes that he is now lost, and the bear returns to help him find his home.

Pretend play, particularly sociodramatic, has a story line and thus provides natural opportunities for developing narrative competence. Children's play and narrative are closely intertwined (Nicolopoulou, 2006). As children enact stories, they learn about the structure of stories. Children who form a sense of story through make believe more readily grasp the organization and meaning of new stories and therefore are more likely to remember them (Pellegrini & Galda, 1982; Silvern et al., 1986). Young pretenders also impose the story organization on the way they recall and explain their experiences to others. Their verbal narratives are more cohesive than those of peers who do not engage in this type of play (Pellegrini, 1982, 1985a, 1985b). Five- to seven-year-olds who engaged in story enactments with their peers and teachers along with story discussion showed significantly greater improvement in narrative length, cohesion, and comprehension compared to children whose teachers read the same book and engaged the children in discussion only (Baumer, Ferbholt, & Lecusay, 2005).

Despite the potential value of play in early childhood education, the current emphasis on early literacy skills has put the educational and therapeutic use of play under siege. Hirsh-Pasek and colleagues (2009) argue in their book *A Mandate for Playful Learning in Preschool* that children are being robbed of playtime at home and school in an effort to give them a head start on academic skills. Yet research suggests that eliminating play from the lives of children is taking preschool education in the wrong direction. What children need is more play rather than less.

Play Dimensions for Literacy

Smilansky (1968) suggested that play is essential for success in school:

> Problem solving in most school subjects requires a great deal of make-believe: visualizing how the Eskimos live, reading stories,

imagining a story and writing it down, solving arithmetic problems, and determining what will come next. History, geography, and literature are all make-believe. All of these are conceptual constructions that are never directly experienced by the child. (p. 25)

Pretend play develops along several dimensions (Westby, 2000):

◆ *Theory of mind*, which initially frees play from the concrete immediate environment and later frees symbolic actions from children's own bodies, allowing them to adopt the roles of others in pretend activities.
◆ *Decontextualization*, which allows play to occur with decreasing environmental support or changing reliance on props (from the use of realistic props to abstract or substituted props [a block is a car], to play using only language).
◆ *Thematic content*, which involves the schema information children have for people, animals, objects, and events.
◆ *Organization*, which allows thematic content in play to be gradually organized into increasingly complex temporal and causal sequences with greater coherence and complexity of action representations.

Each of these play dimensions can contribute in different ways to literacy development via the building of mental models.

Theory of Mind

Theory of mind is critical for narrative comprehension. Children must recognize how characters in a story feel in response to an initiating event, what the characters plan to do about this, and how they feel about the outcomes of their plans. The nature of pretend play is in itself an aspect of theory of mind. When children pretend, they are creating a mental representation in their minds of something that does not exist in the real world. In doing this, children realize that they can think about things that do not exist in the real world. They are aware that pretending is something they do in their heads. As they develop this awareness of their own thoughts, they begin to realize that others have thoughts. And through conversations and play they become aware that the thoughts and feelings of others may be different from their own.

Children initially pretend on themselves. They pretend to eat, drink, or sleep and realize that these behaviors are pretend. They then move these pretend behaviors to a doll—talking to the doll and for the doll. By age 4, they engage in sociodramatic play, taking on the roles of others. To do so, they must reflect on what persons in those roles might think and feel. The ability to reflect on the feelings of oneself and others is critical for narrative comprehension. Observing and engaging in pretend behaviors activates the same areas of the brain that are activated in theory of mind tasks, and role playing activates areas associated with narrative comprehension (Gallagher & Frith, 2003; Whitehead et al., 2009).

The distinction between self and others is seen in children's abilities to carry on multiple discourse roles in play (e.g., the roles of characters, stage manager, and narrator). Children may smoothly switch their roles during play, ranging from outside the play frame to within it. They may take the role of a character ("I'm a fireman. I'll save you"), act as a stage manager for the props ("There's not enough fire hose. Can you get some rope?") and speak as the author of the play story ("The fire was really bad, so we called for Superman"). Wolf and Hicks (1989) noted that these three types of discourse are encountered in reading a story: One reads the words uttered by the characters, descriptions of the thoughts and actions in the story, and perhaps the narrator's reflection about the story. For example, in *The Birthday Fish* (Yaccarino, 2005) one reads the spoken discourse of characters and the text in which the discourse is immediately embedded ("They came to a pet store. 'Would you like something to eat?' Cynthia asked the fish") and the narrative told by the author ("So she bought some fish food"). Wolf and Hicks suggested that the ability to use these multiple strands of discourse in play is related to understanding these strands in literature.

Role-playing facilitates internalizations of rules and expectations. Thus role-playing promotes executive function/metaawareness skills. Children must remember what scenario they chose, what role they chose, and what roles the other children chose. They must inhibit behaviors inconsistent with their role (the baby can't suddenly order others around), and they cannot grab nonscenario-related toys, but must honor the plans they have agreed on. Children help regulate one another as they monitor each other's compliance with the rules and assigned roles.

Decontextualization

As children develop, their play becomes increasingly more decontextualized—they talk about what cannot be seen or heard. Gradually they are able to use less representative props, then creatively substitute objects (a box becomes a roast turkey), and eventually use language to set the entire scene. Decontextualized play requires that children develop decontextualized language—the type of language required for academic success in school. Pretend play has been linked to the use of the type of language functions and decontextualized language used in literacy. Higher levels of symbolic play and literacy both require the ability to comprehend and use language without the benefit of contextual support from the environment. Children who exhibit greater decontextualization in their play by substituting objects (e.g., using a chair as a train) or taking on imaginative roles (e.g., I'm an astronaut) also use more explicit decontextualized language involving elaborated noun phrases, temporal and causal conjunctions, past tense and future aspect, and metacognitive verbs (Pellegrini, 1985). They also use language for a wider variety of functions (reporting, predicting, reasoning, and projecting into the thoughts and feelings of others). Inability to use decontextualized language has been associated with lack of academic success (Michaels & Collins, 1984; Zwiers, 2008). Dickerson and Tabors (2001) reported that children who talked more during play in their preschool years had better literacy outcomes in middle school.

Thematic Content and Organization

In play children both display and further their understanding of events in the world. Initially this knowledge is of a scriptal or procedural nature. Scriptal knowledge involves knowledge of the sequence of activities, how to behave and what to say. If children are to reproduce themes in play, they must have represented the experiences or themes in memory. As children integrate emotional information into situations, their play makes greater use of episodic memory, which enables them to develop more flexible themes.

Children initially play at themes or events they have personally experienced every day (e.g., eating, sleeping, cooking). Gradually they begin to reproduce themes of memorable events they experience less frequently (e.g., shopping or doctor play). By 3½ they are engaging in thematic play about events in which they have not been personally involved (e.g., fireman, superhero); and by 5 or 6 years they produce novel themes in their play, combining aspects of other themes in new and different ways.

As the thematic content of play moves from highly familiar scripts to creative topics, the play becomes more organized. Play begins with reproduction of an isolated activity, evolving to a few related activities, to an evolving sequence of activities or an event, then to planned sequences in play. The development of increasing organization or integration in play appears to reflect not only increasing understanding of the spatial, temporal, and cause-effect relationships within the physical and social world, but also increasing metacognitive skills that enable children to plan and monitor their own behavior. Deficits in the organizational dimension of play may represent lack of understanding of the interrelationships within the physical and social world or deficits in the child's metacognitive abilities.

Language is critical for the development of metacognitive self-control and self-monitoring behaviors, for it is largely through language that individuals plan their behavior. Play has been shown to facilitate development of these self-regulatory skills (Berk, Mann, & Ogan, 2006). In play children can use their language skills to plan out play scripts ahead of time. This play planning has been shown to promote development of executive functions. Tools of the Mind (Bodrova & Leong, 2007) is an early childhood program designed to develop executive functions through play. Children learn to use self-regulatory language during play. They are taught to plan the play scenarios together. They might say, "Let's pretend I'm the vet and your dog is sick. You bring your puppy to see me. I'll take an x-ray and give him medicine." The child who has the puppy might add, "I'll drive him there. I'll have to get gas, and I'll need money to pay you." After the children agree, they act out the scenario. Metacognitive abilities are essential for monitoring reading comprehension (Westby, 2004). Readers must set a goal for reading, they must monitor their comprehension, and when they recognize they are not comprehending, they must evaluate the possible reasons for their comprehension failure and then select from a variety of strategies a method to aid their comprehension. Children have practice with these metacognitive skills in play.

The thematic and organizational dimensions of play are dependent on memory. Memory is highly influenced by talk about past events. Talk about events facilitates children's verbal encoding and reporting by providing labels for and descriptions of the experience. Furthermore, adult-child talk may help children understand an event by highlighting its causal and temporal structure and by guiding the child's attention to its salient aspects. Opportunities to discuss experience afterwards are particularly critical in promoting children's memory for and comprehension of events (McGuigan & Salmon, 2004).

There's More to Be Learned Than Literacy

Educators feel the need to justify play by showing how it can contribute to literacy learning. Play and education should not be viewed as dichotomies. Education for children should be playful. But play has value that goes beyond literacy. Play England, an organization that seeks to ensure that children have the opportunity to play freely as part of their daily lives, at school, at home, and throughout the public realm, has commissioned a number of reports that review the literature on play (Play England, 2011a, 2011b). Play England views play as a human right; play influences all aspects of children's lives.

Benefits of play are both immediate and long term and contribute to all aspects of children's health and development, including their physical and mental well-being, educational development, brain development, language development opportunities, spatial and mathematical learning, creativity, and identity formation (Coalter & Taylor, 2001; Wood, 2007; Zigler & Bishop-Josef, 2009). Through playing children learn vocabulary, concepts, problem solving, self-confidence, motivation, and awareness of the needs of others (Zigler, 2009). Play has a particularly strong effect on social relationships. Play and games serve as a social scaffold. In play children learn skills that are pivotal for schooling such as forming friendships, developing social skills and working out how to become part of a group. Play provides a place for children to experiment with new skills by taking risks and thinking about complicated ideas (Hubbuck, 2009). These social abilities have been seen to help collaborative group working and school learning, leading to academic success in later life (Blatchford & Baines, 2010).

Lack of social play can be a contributing factor to mental health issues in children. This is because play is fun and because play can affect children's adaptive systems making them more resilient, which in turn may make them more able to cope with pressures that can lead to mental health issues. Children enrolled in less developmentally appropriate classrooms (i.e., classrooms where only direct instructional practices were used) experienced more stress and behavioral problems and fewer positive academic outcomes at the end of the school year than did their peers in developmentally appropriate classrooms (Hart, Burts, & Charlesworth, 1997; Hart, Yank, Charlesworth, & Burts, 2003). Play can help give children a more positive outlook, increase cortisone in the body, alter stress receptors, change children's attitudes to friends and places, and encourage more creative learning. It has been suggested that rather than play helping to develop specific skills, it helps to build architectural foundations for the adaptive systems that contribute to resilience (Play England, 2011a). Play makes children feel better and consequently engage more, which in turn makes them feel better and creates a positive cycle, leading to healthy children who become healthy adults.

There are three possible positions on the relationship between play and language/literacy learning: (1) play is essential to literacy proficiency, (2) play is nice, but not necessary for literacy development (a middle ground position), and (3) play is one of many routes toward language/literacy development. Research best supports the third position (Roskos, Christie, Widman, & Holding, 2010). If play is not essential, then educators might ask why time should be wasted in play. Although play does not appear to be essential for literacy development, it does have important and beneficial functions. The evidence shows that young children who engage in playful interactions learn what children in direct instruction learn—but they learn more, in areas not necessarily associated directly with literacy, but still important for school success. The Play England (2011a) monograph concludes, "A world without play is a world of robots. Without play we are functional, potentially productive, but not human. Play for children is a freedom that must be protected and should never be taken away" (p. 8).

References

Ackerman, B., Izard, C., Kobak, R., Brown, E., & Smith, C. (2007). The relation between reading problems and internalizing behavior in school for preadolescent children from economically disadvantaged families. *Child Development, 78,* 581–596.

Afflerbach, P., & Cho, B. Y. (2010). Determining and describing reading strategies: Internet and traditional forms of reading. In H.S. Waters & W. Schneider (Eds.), *Metacognition, strategy use, and instruction* (pp. 201–225). New York, NY: Guilford.

Alborough, J. (2000). *Duck in the truck.* New York, NY: HarperCollins.

Baumer, S., Ferholt, B., & Lecusay, R. (2005). Promoting narrative competence through adult-child joint pretense: Lessons from the Scandinavian educational practice of playworld. *Cognitive Development, 20,* 576–590.

Berk, L. E., Mann, T. A., & Ogan, A. T. (2006). Make-believe play: Wellspring for development of self-regulation. In D. G. Singer, R. M. Golinkoff, & K. A. Hirsh-Pasek (Eds.), *Play-learning: How play motivates and enhances cognitive and social-emotional growth* (pp. 74–100). New York, NY: Oxford University Press.

Biancarosa, C.,& Snow, C. E. (2006). *Reading next—A vision for action and research in middle and high school literacy: A report to Carnegie Corporation of New York.* Washington, DC: Alliance for Excellent Education.

Blatchford, P., & Baines, E. (2010) Peer relations in school. In K. Littleton, C. Wood, & K. Staarman (Eds.), *Handbook of educational psychology: New perspectives on learning and teaching.* Oxford, UK: Elsevier.

Bodrova, E., & Leong, D. J. (2007). *Tools of the mind: The Vygotskian approach to early childhood education* (2nd ed.). Upper Saddle River, NJ: Prentice-Hall.

Brown, S. (2009). *Play: How it shapes the brain, opens the imagination, and invigorates the soul.* New York, NY: Avery.

Byers. J. A., & Walker, C. (1995). Refining the motor training hypothesis for the evolution of play. *American Naturalist, 146,* 25–40.

Cazden, C. (1988). *Classroom discourse: The language of teaching and learning*. Portsmouth, NH: Heinemann.

Chomsky, N. (1965). *Aspects of the theory of syntax*. Cambridge, MA: MIT Press.

Diamond, A., Barnett, W. S., Thomas, J., & Munro, S. (2007). Preschool program improves cognitive control. *Science, 218*, 387–388.

Dickinson, D. K., & Tabors, P. O. (Eds.). (2001). *Beginning literacy with language: Young children learning at home and school*. Baltimore, MD: Paul Brookes.

Elliot, E. S., & Dweck, C. S. (1988). Goals: An approach to motivation and achievement. *Journal of Personality and Social Psychology, 54*, 5–13.

Evans, J. (2008). It's all about change: Emergentism and language impairments in children. In M. Mody & E. R. Silliman (Eds.), *Brain, behavior, and learning in language and reading disorders* (pp. 41–71). New York, NY: Guilford.

Fillion, B., & Brause, R. (1987). Research into classroom practices: What have we learned and where are we going? In J. Squire (Ed.), *The dynamics of language learning* (pp. 291–225). Urbana, IL: ERIC

Gallagher, H. L., & Frith, C. D. (2003). Functional imaging of 'theory of mind.' *Trends in Cognitive Science, 7*, 77–83.

Garfield, J. L., Peterson, C. C., & Perry, T. (2001). Social cognition, language acquisition and the development of theory of mind. *Mind and Language, 16*, 494–541.

Glod, M. (2008, May 2). Study questions 'No Child' Act's reaching plan. *Washington Post*. Retrieved from http://www.washingtonpost.com/wp-dyn/content/article/2008/05/01/AR2008050101399.html

Golinkoff, R. M., Hirsh-Pasek, K. A., & Singer, D. G. (2006). In D. G. Singer, R. M. Golinkoff, & K. Hirsh-Pasek (Eds.), *Play = learning: How play motivates and enhances children's cognitive and social-emotional growth*. New York, NY: Oxford.

Gordon, N., Burke, S., Akil, H.,Watson, S.J., & Panksepp, J. (2003). Socially induced brain 'fertilization': play promotes brain derived neurotrophic factor transcription in the amygdala and dorsolateral frontal cortex in juvenile rats. *Neuroscience Letters, 341*, 17–20.

Guthrie, J. T., & Humenick, N. M. (2004). Motivating students to read. In P. McCardle & V. Chhabra (Eds.), *The voice of evidence in reading research* (pp. 329–354). Mahwah, NJ: Erlbaum.

Hart, C. H., Burts, D. C., & Charlesworth, R. (1997). Integrated developmentally appropriate curriculum: From theory and research to practice. In S. H. Hart, D. C. Burts, & R. Charlesworth (Eds.), *Integrated curriculum and developmentally appropriate practice: Birth to age 8* (pp. 1–27). Albany, NY: State University of New York Press.

Hart, C. H., Yank, C., Charlesworth, R., & Burts, D. C. (2003). *Kindergarten teaching practices: Associations with later child academic and social/ emotional adjustment to school.* Paper presented at the meeting of the Society for Research in Child Development, Tampa, FL.

Hoover, W. A., & Gough, P. B. (1990). The simple view of reading. *Reading and Writing: An Interdisciplinary Journal, 2,* 127–160.

Hubbuck, C (2009) *Play for sick children: Play specialists in hospitals and beyond.* London, UK: Jessica Kingsley.

Lester, S., & Russell, W. (2008). *Play for a charge: Play, policy and practice: A review of contemporary perspectives.* London, UK: Play England.

Lifter, K. & Bloom, L. (1998). Intentionality and the role of play in the transition to language. In A. M. Wetherby, S. F. Warren, & J. Reichle (Eds.), *Transitions in prelinguistic communication* (pp. 161–195). Baltimore, MD: Paul Brookes.

Lucariello, J. (2004). New insights into the functions, development, and origins of theory of mind: The functional multilinear socialization (FMS) model. In J. M. Lucariello, J. A. Hudson, R. Fivush, & P. J. Bauer (Eds.), *The development of the mediated mind: Sociocultural context and cognitive development.* Mahwah, NJ: Erlbaum.

McPhail, D. (1993). *Lost!* New York, NY: Little Brown.

McWhinney, B. (1999). *The emergence of language.* Mahwah, NJ: Erlbaum.

Michaels, S.,& Collins, J. (1984). Oral discourse styles: Classroom interaction and acquisition of literacy. In D. Tannen (Ed.), *Coherence in spoken and written discourse* (pp. 219–244). Norwood. NJ: Ablex.

National Assessment of Educational Progress — Reading 2007. Retrieved from http://nationsreportcard.gov/reading_2007

National Evaluation of Early Reading First. (2007). Retrieved from http:// ies.ed.gov/ncee/pdf/20074007_execsumm.pdf

National Reading Panel. (2000). *Report of the national reading panel: Teaching children to read.* Washington, DC: National Institute for Literacy.

Nelson, K. E., & Arkenberg, M. E. (2008). Language and reading development reflect dynamic mixes of learning conditions. In M. Mody & E. R. Silliman (Eds.), *Brain, behavior, and learning in language and reading disorders* (pp. 315–348). New York, NY: Guilford.

Nelson, K. E., Craven, P. L., Xuan, Y., & Arkenberg, M. E. (2004). Acquiring art, spoken language, sign language, text, and other symbolic systems: Developmental and evolutionary observations from a dynamic tricky mix theoretical perspective. In J. M. Lucariello, J. A. Hudson, R. Fivush, & P. J. Bauer (Eds.), *The development of the mediated mind: Sociocultural context and cognitive development.* Mahwah, NJ: Erlbaum.

Newman, S., & Roskos, K. (1992). Literacy objects as cultural tools: Effects on children's literacy behaviors during play. *Developmental Psychology, 41,* 428–442.

Nicolopoulou, A. (2006). The interplay of play and narrative in childen's development: Theoretical reflections and concrete examples. In A. Göncü & S. Gaskins (Eds.), *Play and development: Evolutionary, socio-cultural and functional perspectives* (pp. 247–273). Hillsdale, NJ: Lawrence Erlbaum.

Panksepp, J., Burgdorf, J., Turner, C., & Gordon, N. (2003). Modeling ADHD-type arousal with unilateral frontal cortex damage in rats and beneficial effects of play therapy. *Brain and Cognition, 52*, 97–105.

Pearson, P. D. (2010). The roots of reading. In K. Ganske, & D. Fisher (Eds.), *Comprehension across the curriculum* (pp. 279–321). New York, NY: Guilford.

Pellegrini, A. D. (1982). The construction of cohesive text by preschoolers in two play contexts. *Discourse Processes, 5,* 101–108.

Pellegrini, A. D. (1985a). The narrative organization of children's fantasy play. *Educational Psychology, 5,* 17–25.

Pellegrini, A. D., (1985b). The relations between symbolic play and literate behavior: A review and critique of empirical literature. *Review of Educational Research, 55,* 107–121.

Pellegrini, A. D. (2008). The recess debate: A disjunction between educational policy and scientific research. *American Journal of Play, 1,* 181–191.

Pellegrini, A. D., & Galda, L. (1982). The effects of thematic-fantasy play training on development of children's story comprehension. *American Educational Research Journal, 19,* 443–452.

Perfetti, C. (1997). Sentences, individual differences, and multiple texts: Three issues in text comprehension. *Discourse Processes, 23,* 337–355.

Play England. (2011a, May). *A world without play: Experts discuss the importance of play in children's lives.* Retrieved http://www.playengland.org.uk

Play England. (2011b, May). *A world without play: A literature review.* Retrieved from http://www.playengland.org.uk

Raver, C.C. (2002). Emotions matter: Making the case for the role of young children's emotional development for early school readiness. *SRCD Social Policy Report, XVI,* 3–18.

Reading First Impact Study: Interim Report. (2008). Retrieved from http://ies.ed.gov/ncee/pdf/20084019.pdf

Root, P. (2001). *One duck stuck.* Somerville, MA: Candlewick.

Roskos, K. A., & Christie, J. F. (2011). Mindbrain and play-literacy connections. *Journal of Early Childhood Literacy, 11,* 73–94.

Roskos, K. A., Christie, J. F., Widman S., & Holding, A. (2010). Three decades in: Priming for meta-analysis in play-literacy research. *Journal of Early Childhood Literacy, 10,* 55–96.

Saunders, W. M., & Goldenberg, C. (1999). Effects of instructional conversations and literature logs on limited- and fluent-English-proficient students' story comprehension and thematic understanding. *Elementary School Journal, 99*(4), 277–301.

Skinner, B. F. (1957). *Verbal behavior.* Englewood Cliffs, NJ: Prentice-Hall.

Silvern, S. B., Taylor, J. B., Williamson, P. A., Surbeck, E., & Kelley, M. F. (1986). Young children's story recall as a product of play, story familiarity, and adult intervention. *Merrill-Palmer Quarterly, 32,* 73–86.

Smilansky, S. (1968). *The effects of sociodramatic play on disadvantaged preschool children.* New York, NY: Wiley.

Snow, C. (2003*). Reading for understanding: Toward an R&D program in reading comprehension.* Rand Corporation. Retrieved from http://www.rand.org

Stigler, J. W., & Hiebert, J. (1999). *The Teaching Gap: Best ideas from the world's teachers for improving education in the classroom.* New York, NY: Summit Books.

Stipek, D., Feiler, R., Byler, P., Ryan, R., Milburn, S., & Salmon, J. M. (1998). Good beginnings: What difference does the program make in preparing young children for school. *Journal of Applied Developmental Psychology, 19,* 41–66.

Tomasello, M. (2003). *Constructing a language: A usage-based theory of language* acquisition. Cambridge, MA: Harvard University Press.

Tulving, E. (1993). What is episodic memory? *Current Directions in Psychological Science, 2,* 67–70.

Verhoeven, L, & Snow, C.E. (2001). *Literacy and motivation: Reading engagement in individuals and groups.* Mahwah, NJ: Lawrence Erlbaum Associates.

Vygotsky, L. S. (1978). *Mind and society: The development of higher mental processes.* Cambridge, MA: Harvard University Press.

Westby, C. E. (2000). A scale for assessing development of children's play. In K. Gitlin-Weiner, A. Sandgund, & C. Schaefer (Eds.), *Play diagnosis and assessment* (pp. 15–57). New York, NY: Wiley.

Westby, C. E. (2004). Executive functioning, metacognition, and self-regulation in reading. In E. Silliman & B. Shulman (Eds.), *Handbook of language and literacy development and disorders* (pp. 398–327). New York, NY: Guilford.

Whitehead, C., Marchant, J. L., Craik, D., & Frith, C. D. (2009). Neural correlates of observing pretend play in which one object is represented as another. *Social Cognitive and Affective Neuroscience, 4,* 369–378.

Yaccarino, D. (2005). *The birthday fish.* New York, NY: Henry Holt.

Yuill, N., & Oakhill, J. (1991). *Children's problems in text comprehension: An experimental investigation.* New York, NY: Cambridge University Press.

Zigler, E., & Bishop-Josef, S. J. (2009). Play under siege: A historical perspective. *Zero to Three, 30,* 4–11.

Zigler, E.F., Singer, D.G., & Bishof-Josef, S. J. (2004). *Children's play: The roots of reading.* Washington, DC: Zero to Three.

Zwiers, J. (2008). *Building academic language: Essential practices for content classrooms.* Newark, DE: International Reading Association.

Chapter 3

Learning What Print Means: Print Awareness in School, Home, and Community

Sharon Black

"Children do not learn to read by magic," noted Neuman and Bredekamp (2000, p. 22). "Rather they learn by engaging with other, more accomplished readers around print." First children need to understand what print is, how it functions, and what it can mean in their lives. This awareness develops as they engage with the written word, immersed in a variety of texts (Bromley, 2000), ranging from the sign reading "Science Center" to the books containing stories they enjoy. Gradually they become aware of the purposes and features associated with books and of the regularities that occur in individual words and letters, eventually developing into self-expression through emergent writing (Justice, Kaderavek, Fan, Sofka, & Hunt, 2009). Print knowledge is multidimensional (Justice et al., 2009), and children add to it as they continue to encounter print experiences in "functional, meaningful settings" (Stewart & Lovelace, 2006, p. 327). Neuman and Bredekamp (2000, p. 22) concluded, "Through assisted instruction, caregivers and teachers *teach* children that written words have meaning and power" (emphasis in original).

Of course the most significant power in written words is not in their prevalence, characteristics, and function; power lies in students' capability for using these words for their own receptive and expressive purposes. Many factors influence this development for each child, both external (sociocultural, environmental) and internal (developmental, motivational) to the individual (Justice, Skibbe, & Ezell, 2006). Thus "instruction in [such print aspects] as phonics, sight vocabulary and other word identification skills should always be placed within the larger context of purposeful literacy activity" (Au, 2000, p. 44). Katherine Au referred to this "overarching goal" as "ownership of literacy" (2000, p. 44).

Confident ownership is fairly easy for some children, less so for others, and a daunting challenge for children who may have current or potential delays or deficits in their language development. Children come to preschool, kindergarten, and primary grade classrooms with a variety of personal and background issues that are often far more significant than the scores they might "produce" on official assessments (Strickland, 2000, p. 101).

This chapter examines children's acquisition of print awareness, print concepts, and preliminary print skills in preschool, kindergarten, and first grade classrooms. As print awareness begins with a print-rich environment, ways of creating such an environment are considered, including strategies for teaching children how to recognize and engage with written words. Once the environment has been established, teachers and SLPs may begin with foundational concepts such as what print means and how books are used, then advance to using print knowledge with receptive strategies such as print referencing and shared reading. Benefits are explained, and techniques are explored. A useful way to begin applying print concepts for expressive purposes is shared writing (including language experience approach; LEA), which is also explained. Finally, provisions for special needs children are treated. Specific activities in multiple classroom contexts are interwoven throughout the chapter.

A Print-Rich Environment

Early in their lives, children are attracted by "situationally embedded environmental print," which some consider to be the beginning of reading experience (Justice, Skibbe, & Ezell, 2006). Contexts in which they encounter this print determine how well they come to recognize and learn from it (Justice, Skibbe, & Ezell); thus teachers, SLPs, and other members of the instructional team must deliberately incorporate print into the classroom in realistic, useful ways. Children benefit from experiencing written language in communication contexts, particularly when they encounter both stimuli and contingencies for using it (Hancock & Kaiser, 2006): possibly a label that tells them where to find the pen they need, a poster that reminds them it's library day, or a sign that lets them know whether the class will jump or jog to the snack table.

The presence of print *stimuli* in the classroom helps young students become aware of ways people respond to and read the written word: that print is meant to be read in a specific order (directionality), that letters are combined to form words, and that words are combined to form sentences or phrases. Such understanding provides a context (Stewart & Lovelace, 2006) in which they can begin to process the information print conveys, particularly when the teacher utilizes print as a teaching tool, not merely a way to decorate the room (Reutzel, Fawson, & Young, 2003). The teacher must call children's attention to and provide opportunities for them to interact with the print, particularly children from diverse backgrounds who may not have a variety of print experiences in their homes (Au, 2000).

Contingencies are important as well; children need to experience the involvement of print in meaningful activities. An effective print-rich environment is both engaging and functional.

Print Presence

Words are symbols that label persons, places, and things in the environment, as well as activities and perceptions. By the time they enter classrooms, children know a significant number of sound labels (oral language), but many of them are not as familiar with print labels (written language).

Labeling

To help the children internalize object/word/print relationships, many teachers and SLPs put written labels on spaces and objects that are part of students' school experience: chairs, desks, white board, bulletin board, supply closet, cubbies, book corner, writing center, science center, and so forth. Many children (particularly those with attention deficit disorder, dyslexia, or autism) experience difficulty in mapping words to objects (even very concrete objects) (Hoffman & Norris, 2006). The labeling is especially valuable for these students, particularly if an SLP or the teacher finds occasions to point to and read the labels with them, stretching the sounds for clarity and precision. If shelves and containers are labeled, students can practice reading the words as they gather supplies at the beginning of a project/activity or put things away afterward. ("Who can bring me the 'marker' box?" "Charles, would you please put this package of paper on the 'paper' shelf." "Who can bring me the big bag of blocks from the 'toy corner'?") (Figure 3–1). When Neuman and Roskos (1990) implemented dramatic play centers in preschool classrooms, they found that the children used posted signs such as "post office" and "library" not only to find places but to find spellings for words they needed during play literacy activities.

Actions can be labeled through the use of instructive signs. Charts with roles or "jobs" can be posted so that children can read their responsibilities for the day (particularly if they volunteered). During cleanup time the teacher, SLP, or other adult helper can

Figure 3–1. A student checks the labels on the supply shelves to find something the teacher has asked her to get.

hold up signs telling the children to "stop," "go," "pick up scraps," "put away toys" etc. During transitions children can consult signs to know where they should go ("Go to the science center," "Go to the art center"). Or signs can direct them how to go ("fast," "slow," "tip toe").

Connecting

Teachers and SLPs need to help children connect print they see daily in the classroom with print uses in their homes and communities. Children encounter many forms of print in their daily lives, from labels on food products to identifiers on stores and businesses, from signs on the roads to slogans on their T-shirts and pajamas (Beaty, 2005) (Figure 3–2). In planning classroom print presence and print practice, instructors need to consider that various ethnic (Au, 2000) and socioeconomic (Justice et al., 2009) communities use reading and writing in different amounts and different ways, so what is familiar and comfortable for the children will vary. Communities' values and beliefs as well as practices may be involved (Justice et al., 2006). Parents in some communities take their children for book reading sessions at the library; extended families and social groups in other communities may gather for oral

Figure 3–2. Labels on the ATM machine remind children of signs they see often in the community.

storytelling. When teachers and SLPs teach about the "functions of literacy already likely to be familiar" to their students, they help the children see that their family/community literacy practices can help them learn to read well (see Au, 2000, p. 37).

SLPs and teachers can obtain texts that are part of the students' experience in their homes and communities and extend use of these texts in the classroom (Rivalland, 2000). For example, a collage of labels is a popular way to illustrate the use of print in identifying food, and *salsa* and *soy sauce* are as illustrative as *salad*. Students playing restaurant might order tamales from a Mexican menu or catfish at an African American hangout. Sometimes an advertisement for a festival or cultural event representing a child's nationality could be added to a collection: for example, Anime Showcase (Japan) or Festival of Colors (India).

Additionally, either large or small groups can be taken on "print walks" throughout the community to gather print, perhaps to a supermarket, library, post office, or hospital (Barratt-Pugh, 2000). Children can be encouraged to bring print from home (Harp & Brewer, 2000) to be displayed on a bulletin broad, wall space, or large poster: labels from foods and various household items, newspaper or magazine clippings, pamphlets, etc. Children may participate in deciding where to place their items (e.g., grouping by alphabet letter) (Harp & Brewer, 2000).

Print can be located and referred to in the classroom mimicking ways in which it appears in the children's communities, linking print at school to print in the students' daily lives and developing their "repertoire of literacy practices" (Rivalland, 2000, p. 43). For example, many children are accustomed to watching adults follow printed instructions, from appliance pamphlets to posted procedures for returning a rental car. Thus classroom rules can be posted on chart paper, as can rules or procedures to be followed in special areas of the classroom (e.g., the science center, the snack area). Students may create games and dictate the rules or procedures for an adult to write up so that other children can play.

A dramatic play area offers many opportunities for authentic uses of print. Neuman and Roskos found that setting up a housekeeping corner, a library, a post office, and a business office in preschool classrooms—all containing a variety of literacy props—resulted in children spontaneously engaging in literacy play in these areas, creatively and enthusiastically. For example, two boys playing in the "office" area decided to sign people up to help the homeless. One of the boys went throughout the classroom with a clipboard collecting teachers' and classmates' signatures. They then "entered" their list into the computer, one reading the names from the list and the other typing. Some children scribble-wrote and exchanged letters in the post office. In the library corner a boy filled out a library card to "check out" a book selected by one of the girls, explaining that people did not have to buy the books, "just rent them." Neuman and Roskos concluded, "Literacy was part of the play flow" (p. 219).

Students who are especially strong in visual thinking and struggle in verbal responding and reasoning can benefit from being able to see and handle print props and other printed objects. "People naturally view objects from multiple dimensions and orientations," but those who are extreme visual thinkers, which include many students who have dyslexia or Asperger's syndrome, think primarily by "reorienting and altering features of objects" (Hoffman & Norris, 2006, p. 350; see also Grandin, 1995; Vygotsky, 1978). SLPs can help these students manipulate printed surfaces, an approach that is appropriate to their strong visual learning style (Hoffman & Norris, 2006).

Print Practices

Although environmental print should be included in preschool through first grade classrooms to develop students' awareness of the everyday presence and functions of written language, "its overall use is constrained by the real-life context in which it appears" (Teale & Yokota, 2000, p. 16). Young students need experiences using and interacting with print within classroom communication contexts. Hancock and Kaiser (2006, p. 216) have noted that the setting of the classroom should create "a reason to talk"—"functional reasons for the child to communicate." And simultaneously children need to learn to recognize that words—whether on a page, poster, label, or personal note—can be used to communicate in ways the same as or similar to spoken language. As Donald Graves (1983) expressed it, "Everyone knows something, has something to say, and can represent it on paper" (p. 19).

Promoting Authentic Communication

Preschool through first grade children need to use print to communicate with their teacher and classmates. Print interaction may be as simple as writing their names on a sign-up sheet (Beatty, 2005) for a team or a turn. One preschool teacher had a daily routine in which children signed up to be classroom helpers by placing their nametags on a chart next to the roles they had chosen (Figure 3–3). Children realize that their own desires or feelings can be accepted and considered when expressed in written form, perhaps copying "Get well soon" on a note for a sick classmate. Many teachers and SLPs post a personal note to the class each morning, leaving space around their message for children to respond in writing (Beaty, 2005), in brief phrases or full sentences as desired. Or the instructor may compose a "class events" poster from students' dictation (Au, 2000; Bromley, 2000).

Children also benefit from being involved in individual person-to-person communication. Some classrooms have a "Message Center" equipped with a variety of writing implements and different types, shapes, and colors of paper. Students are encouraged to write notes to each other, place them in envelopes, and either deliver them to a classroom post office or put them directly into classmates' mail boxes. Young children (and their parents) treasure brief personal notes written by the child's teacher or SLP, praising something about the child: personality, ideas, behavior, accomplishments, and so forth. Many of the children are motivated to write

Figure 3–3. A boy places his name card next to the "Helping Friends" role he wants for the day.

notes in return, even those with language delays who may avoid most writing opportunities.

Providing Support

Language difficulties have a variety of causes and take a variety of forms. But regardless of the source of a child's difficulty, empathetic SLPs, teachers, and other classroom helpers can provide supplementary support to help the child learn concepts and skills to function effectively within the print environment of the classroom.

As print participation is involved with their classroom routines, children with language problems may become confused by some of the ways that they need to interact with and respond to print. For example, they may need extra help in responding to posted signs that tell them where to sit, how to line up, etc., or to cards with letters or other symbols indicating what to do or how to do it. Selecting printed words or phrases to place in a posting chart indicating whether they liked the day's snack or perhaps reading a sign that tells them to move to the story rug may be developmentally appropriate for their age mates but linguistically inappropriate for them. To prepare these children for such environmental routines, an SLP might lead a small group in watching videotapes of other children responding, and then practice responses through role play (Owens, 1999). Costumes or props (including print props) can be used to make contexts more realistic and provide extra motivation. After practicing responses to print signals and symbols as a small group, children with language challenges can be prepared to respond to print confidently as part of the larger class unit. To provide the child-friendly humor that helps relieve stress and "encode learning" for struggling children (Murawski & Dieker, 2008), the SLP may want to use engaging puppets or act out print responses in amusing ways.

Children with language difficulties are likely to avoid a communication center. They may not visualize themselves communicating with others in words (even though their classmates may be writing just letters and squiggles), and many children with language disorders have difficulty relating to other children socially (Brinton & Fujiki, 2004). Because these children can benefit from experiencing this form of authentic print communication, the SLP (or other classroom adult) may give very helpful support by writing simple notes expressing individual approval and encouragement to each of them. As one of the teaching team is circulating to give individual help, she can read the note to the child, running her finger beneath the words, then work with the child to put together a return note, perhaps writing from the child's dictation.

Children who need extra support in dealing with print need to experience a variety of its forms and functions in practical contexts. Owens (1999) suggested several. The teacher or SLP may give a child with language weaknesses occasional print-related errands, such as delivering a written message that requires the child to gain attention, initiate conversation, and recognize that the writing conveys a message on which the recipient will act. During class activities, the repetitive, focused use of print—such as word charts for simple songs or finger plays that require intense involvement—can create associations that strengthen memory and comprehension. To provide appropriate pacing as well as a "safe" context, researchers have suggested that this kind of activity be conducted in groups of three to six (Fuchs & Fuchs, 2007; Murawski & Hughes, 2009).

Sharing Books

An important part of the print atmosphere of the classroom involves positive attitudes toward and exposure to books. Teachers and SLPs need to share books they enjoy and let the children feel their enthusiasm "because pleasure and enthusiasm for reading and books is more effectively caught than taught" (Cecil, 2003, p. 50).

According to Cecil (2003), children should learn the following "crucial literacy-related concepts about books" before they enter kindergarten. Teachers and SLPs need to discern how many and which children have not learned these concepts at home and provide (explicitly or indirectly) the necessary instruction at school.

◆ Books are enjoyable.
◆ Books should be handled in special ways.
◆ Book sharing involves a routine.
◆ Illustrations in books represent real things.
◆ *Words in books have meaning.* (List quoted from p. 37, emphasis added)

Modeling enjoyment from and respect for books is an important aspect of a print-favorable environment. All children, but especially those with language delays or disabilities, must understand the relationship between illustrations and words, as many of them tend to read the illustrations because the words are more confusing and difficult. These students have difficulty learning to process print as a language system (Hoffman & Norris, 2006, p. 349). The SLP may want to provide some small group or even one-on-one help for students who are struggling with this relationship.

Focused Introduction of Print Concepts

Daily exposure to a print-rich environment is important but not sufficient in young children's developing literacy. Teachers and SLPs need to provide specific instruction regarding print concepts to clarify and complement the children's observations and experiences with home and classroom print use. Almost all children need instruction, and most need direct instruction. A practical stance is taken by Katherine Au: "a balance . . . between systematic instruction through teacher-directed lessons . . . and . . . motivating activities that allow children choice and promote their ownership of literacy" (p. 44).

Explicit Introduction to Books as Print

Many children go into preschool and some enter kindergarten or even first grade without understanding the meaning of dark squiggles on paper. Some have a basic sense that the squiggles convey meaning, but do not understand the relationship between words and letters. A few do not know that reading goes from left to right, from the top of the page to the bottom (Harp & Brewer, 2000). If children are to learn the skills of reading and writing, they must know "how to look at print and what teachers are talking about as they give them information about print" (Cunningham, 2005, p. 5). These concepts can be taught by direct instruction with big books leading into shared reading experiences (Harp & Brewer, 2000). Specialized knowledge and experience in these areas make SLPs particularly effective in explaining such concepts.

Direct explicit instruction is purposefully structured and sequenced, directed by adults and focused on specific literacy targets, with the adult modeling, demonstrating, providing prompts for child participation, and conducting guided practice (Kaderavek, 2011). The following steps are typical: (1) state the objective, (2) model the behavior, (3) provide playful practice, and (4) review. A wide variety of methods and strategies can be involved, which are described throughout this book.

A first grade teacher named Melissa Marley (quoted by Au, 2000) uses a large puppet who tells the children shyly that he has no books at his house, no one has ever read to him, and he doesn't know anything about books or reading. The puppet asks the children questions about books, and they answer. Children who have such questions themselves learn specific answers from their classmates without the possible embarrassment of admitting that they do not know. Additionally the puppet models how to ask questions to get help, a basic skill from which all children can benefit.

Print Referencing

Once children have some basic book knowledge to provide a context, they need to understand more specifically the way print works. *Print referencing* is an engaging way to demonstrate this to children, with repetition that does not feel repetitious. While reading aloud from a big book or text written on chart paper, the adult runs a finger beneath the text so the child can easily follow, making explicit comments on print concepts and characteristics: "Here's a period. Sam's finished." Sometimes the adult asks questions or makes requests that draw the children's attention to the print: "Now where do we go to read what Ben will say?" (see Justice & Ezell, 2004; Justice et al., 2006). This technique is often practiced by parents in homes; by teachers, SLPs, or paraeducators in classrooms of young children; and by SLPs in clinical settings. It is easily adapted and personalized for children functioning on any level, being easy to simplify and extend for children with language difficulties and delays (Figure 3–4).

In a series of research studies, Justice and colleagues demonstrated that using print referencing techniques while reading stories with young children can substantially impact both their awareness and knowledge of print and their understanding of the alphabetic principle (Justice & Ezell, 2000, 2002, 2004). From basic print con-

Figure 3–4. In a print referencing session, a teacher points out the features on the book cover.

cepts (directionality, etc.), children become aware of the function of letters (graphic awareness), the function of the smallest sound units (phonemic awareness), the correspondence between letters and phonemes, and ultimately word reading (Justice et al., 2006). Print referencing can be introduced successfully in large group sessions (Justice et al., 2009), but is most often studied (Justice et al., 2009) and perhaps most often carried out in small group sessions during school intervention. Justice and Ezell (2002) described an educator who conducted small group print referencing sessions in a Head Start classroom in a rural community, resulting in significant acceleration in students' literacy skills.

Justice and Ezell (2004) mentioned a number of "milestones" in children's emerging and developing print awareness that are facilitated and enhanced by print referencing and accompanied by development of particular skills.

- ◆ *Print interest* emerges as children develop an idea of printed language as worth their attention.
- ◆ *Print functions* become apparent as children recognize what print does.
- ◆ *Print conventions* are learned as children observe how print is organized.

◆ *Print forms* are observed and abstracted as students encounter them in various contexts.

◆ *Print part-to-whole relationships* finally develop as students bring together and synthesize component print aspects.

Storybooks, which are pleasurable to most children, provide a context and an anchor for their exploration of print and ultimate success with literacy skills (Justice & Ezell, 2004; Justice et al., 2009). Picture books are effective if one to three children are involved; big books may be necessary for larger groups.

Effectiveness of print referencing has been studied in children with language deficits and disabilities as well as in children with typical language development. But SLPs may need to emphasize to teachers that, though it may seem very simple, print referencing needs to be differentiated for these children's special needs and that their individual progress must be carefully monitored (Justice et al., 2006). Even when children have major difficulties with language, SLPs and teachers can use print referencing to teach print concepts that are adapted to each child's individual levels of development and skills (Justice & Ezell, 2004). Stewart and Lovelace (2006) examined the results of print referencing by SLPs with five target children, all of whom had language impairments. From the gains of these children, the researchers concluded that "print referencing can be effectively and efficiently implemented within the context of a language intervention program" (p. 335). Within such an intervention, Justice et al. (2006) have added that children with language disorders will need supplementary discrete lessons explicitly focused on code-based elements, but through print referencing the SLP can combine these with the more motivating focus on storybook content—a "hybrid approach" (p. 404). They recommended that the SLP scaffold the child to "a point that reflects the *cutting-edge* of the child's performance" (p. 413, emphasis in original).

Although the strategy is generally applied on an intervention level, SLPs can implement it as part of their work in classrooms, as well as in pull-out programs or clinical interventions. Justice et al. (2009) asserted that SLPs have a "critical role in translating research findings [concerning such techniques as print referencing] to the everyday setting of schools" (p. 77).

Application of Print Concepts

Hall and Robinson (2000) brought out a paradox common in the treatment of literacy in early elementary classrooms:

> [Schools] treat literacy as if it was an object to be analyzed rather than an object to be used. Thus children do exercises rather than engage in literate practices. Literacy is put on boards, in exercise books, and on work sheets; it is broken down into bits which are practiced over and over again. . . . Thus literacy is seldom meaningful and relevant to children's lives as people. (p. 87)

Structuring Receptive Print Experience Through Shared Reading

Shared reading makes a broader application of concepts children can learn with print referencing experiences. This method takes the broken bits disparaged by Hall and Robinson (2002) off of work sheets and puts them together as unified printed texts from which stories of interest are read both to and by the children. During this interactive process, the teacher guides the children through processes of reading texts and making meaning from them. A teacher of young children can begin with short sessions focused on print function. When children are older, shared reading can be used in teaching comprehension, phonics, and story structure, which are developed in Chapters 6 and 8 of this text.

Shared reading should be enjoyable for the children (Beaty, 2005) and for the teacher as well. During shared reading the teacher or SLP is "modeling the message that print is a reliable conveyer of the text's message"(Neuman & Bredekamp, 2000, p. 30), and both the conveyance and the message should be of positive interest. The SLP or teacher reads a large, easily visible text: a big book for a big group, a book with substantial print or individual copies of a text for a small group or center. She points to each word for the group of students to follow, possibly inviting students to join in for words and phrases they recognize, particularly repeated words, phrases, or refrains (McGee & Richgels, 2008). On a subsequent reading the teacher may point to the words again and have the students help read, with some of them taking turns pointing to or placing small sticky note symbols over the words (Figure 3–5).

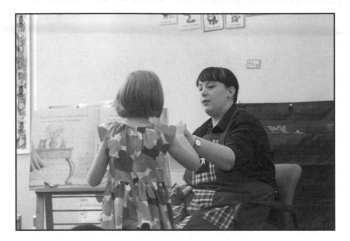

Figure 3–5. During shared reading, the teacher helps a student place a special marker over a target word.

As the teacher models "what fluent readers do," she demonstrates the direction and sequence for reading the print (Tompkins, 1998, p. 99) as letters come together into words, and punctuation marks provide guidelines for interpreting the text (see Tompkins, 1998). Students who have not yet grasped basic, underlying processes of reading observe as the teacher breaks words apart, stressing beginning and ending sounds, and they notice how print conventions can be used in a meaning-making process (Strickland, 2000, p. 104). Although the teacher reads somewhat slowly, she reads expressively; the children are to find meaning and enjoyment in the story (Savage, 2011). When students understand how periods and capital letters can help in making meaning clear, questions marks and exclamation points can be introduced. As they practice making meaning, children understand why it is important to sequence ideas (Cecil, 2003). In addition to reading stories, the teacher may put poems, songs, or chants on the overhead projector for this kind of experience (Nettles, 2006).

In addition to following the functions of print, the teacher or SLP should invite students to respond personally to the book and relate it to their own prior knowledge and experiences. She may make an occasional comment about the conflict in the plot or about one of the characters, or she may stop to explain a vocabulary word (McGee & Richgels, 2008). Students also participate in comprehension skills such as predicting and drawing inferences. They learn to think in terms of choices the author has made while writing the story: things they might have done differently if they had been writing the story themselves. ("Do you like the ending? How would you change it?") The teacher or SLP may lead the children in discussing particular words that the author has used effectively (Nettles, 2006). Additional responses may be invited through creative drama, student-designed puppetry, or visual arts expression (Nettles, 2006), as further discussed in Chapter 11 of this book.

Structuring Expressive Print Experience: Shared Writing

Print awareness is greatly enhanced as children have the expressive experience of putting their own ideas into words, watching those words going into print as the teacher writes them, and ultimately reading those words in their written form. Through this shared writing process, the students internalize the association between spoken and printed words and understand that printed words can express personal meaning. In addition, the teacher is able to illustrate printed language structures and mechanics which students will use in their own writing, which include spacing between words, thinking in terms of sentence units, noticing punctuation, working out conventional spelling, etc., using the children's own words and experiences (see Cramer, 2004; Donoghue, 2009; Miller, 2005). Children see the way the teacher or SLP makes decisions in these areas. The SLP or teacher may stress such aspects as discerning word boundaries, recognizing word structures, and using context clues for meaning (Miller, 2005). Conventions are explored as each sentence is recorded.

Young children particularly benefit from Language Experience Approach (LEA), a form of shared writing generated by a shared experience: perhaps a field trip, a guest speaker (such as a police officer), a playground activity, or a class program. Experiences with books or technology can also generate effective LEA texts (Nettles, 2006), as can caring for a class pet (Donoghue, 2009) or participating in an art, construction or cooking activity (Miller, 2005). The teacher or SLP can structure the experience and/or the introduction/context of the writing to generate words he or she particularly wants to target, such as function words (e.g., *to, of, the*) or past tense use (Nettles, 2006), aspects which can be especially difficult for children with language challenges.

As the children dictate sentences, the teacher or SLP records them on chart paper, an overhead transparency, or a whiteboard in letters large enough to be easily seen by all the students. The adult may record a child's dictation exactly as it is spoken if the child is hesitant to participate in LEA experiences when her own sentences aren't accepted (Miller, 2005). But in most instances, the adult would accept and acknowledge a child's idea, paraphrase or recast it, and record it in a grammatically correct sentence.

The teacher or SLP reads the text to the children, pointing to each word as it is pronounced. A "window bookmark" may be created by cutting a hole in a cardboard square to target particularly important words (Nettles, 2006). Next it is the students' turn to read, as either the adult or a child volunteer points to the words. This reading and rereading of the children's text gives the teacher or SLP opportunities to build students' sentence awareness (Nettles, 2006) as well as word consciousness: "*The* is the first word in the sentence. It begins with a capital letter. This period marks the end of the sentence."

The products of LEA and other shared writing can be used in a number of ways. Class big books may be compiled from LEA writings. Teacher-student journals created through LEA can be a good introduction to journal writing for young students. For advanced groups of students in a small group or at a station, the LEA experience can be extended by rewriting the sentences of the children's text on strips of paper or tagboard and allowing them to re-create and practice reading the text. The sentence strips can then be cut into individual words from which the students can re-create the sentences and form new original sentences (Tompkins, 1998).

Children with language disorders or other special needs may avoid participating in LEA writing with the full class (Miller, 2005). Some may become lost and confused during this kind of language experience and in general dislike activities that require sharing print; thus those who need the most review and practice may receive the least (Brinton & Fujiki, 2004). An SLP can conduct individual and small-group LEA sessions with these children until they feel comfortable with the method. Or topics may be introduced to a small group in advance so that students can preconsider their ideas and use group momentum to find words to express them.

Conclusion

Print can be fun if children perceive it as an interesting part of their home, school, and community environment. They can show off as they identify it; play games with it; enjoy its use in favorite stories; do what it says in order to do, make, or achieve something they want; use it to express their own stories, feelings, and ideas. The classroom should give them opportunities to experiment with all these functions and to develop and hone their capabilities for performing them.

Teachers and SLPs need to make such opportunities available for all students regardless of their divergent backgrounds and varied levels of language development. A print-rich, print-active, print-positive environment with enjoyable, meaningful print interaction is a good place to begin. Print referencing and shared reading help children experience and become sensitive to receptive print functions; shared writing (especially LEA) brings in the expressive dimension.

Specific emphasis, enrichment, and practice should be provided to meet the needs of individual students who have atypical challenges in their language development. Working together, teachers and SLPs can make print into an exciting tool rather than a formidable barrier for communication and accomplishment.

References

Au, K. H. (2000). Literacy instruction for young children of diverse backgrounds. In D. S. Strickland & L. M. Morrow, (Eds.), *Beginning reading and writing* (pp. 35–45). New York, NY: Teachers College Press.

Barratt-Pugh, C. (2000a). Literacies in more than one language. In C. Barratt-Pugh & M. Rohl (Eds.), *Literacy learning in the early years* (pp. 172–196). Philadelphia, PA: Open University Press.

Beaty, J. J. (2005). *50 Early childhood literacy strategies.* Upper Saddle River NJ: Merrill, Prentice-Hall.

Brinton, B., & Fujiki, M. (2004). Social and affective factors in children with language impairment: Implications for literacy learning. In C. A. Stone, E. R. Silliman, B. J. Ehren, & K. Apel (Eds.), *Handbook of language and literacy development and disorders* (pp. 130–153). New York, NY: Guilford Press.

Bromley, K. (2000). Teaching young children to be writers. In D. S. Strickland & L. M. Morrow (Eds.), *Beginning reading and writing* (pp. 111–120). New York, NY: Teachers College Press.

Cecil, N. L. (2003). *Striking a balance: Best practices for early literacy* (2nd ed.). Scottsdale, AZ: Holcomb Hathaway.

Cramer, R. L. (2004). *The language arts: A balanced approach to teaching reading, writing, listening, talking, and thinking.* Boston, MA: Pearson.

Cunningham, P. M. (2005). *Phonics they use: Words for reading and writing* (4th ed.). Boston, MA: Pearson.

Donoghue, M. R. (2009). *Language arts: Integrating skills for classroom teaching.* Los Angeles, CA: Sage.

Fuchs, L., & Fuchs, D. (2007). A model for implementing responsiveness to intervention. *Teaching Exceptional Children, 39*(5), 14–23.

Grandin, T. (2006). *Thinking in pictures.* New York, NY: Vintage Books.

Graves, D. G. (1986). *Teaching writing: Teachers and children at work.* Portsmouth, NH: Heinemann.

Hall, N., & Robinson, A. (2000). Play and literacy learning. In In C. Barratt-Pugh, & M. Rohl (Eds.), *Literacy learning in the early years* (pp. 81–104). Philadelphia, PA: Open University Press.

Hancock, T. B., & Kaiser, A. P. (2006) Enhanced milieu teaching. In R. J. McCauley & M. E. Fey (Eds.), *Treatment of language disorders in children* (pp. 203–236). Baltimore, MD: Paul H. Brookes.

Harp, B., & Brewer, J. A. (2002). Assessing reading and writing in the early years. In D. S. Strickland & L. M. Morrow (Eds.), *Beginning reading and writing* (pp. 154–167). New York, NY: Teachers College Press.

Hoffman, P. R., & Norris, J. A. (2006). Visual strategies to facilitate written language development. In R. J. McCauley & M. E. Fey (Eds.), *Treatment of language disorders in children* (pp. 347–382). Baltimore, MD: Paul H. Brookes.

Justice, L. M., & Ezell, H. K. (2000). Enhancing children's print and word awareness through home-based parent intervention. *American Journal of Speech-Language Pathology, 9,* 257–269.

Justice, L. M., & Ezell, H. K. (2002). Use of storybook reading to increase print awareness in at-risk children. *American Journal of Speech-Language Pathology, ll,* 17–29.

Justice, L. M., & Ezell, H. K. (2004, April). Print referencing: An emergent literacy enhancement strategy and its clinical applications. *Language Speech, and Hearing Services in Schools, 35,* 185–193.

Justice, L. M., Kaderavek, J. N., Fan, X., Sofka, A., & Hunt, A. (2009, January). Accelerating preschoolers' early literacy development through classroom-based teacher-child storybook reading and explicit print referencing. *Language, Speech, and Hearing Services in Schools, 40,* 67–85.

Justice, L. M., Skibbe, L., & Ezell, H. (2006). Using print referencing to promote written language awareness. In T. A. Ukrainetz (Ed.), *Contextualized language intervention: Scaffolding PreK–12 literacy achievement.* Greenville, SC: Thinking Publications.

Kaderavek, J. N. (2011). *Language disorders in children: Fundamental concepts of assessment and intervention.* Boston, MA: Allyn & Bacon.

McGee, L. M., & Richgels, D. J. (2008). *Literacy's beginnings: Supporting young readers and writers* (5th ed.). Boston, MA: Pearson.

Miller, W. H. (2005). *Improving early literacy: Strategies and activities for struggling students (K–3).* San Francisco, CA: Jossey Bass.

Murawski, W. W., & Dieker, L. (2008). 50 ways to keep your co-teacher: Strategies for before, during, and after co-teaching. *Teaching Exceptional Children, 40*(4), 40–48.

Murawski, W. W., & Hughes, C. E. (2009). Response to intervention, collaboration, and co-teaching: A logical combination for successful systemic change. *Preventing School Failure, 53*(4), 267–277.

Nettles, D. H. (2006). *Comprehensive literacy instruction in today's classrooms: The whole, the parts, and the heart.* Boston, MA: Pearson, Allyn & Bacon.

Neuman, S. B., & Bredekamp, S. (2000). Becoming a reader: A developmentally appropriate approach. In D. S. Strickland & L. M. Morrow (Eds.), *Beginning reading and writing* (pp. 22–34). New York, NY: Teachers College Press.

Neuman, S.B., & Roskos, K. (1990). Play, print, and purpose: Enriching play environments for literacy development. *Reading Teacher, 44*(3), 214–221.

Owens, R. E., Jr. (1999). *Language disorders: A functional approach to assessment and intervention* (3rd ed.). Boston, MA: Allyn & Bacon.

Paul, R. (2007). *Language disorders from infancy through adolescence* (3rd ed.). St. Louis, MO: Elsevier.

Reutzel, S. E., Fawson, P. C., & Young, J. R. (2003). Reading environmental print: What is the role of concepts about print in discriminating young readers' responses. *Reading Psychology, 24*(2), 123–162.

Rivalland, J. (2000). Linking literacy learning across different contexts. In C. Barratt-Pugh, & M. Rohl (Eds.), *Literacy learning in the early years* (pp. 27–56). Philadelphia, PA: Open University Press.

Savage, J. F. (2011). *Sound it out: Phonics in a comprehensive reading program* (4th ed.). New York, NY: McGraw-Hill.

Shared reading. (n.d.). Retrieved from http://oe.edzone.net/balanced_literacy

Stewart, S. R., & Lovelace, S. M. (2006). Recruiting children's attention to print during shared reading. In L. M. Justice (Series Ed.), *Emergent and early literacy series: Clinical approaches to emergent literacy intervention* (pp. 327–359). San Diego, CA: Plural.

Strickland, D. S. (2000). Classroom intervention strategies: Supporting the literacy development of young learners at risk. In D. S. Strickland & L. M. Morrow (Eds.), *Beginning reading and writing* (pp. 99–110). New York, NY: Teachers College Press.

Teale, W. H., & Yokota, J. (2000). Beginning reading and writing: Perspectives on instruction. In D. S. Strickland & L. M. Morrow (Eds.), *Beginning reading and writing* (pp. 3–21). New York, NY: Teachers College Press.

Tompkins, G. E. (1998). *50 literacy strategies*. Upper Saddle River, NJ: Merrill, Prentice-Hall.

Tompkins, G. E. (2004). *Teaching writing: Balancing process and product* (4th ed.). Upper Saddle River, NJ: Pearson.

Vygotsky, L. S. (1978). *Mind in society: The development of higher psychological processes*. Cambridge, MA: MIT Press.

Chapter 4

Exploring Squiggles on Paper: Teaching and Practicing Letter Knowledge Skills

Gary Eldon Bingham, Sharon Black,
and Barbara Culatta

"Hey! That is my letter! The letter *L* stands for Lily. That's me." Lily was excited when the preschool teacher held up her name to come and choose a picture (Figure 4–1).

Children like Lily are often excited when they see their names in print. Because names are intensely personal to children, the letters in children's names are the first letters that many children learn, and their names are the very first word many learn to read and write (Clay, 1991; Levin & Ehri, 2009).

Recognizing the letters in one's own name is an important developmental accomplishment, but children must also become proficient in identifying the other letters of the alphabet. Some of the enticement involved in learning the letters in familiar names can be applied in teaching other letters. In fact, a strong correlation

Figure 4–1. Lily proudly shows the letters of her name.

exists between children's ability to read and spell their own name and their developing knowledge of alphabet letters (Blair & Savage, 2006; Levin & Ehri, 2009).

Children benefit from having meaning associated with particular letters and with the skill of learning to identify them. This chapter addresses children's acquisition of letter names, including the nature and importance of this skill, as well as the challenges children face in comprehending and applying it. Ways to introduce letter concepts and letter names to young children are discussed, along with various instructional methods and contexts. Ways for differentiating for children with language difficulties are included.

Nature and Importance of Young Children's Letter Knowledge

In the United States many children enter preschool and most enter kindergarten with the ability to name alphabet letters (Bowman & Treiman, 2004; Ellefson, Treiman, & Kessler, 2009. The initial letters that children learn tend to be those that are most meaningful, such as those in their names or those they come in contact with in the environment (i.e., the letter *M* for McDonalds). Letter knowledge in early childhood is important because it helps children learn to connect letter symbols to sounds and also benefits children as they learn to talk about how the reading process works (Snow et al., 1998; Piasta & Wagner, 2010).

Because similar and overlapping terminology can confuse many literacy issues, some important constructs and definitions are clarified, before and during discussion of the letter knowledge task.

Constructs and Definitions

Multiple labels and constructs have been used to study and explain children's understanding of letters and their sounds. Although such labels generally refer to similar skills, the construct to which they are attached can sometimes be ambiguous.

Three constructs need initial definition: alphabet knowledge, the alphabetic principle, and letter knowledge. *Alphabet knowledge* refers to the knowledge of letter names and the sounds made by letters of the alphabet (McBride-Chang, 1999); this includes the letter recognition concepts discussed in this chapter and application of sounds to letters emphasized in Chapter 5. Alphabet knowledge leads naturally to understanding of the *alphabetic principle*, which can be defined as the mapping of written graphemes to the phonemes in spoken words. Many articles, therefore, use the terms *alphabet knowledge* and *alphabetic principle* interchangeably. In contrast to alphabet knowledge, the term *letter knowledge* represents a narrower construct, which encompasses children's ability to recognize, identify, and write letters. In this chapter letter recognition and naming are considered as an aspect of the alphabetic principle.

Thus the terms *letter knowledge* and *alphabet knowledge* are used to represent their respective constructs.

Role of Letter Knowledge in Literacy Learning

The ability to name letters is a strong predictor of reading achievement and spelling proficiency (Adams, 1990; Catts, Fey, Tomblin, & Zhang, 2002; Hamill, 2002; Muter, Hulme, Snowling, & Stevenson, 2004; Scarborough, 1998; Storch & Whitehurst, 2002; Whitehurst & Lonigan, 1998). In examining skills that contribute to children's reading achievement, the National Early Literacy Panel (NELP, 2008) highlighted alphabet knowledge as one of the five most important predictors of reading ability. In a meta-analysis of literature on alphabet teaching and learning, Piasta and Wagner (2010) found it to be "the best predictor" (p. 8).

Name-Sound Relationships

Although some research suggests a direct link between children's letter-name knowledge and their word reading (Treiman & Kessler, 2003), most studies support the fact that children's knowledge of letters contributes to their ability with letter-sound correspondence, which then contributes to their ability to write and decode words (Levin, Shatil-Carmon, & Asif-Rave, 2006; McBride-Chang, 1999). Many researchers have found that children rely on letter name knowledge when producing letter-sound information, as the phoneme represented by the letter is included in most English letter names (DeJong, 2010; Kim, Foorman, Petscher, & Zhou, 2010; Piasta & Wagner, 2010; Share, 2004). Bowman and Trieman (2004) noted that this may be "a key to encouraging the shift from visual to phonetic reading" and asserted, "Even prereaders can form systematic connections between print and speech when those connections are based on . . . knowledge of the names of the alphabet letters" (p. 297). General consensus in the research is that children's ability to produce letter sounds increases dramatically when they know the letter names (e.g., Kim et al., 2010; Piasta & Wagner, 2009, 2010; Share, 2004). In fact, Piasta and Wagner (2010) found in their meta-analysis "studies providing letter name instruction as the only alphabet component [which] showed reliable, positive impacts on children's letter sound learning" (p. 20).

Share (2004) conducted studies examining possible ways that alphabet knowledge may affect multiple aspects of learning to read. He found that knowledge of letter names accounted for approximately twice the variance in children's progress in early reading as socioeconomic status or parent-child storybook reading and activities. In considering possible reasons for this influence, he suggested, as have many others, that children respond to the similarities between names and sounds of many of the letters and added (1) that having names for the letters helps a child tap into his memory for letter shapes, (2) that recognizing and naming letters helps children understand that "writing represents spoken language rather than directly [representing] meaning," and (3) that knowing letters and their names makes children sensitive to "the fundamental phonological nature of writing" (p. 215). Some research suggests that awareness of letter names and sounds contributes to children's literacy independent of other skills, such as phonological awareness and oral language (Burgess & Lonigan, 1998; McBride-Chang, 1999). Additionally, letter knowledge benefits children as they learn to talk about how the reading process works (Snow, Burns, & Griffin, 1998).

Rapid Letter Naming

In order for children to have well-developed alphabet letter knowledge, they must not only be able to recognize and name the letters, but become "fluent" in their ability to do so. According to the National Early Literacy Panel report (NELP, 2008), children's ability for rapid automatic naming of letters (RAN) is among cognitive skills that have been shown to predict later literacy development. Some preschool teachers may interpret this to indicate that "skill and drill" time should be devoted to promoting this speed; however, highly respected researchers have cautioned otherwise.

Dorothy Strickland, a member of the NELP, cautioned, "Rapid naming . . . is largely a consequence of numerous meaningful exposures to oral language and print. . . . the critical instructional objective should focus on promoting children's deep understanding and ability to apply what is learned" (as quoted in Dickinson, Golinkoff, Hirsh-Pasek, Neuman, & Burchinal, 2009). Others have instructed teachers specifically that they should not spend time directly instructing and drilling children to name letters rapidly (Dickinson et al., 2009; see also Teale, Hoffman, & Paciga, 2010). In a meta-analysis of the literature on "alphabet learning and instruction," Piasta and Wagner (2010) noted that letter name fluency (i.e., RAN) was the only skill that was not affected by instruction.

Barnett and Frede (2009), co-directors of the National Institute for Early Education Research, agreed with Strickland and further explained that where specific skills and literacy are concerned, correlation does not indicate causation—that RAN is only an "indicator of a set of skills and abilities that not only predict later literacy, but are also indicative of better memory skills, higher innate intelligence, and more enriched environments" (as quoted in Dickinson et al., 2009). The ability to automatically recognize letters is beneficial, as it allows children to free up their working memory skills for other tasks. However, drilling for speed alone may be acting via a post hoc causal fallacy. If children are to learn effectively, the learning task must be more than quickly retrieving rote associations.

A Child's View

Morrow (2001) and Nettles (2006) have both suggested that instructors need to look at letter learning through a small child's eyes to gain "a renewed respect for the complexity of the task that lies before the nonreader" (p. 195). Nettles continued:

> How do you answer the question, "What does 'B' mean?" When you attach meaning to this flat, one-dimensional figure printed on the page, you're doing so by associating it with something else—something that is real, personalized, and bigger than it actually looks. The only way that the symbol printed on the page has any meaning is to attach it to something else. (p. 195)

Nancy Lee Cecil (2003) summed up the situation, "In themselves, the letters are meaningless squiggles" (p. 75).

The Challenge

Nettles listed five abstract processes that a child must go through in learning these squiggles:

◆ See each as a "unique, separate entity"

◆ Connect it with a sound that does not make sense
◆ Remember both uppercase and lowercase shapes
◆ Find a way to remember the letter as different from all the other letters (some of which look very much like it)
◆ Connect it to sounds and/or concepts with meaning (Nettles, 2006; see also Gunning, 2000)

Mason (1984, as cited in Bradley & Jones, 2007) included naming the letter and writing it among these "separate yet interconnected components" (p. 452).

As teachers and SLPs help children with these early needs, they may find that students who are English language learners need extra help, as they are less accustomed to the specific sounds related to symbols. Direct instruction is recommended, in homogeneous groups of three to six students, with immediate, clear feedback/error correction (Gersten, Baker, Shanahan, Linan-Thompson, Collins, & Scarcella, 2007). Cooperative work within a group can be beneficial (Barr, Eslami, & Joshi, 2012), with students working together to figure out strategies for recalling letters and making connections.

The Process

A child acquires literacy by gradually accumulating information about the features of language, linguistic as well as orthographic, and this process requires scaffolding and guidance (Bowman & Treiman, 2004). During the *logo-graphic* or *pre-alphabetic* stage, children focus on visual aspects of print and identify letters as they identify pictures: for example, the letter *m* is the humps on *camel* (Bowman & Triman, 2004); the sound of the letter is not involved. Bowman and Triman (2004) explained, "Although children are not actually reading during the logographic stage, they are learning to link a visual configuration to a particular spoken word and are beginning to understand that print and speech are associated" (p. 296). When children move into the *alphabetic phase*, they begin linking the letter (grapheme) to the phoneme that it represents. These stages are not discrete: Sometimes they overlap or interact as children struggle to make sense of what letters are and what they represent.

Early Letter Knowledge Preparation

Children come to preschool with a wide range of letter knowledge experience: Some know no letters at all; others can identify all of the letters in the alphabet; some can write (with varying accuracy) many or all of them. Bridging these gaps as the class begins studying letters is challenging, but teachers have found many successful strategies. Following is a brief discussion of four specific strategies that are widely recognized, useful, and easy to apply: letter-friendly environments, the alphabet song, alphabet books, and children's names.

Letter-Friendly Environments

Learning letter names is a gradual process that moves from recognizing letters to being able to name and produce them (Ehri, 1987, 2005). Thus an effective early literacy curriculum begins with integrated exposure and implicit awareness of letter-sound associations to prepare the children for later explicit instruction. SLPs and teachers should facilitate this learning by making letters and letter learning integral aspects of the environment. Morrow (2001) has suggested that an alphabet chart be posted where children can easily refer to it when they need to remember a letter to identify it or to write it (Figure 4–2). Some teachers use many charts (including word walls) containing high frequency words throughout the room. Au (2000) described a kindergarten teacher who wrote often from her students' dictation and would frequently ask a student to find a particular word on a specific class chart and spell it for her as she wrote it.

Letters are language units that do not carry specific meaning, so children are not exposed to letter names in the same ways they are exposed to object names (Turnbull, Bowles, Skibbe, Justice, & Wiggins, 2010). Associations must be formed between the letter name and the letter in print (Turnbull et al., 2010). Teachers and SLPs need to help children encounter and respond to letters in meaningful ways.

Many researchers and teachers recommend signs and labels for classroom places and items (e.g., Gunning, 2000; Neuman &

Figure 4–2. With letter charts and other print throughout the room, this child can easily check the *B* she is writing next to the picture she has drawn of a bat in her letter journal. She has an illustrated page for each letter as she learns it.

Roskos, 1990; Chapter 3 this text), although signs and labels alone do not promote young children's letter knowledge (see Diamond, Gerde, & Powell, 2008). Thus children use letters they recognize in the words to orient themselves to locations and functions, as they see their parents do in finding a desired business, department, or product in daily life. For example, letter signs can be used in dramatic play to convey meaning and draw children's attention to print (e.g., a big *R* or the word Restaurant to turn a center into a *restaurant* or a *D* next to a cardboard window for a drive-up).

Savage (2011) recommended an "alphabet center," filled with a alphabet letters in a number of different materials: felt, sandpaper, foam rubber, window screen, Styrofoam, plastic, sponge, wood, etc, Magnetic letters with an appropriate board can also be included

(Morrow, 2001). By manipulating letters in a variety of materials, children have a tactile experience, which is a learning style many children respond to well. The center also includes material for tracing and writing letters (e.g., sand, foam, shaving cream) and clay and/or Playdough for forming letters (Rohl, 2000).

If computers are part of the classroom environment, as they are in many preschool and early grade classrooms today, teachers and SLPs can use the very motivating computer keyboards to make children aware of letters. Within the last 10 years technology at home and at school has become part of most children's daily reality, and some classrooms are experimenting with handheld and touch screen tablet devices such as iPads as well. Many interactive letter learning computer programs and mobile applications are available that allow children to work with electronic letter learning activities. Some of these programs encourage children to identify letters in order to solve puzzles or interact with words or pictures. Although the quality of these applications varies widely, teachers who want to give children extra practice with their letter knowledge skills can use apps such as ABC expedition, ABC pop, Alphabet Zoo, Goodnight ABC, Magic Letters, and ABC ZooBorns. Teachers (as well as parents) should be careful about using such technologies with children: for cautions and guidelines, see http://www.naeyc.org/files/naeyc/file/positions/PS_technology_WEB2.pdf. Digital technologies can be powerful in attracting and maintaining children's attention; thus if children want to play these games to the exclusion of more meaningful active learning opportunities, teachers may need to place limits on their use.

The Alphabet Song

Many children respond particularly well when singing is part of the classroom environment and the learning experience. The popular Alphabet Song, which has become for English-speaking children "one of the milestones in the growth of toddlers" (Nettles, 2006), can become part of the letter-rich environment of classrooms. As they learn the song by rote, many children do not perceive the letters as individual entities: "elemenopee" being one long letter (Nettles, 2006; Savage, 2011). Children who have learned the names

Figure 4–3. Children roll letter blocks, naming each letter as it comes up. They may keep a tally to see which letters are "luckiest."

of the letters from the song without learning letter appearance have partial knowledge that can be used as an anchor (Combs, 2002) for learning letter identification. To make use of this mental anchor, an alphabet chart can be placed on the wall with the letters arranged in lines corresponding with the phrases of the song. The entire class or various smaller groups of children could sing the alphabet song, with the teacher or a child with teacher support running a pointer under the letters. In this way, children learn to separate and recognize the letters individually, and they learn the appearance of the various letters as they sing (Nettles, 2006). Nettles noted from her observation that some children who are trying to identify or remember a particular letter will go over to the chart and point-sing the letters to themselves in order to find the letter they need; thus providing themselves with a way of scaffolding their own learning. Since letter shapes have little relationship to letter names (Combs, 2002), multiple exposures to letters and modeling how to use environmental print supports, such as a posted alphabet, can help children internalize letter learning.

Children's Names

Names are also very helpful in learning to recognize letters (Gunning, 2000). Recall the example at the beginning of this chapter: "*L* is Lilly's special letter because it is always at the beginning of her name. Researchers have found that children seem to be exposed more to their first initial than to any other letter, and, as Turnbull et al. (2010) pointed out, "they feel an inherent sense of ownership over this letter" (p. 1759). Many studies have been conducted using young children's names to determine how they process and learn letters and letter names (e.g., Blair & Savage, 2006; Bradley & Jones, 2007; Levin & Ehri, 2009; Turnbull et al., 2010). In looking for ways that the printed name relates to the oral name, children learn to look analytically at the task of associating letters and sounds (Bradley & Jones, 2007).

Marie Clay (1991) suggested that children should begin learning the alphabet letters as soon as they start writing their names, as the process of writing the letters draws attention to them and invests them with meaning that is personal and consistent. Blair and Savage (2006) did not find significant connections between general exposure to environmental print and pre-readers' letter-sound knowledge or phonological awareness, but they did find close connections of these skills to children's ability to recognize and write their own names. If the teacher or SLP writes each child's name on a list and posts it in the classroom, children are able to see their peers' names as composed of specific letters, like their own, and to recognize their friends' "special letters." Levin and Ehri (2009) found that preliterate children could learn to read their classmates' names by using "partial cues" provided by known letters, even if the names contained many unknown letters as well.

Thus, aspects of environment and routines that involve names can be adopted to reinforce the specific partial clues, and exposure expands the number of them that children learn and access. Children could make interesting and creative signs with their own names to place over cubbies or on personal "mailboxes"—using the letters they know best to say, "This is Lily's place." As other children recognize Lily's place, they come to recognize letters in Lily's name as well. A teacher who was having difficulty with young children pushing and shouting for privileges, such as leading a line or being first to be dismissed, was successful with "alphabetic turn taking." She posted a chart of all the children's names in alphabetical order; each time a desired privilege occurred, the marker moved down the alphabetic chart. Before long the children were the ones reminding the teacher, "Let's take alphabet turns" (Durkin, 1987, p. 47).

Opportunities can be provided for children to write their names or use the "special" letters of their initials in authentic contexts. Many children commonly see older family members signing their names on forms, lists, petitions, etc. The children can place their "signatures" on their artwork or dictated stories, or on posted lists to show activities in which they want to participate. Children can create their own identifying nametags for visitors attending an activity such a school field day or a parent event to be hosted by the class (Figure 4–4).

Activities and games can also center on the letters in children's names, possibly adding names that they use during dramatic play and other classroom activities. Simple prompts (disguised as comments) by an interested adult can foster children's imagination for inventing names and finding ways to creatively involve letters and sounds. When seeing a child care for a doll, take a pet for a walk around the classroom, create a bag puppet or build a character from

Figure 4–4. A boy writes his name on a nametag so he can be easily identified.

play dough, the teacher or SLP can playfully engage the children in thinking about names. The adult may furnish sticky notes to "name" the buildings children make in the block center or server nametags for playing restaurant (May, Bingham, & Barrett-Mynes, 2010). She can help children sound out and write the first letter for a made-up name and to attach to play materials. These interactions encourage children to experience letter activities in contexts of their own activities and imagination.

Alphabet Books

Shared reading of alphabet books, like writing names and learning the alphabet song, begins at home in very early childhood for many children. However, teachers can still use them in classrooms to confirm, clarify, and expand the knowledge of all children while providing bridgework for those who did not have earlier exposure. Many researchers and practitioners recommend alphabet books for familiarizing, teaching, and reviewing letter names (e.g., Christie, Enz, & Vukelich, 2007; Combs, 2002; Cunningham, 2005; Gunning, 2000; Nettles, 2006). SLPs can repeat the use of alphabet books presented to the entire class and bring in additional alphabet books to work with individuals or groups needing extra help. Simple alphabet books, with a limited number of words and pictures per page, are particularly helpful for young children who are just beginning with letter sounds or children who are struggling with them (Cunningham, 2005)—less distraction, easier processing. In any alphabet book, letters should be clearly printed; letters integrated into print or obscured by embellishments prevent the children from being able to discern and learn the letter's true shape (Nettles, 2006). When reading alphabet books aloud, the teacher can pause to focus attention on the features of the various letters and let the children fill in the names (Combs, 2002).

Through alphabet books children can become interested in the nature and function of letters and/or learn letter names, visual features, and sounds (Bradley & Jones, 2007). If the purpose of a shared reading is to introduce the nature and function of letters or to attract the children's attention toward learning letters, books like *Chicka Chicka Boom Boom* (Martin & Archambault, 1989) and

Curious George Learns the Alphabet (Rey, 1963) catch attention and provide some initial experience with letter identification. But they do not really focus on individual letters in ways that would help children remember them (Bradley & Jones, 2007). So if the purpose is to help children learn specific letter shapes, names, and sounds, books like *Dr. Seuss's ABC: An Amazing Alphabet Book* (Seuss, 1963) or *Animalia* (Base, 1986) would be more effective, as they emphasize the individual letters more and allow interactive conversation about visual features of the letters as well as their names and sounds (Bradley & Jones, 2007). Bradley and Jones found in their study that teacher talk in both preschool and kindergarten classrooms related mostly to knowledge of the alphabet, features of the text, and child-text involvement in both types of books, but that alphabet knowledge was discussed more with the books specifically written to focus on letters and sounds (e.g., *Dr. Seuss's ABC*).

Alphabet books should be available in the classroom for children to "read" as they choose, especially books with which they are familiar (Cunningham, 2005). Alphabet books can be used in helping children understand the symbolic function of letters, including how letters function in relation to words (Warner & Weiss, 2005). For shared reading, the teacher or SLP can scan and enlarge selected pages from an alphabet book or photocopy pages on a transparency for an overhead projector (Combs, 2002), thus making texts large enough that the processes and relationships are easy to see and talk about. On chart paper the class might make their own alphabet big book to read through in unison as a group.

The children might want to make their own individual alphabet books (Christie, Enz, & Vukelich, 2007). Or they might compile a class book to put in their classroom library, perhaps with each child contributing a page (Tompkins, 2012).

Once children have been introduced to letters—how they look and what they do—children are ready for systematic and explicit letter knowledge instruction, along with multiple opportunities during the day to practice and apply their knowledge. The following section discusses aspects of explicit letter knowledge instruction that teachers and SLPs should be aware of, along with some methods for varying and reinforcing the lessons.

Explicit Letter Knowledge Instruction

Letter skills should be taught explicitly because letters that are not frequently encountered in classroom environments will not become familiar through daily exposure. Additionally, some children struggle more than others in learning to recognize shapes and recall names of the letters. Explicit instruction should be used to increase children's exposure to letters and give them opportunities to write what they see.

Explicit instruction is clear and direct. Lessons are "sequenced, structured, and adult directed"—less naturalistic than many activities that are designed to be child focused (Kaderavek, 2011, p. 317). But explicit does not have to be rote. When explicit instruction is balanced with motivating activities that offer choices, teachers and SLPs can help children learn effectively with this method (Au, 2000). Explicit teaching of letter names should follow a process that includes selecting targets purposefully, introducing the target letter, and modeling/discussing its shape and use. As they administered direct instruction in letter knowledge to three- and four-year-old preschoolers, Lafferty, Gray, and Wilcox (2005) found that children with and without language difficulties developed an increased desire to learn letters—both at home and at school. In planning direct instruction for letter knowledge, teachers and SLPs should select and sequence targets purposefully, select clear, explicit goals for each lesson, and provide repeated modeling of letter recognition and naming.

Purposeful Sequencing

Early childhood curricula approach the sequence for letter learning differently. While there is no prescribed order for teaching letters, following some principle for the sequence of introducing letter names can make it easier for children to acquire them. Instruction should move from recognizing a few personally relevant letters (like those in a child's name), to recognizing and naming frequently occurring letters, to naming less common letters, to naming letters in any order, to matching and recognizing both upper and lower case letters. Researchers and practitioners generally agree on three levels of difficulty or familiarity for the letters. The most frequently encountered consonants have been found to be *M, B, T, S, P, D, K, F, R, C.* The middle level of occurrence contains *L, G, H, J, V, W.* In English, the letters encountered least frequently are *Q, X, Y, Z.* Some teachers have children choose some favorite words that they want to work with (e.g., from a song, poem, story, etc.), and they select letters common in those words to teach during their alphabet instruction (Moustafa, 2000).

Adams (1990) has recommended that uppercase letters be taught before their lowercase equivalents, to avoid initial confusion from two letter forms for each letter name. She noted that children have greater familiarity with uppercase letters and find them easier to discriminate. She advised that preschool teachers or SLPs may even want to postpone lowercase letters until kindergarten. Support for this separation was supplied by Turnbull et al. (2010), who found in their study that students learn lowercase letters much more easily if they already know the uppercase equivalent. These researchers found that similarities between previously learned uppercase letters and new lowercase letters may be a "primary mechanism" for learning lowercase letters (p. 1757). If a preschool curriculum (e.g., Head Start) requires that young children learn both upper- and lowercase letters, the teacher or SLP will need to introduce each letter name as having two symbols, calling attention to the fact that some pairs look alike, and some do not (Bradley & Jones, 2007).

Clear, Explicit Goals

Through explicit instruction students should clearly understand the letter(s) being targeted and taught. Unfortunately, many early childhood classrooms lack clear instructional goals and routines (Justice, Mashburn, Hamre, & Pianta, 2008). One way to make a goal or target clear is to state it and provide striking examples that attract and maintain children's attention. First, the teacher might focus children's attention on the letter, by pointing to a letter on a card or chart and saying, "Today you will learn the letter *M.* It goes up and down and up and down and looks like a mountain."

After naming the letter and pointing to it again, the teacher might ask the children to find the letter *M* among two or three other letters.

To attract further interest in the letter, the teacher may provide a reason to select it. For example, the teacher can read the book *Mouse Mess* (Riley, 1997) and have the children select *M*s from some letter choices to make a mess as they mix and mash *M*s in a big *M*-mess. During the activity the teacher can draw further attention to the letter *M* by having the children select *M*s to mash and mix with macaroni, mud, or mush (flour and water). As the children take turns finding *M*s to mix and mash, the adult reviews the shape and the letter's name. This activity can be done as a whole group with children taking quick turns or in a small group with more participation.

Instructor Modeling

Introducing skills and strategies is not enough to enable most children to use them. Teachers must model and scaffold, showing children what they go through as they think about letter shapes and sounds, then guiding them in going through the processes themselves (Au, 2000). In modeling the letter, the teacher or SLP should use the name and have the children repeat the name.

A variety of ways can be used to draw children's attention to the letter name. For example, the teacher or SLP can ask the children to say the name of the letter each time he puts his finger on it or name the letter multiple times while holding their fingers on it. An additional strategy is to name letters and have children identify them during whole class writing activities. As teachers take down children's dictation, they can have them identify letters they recognize. Children are likely to learn letters more quickly when the teacher or SLP helps them identify and use letters in meaningful contexts rather than through rote practice or instruction.

It is important to consider that the processes of stating and modeling the target help children maintain their attention on the letter, which makes it easier for them to put the letter and its name in short-term (and eventually in long-term) memory. Teachers should point to the letter or tap on it to draw the children's attention to it, making sure the letter is within the children's range of vision and that they are attending to the letter in order to take turns selecting it, moving it, or otherwise interacting with it. Incorporating previously learned letters with new target letters in challenges or games helps build children's visual discrimination.

To focus attention on a letter's visual form, the instructor can point out its distinctive features and talk about how it is written. Comparing the shape of a letter to a common object gives children a visual image to help in remembering it: for example, an *S* looks like a snake; and a *C* looks like a cookie with a big bite taken out of it. The shape of a letter can also be emphasized by discussing the motions involved in making it: for example, an Australian preschooler learned to say, "*M* for mummy goes up, down, up, down" as she practiced drawing the letter in the air (Neumann & Neumann, 2010, p. 91).

Personal experiences with the letter's form can make letter learning relevant. Preschool teachers report that X can be easily acquired if it is used to signal spots or places children can sit on or write their name beside. The teacher or SLP might mark *X*s on the carpet in a circle and let each child take a place, using a catchy phrase to reinforce the letter name—like "*X* marks the spot." *O*s are easily learned because they are associated with circles, which are easy to make and have many uses. They can also be associated with *O*-shaped cereal (Neumann & Neumann, 2010). *O*s can be used in an *O*-toss game in which the objective is to get something in the center of the *O*, which looks like a ring. Children can sit or stand in an *O* shape.

Review

Reviewing what was learned is an important step to cementing children's knowledge and determining the impact of instruction; it should be included in explicit instruction of letter knowledge. Being reminded of letters that they have worked with also gives children a sense of accomplishment as they can see how quickly they are adding to their base of letter knowledge. Reviewing can take a number of forms. The whole class might spend a minute or two each day labeling letters they have already learned, with the teacher pointing on a chart to between three and five letters she has previously taught. Children can identify letters as they draw them from a special container or find them on letter blocks.

As a particular privilege the teacher or SLP might conduct a review with "letter-name basketball." A hoop can be hung at the right height for the children, a soft basketball is provided, and the children line up as two teams. As each child has a turn, the teacher or SLP holds up a flash card with one of the letters being reviewed. If the child identifies the letter correctly, he or she gets to try to shoot a basket (Miller, 2005).

Reviewing letters by labeling them should be presented quickly and enthusiastically. The teacher should use the scaffolding necessary to make sure children are successful and should not let them struggle to remember the correct name of the letter. If a child is slow in responding, the teacher should give the answer or prompt a response by beginning to say the correct letter name and having the child complete then repeat it. Teachers and SLPs need to avoid pressuring the children with review (or any other) "activities that are too formal" (Rohl, 2000, p. 78).

Another way to review letters is to include letters children have already learned into activities designed to teach new letters. For example, letters can be hidden, found, traded, sold, painted, sorted, knocked down, crumpled, thrown, pulled, ripped, or folded. The teacher or SLP might decorate a box with many examples of the new letter on sticky label paper (e.g., lots of *R*s) and also put letters that were already taught on the label paper as well (e.g., stick *M, B, T,* and *D* on the box). Or children might pretend to be mail carriers, writing new and previously taught letters on envelopes, sorting this "mail" for the class post office, and "delivering letters"—old and new—to designated mailboxes.

Despite careful explicit teaching and conscientious review, children acquire literacy knowledge at different rates, particularly if language and its skills do not come easily to them. In all aspects of letter knowledge instruction, the SLP, teacher, and other members of the instructional team must observe and monitor children carefully, making continual adjustments to meet their individual needs.

Differentiation

As many authors have pointed out, alphabet learning is influenced by a number of characteristics and skills of children, including memory, phonological processing, oral language, and print awareness (Piasta & Wagner, 2010b). As many children have weaknesses in such areas, instruction should be adjusted to benefit each.

Needs Assessment

To determine what each child needs and track the child's progress, simple assessment and record keeping are required. Assessment practices that help teachers become aware of which letters children can recognize, name, and produce should be integrated into activities at every step of the instructional process. Many standardized phonics and phonemic awareness tests have subtests or sections that assess letter identification (Savage, 2011), and informal assessment is easy to incorporate. When a teacher or SLP asks children to give the name of a letter or to identify a letter from a choice of several (e.g., on alphabet cards), the responses reveal which each child knows and which need to be re-taught or practiced. The teacher can use simple checklists to keep track of each child's knowledge and progress.

Teachers should look particularly for general fluency in letter naming, noticing which children can name a letter fairly easily in several contexts and which children seem to struggle more with demonstrating this knowledge. Children who learn more slowly or require scaffolding when they respond will need more support and practice. A child has not sufficiently learned the letter until she is able to name it without support in several different contexts over several days, and the SLP should provide small group or individual practice as required. The SLP and the teacher should use both formative assessment practices (such as anecdotal records and checklists) and summative processes (such as benchmark assessment tasks three or four times during the school year) to document children's learning of letter names. However, the most important aspect of assessment for young readers, particularly those who are at risk, is the process of making instructional decisions based on what is assessed and recorded (Strickland, 2000).

Teacher Support and Task Demands

As many authors have pointed out, alphabet learning is influenced by a number of characteristics and skills of children, including memory, phonological processing, oral language, and print awareness (Piasta & Wagner, 2010). As many children have weaknesses in such areas, instruction should be adjusted to benefit each.

Individualization for children requires flexibility for adults. Researchers have found that children can learn letter names as effectively in classrooms as in clinics (Piasta & Wagner, 2010), but teachers and SLPs should share goals and coordinate instruction to maximize the learning situation. Dorothy Strickland (2000) stated firmly, "Large blocks of uninterrupted time in which small-group, personalized instruction is offered should be regularly scheduled for learners who are experiencing difficulty" (p. 103). Teachers and SLPs should willingly arrange adequate time to scaffold children's participation and engagement in activities and pay attention to what children know and where they need support. Children who are having difficulty struggle in different areas for different reasons. Flexible grouping should be adopted so that struggling students experience "varied grouping patterns, varied materials, and varied instructional tasks (Strickland, 2000, p. 104).

Recognition

Children need to learn to notice features of individual letters in order to distinguish and attach names to them (McGee & Richgels, 2000). Gillon (2006) has recommended that for these children SLPs begin with a small number of letters that are "visually distinct" (p. 294). To experience letter shapes vividly, children with this weakness can benefit from specific instructor guidance in the alphabet center. Savage (2011) elaborated that if the instructor and the child(ren) are "talking through the movement of making [or tracing] the letter . . . [they] engage their visual, kinesthetic, and tactual modalities to support visual recognition of letters" (p. 56).

Repetition

Some children require extra repetition: Strickland (2000) explained that many need a second or third iteration of what is presented to the rest of the class. She recommended that SLPs or teachers provide carefully monitored guided practice, which enables them to adjust their instruction to meet children's specific needs. Another suggestion is that some of the instruction and practice involve pairs and that some be delivered in small heterogeneous groups. These structures also allow children the experience of learning from peers (Strickland 2000).

Regardless of particular group structure, using games and activities can make the repetition less tedious. For example, to turn drill with letters into a game with manipulatives, the SLP or teacher can give students loose letter tiles to match to letters printed on a laminated game board (Schickedanz as described in Christie, Enz, & Vukelich, 2007). Or a simple but engaging text can be projected on a wall and the children can take turns running to the text and touching specific letters named by the teacher (Gillon, 2006). If a child is having difficulty discriminating a letter or remembering its name, the SLP or teacher needs to scaffold before the child is frustrated. The adult might begin to pronounce the letter name and let the child finish it or might say the letter name and have the child repeat it. If the child needs to be told the name of a letter, the adult should not hesitate to do so. Adults should provide high levels of support when children are struggling to learn letters and when they hesitate to respond.

For children who continue to struggle, repetition can be embedded multiple times within a variety of activities and contexts. Researchers have found that children with language disorders may need each letter name and sound modeled frequently during letter play activities in order to learn them (Lafferty et al., 2005). As struggling children may be bored easily, repetition should occur within interesting and meaningful activities.

Practice Including Movement

All children enjoy movement, even if it is combined with repeated practice of alphabet letters and names. Simple repetitive activities using movement can be helpful and engaging for the entire class. Thus no one is held up while vivid practice is provided for children who struggle with language, who need to spend more time reviewing and practicing letters but are less interested and motivated for doing it. Mary S. Rivkin (2006), who chairs the Education Department at the University of Maryland, wrote:

> When teachers regard movement as a basic need of children and resolve to work *with* them rather than *against* them . . . it fosters a cooperative atmosphere both in and out of the classroom. Children do not need to feel ashamed of their physicality and restlessness. (p. 36)

Rule, Dockstader, and Stewart (2006) studied the effects of various types of movement on the learning of children who were struggling with emergent literacy, including letters and sounds. These children were placed in two before-school programs: one based on kinesthetic activities involving full body movement (e.g., pantomime, full-arm gestures, stepping stones) and one based on tactile learning involving small manipulatives (e.g., word cards, small objects, environmental print sets). A control group consisted of children without disabilities, whose pretest scores were higher. At the end of the study, the children with difficulties had come up to the level of their typically developing peers.

Acting in Response to Letters

Letters can be used to represent actions and thus give children opportunities for large-muscle movement. Students can move in place in fun or silly ways depending on what "letter" command the teacher gives: "When I hold up the *B* we will bounce right in our spots." The children can pretend to march or dance in place and continue the action as long as the teacher holds up the letter representing the action. Other options can include *H* = hop, *T* = tip toe, *D* = drive, *F* = fly, *W* =wave, *J* = jump, *S* = smile, *B* = blink (Figure 4–5). In addition, letters can be used to help children pretend to be creatures that move. Letters representing animals might include *D* = act like a dog, *T* = act like a tiger, or *E* = act like an elephant, and so forth. As an alternative, the teacher can have the children write (or dictate if necessary) their chosen letter on paper to instruct others

Figure 4–5. A student holds up *H*, and her classmates hop.

to follow the directions. A child could have to write *J* three times to tell the other children to jump three times.

Acting on Letters

Additional kinesthetic learning can occur as children act upon letters as if they were objects: using action words that begin with the sound the letter makes. For example, a *P* is poked, punched, pinched, picked, and pasted; an *F* is folded, fit into, fanned, or found. When playing and acting upon letters with actions that represent them, the SLP or teacher can reinforce the letters and sounds taught explicitly. Children might toss a *T* (or tape, tap, touch); mark the *M* (e.g., with a marker); paint a *P* purple (or push, poke, press, or pound on it); fold the *F*; mash and mush the *M*; rip the *R*; or pop the *P* (i.e., from a large bubble pack with *P*s strategically written on them). Allowing children to act on letters in multiple ways keeps things interesting while explicitly calling attention to the letter. Rivkin (2006) referred to a statement by Mimi Chenfeld reminding teachers that many children who do not succeed very often during typical classroom practice learn more effectively when a skill is associated with movement.

When using engaging materials or activities, adults must be careful to keep children's focus on the letters and not on the medium being used to produce them or the manner of acting on them, particularly if struggling children try to avoid the letter-relevant aspect of the lesson. If a particular material is too engaging, the teacher can require students to perform a task (e.g., identifying letters before playing with them) or set some limits on how the material is to be used (perhaps that the dough is only for making letters).

Looking for Letters

Young children often enjoy activities that involve hiding and finding. Teachers can hide letters written on cards (the letter targeted and one or two other letters being reviewed) in the instruction area. They can ask the children to search for a particular letter or letters, which will be discussed and counted together at the end of the sequence. A variation of this activity is to pretend to lose letters: "I had some letters here in my pocket. I lost letters that were on white cards. They are *K, M,* and *D.* Can you help find them?" One child can be asked to find the *K*s, another to find the *D*s, and another to find the *M*s. Children search for their assigned letter and trade when they find a letter assigned to someone else. The instructor names the letters as the children find them and asks, "What letter did you find?" "Oh, you have an *M.* Peter is looking for the *M*s." If some of the children are having more trouble differentiating letters than their classmates, children can do these activities in purposefully arranged pairs.

A final format for finding letters is to find a letter matching the one another child has. The SLP or teacher can give out cards or slips of paper with a few different letters on them (e.g., *M, D, S*). Holding up a letter on a large card, she might say, "This is an *M.* If you have an *M,* see if you can find a buddy who also has an *M,* and you two can go to lunch together." This activity can also be done to assign partners for working together on an activity or for moving between activities. Children who know fewer letters can be given letters from their own names, which will be among the few with which they are most confident.

Sorting, Labeling, and Matching

Manipulating letters has been found to be as effective as total movement in helping children with alphabet skills (Rule et al., 2006). Children can practice discriminating letters by sorting, labeling, or matching them. Letters can be written on envelopes in a "post office" or a "card shop," or the SLP or teacher can introduce the idea that certain animals like certain letters.

In sorting activities, the adult can select a new target letter to introduce and a few letters to review, then label a container for each letter, either a generic container such as a box or sack or a container that starts with the letter to be contained (*B*-basket, *S*-sack, *P*-pail, etc.). The children can sort slips of paper with letters on them into the appropriate containers, naming the letters as they do so, with prompts as needed.

Children can participate enthusiastically in activities that challenge them at the developmental level at which they are competent (Gagen & Getchell, 2006), physically and cognitively. The next section moves into alphabet practice opportunities that involve less physicality and more mental manipulation.

Opportunities for Applying and Practicing

Letter recognition, names, and knowledge should be interwoven in all aspects of classroom instruction, occurring daily as part of class routines (Rohl, 2000). Students need varying amounts and intensities of small group instruction and frequent casual practice. During such instruction, teachers should implement activities involving letters in an organized and systematic way that is differentiated to meet needs of individual children and presented with creativity and joy.

Communication and Expression

As letters will eventually form words that children will use to communicate, they can begin to make connections by using letters to stand for the words they want to express. Observers (e.g., Walsh, Sproule, McGinness, & Trew) have found that effective learning occurs as teachers are "breaking down the dichotomies between informal and formal learning, and between play and work" (2011, p. 107). Learning letters while communicating with each other can be one way of integrating informal purposes with learning experience. Authentic reasons to communicate can be arranged to engage children in instruction and to increase their interest and motivation in learning letter names. Letters can be manipulated to communicate as children are given opportunities to use letters to request actions, turns, or objects; to stand for objects; or to communicate ideas or preferences.

Making Requests

Although teachers and SLPs try to make literacy relevant in children's lives, many of them do not realize that they are in effect creating a gulf between "using literacy and learning about literacy" (Hall & Robinson, 2000, p. 26). Children respond well to opportunities to use literacy to make something happen or obtain something they want. Many children are highly motivated by getting a turn during an activity or a share of a resource or supply. Letters can be linked by sound to children's requests. For example, the child must point to a particular letter (or copy it, say it, or give its name) to get a chance to work with interesting materials: possibly marking *D* to play with dough or writing *S* for a chance to stretch silly putty. During snack time, letter requests may include *P* for "please pass," *C* for crackers, and *J* for juice.

Expressing Choices

Polly Greenberg, formerly with the U.S. Department of Education, the Department of Health and Human Services, and the War on Poverty, wrote that it is important for early childhood teachers to "feature activities and projects that children of this age find meaningful" (p. 21). What could be more meaningful to young children than making choices and expressing opinions? Taste tests, surveys, and opinion polls are among the activities that enable class members to do so.

Taste Tests. Taste tests can be real or pretend (using gestures or paper props to stand for food items to try). The teacher or SLP emphasizes letter names as children use letters to request a turn to try an item or take a small bite of a food: for example, writing, tracing, or identifying an *F* to try "free fun fish food" (small fish crackers). They might do a commercial-style taste test comparing plain fish crackers to cheese fish crackers, voting for their choice and even defending it. In addition to writing the letter on paper to indicate their choice, children could write the letter multiple times to signal how many small pieces of a food item they want: possibly three *B*s for three (gummi) bears.

Opinion Polls and Surveys. In efforts to connect literacy to children's daily lives (see Hall & Robinson, 2000), teachers and SLPs might remember that opinion polls and surveys are delivered to mailboxes or over telephones in a number of children's homes, and many see references to these items on television or online, ranging from newscasts to advertising. Children can participate in opinion polls or surveys using letters to represent answers to questions. For example, children could use *Y* for *yes* and *N* for *no* on charts or individual papers to indicate that they agree or disagree with a question that is being discussed. Or they could signal favorite foods, pets, etc. by writing a letter that represents their preference (*T* for taco, *H* for hamburger, etc.). Teachers can make up a survey form and have children mark on a clipboard or piece or paper their opinion of an activity or story: *N* = no (don't like); *S* = silly; *F* = fun. A pet survey might catch the children's attention: "Mark *P* if you have a pet. Which pet would you like to have? *D* = dog, *M* = mouse, *B* = bird, etc."

Reading and Writing Experiences

Teachers or SLPs should call children's attention to letters used in books or the letters of vocabulary words being introduced during story time. As children encounter letters meaningfully in print-rich environments or storybook reading contexts, they have opportunities for learning the letter names as part of purposeful or functional uses of print (Justice, Kaderavek, Fan, Softa, & Hunt, 2009).

Participating in Shared Reading

Whenever possible children should learn and apply letters with their names and sounds through motivating stories and information books (Miller, 2005). When print is large enough to notice, the adult can point out letters during shared reading or read alouds. ("This says *Sam*. Sam is the dog in the story. Sam's name starts with *S*.") Big books are particularly helpful for children who are learning letters, as they range from 14 × 20 inches to 24 × 30 inches and are usually set on a stand or easel so that all can see both text and pictures (Morrow, 2001, p. 204). The SLP or teacher might want to place a sheet of acetate over the words and have the children take turns circling specific letters (Combs, 2002). Or the teacher might choose a poem or song that has high frequency use of a targeted letter (e.g., the initial letter in a repetitive word). She tells the students that they are learning the letter *B*, and the poem, song, or story they're going to hear has a lot of that letter in it. She can then encourage the children to help "read" the poem or lyrics.

Contributing to Shared Writing

Along with shared reading of big books or enlarged texts, shared writing on large chart paper can "involve children in literate behavior and help make explicit the connection between the spoken and written word" (Beach & Young, 1997, p. 261). As a shared writing activity, an adult can lead the children in generating a text about a shared experience that will naturally result in use of the targeted letter (e.g., a special time for tasty treats under a tall tree). Because the children are dictating the words about their experience, both the content and the word choice are their own, and the personal connection helps them to predict identity of personally unfamiliar words as the teacher adds each (see Christie, Enz, & Vukelich, 2007).

After shared reading of the text, special attention is called to the target letter(s). Small pieces of colored transparent plastic can be cut to place over the letters (but removed when the text is read interactively in order to show the letter in the context of the entire word). In this way teachers or SLPs can draw some attention to individual letters within the shared writing experience. Some teachers hang the finished story in a center at the children's eye level so that children can copy it if they want to do so (Christie, Enz,

& Vukelich, 2007) and perhaps take it home to share with their parents and siblings.

Children who have language difficulties may avoid participating in shared writing as a whole class or large group activity; however these children can benefit significantly from this experience as they watch their words represented as letters and have the teacher identify the letters while writing them. Wilma Miller (2005), who specializes in working with struggling children, recommended that a small group share an experience that is straightforward, direct, and easy to discuss: for example, a simple craft or baking activity, or perhaps a story all of them enjoy. Afterward the group discusses the experience (which helps them recall details and generate language). Each child then contributes one sentence to the short shared writing of the group.

Letter Practice Throughout the Day

The roles of teachers and SLPs in scaffolding and co-constructing children's literacy (Walsh et al., 2011) do not need to pause during routines and times of day that are not traditionally used for instruction. When playfulness is characteristic in the interactions of adults and children, as recommended by Walsh et al. (2007), even academic knowledge and skills such as letter knowledge can be slipped into contexts occurring throughout the school day.

Morning Business

Many teachers like to begin the day with a "morning message," which can be adapted to emphasize alphabet letters. Some simply choose to emphasize target letters when writing about the day: for example, having children provide ideas about what could be special about the day and writing their contributions on chart paper, highlighting initial letters or asking the children to write the first letter for particular words. Children respond well to opportunities to use letters to signal a response: possibly taking part in an "opinion poll" to indicate which of two books (shown by the teacher) they would like to have read to them—marking *P* for the book about plants or *M* for the book about magnets. The children may choose a letter card to indicate which activity they want to engage in first at the end of morning business (e.g., *B* to make a b-band with buttons and bows or *M* to make a marvelous mitten with magazines and markers).

Talking During Snack Time

Cunningham (2005) quipped, "Children remember what they do and what they eat" (p. 44). Snack time, which involves both doing and eating, is a particularly authentic context for using letters. For example, letters can make an appearance as snack items, menu components, symbols for requests, or a subject for casual table chatter. For a particularly motivating review, a member of the instructional team or a helpful parent could make cookies in the form of particular letters the children have been learning. During snack time, letters can make appearances in a variety of ways. To the teacher's surprise, children may discover letters under a cup or on a plate. Or they may be asked to write a *B* to get bits and bites of banana bread or a *P* for pieces of pretzels.

Reinforcing Letters During Transitions and Routines

Among classroom contexts in which letter encounters can be arranged with some intentionality (Justice, Kaderavek, Fan, Sofka, & Hunt, 2009) and frequency are transitions and other classroom routines. Using letters to symbolize objects or actions in daily classroom happenings gives opportunities to increase exposure and perceived prominence.

Transitions enable quick exposures that do not seem to be drill, and teachers and other instructional team members can slip in brief but engaging activities. For example, a teacher or SLP can use the beginning letter in each child's name to excuse children one at a time from large group to go to free choice activities, snack, centers, etc. In this way children enjoy having attention called to their "special letter," and they learn to recognize the first letters in names of their friends. Associating the letter with turns and privileges might even strengthen children's positive alphabet association. Or the instructor might pass out letters the children have been learning, using sticky notes, stamp pads, alphabet cards, or label paper, and excuse students from the carpet when the letter they are holding is called. Occasionally children could pass from place to place with a hopscotch activity (Savage, 2011), hopping across a hopscotch or some other sort of "lettered" grid formed from masking tape on the floor. As they land on each letter, they say its name. Sometimes it is the "little things," like playing hopscotch or watching as each classmate is excused according to his or her special letter, that can reinforce and solidify some of the letters and sounds children need to internalize so they can learn to read fluently.

Conclusion

This chapter has considered both the role of children's letter knowledge in their literacy development and ways teachers and SLPs can facilitate the development of this letter knowledge. Although letter knowledge is a narrow aspect of the written language system that does not focus on meaning, ways have been described for teachers to embed into their classroom environments, routines, and instruction a variety of letter practice activities that allow children to apply their alphabet knowledge in meaningful and engaging ways.

In addition, this chapter demonstrates the need for systematic and explicit letter knowledge instruction. Explicit teaching of letter names can follow a process that includes stating and modeling the target letter, providing practice, and reviewing and monitoring children's learning. This type of instruction is particularly needed when children struggle to learn letter names. As noted in this chapter, teachers and SLPs should implement a letter knowledge instructional program that provides all children with appropriate lessons and practice to meet their individual needs. Further, such exposure should be fun and engaging for young children. By making activities explicit and fun, the teacher is able to recruit each child's attention while helping him or her learn the targeted letters.

References

Adams, M. J. (1990). *Beginning to read: Thinking and learning about print*. Cambridge, MA: MIT Press.

Au, K. (2000). Literacy instruction for young children of diverse backgrounds. In D. S. Stickland & L. M. Morrow (Eds.), *Beginning reading and writing* (pp. 35–57). New York, NY: Teachers College Press.

Barr, S., Eslami, Z. R., & Joshi, F. M. (2012). Core strategies to support English language learners. *Educational Forum, 76,* 105–117. doi: 10.1080/00131725.2012.628196

Beach, S. A., & Young, J. (1997). Children's development of literacy resources in kindergarten: A model. *Reading Research and Instruction, 36*(3), 241–265.

Blair, R., & Savage, R. (2006). Name writing but not environmental print recognition is related to letter-sound knowledge and phonological awareness in pre-readers. *Reading and Writing, 19,* 991–1016.

Bowman, M., & Treiman, R. (2004). Stepping stones to reading. *Theory Into Practice, 43*(4), 295–303.

Bradley, B. A., & Jones, J. (2007). Sharing alphabet books in early childhood classrooms. *Reading Teacher, 60*(5), 452–463.

Burgess, S. R., & Lonigan, C. J. (1998). Bidirectional relations of phonological sensitivity and prereading abilities: Evidence from a preschool sample. *Journal of Experimental Child Psychology, 70,* 117–141.

Catts, H. W., Fey, M. E., Tomblin, J. B., & Zhang, X. (2002). A longitudinal investigation of reading outcomes in children with language impairment. *Journal of Speech, Language, and Hearing Research, 45,* 1142–1157.

Cecil, N. L. (2003). *Striking a balance: Best practices for early literacy* (2nd ed.). Scottsdale, AZ: Holcomb Hathaway.

Christie, J. F., Enz, B. J., & Vukelich, C. (2007). *Teaching language and literacy: Preschool through the elementary grades* (3rd ed.). Boston, MA: Pearson.

Clay, M. M. (1991). *Becoming literate: The construction of inner control.* Portsmouth, NH: Heinemann.

Combs, M. (2002). *Readers and writers in primary grades: A balanced and integrated approach* (2nd ed.). Upper Saddle River, NJ: Merrill, Prentice-Hall.

Cramer, R. L. (2005). *The language arts: A balanced approach to teaching reading, writing, listening, talking, and thinking.* Boston, MA: Pearson, Allyn & Bacon.

Cunningham, P. M. (2005). *Phonics they use: Words for reading and writing* (4th ed.). Boston, MA: Pearson Allyn & Bacon.

DeJong, P. F. (2012). Phonological awareness and the use of phonological similarity in letter-sound learning. *Journal of Experimental Child Psychology, 105*(4), 324–344.

Diamond, K. E., Gerde, H. K., & Powell, D. R. (2008). Development in early literacy skills during the pre-kindergarten year in Head Start: Relations between growth in children's writing and understanding of letters. *Early Childhood Research Quarterly, 23,* 467–478.

Dickinson, D. K., Golinkoff, R. M., Hirsch-Pasek, K., Neuman, S. B., & Burchinal, P. (2009). *The language of emergent literacy: A response to* the *National Institute for Literacy Report on Early Literacy*. Retrieved from http://nieer.org/psm/index.php?article=294

Durkin, D. (1987). *Teaching young children to read* (4th ed.). Boston, MA: Allyn & Bacon.

Ehri, L. C. (1987). Learning to read and spell words. *Journal of Literacy Research, 19*, 5–31.

Ehri, L. C. (1998). Grapheme-phoneme knowledge is essential to learning to read words in English. In J. L. Metsala & L. C. Ehri (Eds.), *Word recognition in beginning literacy* (pp. 3–40). Mahwah, NJ: Erlbaum.

Ehri, L. C. (2005). Learning to read words: Theory, findings, and issues. *Scientific Studies of Reading, 9*, 167–188.

Ellefson, M. R., Treiman, R., & Kessler, B. (2009). Learning to lavel letters by sounds or names: A comparison of England and the United States. *Journal of Experimental Child Psychology, 102*, 323–341. doi:10.1016/jecp.2008.05.008

Gagen, L. M., & Getchell, N. (2006). Using "constraints" to design developmentally appropriate movement activities for early childhood education. *Early Childhood Education Journal, 34*(3), 227–232. doi:10.1007/s10643-006-0135-6

Gersten, R., Baker, S. K., Shanahan, T., Linan-Thompson, S., Collins, P., & Scarcella, R. (2007). *Effective literacy and English language instruction for English learners in the elementary grades: A practice guide* (NCEE 2007–4011). Washington, DC: National Center for Education Evaluation and Regional Assistance, Institute of Education Sciences, U.S. Department of Education. Retrieved from http://ies.ed.gov/ncee

Gillon, G. T. (2006). Phonological awareness intervention: A preventive framework for preschool children with specific speech and language impairments. In R. J. McCauley & M. E. Fey (Eds.), *Treatment of language disorders in children* (pp. 279–307). Baltimore, MD: Paul H. Brookes.

Greenberg, P. (2006). "I'm doing this!" *Early Childhood Today, 21*(3), 21.

Gunning, T. G. (2000). *Creating literacy instruction for all children* (3rd ed.). Boston, MA: Allyn & Bacon.

Gunning, T. G. (2005). *Creating literacy instruction for all children* (5th ed.). Boston, MA: Allyn & Bacon.

Hall, N., & Robinson, A. (2000). Play and literacy learning. In C. Barratt-Pugh & M. Rohl (Eds.), *Literacy learning in the early years*. Buckingham, UK: Open University Press.

Hammill, D. D. (2004). What we know about correlates of reading. *Exceptional Children, 70*, 453–468.

Justice, L. M., Kaderavek, J. N., Fan, X., Softa, A., & Hunt, A. (2009). Accelerating preschoolers' early literacy development through classroom-based teacher-child storybook reading and explicit print referencing. *Lan-*

guage, Speech, and Hearing Services in Schools, 40, 67–85. doi:10.1044/ 0161-1461(2008/07-0098)

Justice, L. M., Mashburn, A., Hamre, B., & Pianta, R. (2008). Quality of language and literacy instruction in preschool classrooms serving at-risk pupils. *Early Childhood Research Quarterly, 23,* 51–68. doi:10.1016/j .ecresq.2007.09.004

Kaderavek, J. N. (2011). *Language disorders in children.* Boston, MA: Allyn & Bacon.

Kim, Y., Foorman, B. R., Petscher, Y., & Zhou, C. (2010). The contributions of phonological awareness and letter-name knowledge to letter-sound acquisition—A cross-classified multilevel model approach. *Journal of Educational Psychology, 102,* 313–326. doi:10.1037/a0018449

Lafferty, A. E., Gray, S., & Wilcox, M. J. (2005). Teaching alphabetic knowledge to pre-school children with developmental language delay and with typical language development. *Child Language Teaching and Therapy, 21*(3), 263–277.

Levin, I., & Ehri, L. C. (2009). Young children's ability to read and spell their own and classmates' names: The role of letter knowledge. *Scientific Studies of Reading, 13*(3), 249–273.

Levin, I., Shatil-Carmon, S., & Asif-Rave, O. (2006). Learning of letter names and sounds and their contribution to word recognition. *Journal of Experimental Child Psychology, 93,* 139–165. doi:10.1016/j.jecp.2005.08.002

May, L., Bingham, G. E., & Barrett-Mynes, J. (2010). Name games: Literacy and play in the pre-Kindergarten classroom. *Focus on Pre-K & K, 1,* 5–7.

McBride-Chang, C. (1999). The ABCs of the ABCs: The development of letter-name and letter-sound knowledge. *Merrill-Palmer Quarterly, 45,* 285–308.

McGee, L. M., & Richgels, D. J. (2000). *Literacy's beginnings* (3rd ed.). Boston, MA: Pearson, Allyn & Bacon.

Miller, W. H. (2005). *Improving early literacy: Strategies and activities for struggling students (K–3).* San Francisco, CA: Jossey Bass.

Morrow, L. M. (2001). *Literacy development in the early years* (4th ed.). Boston, MA: Allyn & Bacon.

Moustafa, M. (2000). Phonics instruction. In D. S. Stickland & L. M. Morrow (Eds.), *Beginning reading and writing* (pp.121–133). New York, NY: Teachers College Press.

Muter, V., Hulme, C., Snowling, M. J., & Stevenson, J. (2004). Phonemes, rimes, vocabulary, and grammatical skills as foundations of reading development: Evidence from a longitudinal study. *Developmental Psychology, 40,* 665–681.

National Association for the Education of Young Children and the Fred Rogers Center for Early Learning and Children's Media at Saint Vincent College. (n.d.). *Technology and interactive media as tools in early child-*

hood programs serving children from birth through age 8. Retrieved from http://www.naeyc.org/files/naeyc/file/positions/PS_technology_WEB2.pdf

National Early Literacy Panel. (2008). *Developing early literacy: Report of the National Early Literacy Panel*. Washington, DC: National Institute for Literacy.

Nettles, D. H. (2006). *Comprehensive literacy instruction in today's classrooms: The whole, the parts, and the heart*. Boston, MA: Pearson, Allyn & Bacon.

Neuman, S. B., & Roskos, K. (1990). Play, print, and purpose: Enriching play environments for literacy development. *Reading Teacher, 44*(3), 214–221.

Neumann, M. M., & Neumann, S. L. (2010). Parental strategies to scaffold emergent writing skills in the pre-school child within the home environment. *Early Years, 30*(1), 79–74. doi:10.1080/09575140903196715

Piasta, S. B., & Wagner, R. K. (2009). Learning letter names and sounds: Effects of instruction, letter type, and phonological processing skill. *Journal of Experimental Child Psychology, 105*, 324–344.

Piasta, S. B., & Wagner, R. K. (2010). Developing early literacy skills: A meta-analysis of alphabet learning and instruction. *Reading Research Quarterly, 45*(1), 8–38.

Riley, L. A. (1997). *Mouse mess*. New York, NY: Blue Sky Press.

Rivkin, M. S. (2006). Let's move together! Moving and learning together. *Early Childhood Today, 20*(6), 32–38.

Rohl, M. (2000). Learning about words, sounds and letters. In C. Barratt-Pugh & M. Rohl (Eds.), *Literacy learning in the early years* (pp. 57–80). Buckingham, UK: Open University Press.

Rule, A. C., Dockstader, C. J., & Stewart, R. A. (2006). Hands-on and kinesthetic activities for teaching phonological awareness. *Early Childhood Education Journal, 34*(3), 195–201. doi:10.1007/s10643-006-0130-y

Savage, J. F. (2011). *Sound it out: Phonics in a comprehensive reading program* (4th ed.). New York, NY: McGraw-Hill.

Scarborough, H. S. (1998). Early identification of children at risk for reading disabilities. In B. K. Skapiro, P. J. Accardo, & A. J. Capute (Eds.), *Specific reading disability: A view of the spectrum* (pp. 75–120). Timonium, MD: York Press.

Share, D. L. (2004). Knowing letter names and learning letter sounds: A causal connection. *Journal of Experimental Child Psychology, 88*, 213–233. doi:10.1016/j.jeep.2004.03.005

Snow, C. E., Burns, M. S., & Griffin, P. (Eds.). (1998). *Preventing reading difficulties in young children*. Washington, DC: National Academy Press.

Storch, S. A., & Whitehurst, G. J. (2002). Oral language and code-related precursors to reading: Evidence from a longitudinal structural model. *Developmental Psychology, 38*, 934–947.

Strickland, D. S. (2000). Classroom intervention strategies: Supporting the literacy development of young learners at risk. In D. S. Stickland & L. M. Morrow (Eds.), *Beginning reading and writing* (pp. 99–110). New York, NY: Teachers College Press.

Teale, W. H., Hoffman, J. L., & Paciga, K. A. (2010). Where is NELP leading preschool literacy instruction? Potential positives and pitfalls. *Educational Researcher, 39*, 311–315. doi:10.3102/0013189X10369830

Tompkins, G. E. (2012). *Teaching writing: Balancing process and product* (6th ed.). Boston, MA: Pearson.

Treiman, R., & Kessler, B (2003). The role of letter names in the acquisition of literacy. In R. Kail (Ed.), *Advances in child development and behavior* (Vol. 31, pp. 105–135). San Diego, CA: Academic Press.

Turnbull, K. L. P., Bowles, R. P., Skibbe, L. E., Justice, L. M., & Wiggins, A. K. (2010). Theoretical explanations for preschool lowercase alphabet knowledge. *Journal of Speech, Language, and Hearing Research, 53*, 1757–1768.

Walsh, G., Sproule, L., McGinness, C., & Trew, K. (2011). Playful structure: A novel image of early years pedagogy for primary school classrooms. *Early Years, 31*(2), 107–119. doi:10.1080/09575146.2011.579070

Warner, L., & Weiss, S. (2005). Why young children need alphabet books. *Kappa Delti Pi Record, 41*(3), 124–127.

Whitehurst G. J., & Lonigan, C. J. (1998). Child development and emergent literacy. *Child Development, 69*, 848–872.

Children's Books Cited

Base, G. (1986). *Animalia*. New York, NY: Penguin.

Martin, B., Jr., & Archambault, J. (1989). *Chicka chicka boom boom*. New York, NY: Simon & Schuster.

Rey, H. A. (1963). *Curious George learns the alphabet*. New York, NY: Houghton Mifflin.

Chapter 5

Recognizing and Manipulating Sounds: Phonological and Phonemic Awareness

Kendra M. Hall-Kenyon and Barbara Culatta

Children can learn to hear, identify, and manipulate sounds in language when they learn about these sounds through engaging lessons and activities (Bingham, Hall-Kenyon, & Culatta, 2010; Justice & Kaderavek, 2004; Verhoven, 2001). Even very young children enjoy playing with sounds by repeating the same sound in a variety of words (e.g., "big, burly bear bringing blueberries for breakfast"), enjoying the rhyming words in books, or making real and nonsense words that sound the same (e.g., *hit, rit, dit, sit, pit, lit*). As children notice similarities in words, they can more easily move toward identifying the sounds they hear and blending words by onset and rime (*h-it, s-it*). Eventually, they are able to participate in complex sound awareness activities where they change, add, or delete the sounds in words. ("I can pat a cat. What would I pat if I changed the /k/ in *cat* to /b/?")

Playing with, identifying, and manipulating sounds can help children develop *phonological awareness,* the awareness of sounds in words separate from meaning. A robust relationship has been found between phonological awareness and later reading success (Catts, Fey, Zhang, & Tomblin, 2001; Lonigan, Burgess, & Anthony, 2000; Scarborough, 2001; Snow, Burns, & Griffin, 1998; Torgesen, Al Otaiba, & Grek, 2005; Whitehurst & Lonigan, 1998). This is likely because phonological awareness permits children to understand that words are made of sounds, which leads to understanding that letters represent sounds that can be combined into words. This chapter explores the nature and development of phonological awareness, explains some instructional strategies that explicitly teach phonological awareness in meaningful and engaging ways, and discusses the progression of phonological awareness skills as they build on each other to lay the foundation for early reading.

Nature and Development of Phonological Awareness

Before children begin the processes involved with reading, they first become aware of the ways sounds function in producing words. In order to help children progress through the development of these skills, SLPs and teachers must understand differences in terminology, constructs, and development.

Term Distinctions

Terms involved with phonological awareness and development can be confusing, due to concept overlap and word similarities. To communicate effectively with colleagues, SLPs and teachers should discuss significant term distinctions, particularly as they relate to instruction.

Phonological Versus Phonemic Awareness

Although they are related skills, there is an important distinction between phonological awareness and phonemic awareness. *Phonological awareness* is a broad term that refers to knowledge of the sound structure of language (Gillon, 2004).

> [It] includes identifying and manipulating larger parts of spoken language, such as words, syllables, and onsets [initial consonant or

consonant cluster] and rimes [vowel and rest of the syllable], as well as phonemes [smallest unit of sound]. It also encompasses awareness of other aspects of sound, such as rhyming and alliteration. (Armbruster, Lehr, & Osborn, 2001, p. 3)

Phonemic awareness, a narrower term, refers to a subcategory of phonological awareness, a specific aspect of sound knowledge: the awareness of individual phonemes in words. More specifically, phonemic awareness refers to the ability to hear, identify, and manipulate individual phonemes in words (Armbruster et al., 2001). Since the phoneme is the smallest individual unit of sound, the phoneme is what students need to initially identify or manipulate. Phonemic awareness tasks include identifying phonemes ("What is the first sound in *pig*?"), blending and segmenting individual sounds in words ("What word is *p-e-n*?"), and manipulating sounds (e.g., substitution—"What new word would we have if we changed the /*n*/ sound in *pen* to the /*t*/ sound?).

Implicit Versus Explicit Awareness

Early phonological awareness skills are implicit, meaning children are sensitive or attentive to sound patterns but lack the metalinguistic ability to consciously manipulate or talk about them. Children with latent awareness of sound patterns may play with sounds in patterns such as rhyming and alliteration and even generate rhyming words spontaneously before they have any idea how or why sound patterns may be deliberately changed (Bradley & Bryant, 1983; Brady & Shankweiler, 1991; Goswami & Bryant, 1990; Muter, Hulme, Snowling, & Stevenson, 2004).

Explicit phonological awareness is revealed when students can talk about the structure of words. Although phonological awareness skills such as rhyming and alliteration can occur at a sensitivity level, they become more metalinguistic as students are able to generate rhyming words upon request, label word pairs that rhyme, or state why words do not rhyme. By the time children are using phonemic awareness skills, they are able to identify individual phonemes and become more conscious of how individual sounds in words can be manipulated. For example, they are able to isolate and change sounds in words, analyze words into individual sounds, and comprehend what others say about the process.

Factors Influencing Development of Phonological Awareness

Factors such as the size of the sound unit, the demands of the task, and the nature of stimuli influence children's development and performance in phonological awareness. Though it is impossible to completely separate the influence of these factors, for the purpose of clarity each factor will be discussed individually.

Component Skills

An array of skills and abilities is included under the category of phonological awareness: rhyme, alliteration, phoneme identification, sound blending and segmenting, and sound manipulation. Although the development of these tasks is not linear, children typically master rhyming and alliteration earlier than the other skills (Vloedgraven & Verhoeven, 2007). Table 5–1 describes and exemplifies each of the skills.

Size of Sound Unit

Within the development of phonological awareness, children recognize larger holistic sound units before detecting smaller sound structures (Anthony, Lonigan, Driscoll, Phillips, & Burgess, 2003; Gillon, 2006; Phillips, Clancy-Menchetti, & Lonigan, 2008; Schuele & Boudreau, 2008). Children will likely acquire phonological awareness initially at the sentence level and move to the word level.

Children demonstrate phonological awareness on the sentence level when they detect the words that compose a sentence: for example they are able to clap out or count the number of words in a sentence. Once children are aware of how words compose a sentence, they may develop an awareness how sounds compose words.

Phonological awareness at the word level is believed to actually occur at several levels: the syllable level, the onset-rime level (which is intrasyllabic), and the phoneme level (Gillon, 2004). Children have attained phonological awareness at the *syllable level* when they recognize the syllables that compose a word, demonstrating that they understand that words can be divided into different sound units (Gillon, 2004). For example, they may recognize that *baby* is composed of two syllables: *ba-by*. Once awareness of syllables is established, children may progress to awareness within

Table 5–1. Phonological Awareness Skills

Term	*Definition*	*Example*
Rhyming	Ability to identify words that sound the same at the end, or words with a different onset (initial consonant or consonant cluster) and the same rime (final vowel and consonants)	*s* (onset) + *it* (rime) = *sit* *b* (onset) + *it* (rime) = *bit*
Alliteration	Ability to identify the same initial sound in a series of words	Big, beautiful, bright, blue banner
Phoneme identification	Ability to identify a particular sound (phoneme) in a word	/k/ is the first phoneme in *cat*; /t/ is the last phoneme
Sound blending	Process of combining smaller sound units to create words: may be done with units of various sizes	At onset-rime level "What word is *s-it*?" At phoneme level "What word is /s/-/ĭ/-/t/?"
Sound segmentation	Process of separating words into their component sounds, opposite of blending	What are the sounds in *sit*?
Sound manipulation	Substituting, adding, or deleting sounds in words	"If you change the /p/ in *pit* to /s/, what word do you have?"

syllables: for example, at the *onset-rime level* they may detect sound structures within syllables (*c-at, d-ot, sh-ed*).

Phonological awareness at the syllable or onset-rime level deals with relatively large sound units (because syllables and rimes are composed of several sounds), whereas phonological awareness at the phoneme level deals with the smallest unit of speech. Children who demonstrate phonological awareness at the phoneme level may show that they are aware of individual sounds that compose a word, which was defined earlier as phonemic awareness. Phonemic awareness is more mature than syllable or rhyme awareness because smaller units must be noticed and identified; this awareness is needed for some higher-level phonological tasks: for example, identifying the final sound or blending and segmenting words at the individual phoneme level.

Task Demands

In addition to the size of the sound unit, children's phonological awareness abilities are influenced by the demands of the phonological task. Various tasks demand a range of phonological skills. Children move from simple implicit to more complex explicit or metalinguistic tasks (Adams, 2001; Gillon, 2004; Goswami, 2001; Troia, 2004; Whitehurst & Lonigan, 2001). Phonological skills do not generally develop at the same time; rather they progress from an awareness of sounds, including sound play, to higher metalinguistic manipulation of sounds, including deletion of one phoneme to make a different word. Tasks that include various sound unit sizes relate to both phonological and phonemic awareness. Teachers and SLPs should follow this developmental sequence when planning phonological awareness tasks for young children: beginning with sound play and progressing to sound manipulation. A more complete illustration of this developmental sequence is available on the SEEL Web site, see the PreK and K curriculua.

Sound Play. Sound play is an early phonological task that allows children to show awareness of sounds through play. For example, they may make up words for objects or play with nonsense words (Snow et al., 1998). Some tasks may prime sound awareness but not require children to respond in a particular way: for example, exposing them to rhyming words in a song and giving them an opportunity (without directly asking them) to add rhyming words of their own. Some teachers model sound play by highlighting interesting sounds: McGee and Richgels (2000) recommend "word play books," which have "a bit of a story line" but are written particularly to stimulate sound awareness and sound play. For example, children enjoy *One Duck Stuck* by Phyllis Root (2001), which has both rhyme and rhythm and includes "sound" words, like *pleep, plop,* and *plunk,* to describe the ways the animals move. Resources, activities, and tasks that evoke such responses may tap into children's implicit awareness when they first become sensitive to sound structures. Sound play is often spontaneous as children enjoy repeating or listening to tongue twisters or even real and made up words that sound the same.

Many children demonstrate implicit awareness of rhyme before entering school (MacLean, Bryant, & Bradley, 1987). Some as young as three years old show this sensitivity as they gravitate toward, play with, and demonstrate enjoyment in rhyme, experimenting with both real and nonsense words. Even some 2-year-olds have been found playing with sounds such as "pancake, cancake, and canpake" (Snow et al., 1998, p. 51). This type of sound play is considered to be implicit: Although children seem to hear or recognize rhyme, they are not likely to be able to talk about why these words sound alike.

Recognition and Generation. Explicit or metalinguistic awareness of sounds in words, a more sophisticated level of phonological awareness, is characterized by an ability to recognize and generate sound patterns. Children who can recognize sounds can identify sounds (e.g., choose the word that does not belong—*bed, cat,* and *hat*), sort them (e.g., place objects or pictures that start with the same sound in one group and those that do not start with that sound in another group), and recognize whether or not a pair of words rhyme (Figure 5–1). Children who can generate sounds can respond to a request to think of a word that starts with /*b*/ (an initial sound task) or produce words that rhyme (a rhyming task).

Figure 5–1. Children can sort objects in a variety of ways as they practice and demonstrate their ability to recognize rhyming words.

Word Analysis and Phoneme Manipulation. Word analysis includes the ability to blend and segment words as well as manipulate individual sounds in words. When done at the phoneme level, blending and segmenting are part of the most mature form of phonological awareness: phonemic awareness. The ability to add, delete, or change individual phonemes to create and deconstruct words represents the most advanced level of phonological awareness (Schuele & Boudreau, 2008).

Nature of the Stimuli

In addition to familiarity with particular sound patterns in words, there are semantic and contextual factors that influence children's phonological awareness performance. Children begin recognizing sounds in familiar words and move to finding the sounds in less familiar words; with some practice identifying sounds and words in familiar contexts, they can advance to less familiar applications. Teachers and SLPs manipulate instruction or intervention so that sound awareness tasks begin with familiar words and contexts.

Neighborhood Density

An individual's exposure to similar sounding words, referred to as *neighborhood density*, can also influence a child's performance in phonological awareness. As a child's vocabulary grows, the number of words with similar sounds in his or her mental lexicon is greater. Neighborhood density affects children's ability to handle phonological awareness tasks such as detecting onset and rime, since words with common rimes may be more familiar. Some studies have shown that words used in an assessment are easier for children whose exposure to similar sounding words is dense (Carroll & Snowling, 2001; De Cara & Goswami, 2003). However, other research has found that neighborhood density does not influence children's rhyming ability (Stadler, Watson, & Skahan, 2007). Despite some disagreement in the literature, strong theoretical and practical results show that making targeted stimuli or other particular features salient for children is an important instructional practice.

Semantic Context

As stated earlier in this chapter, early phonological awareness tasks, such as rhyming and alliteration, are appropriate for preschool children (Carroll & Snowling, 2001; Byrne & Fielding-Barnsley, 1993, 1995). However, semantic associations may distract young children from focusing on phonological associations. For example, *bread* and *jam* have high semantic associations because they often go together (Carroll & Snowling, 2001; Moss, Hare, Day, & Tyler, 1994). In an alliteration sort task, children may associate words that go together in the environment rather than those that sound the same (e.g., *bread* with *jam* rather than *bread* with *ball* and *bug*), particularly when the semantic association is more common to the child than the sound pattern. Thus it is important for teachers and SLPs to consider possible semantic distractions in finding ways to emphasize the sound pattern. But if distraction can be compensated or controlled, some semantic relationships can be effective in helping children with low entering language or meta-language skills to find meaning in the sound awareness activity/task.

For example, children who have been successful with rhyme in supportive contexts where semantic associations are high can learn to disembed sound play from context, first with familiar words and then with unfamiliar ones (Culatta, Kovarsky, Theadore, Franklin, & Timler, 2003). Head Start children who could not rhyme even in familiar contexts began repeating and recognizing rhymes within contexts they enjoyed (e.g., rhyming *dip, rip, clip, drip* and *tip* as they dipped tips of strips of paper in paint). They learned to identify those same familiar words out of context and eventually were able to rhyme with unfamiliar words without semantic or contextual support. The sematic association was a factor that helped the children at first but could be gradually faded.

Playful and Engaging Ways to
Build Phonological Awareness Skills

Because phonological awareness skills include a wide range of difficulty, teachers must begin with those that are most basic (typically larger sound units) and build to those that are more challenging (generally smaller sound units) (Schuele & Boudreau, 2008; Ziolkowski & Goldstein, 2008). But because of overlap in this developmental sequence, the earlier skills can be revisited to scaffold children as they move on to more complex tasks or higher level skills (Anthony et al., 2003). The actual timing for teaching any one of these skills can depend on a number of factors: for example, developmental level of the children, results from assessment data, and/or the mandated core curriculum standards (Schuele & Boudreau, 2008). However, most agree that teachers should introduce basic phonological awareness skills, such as rhyming and alliteration, in preschool and early kindergarten and more complex blending, segmenting, and manipulating in late kindergarten to early first grade (Good & Kaminski, 2002; Invernizzi, Meier, Swank, & Juel, 2001).

Ultimately, the goal of all phonological awareness instruction is to provide a strong foundation that leads to success with early reading skills. This section discusses (a) how to teach those skills in playful and engaging ways, and (b) how to build from sound awareness to early reading skills within each of the critical components of phonological awareness (rhyming, alliteration, sound identification, blending, segmenting, and manipulation).

Rhyme Skills

Although some research has suggested that rhyming instruction does not produce significant long-lasting gains in phonological awareness (Yeh, 2003), rhyme sound play can be a foundation for building deeper phonological awareness skills such as onset + rime blending of word family words (*h-op, t-op, p-op, m-op*) (Goswami, 2001) and other early literacy skills (Majsterek, Shorr, & Erion, 2000; Snow et al., 1998). The next sections provide ideas for teaching rhyming in playful and engaging ways and for building on rhyming capability to develop more complex literacy skills.

Playful and Engaging Activities

Teachers and SLPs can introduce and review rhyming words in a variety of playful ways. For example, the teacher can use and repeat rhyming words and phrases along with actions to tell a story, as illustrated in Table 5–2. Rhyming can also be taught in a movement or action routine (e.g., *tap* [feet], *clap* [hands], *flap* [arms], and *snap* [fingers]). Teachers and SLPs may also emphasize rhyming words as children engage in an activity in which they create something: for example, making a pig wig out of paper. ("Make a wig for a pig.

A big wig for the pig.") Before, during, and after these hands-on activities, the teacher specifies the goal, calls attention to words that rhyme, and models how to talk about or respond to rhyme tasks (e.g., we will rhyme with *-ig* words like *pig* and *wig*. The words *pig* and *wig* rhyme. Do *pig* and *wig* rhyme?).

These examples are only a sample of the kinds of activities that help support young children's ability to recognize and generate rhyme. More playful and engaging rhyming activities can be found on the Web site for SEEL, a formal program based on information and applications described throughout this book: education.byu. edu/seel/. Teachers and SLPs can use these and many other activities to engage children in sound play, move them to rhyme recognition and generation tasks, and eventually help them blend and segment simple word family words.

Relationship to Reading

When building early awareness of rhyme, teachers and SLPs concentrate on teaching children to understand ways to identify and generate rhyming words. But as children get older, teachers and SLPs scaffold them in identifying the same sound pattern in words, analyzing words into onsets and rimes, and attaching those sound patterns to print. ("Why do *cap* and *map* rhyme?" What do you hear that is the same in *cap* and *map*?") Initially children need a

Table 5–2. An Action Rhyming Story

Wake	Stretch and yawn
Cake!	Point to head to indicate getting an idea
Take and shake	Shake in sugar, salt, and water
Break	Crack an egg
Bake the cake	Place "cake" in box oven
Take the cake	Take cake out of oven
Make a flake for the cake	Put chocolate flake on cake
Take and break the cake	Break the cake in pieces and pass them out

great deal of support from the teacher through cues, exaggeration, intonation, and varied opportunities to practice (McGee & Ukrainetz, 2009). However, with practice children can move forward effectively.

Children can also analyze rhyming words. For example, the children can begin by orally segmenting and blending familiar rhymed words into their onsets and rimes (e.g., "What am I saying? *Fl-ap?*") or change the onset to make new words (e.g., "If I say *lap*, what word do I get if I change the /l/ to an /n/?"). As children become more familiar with a set of words with the same rime ending, the teacher can then shift the focus to print. For example, the teacher or SLP might write the onsets *cl*, *m*, *t*, *fl*, and *sn* on the board can let the children write in the *-ap* ending to make the words they have been talking about, illustrating how the words that sound alike look alike in print and are written in similar ways.

The teacher can also highlight the rime ending by recording the onset of the rhyming words (initial consonant or consonant cluster) and their rime ending with different colored markers or with spaces (e.g., *c ap*, *cl ap*, *t ap*) or having the children create rhyming word sets by matching up onset and rime cards. By noticing similarities in printed and spoken words and analyzing words into their onsets and rimes, children move toward reading by analogy (Torgesen et al., 2005). For instance, the child who recognizes the rime unit *-ap* in *map* may use the strategy of analogy to read *cap* (Goswami, 2002). After blending a particular word at the onset + rime level, the teacher can then model how to change the onset to make new words (take the *f* off *flap* to make *lap*). For variety, children may sing a song with rhymed lyrics which they read from a song chart, then change beginning sounds: for example changing "Row Row Row Your Boat" to something like "Float, float, float your boat gently through the moat" (adapted from Harp & Brewer, 2000). As children learn how to figure out new words from these onsets and rimes, they develop "a strategy to deal with other unknowns" (Morrow, 2001. p. 261).

Alliteration

Like rhyming, alliteration sound play is a lower level phonological awareness task that can lay a critical foundation for more complex phonological awareness skills and early word reading (Bryant, MacLean, & Bradley, 1990). Teachers and SLPs can first engage in playful and engaging alliteration activities that highlight the same first sounds in words. These activities then build to identifying the initial sound in familiar CVC words. Thus this awareness can lead to identification of the initial phoneme in words as the adult gradually does more to isolate and talk about the same first sound (Gillon, 2004). This knowledge of initial sounds is also helpful when teaching children to associate letters with their sounds.

Playful and Engaging Activities

Alliteration comes more naturally to some children than to others. To allow children who may be learning more slowly to practice recognizing the "same first sound" in words, the instructor needs to infuse playfulness into activities that are actually quite structured (Walsh, Sproule, McGinness, & Trew, 2011), using multiple examples in playful contexts. For example, the teacher can emphasize the alliteration that occurs in the book *No Mail for Mitchell* (Siracusa, 1990) and create additional /*m*/ alliterative phrases in telling a part of the story:

> Mr. Mitchell mails many magazines. Mr. Mitchell's mail has M marked on the mail. Mail and magazines with M's go to Mr. Mitchell's messy mailbox. This mailbox has Mr. Mitchell's mail and his many, marvelous, magnificent magazines. It's all mucky and muddy [because it's raining heavily in the story] and Mr. Mitchell's mail gets all muddy.

The children also enact the story by making mail for Mitchell and marking the mail with *M*s so the mail can be delivered into Mr. Mitchell's mailbox.

Teachers can also use activities such as movement or crafts to highlight initial sounds: for example, in an activity designed to identify the onset /*sp*/, children hear many examples as they *spill*, *spin*, *splat*, or *splatter spools* and *spouts* [cut from tops of water bottles] on *spaces* and *spots*. Or in a craft activity designed to focus on initial /*b*/ sound, children can create "*B* bracelets" by adding *B* items (*balloons*, *beads*, *beans*, *butterflies*, and *B*s). A variety of playful alliteration activities is available on the SEEL Web site (education.byu.edu/seel/).

Relationship to Reading

As with rhyming, activities to practice alliteration begin with an emphasis on sound play, move to the more complex tasks of recognition and generation, and finally work into letter-sound associations. Thus when beginning to emphasize alliteration, teachers repeat alliterative phrases, extending continuant sounds when they are the target first sounds (e.g., /f/, /m/, /s/) or laughing at or tripping up when producing "tongue twister" alliterative phrases (e.g., Feed a few of the fish with flapping, flashy fins four or five fish food flakes). The teacher can build from this sound play by leading children to identify and then generate words with the same initial sounds ("Remember when you fed the fish with flapping, flashy fins? We fed them fish food flakes. Let's remember some of those words that begin with /f/"). Once children have had some experience playing with, identifying, and generating words with the same first sound, the teacher can support them in associating the sound with its letter ("Mark *f* for /f/ on the fish food, and fit Fs on the fish fins").

When a teacher conducts activities with a playful manner, the learning experience seems like play, which can contribute to its overall quality (Walsh et al., 2011). Using a well loved book can be an effective way of bringing playfulness into phonological awareness. In an activity based on the popular children's book *Mouse Mess* (Riley, 1997), the teacher playfully leads the children in the process of moving from alliteration sound play, to identification and generation of beginning sounds, to letter-sound associations. After enjoying the story with the children, the teacher first highlights the initial /m/ sound as children make a mess with *M*-items. ("We're going to make a mess with things beginning with the /m/ sound. Only things [real, pretend, or pictured] that start with the /m/ sound can go in our mess.") As the children play with the mouse mess, the teacher comments on the items and highlights the /m/ sound. ("Make a mess with macaroni." "Should we mix in mustard with our mouse mess?") The teacher supports the children as she asks them to identify words with the same first sound. ("Could mud go in our mouse mess? What about marshmallows? Yes, mud and marshmallows both start with the /m/ sound so they can go in our mouse mess.") The teacher can also ask the children to generate words that begin with the same initial sound. (What else could we put in our mess?)

In addition to providing many opportunities to play with the sound and identify and generate words with it, children should have many opportunities to connect the sound of the letter *M* to print as the teacher explicitly makes the letter-sound association. "We can put a letter *M* on this mess or mix *M*s into the mess, since the mess begins with the sound the letter *M* makes—/*m*/. The *M* makes the /*m*/ sound." The teacher allows the children to have additional practice with this letter-sound association as she helps the children identify the letter *M* in the list of words identifying the objects included in the mess. ("We made a *mess*. We made a *mess* with *macaroni, mustard* and *markers*. We *mixed* and *mashed* and *moved* the *marshmallows* to make a very big *mess!*) Children begin to learn letter-sound associations when the letter is associated with repeated sounds in alliteration activities. Additional ideas for building from a playful alliteration activity to making letter-sound associations in more independent and less supported contexts can be found in the initial sound identification suggestions below.

Sound Identification

Teaching children to identify and isolate the initial and final consonants and medial vowel sounds in CVC words prepares them to analyze words at the phoneme level and read simple short vowel words. Teachers typically begin with identifying the initial sound, move to the final sound, and then to the medial vowel. The following sections illustrate how teachers and SLPs can teach children identification skills for these sounds in engaging ways and then how those skills lead to early reading.

Playful Sound Identification Activities

Children benefit from engaging activities that teach sound identification separately in the three common sound positions: initial consonant, final consonant, and medial vowel. Since identifying and isolating the medial vowel in CVC words can be the most challenging of the three sound identification tasks, it is typically taught after children can identify the beginning and ending consonants. Identification of sounds in words, respective of the positions, should begin with engaging sound play (rhyme and/or alliteration), move toward modeling the way to talk about sounds heard in words and isolating individual sounds from words.

Initial Sound Identification. Identifying sounds as they appear in different positions usually begins with the initial sound because it generally can be identified most easily (Savage, 2011). Initial sound identification can follow sound play with both alliteration and rhyme. As mentioned above, alliteration sound play draws attention to words that share the same onset, and rhyming sound play draws attention to words with the same rime but different onsets. The following two examples of playful activities can be used to teach initial sound identification: one with alliteration and one with rhyming.

An alliteration sound play can follow a telling of *Stone Soup* (Brown, 1947), an old tale about soldiers who trick the people in a peasant village into making them some food. The children make some "*S* soup" with *S*s, snakes, stones, snails, straw, string, soap, sparkles, stars, socks, and so forth, identifying and isolating the first sound as they put in the ingredients. After they create their soup, the teacher leads the children through the process of writing a "recipe" for it, while commenting on the same initial sound. ("You need six snakes and seven stones, some snails, some string, sparkling stars and a pair of stinky socks. All of these things in our s-soup start with the /s/ sound. Sssix sssssnakes and ssssseven sssstones.")

Rhyming sound play can take many forms, such as making lots of dots on spots, putting lots of dots on pots, or following dots to a spot; one could even create a parking lot with slots, spots, or dots, then trot to the spots in the lot, and trot on lots of dots and spots that are "hot" (pretend) to get to the lot. After the activity the teacher writes the rime ending -*ot* (on the board or on disks or lids that can slide), and the children write or select single initial consonants to slide into the initial slot to make different words. Thus children are told the sound that a small core of letters makes and then shown how to pay attention to the initial letter-sound in order to make new words. ("Let's think about the sound of these letters [e.g., *L*, *D*, *S*, *H*, or *P*]. We can slide the *l* to the -*ot* to make the word *lot*.")

Final Sound Identification. Although initial sound identification can follow from sound play focused on either alliteration or rhyming, final sound identification evolves only from experience with rhyming. After children can already rhyme with a set of word family words, they are exposed again to the words in order to more explicitly analyze the final sound. For example, after children play with –*ip* rhyme words, the teacher places emphasis on the final /*p*/ in the target words with stress and repetition of the words, along with comments. For example, /*p*/ can be presented and practiced in an activity in which the teacher gives children a little drink of water:

◆ The teacher will *snip* straws (in half)—*clip* and *snip* the *tip* of the straw.
◆ The children *dip* the *tip* (in water) to *drip*; then *drip*, *drip* on their *lip*.
◆ They *drip* and *drip* (in a little cup); *tip* to *drip* (from the cup), *sip* the *drip* (from the cup).
◆ Then they *drip* (a few drops of water) on the floor.
◆ The teacher warns them, "Don't *slip*, don't *slip* on the *drips*!"

Before, during and after the -*ip* activity, the teacher can call attention to the final /*p*/ sound ("I hear /*p*/ and the end of *tip*. ("I hear /*p*/ at the end of *drip* and *sip*. Tip (a cup), sip a drip. I hear the /*p*/ sound at the end of *tip*, *dip*, *drip*, *sip*, and *lip*. Do you hear /*p*/ in *clip* and *snip*?") In this way, the teacher or SLP reviews word family words and then introduces final sound identification as she places emphasis on the final consonant by repeating the examples and commenting on and stressing the final /*p*/.

After children identify the final sound in a single set of word family words (*tip*, *sip*, *drip*, *tip*), the teacher or SLP can mix up, compare, or identify a target ending sound from words with different vowels, still calling attention to and placing emphasis on identifying the phoneme at the end of the word:

◆ *tap* a *top* (a spinning toy top or bottle top),
◆ *tip* a *top* (tip a bottle top on its end to spin it),
◆ *slap* the *top*,
◆ *tap* or *slap* the *top*,
◆ to make it *stop*.

The teacher calls attention to the sound at the end of the short vowel words: "I hear that /*p*/ at the end of *tap* and /*p*/ at the end of *top* and *stop*; I hear /*p*/ at the end of *tip*, *top*, and *stop*. Do you hear /*p*/ at the end of *top*?"

Once children are able to recognize (with high levels of support) the final sound in a series of words that all have the same ending, they are ready to practice (a) stating what sound they hear in the final position and (b) contrasting words that end in different final sounds. For example, the teacher or SLP might give each child two paper cups, one labeled *beginning* for the beginning sounds of words the other marked *end* for the sounds at the ends. The instructor reads a series of words, and before each she previews a sound (e.g., "Listen for the /p/ sound in the word"). The children drop a token (e.g., paper clip, M & M, goldfish cracker) in the right cup to indicate whether the chosen sound is at the beginning or at the end of the word. ("If the /p/ sound is at the beginning of the word, drop the token in the first cup. If you hear it at the end, drop it in the second cup. Where do you hear the /p/ sound in *cap*?") (Savage, 2011).

The teacher can also illustrate the sound placement process by placing out or drawing three blocks in a left to right sequence (each block representing one sound in a CVC word) and leading children in a chant:

- *Pit, pat, pot—*
  hear that /t/?
  It's in the end spot. [Point to the third block]

- *Lip, lap, lot—*
  hear a /t/ in *lot*?
  It's in the end spot. [Point to third block]

- *Slip, slap, slot*
  hear a /t/ in *slot*
  It's in the end spot. [Point to third block]

The teacher or SLP can then review each of the words used in the chant and point to the beginning, middle, and end blocks as she says each of the sounds. The teacher then moves into having children state the final sound heard in words. ("What sound do you hear at the end of *lip*?") Finally, he has the children identify or differentiate final sounds from a larger variety of words. ("Does the word *slot* end in /p/?" "Which of these words ends in /p/? *Slap, slot*?")

Medial Sound Identification. To lead toward identifying the medial vowel, the teacher or SLP can set up an identification and discrimination sequence beginning with rhyme-based sound play activities. After exposing children to a particular set of rhyming words in a facilitative, playful context, the adult calls attention to the vowel sound heard: for example isolating or calling attention to the initial sound in an activity that uses the /ă/ in -ag.

> We will make some rags for a rag bag.
>
> You can hear /ă/ in the words rag and bag.
>
> Make a rag, a rag! a rag! (ripping an old cloth into rags).
>
> Here is a bag for the rags, a rag bag,
>
> Drag the rags to the rag bag,
>
> Put a tag on the rag,
>
> The tag says "tag."
>
> Put a rag on the rag bag,
>
> The tag says "rag bag."
>
> I hear /ă/ in rag, bag, tag, and drag.

The teacher then exposes children to the /ă/ medial vowel in words that share the /ă/ but differ in final consonant.

> I heard the /ă/ in rag and bag, but I can also hear the /ă/ in words like *rat*, *bat*, and *cat* or *bad*, *sad*, and *mad*. Can you hear the /ă/ in *bat* and *bag*? — /b/-/ă/-/t/ and /b/-/ă/-/g/. What about in *cat* and *bag*?).

In the discrimination phase the teacher exposes children to repeated and salient examples of words that differ with the exception of the vowel, helping them in discriminating and labeling the vowel sound heard in different words. For example, the SLP or teacher might say, "We'll play with words that have different middle vowel sounds: tick-tock, tick-tock [repeat stressing the different vowels]; click-clack; snip-snap, zip-zap. I hear /ĭ/ in *tick*. I hear /ŏ/ in *t-o-ck*. Tick-tock, tick-tock, tick-tock. During this instruction, children are exposed to and learn to discriminate between words in a pair that vary in one phoneme and have different meanings.

In this example the change in the vowel sound creates two different words.

After an activity in which children play with simple words that contrast or vary only in the vowel, they can be taught to differentiate examples of words with a targeted medial vowel from non-examples. Table 5–3 represents a sequence that might be used.

Relationship to Reading

Children's experience playing with and identifying sounds in words can support their ability to hear the individual sounds in words and then associate those sounds with letters, through either alliteration or rhyming activities. The following example illustrates how a rhyming activity can lead to initial, final *and* medial sound identification. When children start to become more analytical, rhyming provides a base for moving from the larger (onset and rime) sound unit to the

Table 5–3. A Sequence for Teaching Children to Identify the Medial Vowel in *-at* Family Words.

Highlight *–at* words in an activity.	Using a stuffed animal or a cat-shaped balloon, let the children *pat* the *fat cat*, put a *hat* on the *fat cat*, and make it so the *fat cat* with the *hat sat* on a *mat*.
Let children play a game where each becomes a cat, bat, or rat.	The "animals" move along a path to get to a *mat*, but have to pass pictures and word cards representing *hat*, *fat*, *pat*, and *sat*. At each picture or word card they must state the word stressing the medial vowel sound /ă/.
Include non-items on the path (e.g., a mit, a ball, a fish, a frog).	Children must jump over the items that do not have the /ă/ sound.
Model breaking the words into the component sounds.	Children may need a high level of support. As children get to an *–at* word along the path, the teacher models the individual sounds in words (e.g., "You landed on *pat* /p/ /ă/ /t/"). And then when children are ready the teacher can ask the children about the individual sounds. "What sound do you hear at the beginning of *cat*?" or "What sound do you hear in the middle?" or "What is the sound at the end?")

phoneme level. The example in Table 5–4 illustrates how a rhyming activity can lead from playing with sounds to identifying initial sounds, then to identifying medial and final sounds, and finally to identifying all three letter-sound associations in CVC words.

Table 5–4. A Rhyming Activity Leading from Sound Play to CVC Sound Identification

Play with a rhyme ending.	Tie strings on a plastic bug, jug, and mug. Have children *tug* the *bug*, *jug*, and *mug* to a *rug*. Manipulate the bug to tug the mug and jug to the rug. Then let the bug get *snug* on the *rug*.
Give the children choices.	"Do you want to *tug* the *mug?*" "Would you rather *tug* the *bug* or the *mug?*"
Comment on the different onsets and familiar rime ending.	"*Mug* is an –ug word that begins with M. I hear /m/ in *mug*. *Bug*—I hear /b/ in *bug*. What sound does the word *bug* start with?"
Adapt to emphasize the final sound.	Demonstrate that the final sound is the same in all -ug words. "*Bug*, *mug*, and *tug* all end with the same sound. *Mug* ends with the /g/ sound. I also hear /g/ in *bug*."
Emphasize the medial sound.	"*Bug*, *mug*, and *tug* all have the same sound in the middle—the /ŭ/ sound. *Mug* has the /ŭ/ sound in the middle. I hear /ŭ/ in *mug*."
Have children generate the sounds.	"What is the last sound in *bug*? What other words have the same sound at the end?" (Support as necessary.)
Provide discrimination practice.	Cut a picture of a bug into three parts: head, first sound; body, medial sound; tail, final sound. Prepare picture cards of words with the same medial sound that children can place under the body of the bug. The same can be done with first or final sounds, with cards placed under the appropriate bug part.
Distribute letter cards	Have children form words using the letter cards. As they connect sounds to appropriate letters, they shift focus from phonemic awareness to letter-sound associations and then to reading a well-practiced set of word family words.

Sound Blending, Segmenting, and Manipulating

Any of the activities and skills that are practiced and acquired in the final and medial sound identification activities are similar to blending, segmenting, and manipulating activities when they are done at the phoneme level. However, the next section begins with some discussion of blending, segmenting and manipulation activities at the onset-rime level, which is easier, and then provides examples of these activities at the phoneme level. Most would agree that the processes of blending, segmenting, and manipulating at the phoneme level represent the most advanced stage of phonological awareness (Philips et al., 2008; Schuele & Broudreau, 2008).

Playful activities can be applied to blending and segmenting and also to manipulating sounds and sound patterns. Some suggest that these activities occur in short gamelike contexts in which children have the opportunity to explore and play with the sounds in words (Yopp & Yopp, 2009). Blending, segmenting, and manipulating sounds in words lead children toward decoding predictable words (Gillon, 2004; Goswami & Bryant, 1992; Torgesen et al., 2005).

Playful Activities for Blending, Segmenting, and Manipulation

As the natural sequence is for children to move from simple to more complex tasks (Adams, 2001; Troia, 2004; Whitehurst & Lonigan, 2001), when teachers and SLPs teach sound blending, segmenting and manipulation, they emphasize the sounds in words orally and then move to the same process attached to print. For example, as part of a movement activity children can clap, march, count, or tap out parts of a word, blending sounds to the rhythm of movement or music (Figure 5–2). Simple games can provide additional practice. For example, a blending game may include creating a special store where the prices are determined by numbers of sounds in the words. So either a *mop* or a *hat* costs three tokens; a *shoe* is cheaper. Some sort of "cash register" can be invented to click out the number of sounds.

Another activity that emphasizes sound manipulation is played like a shell game with cups that have letters hidden under them. The student can move only the cups in a particular position (i.e.,

Figure 5–2. In a small group activity, the teacher supports children's phonemic awareness as they blend and segment familiar CVC words by tapping out each of the individual sounds (e.g., /b/ /ă/ /t/ is bat; /p/ /ă/ /t/ is pat).

initial, medial, or final) in a row to make new words (e.g., any cup in the first position can be switched with any other cup in the first position, etc.); for example, *p-a-t* can become *bat* or *t-a-p* can become *top*. When children are ready to connect sounds to print, they can create a list of the words they can make by switching the letters in the various positions. See the SEEL Web site (education. byu.edu/seel/) for more examples of blending, segmenting and manipulating sounds taught in playful and engaging ways.

Relationship to Reading

Children typically begin blending and segmenting activities with larger sound units and move to the smallest unit. When manipulating phonemes, children are first given experiences just changing the initial sound. With more experience, children then practice manipulating the final and medial sounds in familiar CVC words. At first, teachers would only expose children to blending and segmenting as a method of sound play but would not necessarily require the children to blend and segment words into onset + rime or phonemes or to attach print to the sounds or sound patterns in words. Following a sound play activity focused on a set of words with the same rime ending (e.g., nut, hut, cut, shut), children can engage in supported practice blending and segmenting words into onsets and rimes. They may use unlettered bottle caps to stand for word parts, move them together while saying the sounds (e.g., touch one cap and say the /n/ sound and another cap and say -*ut*, then push them together to make *nut*). Teachers then support children in learning to manipulate by changing the onset in these known words to create new words. Children might move the bottle cap in the first position around to create new words (e.g., replace /n/ in *nut* to /k/ to make *cut*). At this point, teachers move to blending and segmenting words into phonemes.

For blending, children may pull cards that represent the sounds in CVC words out of a three-pocket apron. The SLP or teacher reads the sounds. All words can be real, or some words can be real and others nonsense. The SLP or teacher comments on the meaning of the real words and laughs at the "silly" words or says, "I don't know what that is!" Children then move to manipulating beginning, medial, or final sounds in simple CVC words as the teacher changes the sounds that are pulled out of the apron pockets. ("Here is the word cut. /k/ /ŭ/ /t/. If I change the /k/ to /n/, what word do I have?" or "If I change the /t/ to /p/ what word do I have?")

Once children have analyzed the sounds in words orally, they can repeat similar activities with printed onsets and rimes or can use letters for phonemes to create simple CVC words. Children can then move the cards around to make new words with emphasis on either the beginning, middle, or ending sound. Thus they practice blending, segmenting, and manipulating sounds in words in preparation for creating and reading simple CVC words.

After large and small group practice with oral blending, segmenting, and manipulating, students can be involved in some individual manipulation as well. Lesley Morrow (2001) describes how a "word-study center" can be created with a variety of manipulatives for practicing letter-sound manipulation in creating words: These include magnetic board and letters, wooden and/or foam rubber letters, flash cards (with word part coded by color) to line up in a pocket chart, white boards and marker, word wheels, letter stamps, and word-study games.

Utilizing All Instructional Contexts

Traditionally teachers and SLPs present and practice phonological targets during time periods labeled as "instructional": most often whole class or small group sessions. The examples presented in the chapter to this point primarily illustrate those kinds of activities. But if teachers and SLPs are to provide high levels of exposure to target skills, they should consider using all contexts throughout the day. Classroom routines and transitions are considered non-instructional times—necessary but rarely productive. However, members of the instructional team may use these contexts to offer children additional exposure to and practice with targets. A few examples for the non-instructional contexts are described below. The SEEL Web site (education.byu.edu/seel/) includes many additional engaging activities.

Snack

Researchers have called attention to the importance of "oral interaction among students," particularly heterogeneous groups in various aspects of literacy learning (see Morrow, 2001). As snack seems to be a motivating, relaxing, and conversational time for most children, the teacher or SLP can include a little playful phonological awareness practice as children are preparing for and enjoying snack time.

For example, events during snack time can be expressed orally in rhyme, and rhyming word games can be played. The adult and children sitting at a table can think of rhyming words for objects. ("Let's make up a rhyme name for this fork. How about *bork?*") Real, pretend, or paper food items can be used. Little circles of green paper can be peas, and squares of yellow paper can be cheese. "Please pass the peas, don't sneeze on the peas. Are there peas on your knees? No! Would you like some cheese with your peas? Cheese and peas? Peas and cheese? Don't squeeze the peas. And don't sneeze on the peas or cheese!"). Alliteration games can also be used. Children can put real and pretend /p/ items on the "pink paper plate": potatoes, peas, pasta, pudding, popcorn, pizza, pop, popsicles, pretzels, and pickles.

Another way to play literacy games during snack is by blending and segmenting words related to snack items. ("Guess what we will have for our snack. I'm going to say a word, and you figure out what I am saying. We will have *cra-ckers*.") Segmented words can be presented as a guessing game, with the SLP or teacher giving semantic and phonological clues: "I'm thinking of something we need during snack — *c-ups*."

Transitions

The range of classroom contexts and activities in which classroom instructors can embed playful learning activities (Walsh et al., 2011) includes even transitions. During transitions children are moving, and they can learn and move at the same time. For example, as they move from place to place within the classroom they can depict alliteration phrases with their bodies. They can be "tyrannosauruses that tramp and trek on tracks and tromp on tall trees." Children can also "act out" alliteration phrases with characters (people, animals, vehicles) performing movements or actions that can be expressed with words that alliterate: for example, "Bear bends backward before beginning to burrow" (a nice way of getting in a necessary stretch between curricular subjects).

As children are waiting in line, SLPs or teachers can have them clap, march, or count out parts of sentences or words. Children can blend or segment a word (with imitative support) or say a word in its segmented parts as a "password" to move to the next station or activity. Blending or segmenting a word may be their "ticket" to make the transfer. Familiar words (e.g., words that have been used frequently that day, their own names, or common clothing items) can be used for children who need more support. As children are waiting, the SLP or teacher can talk in a "funny way": stretching sounds out like a snail or talking in slow motion. The adult can give information or directions in words segmented into syllables or onset-rime.

Summary

To ensure reading and academic outcomes in early childhood education settings, young children should be provided with intense and systematic instruction in phonological awareness. Furthermore, all children can benefit from training in phonological awareness and from intervention that is interesting, including interactive and playful activities that provide frequent opportunities to practice using phonological awareness skills (Lyon, 1999; Verhoeven, 2001; Yopp, 1992). Early achievements in phonological awareness include rhyming and alliteration, whereas later achievements include isolating and substituting individual phonemes in words (promoting *phonemic* awareness). Phonological awareness instruction should follow a developmental sequence of instruction in four main areas: rhyming, alliteration, sound blending and segmenting, and manipulating. Development of these skills, along with attachment of letters to sounds, enables children to progress from phonological awareness to phonic attainments, which include reading regular short vowel family words.

References

Adams, M. (2001). Alphabetic anxiety and explicit, systematic phonics instruction: A cognitive science perspective. In S. B. Neuman & D. K. Dickinson (Eds.), *Handbook of early literacy research* (pp. 66–80). New York, NY: Guilford Press.

Anthony, J. L., Lonigan, C. J., Driscoll, K., Phillips, B. M., & Burgess, S. R. (2003). Phonological Sensitivity: A quasi-parallel progression of word structure units and cognitive operations. *Reading Research Quarterly*, *38*, 470–487.

Armbruster, B., Lehr, F., & Osborn, J. (2001). *Put reading first: The research building blocks for teaching children to read.* Center for the Improvement of Early Reading Achievement. Retrieved from http://www.ciera .org/library/products/others/putreadingfirst/index.html

Bingham, G. E., Hall-Kenyon, K. M., & Culatta, B. (2010). Systematic and engaging early literacy: Examining the effects of paraeducator implemented early literacy instruction. *Communication Disorders Quarterly*, *32*(1), 38–49.

Bradley, L., & Bryant, P. E. (1983). Categorizing sounds and learning to read: A causal connection. *Nature*, *301*(3), 419–421.

Brady, S. A., & Shankweiler, D. P. (1991). *Phonological processes in literacy: A tribute to Isabelle Y. Liberman.* Hillsdale, NJ: Lawrence Erlbaum Associates.

Bryant, P. E., MacLean, M., & Bradley, L. (1990). Rhyme, language, and children's learning. *Applied Psycholinguistics, 11*, 237–252.

Byrne, B., & Fielding-Barnsley, R. (1993). Evaluation of a program to teach phonemic awareness to young children: A 1-year follow-up. *Journal of Educational Psychology, 85*, 104–111.

Byrne, B., & Fielding-Barnsley, R. (1995). Evaluation of a program to teach phonemic awareness to young children: A 2- and 3-year follow-up and a new preschool trial. *Journal of Educational Psychology, 87*(3), 488–503.

Carroll, J. M., & Snowling, M. J. (2001). The effects of global similarity between stimuli on children's judgment of rime and alliteration. *Applied Psycholinguistics, 22*, 327–342.

Catts, H. W., Fey, M. E., Zhang, X., & Tomblin, J. B. (2001). Predicting reading disabilities: Research to practice. *Language, Speech, and Hearing Services in Schools, 32*, 38–50.

Culatta, B., Kovarsky, D., Theadore, G., Franklin, A., & Timler, G. (2003). Quantitative and qualitative documentation of early literacy instruction. *American Journal of Speech-Language Pathology, 12*, 172–188,

De Cara, B., & Goswami, U. (2003). Phonological neighborhood density: Effects in a rhyme awareness task in five-year-old children. *Journal of Child Language, 30*(3), 695–710.

Gillon, G. T. (2004). *Phonological awareness: From research to practice.* New York, NY: Guilford Press.

Gillon, G. T. (2006). Phonological awareness intervention. In R. J. McCauley, & M. E. Fey (Eds.), *Treatment of language disorders in children* (pp. 279–308). Baltimore, MD: Brookes.

Good, R. H., & Kaminski, R. A. (2002). *Dynamic indicators of basic early literacy skills* (6th ed.). Eugene, OR. Institute for the Development of Educational Achievement.

Goswami, U. (2001). Early phonological development and the acquisition of literacy. In S. B. Neuman & D. K. Dickinson (Eds.), *Handbook of early literacy research* (pp.111–125). New York, NY: Guilford Press.

Goswami, U., & Bryant, P. E. (1990). *Phonological skills and learning to read.* Hillsdale, NJ: Lawrence Erlbaum Associates.

Goswami, U., & Bryant, P. (1992). Rhyme, analogy, and children's reading. In P. Gough, L. Ehri, & R. Treiman (Eds.), *Reading acquisition* (pp. 49–63). Hillsdale, NJ: Lawrence Erlbaum Associates.

Harp, B., & Brewer, J. (2000). Assessing reading and writing in the early years. In D. S. Strickland & L. M. Morrow (Eds.), *Beginning reading and writing* (pp. 154–167). New York, NY: Teachers College Columbia University.

Invernizzi, M., Meier, J., Swank, L., & Juel, C. (2001). *Phonological Awareness Literacy Screening (PALS–K).* Charlottesville, VA: Virginia State Department of Education and the University of Virginia.

Justice, L. M., & Kaderavek, J. N. (2004). Embedded-explicit emergent literacy intervention I: Background and description of approach. *Language, Speech, and Hearing Services in Schools, 35*, 201–211.

Lonigan, C. J., Burgess, S. R., & Anthony, J. L. (2000). Development of emergent literacy and early reading skills in preschool children: Evidence from a latent-variable longitudinal study. *Developmental Psychology, 36*(5), 596–613.

Lyon, G.R. (1999). *The NICHD research program in reading development, reading disorders and reading instruction.* Paper prepared for the Keys to Successful Learning Summit in Washington, DC.

MacLean, M., Bryant, P., & Bradley, L. (1987). Rhymes, nursery rhymes, and reading in early childhood. *Merrill–Palmer Quarterly, 33*(3), 255–281.

Majsterek, D. J., Shorr, D. N., & Erion, V. L. (2000). Promoting early literacy through rhyme detection activities during Head Start circle–time. *Child Study Journal, 30*, 143–151.

McGee, L. M., & Richgels, D. J. (2000). *Literacy's beginnings: Supporting young readers and writers* (3rd ed.). Needham Heights, MA: Allyn & Bacon.

McGee, L. M., & Ukrainetz, T. A. (2009). Using scaffolding to teach phonemic awareness in preschool and kindergarten. *Reading Teacher, 62*, 599–603.

Morrow, L. M. (2001). *Literacy development in the early years* (4th ed.). Boston, MA: Allyn & Bacon.

Moss, H. E., Hare, M. L., Day, P., & Tyler, L. K. (1994). A distributed memory model of the associative boost in semantic priming. *Connection Science: Journal of Neural Computing, Artificial Intelligence and Cognitive Research, 6*, 413–427.

Muter, V., Hulme, C., Snowling, M. J., & Stevenson, J. (2004). Phonemes, rimes, vocabulary, and grammatical skills as foundations of early reading development: Evidence from a longitudinal study. *Developmental Psychology, 40*(5), 665–681.

Phillips, B. M., Clancy–Menchetti, J., & Lonigan, C. J. (2008). Successful phonological awareness instruction with preschool children. *Topics in Early Childhood Special Education, 28*(1), 3–17.

Pufpaff, L. A. (2009). A developmental continuum of phonological sensitivity skills. Psychology in Schools, 46(7), 679–691.

Riley, L. (2000). *Mouse mess.* Glenview, IL: Scott Foresman.

Root, P. (2001). *One duck stuck.* Somerville, MA: Candlewick Press.

Savage, J. F. (2011). *Sound it out!* (4th ed.). New York, NY: McGraw-Hill.

Scarborough, H. (2001). Connecting early language and literacy to later reading (dis)abilities: Evidence, theory, and practice. In S. B. Neuman & D. K. Dickinson (Eds.), *Handbook of early literacy research* (pp. 97–110). New York, NY: Guilford Press.

Schuele, C. M., & Boudreau, D. (2008). Phonological awareness intervention: Beyond the basics. *Language, Speech, and Hearing Services in Schools, 39,* 3–20.

Siracusa, C. (1990). *No mail for Mitchell.* New York, NY: Random House.

Snow, C., Burns, S., & Griffin, P. (1998). *Preventing reading difficulties in young children.* Washington, DC: National Academy Press.

Stadler, M. A., Watson, M., & Skahan, S. (2007). Rhyming and vocabulary: Effects of lexical restructuring. *Communication Disorders Quarterly, 28*(4), 197–205.

Thatcher, K. L. (2010). The development of phonological awareness with specific language–impaired and typical children. *Psychology in the Schools, 47*(5), 467–480.

Torgesen, J. K., Al Otaiba, S. A., & Grek, M. L. (2005). Assessment and instruction for phonemic awareness and word recognition skills. In H. W. Catts & A. G. Kamhi (Eds.), *Language and reading disabilities* (pp. 127–156). Boston, MA: Pearson Education.

Troia, G. A. (2004). Phonological processing and its influence on literacy. In C. A. Stone, E. R. Silliman, B. J. Ehren, & K. Apel (Eds.), *Handbook of language and literacy* (pp. 271–301). New York, NY: Guilford Press.

Verhoeven, L. (2001). Prevention of reading difficulties. In L. Verhoeven & C. Snow (Eds.), *Literacy and motivation: Reading engagement in individuals and groups* (pp. 123–134). Mahwah, NJ: Lawrence Erlbaum Associates.

Vloedgraven, J. M. T., & Verhoeven, L. (2007). Screening of phonological awareness in the early elementary grades: An IRT approach. *Annals of Dyslexia, 57,* 33–50.

Walsh, G., Sproule, L., McGinness, C., & Trew, K. (2011). Playful structure: A novel image of early years pedagogy for primary school classrooms. *Early Years, 31*(2), 107–119.

Whitehurst, G. J., & Lonigan, C. J. (1998). Child development and emergent literacy. *Child Development, 69,* 335–357.

Whitehurst, G. J., & Lonigan, C. J. (2001). Emergent literacy: Development from prereaders to readers. In S. B. Neuman & D. K. Dickinson (Eds.), *Handbook of early literacy research* (pp. 11–29). New York, NY: Guilford Press.

Yeh, S. S. (2003). An evaluation of two approaches for teaching phonemic awareness to children in Head Start. *Early Childhood Research Quarterly, 18,* 513–529.

Yopp, H. K. (1992). Developing phonemic awareness in young children. *Reading Teacher, 45*(9), 696–706.

Yopp, H.K., & Yopp, R.H. (2009). Phonological awareness is child's play. *Beyond the Journal: Young Children on the Web.* Retrieved from http://www.naeyc.org/files/yc/file/200901/BTJPhonologicalAwareness.pdf

Ziolkowski, R. A., & Goldstein, H. (2008). Effects of an embedded phonological awareness intervention during repeated book reading on preschool children with language delays. *Journal of Early Intervention*, *31*(1), 67–90.

Chapter 6

Putting Letters and Sounds Together: Phonics and Decoding Strategies

Barbara Culatta,
Kendra M. Hall-Kenyon, and Sharon Black

Phonics, the ability to recognize letters, identify their sounds, and connect them to decode words, is widely accepted as one of the most important factors in children's reading success (Beatty, 2005; Ehri, Nunes, Stahl, & Willows, 2001; McGee & Richgels, 2003; Savage, 2011). As researchers continually point out, children who do not develop these foundational early literacy skills are at risk for subsequent reading difficulties (e.g., Catts, Fey, Zhang, & Tomblin, 2001; Cunningham & Stanovich, 1998). Those who have these basic tools are able to gain the abilities they will need to access not only reading as a skill area, but ultimately the general school curriculum (Foster & Miller, 2007).

Chapter 4 discussed the importance of alphabet knowledge, along with ways it can be taught. Chapter 5 described areas of phonological and phonemic awareness, explaining how these skills develop and interrelate with others, suggesting ways teachers and SLPs can promote and guide these processes. This chapter introduces readers to the further application and development of these skills as they relate to the nature of phonics and decoding instruction. Both synthetic and analytic approaches for teaching phonics are introduced; however, the authors of this chapter feel that these approaches can be complementary and interactive and that they should be combined as phonics is introduced in preschool and taught in kindergarten through second grade. Throughout the chapter, specific activities are suggested to bring both meaning and engagement to phonics learning. Studies and suggestions involving children with language difficulties are described as well.

The Nature of Teaching Phonics

When children begin to realize that words are made up of sounds and sounds can be represented in print, they are beginning to develop some basic emergent literacy skills (Clay, 2002). At the end of preschool or beginning of kindergarten, they start to realize that sounds and words can be talked about, manipulated, and deliberately chosen. Children at this stage are able to begin to learn tools like phonics skills because they can "focus on language . . . talk about such things as words, sentences, letters and sounds" (Rohl, 2000, p. 67). The term *phonics* is generally applied to teaching letter-sound correspondences, demonstrating how letter-sound relationships are applied in decoding, and practicing use of letter-sound knowledge to pronounce written words (Shanahan, 2006).

Research has provided no "best way" for teaching phonics, but studies and observations have indicated that engaging in a variety of activities and doing a lot of reading and writing help children to learn more effectively (Cunningham, 2005). Before exploring specific approaches, methods, contexts, and activities for teaching phonics, some general perspectives affecting these aspects are treated.

Phonics in Perspective

Students' ability to recognize letters and identify their sounds is widely acknowledged to predict children's reading success (Zucker, Justice, & Piasta, 2009, p. 377; see also McGee & Richgels, 2000; Savage, 2011). Capability with phonics is recognized as contributing to "a large fluent reading vocabulary," as well as skill in recognizing known words and in breaking unfamiliar words apart in order to decode them (Donoghue, 2009, p. 122). Students can consider letter sounds separately and additionally recognize chunks that create familiar sounds within words. Although eventually they will recognize words from memory, "in order to bond words in memory" students must initially be able to analyze a word in terms of all of its sounds (Gunning, 2000a, p. 30).

However, SLPs and teachers must remember that phonics is a significant *part*, but not all, of a reading program (Ehri et al., 2001; Eldredge, 2005). Eldredge (2005) referred to it as "the form of a written text, not its function" (p. 124). He noted that phonics should be taught as a strategy for decoding; it should not be allowed to eclipse other important aspects of literacy preparation. Ehri et al. (2001) concluded, after a substantial meta-analysis, that phonics instruction must be taught in combination with other critical components in a "complete and balanced" program of reading instruction.

Because children come to a reading program with such significant differences (Curby, Rimm-Kaufman, & Ponitz, 2009; Hovland, Gapp, & Theis, 2011; Ukrainetz, Ross, & Harm, 2009), phonics experiences and activities need to be multilevel as well as multifaceted so that every child learns something compatible with his or her level of word knowledge (Cunningham, 2005).

Interrelated Skills and Components

Phonics and decoding are so closely interrelated with other aspects of literacy that they need to be considered in the context of this body of knowledge and skills (Camilli, Kim, & Vargas, 2008). These skill areas include phonological awareness, spelling, word analysis, word recognition, and comprehension. Although these areas are discussed elsewhere in this book, they are applied here in terms of their relationship to phonics instruction.

Phonological Awareness

Children may begin learning letters and sounds before they become conscious of phonemes and begin to understand how they come together to form words (Cunningham, 2005). But once phonological awareness begins to develop, instruction and practice in phonological awareness and in phonics knowledge and skills are interactive and complementary (Stahl, Duffy-Hester, & Stahl, 1998). Several studies have indicated that combining instruction in these two areas can result in greater gains in reading (Ball & Blachman, 1988, 1991; Bradley & Bryant, 1983; National Reading Panel, 2000). Children need to be aware of the relationship of sounds to letters and words (phonological awareness) and to be able to apply this knowledge to printed representation (phonics) if they are to understand how reading works (Byrne & Fielding-Barnsley, 1991). Teachers can blend these processes by attaching letters to sounds after or during phonological awareness activities that teach rhyme, alliteration, sound blending, and word analysis, as discussed and described in Chapter 5.

Spelling

In addition, spelling is integrally linked to phonological awareness and phonics instruction. Although some teachers may feel that spelling instruction should come after letter-sound and decoding skills are well developed (Shanahan, 2006), actually the processes that children use as they attempt to spell and write words solidify phonological awareness and phonics skills. As children learn to represent the sounds they hear in words with a sequence of letters, they internalize ways the alphabetic system works (Armbruster, Lehr, & Osborn, 2001), and as they hunt in their minds for the specific letters they have learned, they strengthen letter-sound associations.

Early spelling experience also teaches students to segment the sounds in words and then blend them to write in whole-word form. Spelling development begins as students learn that word family words can be spelled by changing only beginning sounds and that many rhyming words are easy to spell once children learn the pattern of the rhyme (Cunningham, 2005).

Word Building/Analysis

Word building and word analysis, which identify or change word parts in the process of creating other words, also support phonics and decoding (Beck, 2006; Savage, 2011). Children are given opportunities to create words by changing the arrangement of letters. The procedures require students to focus attention on the individual letters in words and the different sequences of letters that make up words (Beck, 2006). For example, Cunningham (2005) suggested an activity she called "Using Words You Know," in which several words children have learned are written at the heads of columns. The teacher pronounces words that rhyme with the given words, and the children figure out how to spell each and write it in the correct column. For example, Cunningham showed *ice* (a word the children took from an ice cream label) at the head of a column containing *nice, mice, slice, twice,* and *dice* (p. 105).

Word Recognition

Using phonics to decode should eventually lead to the automatic word recognition necessary for fluent reading. Once students have repeatedly broken a familiar word into parts and blended the parts into the word's sound(s), they recognize the word and it becomes part of their reading as well as oral vocabulary (Ehri, 2002).

Once children have had sufficient experience decoding words, they develop the ability to instantly recognize key letter sounds and patterns and can identify words without having to sound them out (see Ehri & McCormick, 1998; Gunning, 2000a). Thus letter-sound and decoding skills influence fluency (smooth, expressive reading) by contributing to effortless word recognition. The goal is to promote automatic word recognition so that children can read with their focus on meaning, not on figuring out individual words.

Comprehension

The ultimate goal of reading instruction is, of course, comprehension. Phonics should enhance but not detract from functional classroom reading experiences (Eldredge, 2004). Comprehension is facilitated by effortless word recognition, which depends on well-developed phonics and decoding skills. Thus the lower-level skills of attaching letters to sounds, decoding words, recognizing words, and reading sentences fluently will influence children's ability to understand and interpret the meaning of a text. Children will have difficulty comprehending what they read if the reading process is slow and laborious. Effortful decoding ties up cognitive processes that are needed for connecting and attaching meaning to ideas in texts (Perfetti, 1985). Thus comprehension and decoding instruction can and should both be addressed in early literacy instruction (Pearson & Duke, 2002).

Instruction in Phonics Skills

Teaching phonics is a multifaceted endeavor, and facets are interrelated and interactive. Instruction begins by emphasizing letter-sound associations, first in isolation and then in the context of words. These skills then lead to decoding, or the actual reading of words. Decoding skills are first taught using individual words and simple texts. As word identification skills become more automatic, children are ready to move to more challenging texts. This section looks at methods and strategies for teaching basic phonic skills, and the next section focuses more extensively on the application of those skills in the context of reading and writing simple connected texts.

Methods and Approaches

Many methods and approaches have been applied to teaching phonics. Out of this multiplicity, the National Reading Panel (NRP, 2000) has drawn some basic conclusions that can be helpful to teachers and SLPs in making decisions about overall plans for instruction, including the necessity for systematic and explicit instruction, and the efficacy of some of the approaches.

Systematic and Explicit Instruction

The National Reading Panel (NRP; 2000) stated that the most effective approach to phonics instruction is one that is systematic and explicit. It reports that this instruction "provides practice with letter-sound relationships in a predetermined sequence," specifying, "Children learn to use these relationships to decode words that contain them" (p.14). The Panel further stated that systematic and explicit instruction in phonics "significantly improves children's reading comprehension" (p. 14), "is effective for children from various social and economic levels" (p. 12), and "is more effective than nonsystematic . . . instruction" (p. 13). This endorsement by the NRP is supported by others, including the meta-analysis of Ehri et al. (2001) and the experimental work of deGraff, Bosman, Hasselman, and Verhoeven (2009).

Thomas Savage (2011) commented that "systematic and explicit instruction leaves little to chance" (p. 128). All aspects of instruction are deliberately planned and carefully structured. Letter-sound relationships are taught in cumulative sequence in "systematic and prespecified sets" (deGraff et al., 2009). Teachers have a clear plan for moving children from skill to skill (Shanahan, 2006), and they are careful to teach prerequisite letter and decoding skills before introducing more complex skills and applications. A particular plan for the order of letters and sounds has not been established, but most teachers like to start with the sounds found most often in the words children are reading and writing (Donoghue, 2009). In systematic instruction, words that are regular graphophonically should be approached by teaching predictable letter-sound correspondences and patterns so that children can segment and blend sounds and chunks of sounds to discern or form words (Eldredge, 2005). The methodology involved in systematic and explicit instruction is grounded in the philosophy that young children need to "master the code early" (Eldredge, 2005, p. 45). (See Appendix 6–A for an example of a systematic phonics curriculum for kindergarten.)

Synthetic, Analytic, and Combined Approaches

The particular approach selected to teach phonics to children can vary as long as the elements of systematic and explicit instruction are maintained (NPR, 2000). Two commonly used instructional approaches are synthetic and analytic (NRP, 2000). The synthetic approach teaches grapheme-sound combinations in a logical order and guides children in blending these sounds to form words. Emphasis in the synthetic method is on having children read or decode words without relying on context or on prior knowledge of a word's pronunciation for clues (Beck, 2006). With analytic phonics children learn patterns of letters (e.g., the word family ending of -*ot* in *pot* and *dot*) and then go on to locate the pattern in additional words (e.g., discover that they can also read *not, got,* and *lot*). With the analytic approach, meaning and context can support children's ability to figure out what a word says when they are initially learning to read.

Many educators and researchers advocate combining the approaches to give children the benefits of both methods (Shanahan, 2006). Combining the synthetic and analytic methods allows teachers different options for meeting the literacy needs of children (Shanahan, 2006). Drawing upon procedures from synthetic and analytic approaches, teachers and SLPs can help children associate letters with sounds, decode words, read connected texts, and engage in spelling and writing to strengthen phonics skills.

The remainder of this chapter describes how educators can systematically and explicitly implement a combined synthetic/ analytic approach in kindergarten and first grade settings. The following section suggests ideas and examples for teaching letter-sound association, focused on recognizing and manipulating initial letter sounds. The subsequent section is concerned with decoding instruction, including examples that treat medial and final sounds.

Letter-Sound Association

Using both analytic and synthetic strategies enables teachers to make letter-sound instruction meaningful to children (Jalongo, 2000) without losing the advantage of systematically teaching individual letters and sounds. Teachers and SLPs can help children associate letters with sounds by highlighting letter-sound associations both in isolation and in words, providing opportunities to use and act on letter sounds in communicative contexts.

Individual Letter Sounds

When teaching letter sounds in isolation, the teacher or SLP should offer a clear explanation of the association. For example, the teacher might show a large *P* and begin, "Today we're going to learn about the letter *P*. *P* makes the sound /*p*/." The teacher and class may practice making the /*p*/ sound, with the children responding in unison to the teacher's examples: "When you see me touch the *P*, all of you say /*p*/" (see Denton, Parker, & Hasbrouck, 2003).

Games and routines can be used to call children's attention to individual letters and sounds in engaging ways. The teacher might show a large cutout of a pig sitting on a pile of *P*s and have the children say the sound /*p*/ as they add more *P*s to the pile. "This is Pat Pig; Pat the pig puts *P*s in a pile—a pile of *P*s. Make the /*p*/ sound for the *P* you put on the *P* pile." Children say the /*p*/ as they put paper *P*s on Pat Pig's pile. The children can also say the /*p*/ sound as they pull the *P*s off the pile and put them in a package, a pan, or a paper pouch.

After introducing the letter and sound explicitly, the teacher or SLP may highlight the letter-sound relationship in the initial position in words (Gunning, 2000b). If Pat the Pig has a pile of *P*s, she may also have a pail full of words that begin with *P*, and the teacher can point out the letter and call attention to the sound (or segment the sound from the word) as the children take an object or picture from the pail: "*Pig, pants,* and *potatoes* all start with the /*p*/ sound, and we use this letter *P* to stand for the /*p*/ sound. What else do you think we'll find that begins with the /*p*/ sound?" Children may suggest other words that start with *P*, which the teacher can write on word cards to put in the pail. She can hold up the card, point to the initial letter, and highlight the sound, breaking it from the rest of the word as she clearly emphasizes the initial sound.

Letters as Sound Symbols

Letter-sound instruction can be embedded into activity contexts in which letter sounds are related to the context and letters may symbolize ideas or words. Initial letter sounds can be applied in engaging activities for recognition practice or used to differentiate words with the same rime ending.

Application and Practice with Initial Sounds. Letters representing the beginning sounds in key words may be used to communicate ideas in a simple situation, such as using *B* in a "birthday bash" for a big brown bear named Buzz. The students all write a *B* (Buzz's special letter) on a big birthday card. They also write *B*s on envelopes or wrapped packages so Buzz can know that the gifts are for him and that the presents (pictures and objects) inside begin with the /*b*/ sound (ball, bat, book, bell, bag, beads, bows, etc.). The children write *B*s on a big blue banner they make for Buzz and say the sound each time they write the letter *B* (Figure 6–1).

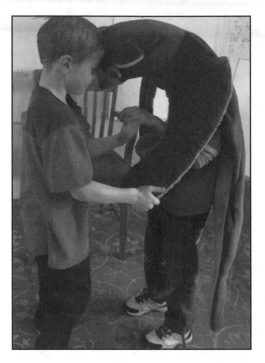

Figure 6–1. Buzz, the big brown bear, thanks children for the *B*-things they have given him for his birthday bash. (Any large teddy bear or bear puppet will do.)

The sounds of initial letters in words can also be emphasized while reading a simple text. The children can "read" the initial letter *B*, for example, in a teacher-made or teacher-student co-constructed text about what Buzz the bear got for his birthday or what he ate. "Every time you see the letter *B* at the beginning of the word as we read about Buzz bear's birthday, you read the /*b*/ sound."

Use of Initial Sounds to Distinguish Words. After applying initial sounds to represent words in a context, children can focus on identifying the sound of the initial letter to distinguish among words with the same rime or word family ending. They learn to use the initial letter sound along with contextual and verbal support to identify written words in terms of meaning. For example, the children may pretend to cook an egg, with actions or gestures, as they read with the teacher or SLP a text telling them how to do this. The text includes many -*op* word family words, which the children distinguish by focusing on the initial consonant.

> Pop! Break open the egg. Plop the egg in a cup. Slop the egg in the cup. Oops! Mop up the slop, the sloppy egg that dropped. Drop the egg in the pan. Flip-flop the egg. Chop some tomato. Top the egg with the tomato. Yum! Yum! Eat the egg.

After the reading, the teacher can highlight some of the words for -*op* actions the children performed while making the egg. "Here are some things we did to make our egg: *pop* it open, *top* it with tomato, and *mop* it up." With modeling and support, the children read the first letter of the -*op* words in the list, and the teacher blends the initial sound with the -*op* ending. When producing the sound of the initial consonant in isolation, before blending it into a word, the teacher must be careful not to add a stressed vowel, so that /*p*/ does not become *puh*, for example. This can be done by softly repeating plosive sounds (e.g., /*p*/, /*b*/, /*d*/, /*t*/) or extending sounds that can continue (e.g., /*s*/, /*f*/, /*m*/, /*n*/).

Word Decoding

In addition to associating letters with sounds, instruction in phonics must teach children to decode words. An important part of decoding words is the capacity to segment a printed word into component parts and blend the sounds to produce words. As teachers support decoding, they must consider the size of the sound unit that the children encounter as well as the context within which word decoding occurs.

Contextualized Instruction

Researchers and practitioners recommend that teachers and SLPs embed instruction into interesting contexts that provide reasons for children to read, particularly for children with language deficits (Justice & Kaderavek, 2004). Children are attentive as they construct meaning with adults while they read in engaging contexts

(Bromley, 2000; Justice & Kaderavek, 2004; Kaderavek & Rabidoux, 2004; McGee & Richgels, 2000; Zucker, Justice, & Piasta, 2009).

For example, a first grade teacher engaged children in reading long *i* words spelled with *y* by having them enact a skit with gestures and a paper props. The teacher overviewed target words and had the children read their 'lines' on cue cards:

> I spy a fly in the sky. (*Point up.*) Do not try to get my fry, fly. (Shake finger.) Oh my, the fly is on my fry! (*Look mad.*) Why are you on my fry, fly? (*Scratch head.*) "That is my fry," I cry. (*Pat chest.*) "Fly away, fly!" (*Shoo the fly.*) The fly is in the sky. (*Point up.*) Now I can eat a fry! (*Pretend to eat.*) But I won't eat the fry that had the fly!

After illustrating the story, the children decode the key words in the text. The teacher decides how much support they need but gradually fades that support.

Not all sound blending and word reading should be placed in highly contextualized settings, however. Once children have ample experience and practice with particular phonic patterns, they need opportunities to blend sounds and read words with decreasing amounts of support. One way this can be done is by providing texts that are clearly at the children's independent reading levels so that they can solidify their recognition of familiar phonic patterns and practice reading words in a connected text.

Practice with Blending and Analyzing Words

In early literacy instruction, children should first blend simple CVC words at the larger onset and rime level and then blend individual phonemes into words (Cunningham, 2005). Activities that support blending and segmenting at the onset + rime level include reading words from word wheels, pushing written onsets together with rime endings to produce words, and changing initial or final letters and/or rime endings to make different words. At the onset + rime level, children can be expected to read word family words and then analyze those words afterward.

After being introduced to a set of word family words in which they blend and segment the onsets and rimes, children should be supported in analyzing the same words at the phoneme level. A teacher or SLP may guide children in identifying the final consonant and medial vowel in CVC words (e.g., pointing to, stating, and sorting words by their individual sounds). She may ask children to state the individual sounds they hear in a particular word or set of words (*zip* = *z-ĭ-p*) or to analyze and build new CVC words: for example, switching around the initial and final consonants to make new words (*pot* becomes *top*), and changing the medial vowel (e.g., *bug* becomes *big* or *bag*) (Figure 6–2).

   Practice connected to engaging conversations enables children to use the skill in a context. The teacher or SLP might begin a conversation on the idea that all people have things they can't do and things that they can. A controlled text like the following could then be read from chart paper, first in unison and then by individuals. The adult would demonstrate for the children how the short *i* is used with multiple initial and final sounds.

Are you a big kid?

Big enough to. . . .

 kick a stick?

 dig with a twig?

 spin and skip?

 do a flip?

 do a jig?

 take a trip on a ship?

You are big enough to kick, dig, spin, skip, do a jig, and take a trip.

You are big enough to do a flip. But it is not easy to do a flip.

I am big, but I can **not** do a flip.

When children learn to identify the vowel and trade around final as well as initial letters to make new words, they are able to manipulate words at the phoneme level because the rime pattern is broken apart (Cunningham, 2005). Table 6–1 illustrates how kindergarten teachers can systematically use this basic sequence to introduce skills and gradually move children from lower to higher levels.

Figure 6–2. Children construct words with letter blocks by keeping a vowel constant and changing the initial and final consonants.

Support for Decoding Within Texts

Instruction in phonics should operate at the text as well as word level. A teacher or SLP can implement various supports for decoding while reading texts together with the children. As children encounter different texts, the instructor can embed appropriate strategies into the decoding experience. A list of supportive actions teachers and other adults can include while reading with children follows:

◆ Determine which phonic patterns are targeted and decide what the child will be asked to "read" and where the teacher will provide support. Within the text, point to the target pattern or word and wait for the child to decode it. If the child does not produce the correct sound within a second or two, supply the sound, sound pattern, or word, and provide a chance for the child to re-read the word or phonic pattern and to encounter other examples of the same word or pattern after reading the text.

Table 6–1. Application of Kindergarten Skill Sequence for Words with Simple CVC Structure

Teach a core of letter-sound associations.	e.g., /f/, /b/, /t/, /m/, /s/, and /ă/
Help children decode words using these sounds: e.g., word family words. For motivation, you may attach an activity.	Draw a bat on a large balloon. Slowly blow up the balloon, making the bat fat, as the children read the words "fat bat" from chart paper or white board. Place the bat on a mat, and add *mat* and *sat* to the list of words. Let the children practice reading, first in unison and then individually as you point to the words: "The fat bat sat on a mat."
Segment and blend CVC words.	Show a copy of the sentence leaving off the word family sounds: "The f__ b__ s__ on a m__." As you read the sentence together, let children fill in the missing letters in a different color marker. Read the sentence in segmented form: "The f—at b—at s—at on a m—at."
Sound out each letter and read the words at the phoneme level (smallest unit of sound).	"Let's say all the sounds in our *at* words: fat, f-a-t; mat, m-a-t; bat, b-a-t ; sat, s-a-t."
Analyze or build new words.	Introduce more *-at* family words: e.g., *cat, pat, hat, rat*, etc. If students have learned other short-vowel word families, there will be a greater variety of ways they can change letters around to form new words: e.g., *mat* becomes *mop*, *pat* becomes *tap*, or *top* becomes *tap*.
Read familiar words in connected texts.	1. Use the new words among others in a brief story (The Fat Cat's Hat), class message ("Get a mat to use at snack"), or some sentences related to informational content (contrast some facts about bats, cats, or rats) and write the text on chart paper. Read it with the students and let several volunteers read it as well. 2. Help the children compose a story (on chart paper) using words they have learned. Let various students write words or parts of words that they know. Sound out words together, and discuss how new words are being made from old sounds. Let the children read the story separately and in unison.

◆ Prime the students to identify a particular pattern that they will encounter in the text; practice decoding the pattern out of the text and call attention to it when it comes up in the text.

◆ Provide initial sound prompts by forming the sound as the child approaches an unfamiliar word. If the child is unable to continue, model segmentation of the word or begin to produce the sounds, the letters, or phonic pattern and wait for the child to join in.

◆ Help the child segment words. Point to a pattern or letter the child will recognize, and encourage the child to decode that portion of the word.

◆ Model the segmenting and reading of consonant blends (e.g., sounds of *br*, *fl*, *st*). Kindergarten children should be given extra support to segment blends. The adult should "read" the blend and ask the child to read the rime ending (e.g., for *flop*, the teacher reads *fl-* and child reads *–op*).

◆ Provide practice segmenting and blending any multisyllable words. Point out parts (syllable or letter patterns) in a multisyllable word that the child may recognize; assist in breaking the word into its syllables, and then blend the parts into the word

Connected Texts for Reading and Writing

Young children's decoding will be slow at first, and they will require high levels of support. The teacher's goal is to move children from labored and highly supported decoding to more efficient, independent reading (even at very simple text levels) and automatic word recognition. As decoding and word recognition improve, text comprehension will likely improve as well (Shankweiler et al., 1999).

Writing and reading are complementary and interactive; they approach the language medium from different directions, but they utilize and develop the same skills. Cunningham (2005) noted, "In addition to lots of reading, lots of writing helps children become better decoders and spellers" (p. 58). This section first discusses the use of texts that children can read with appropriate adult support, and then moves into writing techniques that complement and extend the phonics experience.

Texts Children Can Read

In a joint position statement the International Reading Association and the National Association for the Education of Young Children (1998) have advocated "meaningful connected reading," which includes "systematic code instruction" (as cited in Cassidy, Brozo, & Cassidy, 2000). Teachers can use decodable, hybrid, or leveled texts that are commercially available, or they can make up their own decodable or hybrid texts tailored specifically to their students' needs and experiences.

Decodable Texts

Decodable texts highlight certain phonic patterns, giving children frequent opportunities to practice particular decoding skills: for example, a certain short or long vowel, a word family, or a specific vowel variant (combination) such as the sound of *oo* in moo and coo or the sound of *oo* in book and look. Many decodable texts are currently available to support the development of early reading. In reviewing types of reading texts and examining studies on them, Hiebert and Martin (2001) commented,

> Students who read from the decodable preprimers were more likely to learn the letter-sound correspondences early, including ones not explicitly taught, and to use decoding knowledge when encountering unfamiliar words. Use of decodable texts for a particular part of the reading acquisition period seems to help, but this study does not indicate how long this period extends. (p. 363)

An example of an appealing decodable text is the book *The Mix* by Mary Beth Spann. The text was written to teach short *i*, and every word except *the*, *on*, and *her* contains short *i*. The story is limited to children mixing a drink and drinking it, but the pictures are cute, and children can easily relate to the drink experience.

Decodable texts vary, and teachers' practical experience shows that effectiveness varies as well. Some have very tightly controlled vocabulary, and this can result in contrived, unnatural language in addition to limiting the story or other content. *The Mix* is not badly damaged in these ways as it uses playful repetition of the pattern "Mix, mix, mixing" (p. 5) or "Sip, sip, sipping" (p. 11) to call attention to target words. However, regardless of how well the decodable text is written, teachers should remember that it serves a particular purpose—to highlight a particular phonic pattern. As such, some suggest that while decodable books offer some benefits, particularly for struggling students, teachers should limit their use with advanced readers (Cunningham, 2005; Donoghue, 2007; Eldredge, 2005; Savage, 2011) unless elaboration and discussion are included (Figure 6–3).

Many texts written for young children to read may be labeled as *hybrid*, having much of decodability but including some words (and thus potential for interesting content) outside the narrow strictures of many of the decodable texts. They highlight phonic patterns but with natural language and meaningful, interesting content (Hiebert & Martin, 2001), as do leveled texts, which are described in the following subsection (hence the term *hybrid*). For example, *Bees' Tea Party* was written to emphasize long *e* (*ee* and *ea* pattern) with frequent use of words like *queen, bee, tea, peach, tree, sweep, green, seats*, and many more. But this text also adds words such as *busy, shout,* and *surprise* to fit the ideas presented in the text. The book tells a story about a group of bees putting together a tea party as a surprise for their queen who, while the workers are out looking for her, finds the feast and makes herself at home.

In addition to using commercially produced texts, SLPs and teachers can construct their own decodable texts to meet the spe-

Figure 6–3. A group of children read from their own copies of a decodable text with their teacher.

cific needs of students, providing examples of target phonic patterns in varied and interesting ways (Bingham, Hall-Kenyon, & Culatta, 2010; Culatta, Aslett, Fife, & Setzer, 2004; Culatta, Culatta, et al., 2004; Culatta, Reese, & Setzer, 2006; Culatta, Setzer, & Wilson, 2004). Personalized decodable materials can be introduced with experiences arranged to activate meaning and expose children to examples of words and phonic patterns. Children have made progress by reading words in texts that were based on meaningful experiences (Bingham et al., 2010; Marshall, 2011). As children engage in arranged play or hands-on activities designed to highlight a target phonic pattern, they encounter a number of similar-sounding yet relevant phrases or sentences that go with their actions; and then they can read about what they did in the form of a hybrid decodable text.

For example, kindergarten children might read a decodable text about an experience they have as they hop to the shop to get a pop. They hop to a shop, hop back from the shop with the pop, pop off the top (which overflows, of course), and mop up the pop. The context of acting out the skit helps the children engage with target words (i.e., *hop, pop, mop*). Before and after the activity the children decode the key *-op* words from a list, a series of phrases, or a text related to the experience. A teacher-written hybrid text might go something like this:

Want some soda pop?

Let's hop to a shop to get some pop.

Buy the pop at the shop

Then hop back from the shop with the pop.

Pop off the top!

Oops! What a mess!

The pop went all over.

We've got to mop up the pop.

Do not hop with a can of pop!

In another example, a first-grade text drawn from the SEEL site accompanies an activity in which a stuffed or puppet cow shows the children how he can bow and then the children practice bow-ing. The children may read the following sentences on strips, which they can arrange in different patterns.

Here is my cow.

He knows how to bow.

Take a bow, cow.

Do you know how to bow?

My cow will teach you how.

Watch him now and then take your bow.

That's some bow!

Now you know how to bow.

What a cow!

WOW!

Additional examples of decodable texts based on hands-on, playful activities and designed to highlight a target phonic pattern can be found on the Systematic and Engaging Early Literacy (SEEL) Web site (http://education.byu.edu/seel/).

Leveled Texts

The term *leveled texts* refers to a series of books that have been grouped according to different reading or grade levels (Fountas & Pinnell, 1996). Frequent opportunities to practice reading leveled texts supports children's ability to decode and recognize words in a text that closely matches their current readings skills. Both nar-rative and expository texts are available.

Texts can be leveled in a number of ways. For example, books are often classified on low levels because they contain shorter sen-tences and fewer overall words, content closer to children's lived experiences, and/or more high-frequency words and decodable words (Fountas & Pinnell, 1996). Publishers of early reading books sometimes also level their texts. Three books titled *Bats* (Carney, 2012; Iorio, 2005; Wood, 2010) illustrate the differences among books labeled by the publishers as Level 1 ("beginning reader"), Level 2 ("developing reader"), and Level 3 ("confident reader"). These books are from different series with different publishers but use the same designations (mostly the same words) in identifying levels. The books were chosen for comparison because contrasts are easier to see when the same subject is involved. These differences are shown in Table 6–2.

Compared to decodable texts, leveled texts provide children opportunities to decode a wider variety of words, since they are not designed to highlight one particular phonic pattern and thus can mix patterns. This also means that, initially, teachers may need to provide children with high levels of support: filling in words when necessary, modeling the blending and segmenting of words at the phoneme level, and helping children identify familiar phonic patterns the words contain. As is evident in the examples from Table 6–2, with expository texts some preteaching of scientific vocabulary may be desirable.

The teacher or SLP can also support children in reading leveled texts by re-reading; reading simultaneously with the child, fading out and in as needed; and jumping in to decode difficult words. The adult can also comment on the ideas and engage children in dialog about the content to support comprehension while strengthening decoding and word recognition skills.

Cloze Texts to Highlight a Phonic Pattern

Some teachers and SLPs like to practice phonic patterns with a cloze procedure, using simplified versions of a text with key words eliminated. The adult demonstrates an activity, then tells or reads a story containing target words, and gives each of the children a copy with blanks where words are to be filled in. For example, each child can be given a paper hand and can decorate it by rubbing it with a glue stick and sprinkling on a little sand and making a band for the hand; they can let the hand stand, do a hand stand, pick up the word *and*, shake hands, give a helping hand, lend a hand, and fall and land in sand. After the experience, the children complete their own stories by writing words they remember from the model to complete the cloze text. The children will have heard target words during lessons and activities, so they should easily recall

Table 6–2. A Comparison of Three Levels of Texts on Bats

Characteristic	Level 1	Level 2	Level 3
Sentence length	"Bats live in caves. Some bats can be found inside trees. Other bats live in attics." (pp. 4–5) **Short, simple sentences.**	"Bats are nocturnal, meaning they're active at night. This way of life has many advantages for a bat. Insect-eating bats often feast on bugs that come out after dark." (pp. 10–11) **Longer sentences, but simple sentence structure.**	"Night has fallen. It is time for this little bat to spread its wings and soar away. Like all bats, this creature is nocturnal. It sleeps all day and rises when it is dark. When daylight comes, it folds up its wings and eats." (p. 5). **Sentences varied in length and structure—some complex**
Vocabulary	Words are simple: short, conversational very concrete. Some more advanced terms are used (e.g., *hibernate, migrate, colonies,* and, perhaps oddly, *echolocation*), but they are highlighted, discussed specifically in the text, and also defined in the glossary.	Words are a little more sophisticated, but still concrete. Similar scientific terms, adding *mammal, nocturnal, nectar, roost. Echolation* is found in this text as well. The more sophisticated words and scientific terms are defined in footnotes on pages on which they are used.	Words basically are still concrete, but they involve more complex thinking (e.g., comparing bat to other mammals and bat bite to bee sting) and more descriptive sensory language ("syrupy nectar," "scoops up bugs as it soars through the air.") *Echolation* as a process is described in detail. Word meanings are inherent in context.
Content	The text is a very basic description of habits. Details are mostly visual—richly illustrated.	This text contains many lesser known facts about bats with more detail. Causal relationships are often explained, also processes. Analogies are also used to relate to children's lives.	There are more detailed processes and comparisons. Some rare bats are described, and worldwide variety is stressed. Photos are more exotic.

170

many of the specific target words to use in the stories (e.g., I put some ____ and a band on my ____. I let my hand do a ____ stand). If they need scaffolding, the adult may coach the children in remembering the key words, or he may have the children choose words from a list of several alternatives (Culatta, Culatta, et al., 2004). When cloze texts are used, the children are able to have their own copies of stories with words they have written in themselves.

Texts Children Write or Co-Construct

Back in 1986, Donald Graves surprised many people by stating boldly that children's first literacy impulse is to write, not to read. At that time many people thought that children shouldn't begin to write until they could read (and, of course, knew phonics well). Graves demonstrated that children learn phonic skills as they use them in order to write, and that this process interacts with reading skills and significantly benefits learning to read. Jones, Reutzel, and Fargo (2010) expressed this relationship: "The concrete task of creating written text serves as a bridge to the more abstract task of reading" (p. 327).

Shared Writing

Phonics instruction can be easily embedded into shared writing activities, as the teacher or SLP writes from the dictation of a group of children. A small group or class of children dictate a text—story, shared experience, list, procedure, group journal, note to be copied and sent to parents, and so forth—and the teacher or SLP writes their words. The instructor practices "writing aloud" (Nettles, 2006), telling the children what is going through her mind as she chooses the letters and writes the words. ("That's a hard word so spell. I usually start by figuring out the first letter. What letter makes the /d/ sound?") The shared writing approach allows the students to work with their peers and their teacher to write on a level they could not accomplish by themselves (Read, 2010).

Shared writing developed from the language experience approach (LEA), a process in which children share an experience that becomes the subject of their composition (Tompkins, 2005). As the LEA writing describes a classroom event or shared experience, the writing product becomes a sequentially organized written account containing the key words the students spontaneously chose to represent it (Tierney & Readence, 2000). If the event is structured to naturally include words containing the target sounds, the writing experience becomes an equivalent of a hybrid text, containing but not limited to the sounds the children have been learning. For example, a kindergarten teacher gave the children tops from water and juice bottles to spin and drop on a surface marked with spots and dots. The goal was to see if the top would drop and stop on a spot or dot or a picture of a pot. The children also dropped the top into a real pot to watch it spin or stop. Afterwards, the children composed a brief writing, which they titled *Drop the Top*: "Drop the top to see it stop. Did it stop on a dot? Did it stop on a spot? Did it drop on a lot of dots and spots? Did it spin or stop in a pot?"

Interactive Writing

As children are becoming more accustomed to using letter sounds to figure out words, they are getting ready to share the pen rather than having the adult write everything they say. They become apprentices, jointly producing texts supported by the modeling and guidance of their teacher, continually interacting with meaning and purpose (Read, 2010). Traditionally, group interactive writing is done on chart paper so students can easily watch and follow what is being written.

Cunningham (2005) mentioned that early interactive writings should be short, no more than two sentences. The group members decide what they want to say and choose words to express their content. Children often find interesting words on the word wall that they can include in their writing (Paquette, 2007). The teacher can be sure that words containing the target phonic patterns are prominently featured.

As messages get a little longer and more complex, the teacher models the process by which she figures out how to arrange and spell the words as the students take turns writing them (Nettles, 2006). She may segment syllables and blend them or call attention to words with similar sound patterns. Or she may help the children with the medial vowel in CVC words and have the children figure out the initial and final letters. During an interactive writing experience the teacher can decide how much support the children need. Some children will contribute one letter or rime ending to the text. Other children will be ready to write whole words and even entire phrases or sentences.

Teachers can set up a particular activity as a subject for interactive writing in order to generate words using sounds or sound units they want to stress. For example, a kindergarten class that was learning *-ub* word family words enjoyed a lively session in which they learned to scrub and rub a cub in a tub. The teacher provided a teddy bear, a small tub, a scrub brush and a towel. As the bear was repeatedly scrubbed and rubbed (in each child's individual style), the teacher and children talked about the experience. "I gave that cub a big scrub!" "Let's rub and rub and rub the cub!" "Don't dump the cub out of the tub!" With those words and sounds in mind, the class wrote an interactive story about their experience, each adding a series of words or a sentence. As the pictures show, the children enjoyed the experience, and they were able to write about it. The children learned the *-ub* letters and sound, the teacher was gratified by the students' developing skills, and the cub was a little bedraggled from the experience (Figures 6–4A and 6–4B).

A   B

Figure 6–4. A. Children engage in and talk about their "Scrub the Cub" activity. They are learning *-ub* family words in a memorable way. **B.** A child contributes to an interactive writing about scrubbing and rubbing the cub, using the sounds and words he learned during the activity.

Story Prompts

As children move in the direction of more independent writing, they can begin to generate individual written texts based on experiences arranged to highlight a pattern. They will need lots of support, particularly if the teacher wants to prime them with words involving the target pattern. The teacher might begin by presenting her version of a shared experience and ask the children to write their own accounts of what they experienced. Although she will have included words she hopes the children will use somewhere in their stories, and she may list these words on a chart or as part of a word wall, she should *not* instruct the children to imitate what she has written. The voice and selection of details should be their own. The teacher might scaffold children's memory of the experience (and of relevant words) by asking questions about what they did or how they felt, providing an oral review of what took place. Many teachers begin by asking the review questions rather than presenting their own story.

One teacher provided an activity in which she gradually blew up a balloon with a cat drawn on it to make the cat fat; she let the children pat the fat cat, let go of the balloon to make the fat cat go splat, and sat the flat cat on a mat. The teacher reviewed the experience and then let the children write their own story about making the cat fat. She said, "We made a cat get fat and we got to pat the cat. We let the cat go splat and get flat! Then the flat cat sat on a mat. We read a story about what we did. Now it's your turn to write a story about what we did with the fat cat." One five-year-old girl wrote the following:

Mec a cat fat. Pat thi fat kat. Splat thi fat kat. Put thi kat on thi mat.
(Make a cat fat. Pat the fat cat. Splat the fat cat. Put the cat on the mat).

Not a teacher text, of course—but for a five-year-old writing her own version, it's just fine.

Differentiation to Meet the Needs of All Students

A teacher described a breakthrough in her understanding of struggling readers: "But for our students, it's not easy at all. . . . I had been thinking like a person who could read, rather than thinking like a person who was learning to read and who was finding this learning very difficult" (Hovland, Gapp, & Theis, 2011). SLPs and teachers need to understand what individual children with language and reading difficulties are going though in the learning process and what they need to progress.

Students can be behind in their reading for many reasons, among them impairments in oral language or phonological processing, lack of experiences with language and literacy, and limits in proficiency with the English language (Ukrainetz, Ross, & Harm, 2009). With these difficulties added to the variety in growth patterns of young children, teachers of kindergarten and first grade classes may have students who are more than a year apart academically (Curby, Rimm-Kaufman, & Ponitz 2009).

Although classroom teachers are primarily responsible for teaching phonics, SLPs should incorporate phonics-related skills and support decoding as they work with children who have deficits in phonological awareness or other aspects of language development. Sharing the curriculum and knowing the classroom goals and objectives can help SLPs support phonological awareness, reading, and writing, during their interventions. This is particularly important as children with language difficulties often have phonological awareness deficits and reading and writing problems as well.

Ideally the SLP and teacher will work together to serve these students and closely coordinate intervention with the full-class program (Gunning, 2000b). Coordinated intervention can ensure that children receive relevant instruction as they work with different service providers. This section deals with ways teachers and SLPs can differentiate for children's needs: supplementing instruction in a variety of contexts, and collaboratively selecting appropriate methods to support learning.

Multiple Contexts

Because children come to a reading program with such significant differences (Curby, Rimm-Kaufman, & Ponitz, 2009; Hovland, Gapp, & Theis, 2011; Ukrainetz, Ross, & Harm, 2009), phonics experiences and activities need to be multilevel as well as multifaceted so that every child learns something compatible with his or her skill level (Cunningham, 2005). Some children will need more instruction, while others need modified objectives and supports.

Implementing instruction in a variety of contexts can provide multiple opportunities for supplementation and differentiation. Skills can be introduced in one context and practiced in others, or children who didn't acquire or thoroughly master skills as quickly as most of their classmates can have opportunities to work on them during supplemental small group instruction. If objectives have to be adjusted for students with significant difficulties, one-on-one or very small group interventions can be provided while other students are engaged in centers, small group projects, or individual work. Contexts for differentiated instruction can include large group, small group, one-on-one interaction, transitions, and class routines.

Large Group

Letter-sound associations and phonic patterns are often introduced in a large group setting. Good whole group instruction is essential to a differentiated classroom. Focused brief lessons in large groups highlight skills and provide multiple opportunities to practice them. The children can respond in unison or can take quick individual turns to experience the multiple examples necessary for mastering phonics information and skills. Even very capable students need for large group instruction to be reinforced by practice in additional contexts. But SLPs and teachers need to monitor struggling students' responses during large group experiences in order to gather important information about how much support individual children may need in order to be successful and/or what areas to focus on during follow-up instruction (e.g., more support for blending skills or more practice with letter sounds previously taught).

Small Group

Supplemental small group instruction is critical for children who are having difficulty meeting curricular expectations. Specific needs of children with language difficulties can be served effectively in small groups, which provide them with plenty of opportunities to practice skills previously mastered by many peers. Group rotations or use of centers can be particularly useful for providing practice for target skills (Adams, 2001). Additional supported opportunities for learning target phonic patterns and words and for reading practice can be provided for small groups of children who are struggling (Foorman &

Torgesen, 2001; Kaderavek & Justice, 2004; Kaderavek & Rabidoux, 2004). Although there is variety in how the groups are assigned, a maximum group size of five or six has been recommended, with smaller groups being formed for more serious problems (Gunning, 2000b). Some experts have recommended that intervention groups meet daily, but if circumstances and resources do not enable daily work, they should meet at least three times a week (Gunning, 2000b).

Classroom Routines and Other Noninstructional Contexts

Practice within classroom routines and noninstructional contexts (snack time, departure, cleanup, welcome) can reinforce skills and also permit students to transfer use to more authentic contexts. Frequent encounters with targeted skills keep the patterns forefront in the children's minds and provide extra exposure for students who struggle. Practice can be slipped into almost any classroom context during the school day (Richgels, 2001), although some teachers overlook less conspicuous instructional opportunities. For example, letter sounds or phonic patterns can be reviewed during transitions. One kindergarten teacher incorporated reading experiences with -*ot* in transition following a lesson about shapes. The children had made robots out of shapes, so the teacher made dots containing -*ot* words for the robots to follow. As the robots followed dots to certain spots in the classroom for their next activity, the children reviewed -*ot* words by reading the words on the dots as they would trot from dot to dot to their next spot. Not only was this an enjoyable game for the children, it also provided some helpful review for those who needed more practice with the -*ot* sound.

Departure is a strategic time for review. As the children prepare to leave at the end of the day, the SLP may hold up a card or sign that says *hat*, ask them if they want a hat to wear, let them read the word *hat*, and then place a pretend hat on each child as he or she leaves. The instructor may say, "Better put on your hat. Ready for your hat? Read the word 'hat' with me and I'll give you your hat to wear." Thus the teacher reviews the skill by calling attention to an example in an authentic but playful context. The playfulness enables the class to leave on a positive, friendly note, and it also provides a review for students needing more practice with the -*at* sound, giving them a key word for remembering the sound as it sends them home with *hats* on their minds.

"Review, Reteach, Reinforce"

Struggling students need intense instruction, but intense instruction cannot be maintained when students are inadequately engaged; thus, teachers and SLPs must plan motivating lessons and activities (Dickinson, McCabe, Anastasopoulos, Peisner-Feinberg, & Poe, 2003; Guthrie, Wigfield, & Von Secker, 2000; Gutierrez-Clellen, 1999; McCardle, Scarborough, & Catts, 2001; McKenna, 2001; National Reading Panel, 2000; Storch & Whitehurst, 2002), enabling children with a range of interests and needs to maintain high levels of active processing. Research has shown that even children who have disabilities have been able to achieve significant growth in emergent literacy when immersed in appealing and positive literacy instruction and activities (Kaderavek & Rabidoux, 2004), "including (but not limited to) the social, functional, physical, and emotional contexts of the literacy event [focusing on] both oral and written communication and language development" (p. 239).

During their meta-analysis, Ehri et al. (2001) found systematic instruction to be best for children with reading problems. Children with difficulties need practice opportunities that allow them to implement the skills more frequently than their classmates do (Gunning, 200b). Savage (2011) suggested a three-step strategy: "Review, reteach, reinforce" (p. 103).

Review

Review involves repeating skills that have been previously taught, which means providing additional and varied opportunities to practice without rote recitation. Researchers have found that if teachers and SLPs provide activities that will interest and stimulate the children at their "developmental level of competence," children will become enthusiastically involved (Gagen & Getchell, 2006). Savage (2011) explained that even letting the children place word cards on clotheslines rather than manipulating them on desks can add variety, and he adapted "Simon Says" to use actions beginning with target letters. Additionally, children can engage in riddles and guessing games for words beginning with certain letters or ending in certain rhymes. A variety of word sorts can be used, as can adaptations of card matching games (e.g., Old Maid, Hearts, Go Fish, or even simplified Bananagrams) using both sounds and pictures.

One way to supplement and adapt instruction is to provide targeted students with modified versions of texts related to texts and content the entire class is using. Additional instructional activities and materials within the class theme and similar in content to the curricular texts can be appropriate for children who are functioning at a lower reading level. For example, a first grade teacher planned an activity of making pizza and introduced two engaging leveled books to go with the theme: *The Pizza That We Made* (Holub, 2002) and *Pizza Party* (Maccarone, 1994). Children participated in supported reading of the books and made a simple pizza with pita bread (prepared biscuit dough could also be used). For a few children who were reading at an early kindergarten level, the teacher provided a supplemental activity that highlighted *-ip* words as students made a paper pizza by *flip*ping the dough (paper plate), *clip*ping, *snip*ping, and *tip*ping a sauce packet (red paint), and *rip*ping strips of pepper and cheese (green and yellow paper), practicing word sounds as they did so. The children then read a decodable text about their experience. This text was closer to their actual reading level than the books they had enjoyed listening to but had been unable to read effectively with their classmates.

Making Pizza

Flip the dough.

Snip and clip the sauce packet.

Tip and drip the sauce on to the pizza.

Rip a strip of pepper.

Rip a strip of cheese.

Pizza!!

Review can lead to overlearning and thus to speed and automaticity of phonic skills (Cruickshank, Bainer, & Metcalf, 1999).

Reteach

Children who have not learned important material during an initial full-class presentation need to be retaught with engaging practice opportunities. Researchers have found that struggling children need variety in their lessons and activities, ranging from dramatic play to specifically targeted skill instruction (e.g., Justice & Kader-avek, 2004; Zucker, Justice, & Piasta, 2009).

Some teachers involve action, valuable for engaging all children, but particularly for alleviating the intensity of reteaching children who are struggling with delays and disabilities. Kindergarten children like moving through classroom space (Gagen & Getchell, p. 232). In fact, Polly Greenberg, a former child/parent/ staff development specialist with the U.S. Department of Education, has recommended "movement while learning" as integral to developmentally appropriate teaching of young children. For example, teachers have had success with having children "ride" on the big, bulky blue (cardboard) bus that bumps and bangs into objects that begin with *B* on its way to buy bread and buns at a bakery. Rule, Dockstader, and Stewart (2006) suggest some types of large muscle movement can serve as accompanying actions to illustrate word components and/or features (e.g., extending and shortening arms according to whether the vowel in a word is long or short).

Engaging children imaginatively is another way to make reteaching a positive experience. Binding sounds and symbols to an imaginative experience is a way of binding them to memory. For example, a small group of first grade students who need reteaching of the *kl* blend can respond well to imagining clutter. The students in this group gather around the "cluttered classroom closet" and "clear that closet of clutter." First they take turns stepping into the closet and taking something out that begins with the *kl* sound (planted by the SLP or teacher, of course): clock, clay, clippers, clam, clothes, cloak, and so forth. Next the teacher and group members could use their imaginations to think of funny things that start with the *kl* sound that *could* be in a cluttered closet (e.g., clown, cliff, clarinet). The adult might want to give clues or have some pictures available to suggest items. She writes the children's words on cards that are placed, along with the names of items actually found, on a large closet picture to go on the word wall.

Reinforce

To effectively reinforce reading skills, teachers need to provide struggling students with plenty of practice that can include opportunities for success. These strategies are best applied and practiced through "real reading" experiences (Gunning, 2000b). Struggling students need more practice with decodable texts than their classmates (Savage, 2011). Because these texts have tightly controlled vocabulary selected to illustrate regular phonic patterns, students have repeated opportunities to decode simple words and to store sound combinations, word chunks, and word families in memory. Keeping a record of the number of "books completed" and allowing the students to take books they can read home to share with their parents give additional feelings of accomplishment.

Sometimes children can each create an illustrated page with minimal text for a group book, based on a meaningful theme, a favorite story, or a classroom "happening." It can be constructed with chart paper, published as a class book, or converted into a digital format (Culatta, Culatta, Frost, & Buzzell, 2004; Hales, 2012). This book, like the decodable books read, can be enthusiastically shared with parents; afterward, it may be added to a classroom library. In a project conducted in kindergarten classrooms, children made gains on trained as opposed to untrained phonic targets when provided with opportunities to practice reading the targeted words presented in personally created digital books using a story creation iPad application (Hales, 2012; Cole, 2012).

Additional review and reinforcement sessions may be devoted to books that have been read and enjoyed earlier with the entire group, giving some children more experience with decoding. Zucker, Justice, and Piasta (2009) advise SLPs specifically to take more interest in "studying the efficacy of [joint or supported reading] as a vehicle" (p. 376). Learners who are having difficulty need additional opportunities to respond to initial sounds, word endings, and sound combinations within words (Strickland, 2000).

When processes such as reviewing, reteaching, and reinforcing are carried out in planned, systematic early interventions, students who are initially behind are more likely to be able to make significant gains in reading and connect sounds with print by the end of their kindergarten year (Ray & Smith, 2010). Teachers and SLPs need to collaborate to make this happen.

Conclusion

Most teachers, SLPs, and researchers consider phonics to be one of many interrelated aspects of early literacy instruction. Phonics is a set of tools students use to decode words they do not know and to recognize words they have learned. The next chapter, which is focused on spelling, explains how these letter-sound connections gradually develop into the ability to spell words as well as read them. The goal of teaching phonics is not proficient phonics; it is use of phonics to fluently decode or encode words so that students' attention can be focused on meaning as they read or write.

This chapter has provided descriptions, mentioned benefits, and included multiple examples of an approach that combines both synthetic and analytic phonics within systematic and explicit curricula. As with other aspects of early literacy, learning phonics will be more difficult for some children than for others. Children who have delays or deficits in language development need early intervention to prevent early difficulties from becoming long-term stumbling blocks. Suggestions for ways teachers and SLPs can help these children are included as well.

The most important element, of course, is the human element. Recent studies on classroom environment and communication have shown that skilled teachers and SLPs can infuse into most topics a childlike playfulness that keeps even a skill-based component of literacy like phonics from seeming contrived. Indeed the goal of a teacher or SLP should be to be "approachable, so that even a child with a speech difficulty has no hesitation in contributing to the discussion" (Walsh, Sproule, McGinness, & Trew, 2011, p. 111).

References

Adams, M. J. (2001). Alphabetic anxiety and explicit, systematic phonics instruction: A cognitive science perspective. In S. B. Neuman & D. K. Dickinson (Eds.), *Handbook of early literacy research* (pp. 66–80). New York, NY: Guilford Press.

Armbruster, B., Lehr, F., & Osborn, J. (2001). *Put reading first: The research building blocks for teaching children to read.* Jessup, MD: National Institute for Literacy.

Au, K. H. (2000). Literacy instruction for young children of diverse backgrounds. In D. S. Strickland & L. M. Morrow (Eds.), *Beginning reading and writing* (pp. 35–57). New York, NY: Teachers College Columbia University.

Ball, E. W., & Blachman, B. A. (1988). Phoneme segmentation training: Effect on Reading readiness. *Annals of Dyslexia, 38,* 208–225.

Ball, E. W., & Blachman, B. A. (1991). Does phoneme awareness training in kindergarten make a difference in early word recognition and developmental spelling? *Reading Research Quarterly, 26,* 49–66.

Beaty, J. J. (2005). *Fifty early childhood literacy strategies.* Upper Saddle River, NJ: Pearson Merrill Prentice-Hall.

Beck, I. L. (2006). *Making sense of phonics: The hows and whys.* New York, NY: Guilford Press.

Bingham, G., Hall-Kenyon, K., & Culatta, B. (2010). Systematic and engaging early literacy: Examining the effects of paraeducator implemented early literacy instruction. *Communication Disorders Quarterly, 32*(1), 38–49.

Bradley, L., & Bryant, P. E. (1983). Categorizing sounds and learning to read: A causal connection. *Nature, 30,* 419–421.

Bromley, K. (2000). Teaching young children to be writers. In D. S. Strickland & L. M. Morrow (Eds.), *Beginning reading and writing* (pp.111–120). New York, NY: Teachers College Columbia University.

Byrne, B., & Fielding-Barnsley, R. (1991). Evaluation of a program to teach phonemic awareness to young children. *Journal of Educational Psychology, 83,* 451–455.

Camilli, G. C., Kim, S. H., & Vargas, S. (2008). A response to Steubing et al., "Effects of systematic phonics instruction are practically significant": The origin of the National Reading Panel. *Education Policy Analysis Archive, 16*(16), 1–20.

Cassidy, J., Brozo, W. G., & Cassidy, D. (2000, June). *Literacy at the millennium.* Retrieved from http://www.readingonline.org/past/past_index .asp?HREF=../critical/cassidy/index.html

Catts, H. W., Fey, M. E., Zhang, X., & Tomblin, J. B. (2001). Predicting reading disabilities: Research to practice. *Language Speech and Hearing Services in Schools, 32,* 38–50.

Cecil, N. L. (2003). *Striking a balance: Best practices for early literacy* (2nd ed.). Scottsdale, AZ: Holcomb Hathaway.

Clay, M. M. (2002). *An observation survey of early literacy achievement* (2nd ed). Portsmouth, NH: Heinemann.

Cole, H. (2012). Evaluating the effectiveness of Systematic and Engaging Early Literacy (SEEL) intervention on the reading of consonant-vowel-consonant (CVC) words by kindergarten students. (Unpublished master's thesis). Brigham Young University, Provo, UT.

Cruickshank, D. R., Bainer, D. L., & Metcalf, K. K. (1999). *The act of teaching* (2nd ed.). Boston, MA: McGraw-Hill.

Culatta, B., Aslett, R, Fife, M., & Setzer, L. A. (2004). Project SEEL: Systematic and engaging early literacy instruction. *Communication Disorders Quarterly, 25*(2), 79–88.

Culatta, B., Reese, M., & Setzer, L. (2006). Early literacy instruction in dual language (Spanish/English) kindergarten. *Communication Disorders Quarterly, 27,* 67–82.

Culatta, B., Setzer, L. A., & Wilson, C. (2004). Project SEEL: Children's engagement and progress attainments. *Communication Disorders Quarterly*, *25*(3), 127–144.

Culatta, R., Culatta, B., Frost, M., & Buzzell, K. (2004). Project SEEL: Using technology to enhance early literacy instruction in Spanish. *Communication Disorders Quarterly*, *25*(2), 89–96.

Cunningham, A. E., & Stanovich, K. E. (1998, Spring/Summer). What reading does for the mind. *American Educator*, *22*, 8–15.

Cunningham, P. M. (2005). *Phonics they use* (4th ed.). Boston, MA: Pearson, Allyn & Bacon.

Curby, T. W., Rimm-Kaufman, S. E., & Ponitz, C. C. (2009). Teacher-child interactions and children's achievement trajectories across kindergarten and first grade. *Journal of Educational Psychology*, *101*(4), 912–925. doi:10.1037/a0016647

deGraaff, S., Bosman, A. M. T., Hasselman, F., & Verhoeven, L. (2009). Benefits of systematic phonics instruction. *Scientific Studies of Reading*, *13*(4), 318–333. doi:10.1080/10888430903001308

Denton, C., Parker, R., & Hasbrouck, J. E. (2003). How to tutor very young students with reading problems. *Preventing School Failure*, *48*(1), 42–44.

Dickinson, D. K., McCabe, A., Anastasopoulos, L., Peisner-Feinberg, E. S., & Poe, M. D. (2003). The comprehensive language approach to early literacy: The interrelationships among, vocabulary, phonological sensitivity and print knowledge among preschool-aged children. *Journal of Educational Psychology*, *95*(3), 465–481.

Donoghue, R. M. (2009). *Language arts: Integrating skills for classroom teaching*. Thousand Oaks, CA: Sage.

Ehri, L. C. (2002). Phases of acquisition in learning to read words and implications for teaching. In R. Stainthorp & P. Tomlinson (Eds.), *Learning and teaching reading* (pp. 7–28). London, UK: British Journal of Educational Psychology Monograph Series II.

Ehri, L. C., & McCormick, S. (1998). Phases of word learning: Implications for instruction with delayed and disabled readers. *Reading and Writing Quarterly: Overcoming Learning Disabilities*, *14*, 135–163.

Ehri, L. C., Nunes, S. R., Stahl, S. A., & Willows, D. M. (2001). Systematic phonics instruction helps students learn to read: Evidence from the National Reading Panel's meta-analysis. *Review of Educational Research*, *71*, 393–447.

Eldredge, L. C. (2004). *Phonics for teachers: Self-instruction, methods, and activities* (2nd ed.). Upper Saddle River, NJ: Pearson, Merrill, Prentice-Hall.

Eldredge, J. L. (2005). *Teach decoding: Why and how* (2nd ed.). Upper Saddle River, NJ: Pearson, Merrill, Prentice-Hall.

Foorman, B. R., & Torgesen, J. K. (2001). Critical elements of classroom and small-group instruction promote reading success in all children. *Learning Disabilities Research and Practice, 16*(4), 203–212.

Foster, W. A., & Miller, M. (2007, July). Development of the literacy achievement gap: A longitudinal study of kindergarten through third grade. *Language, Speech and Hearing Services in Schools, 38,* 173–181.

Fountas, I., & Pinnell, G. S. (1996). *Guided reading: Good first teaching for all children.* Portsmouth, NH: Heinemann.

Gagen, L. M., & Getchell, N. (2006). Using 'constraints' to design developmentally appropriate movement activities for early childhood education. *Early Childhood Education Journal, 34*(3), 227–232.

Graves, D. G. (1986). *Teaching writing: Teachers and children at work.* Portsmouth, NH: Heinemann.

Greenberg. P. (2006). I'm doing this. *Early Child Today, 21*(3), 21.

Gunning, T. G. (2000a). *Creating literacy instruction for all children* (3rd ed.). Boston, MA: Allyn & Bacon.

Gunning, T. G. (2000b). *Phonological awareness and primary phonics.* Boston, MA: Allyn & Bacon.

Guiterrez-Clellen, V. (1999). Mediating literacy skills in Spanish-speaking children with special needs. *Language, Speech, and Hearing Services in Schools, 30,* 285–292.

Guthrie, J. T., Wigfield, A., & VonSecker, C. (2000). Effects of integrated instruction on motivation and strategy use in reading. *Journal of Educational Psychology, 92*(2), 331–341.

Hales, A. (2012). *Using Systematic and Engaging Early Literacy Instruction and digital books to teach at-risk kindergarteners target vocabulary and literacy skills.* Unpublished master's thesis, Brigham Young University, Provo, UT

Hiebert, E. H., & Martin, L. A. (2001). The texts of beginning reading instruction. In S. B. Neuman & D. K. Dickinson (Eds.), *Handbook of early literacy research* (pp. 361–376). New York, NY: Guilford Press.

Holub, J. (2002). *The pizza that we made.* New York, NY: Scholastic.

Hovland, M. R., Gapp, S. C., & Theis, B. L. (2011). LOOK: Examining the concept of learning to look at print. *Reading Improvement, 48*(3), 128–138.

International Reading Association. (1998). Learning to read and write: Developmentally appropriate practices for young children. A joint position statement of the International Reading Association (IRA) and the National Association for the Education of Young Children (NAEYC). *Reading Teacher, 52*(2), 193–216.

Jalongo, M. R. (2000). *Early childhood language arts* (2nd ed.). Boston, MA: Allyn & Bacon.

Jones, C. D., Reutzel, D. R., & Fargo, J. D. (2010). Comparing two methods of writing instruction: Effects on kindergarten students' reading skills. *Journal of Educational Research, 103*, 327–341. doi:10.1080/002 20670903383119

Justice, L. M., & Kaderavek, J. N. (2004). Embedded-explicit emergent literacy intervention I: Background and description of approach. *Language, Speech, and Hearing Services in Schools, 35*(3), 201–211.

Kaderavek, J. N., & Justice, L. M. (2004). Embedded-emergent Literacy Intervention II: Goal selection and implementation in the early childhood classroom. *Language, Speech, and Hearing Services in Schools, 35*(3), 212–228.

Kaderavek, J. N., & Rabidoux, P. (2004). Interactive to independent literacy: A model for designing literacy goals for children with atypical communication. *Reading and Writing Quarterly, 20*(3), 237–260. doi:10.1080/10573560490429050

Maccarone, G. (1994). *Pizza party*. New York, NY: Scholastic.

McCardle, P., Scarborough, H. S., & Catts, H. W. (2001). Predicting, explaining, and preventing children's reading difficulties. *Learning Disabilities Research and Practice, 16*(4), 230–239.

McGee, L. M., & Richgels, D. J. (2000). *Literacy's beginnings: Supporting young readers and writers* (3rd ed.). Boston, MA: Allyn & Bacon.

McGee, L. M., & Richgels, D. J. (2003). *Designing early literacy programs: Strategies for at-risk preschool and kindergarten children*. New York, NY: Guilford Press.

McKenna, M. (2001). Development of reading attitudes. In L.Verhoeven & C. Snow (Eds.), *Literacy and motivation: Reading engagement in individuals and groups* (pp. 135–158). Mahwah, NJ: Lawrence Erlbaum Associates.

Marshall, E. (2011). *An examination of the effects of using systematic and engaging early literacy instruction to teach tier 3 students to read consonant-vowel-consonant (CVC) words*. Unpublished master's thesis, Brigham Young University, Provo, UT.

National Reading Panel. (2000). *Put reading first: Kindergarten through Grade 3*. Retrieved from www.nichd.nih.gov/publications/nrp/upload/report.pdf

Nettles, D. H. (2006). *Comprehensive literacy instruction in today's classrooms: The whole, the parts, and the heart*. Boston, MA: Pearson: Allyn & Bacon.

Neuman, S. B. (2006). Connecting letters and sounds. *Early Childhood Today, 20*(6), 20–21.

Paquette, K. R. (2007). Encouraging primary students' writing through children's literature. *Early Childhood Education Journal, 35*(2), 155–165. doi:10.1007/s10643-007-0183-6

Pearson, P. D., & Duke, N. K. (2002). Comprehension instruction in the primary grades. In C. C. Block & M. Pressley (Eds.), *Comprehension instruction: Research-based practices* (pp. 247–258). New York, NY: Guilford Press.

Pellegrini, A. D. (2001). Some theoretical and methodological consider-ations in studying literacy in social context. In S. B. Neuman & D. K. Dickinson (Eds.), *Handbook or early literacy research* (pp. 54–65). New York, NY: Guilford Press.

Perfetti, C. (1985). *Reading ability.* New York, NY: Oxford University Press.

AssistiveWare. (n.d.). Pictello. Retrieved from http://www.assistiveware .com/product/pictello

Ray, K., & Smith, M.C. (2010). The kindergarten child: What teachers and administrators need to know to promote academic success in all children. *Early Childhood Education Journal, 38,* 5–18. doi:10.1007/ s10643-010-0383-3

Read, S. (2010). A model for scaffolding writing instruction: IMSCI. *Reading Teacher, 64*(1), 47–52. doi:10.1598/RT.64.5

Richgels, D. J. (2001). Invented spelling, phonemic awareness, and read-ing and writing instruction. In S. B. Neuman & D. K. Dickinson (Eds.), *Handbook of early literacy research* (pp. 142–158). New York, NY: Guilford Press.

Rohl, M. (2000). Learning about words, sounds and letters. In C. Barratt-Pugh & M. Rohl (Eds.), *Literacy learning in the early years* (pp. 57–80). Philadelphia, PA: Open University Press.

Rule, A. C., Dockstader, J., & Stewart, R. A. (2006). Hands-on and kines-thetic activities for teaching phonological awareness. *Early Childhood Education Journal, 34*(3), 195–201.

Savage, J. F. (2011). *Sound it out.* New York, NY: McGraw-Hill.

Shanahan, T. (2006). *The National Reading Panel report: Practical advice for teachers.* Naperville, IL: Learning Point Associates.

Shankweiler, D., Lundquist, E., Katz, L., Stuebing, K. K., Fletcher, J., Brady, S., . . . Shaywitz, B. A. (1999). Comprehension and decoding: Patterns of association in children with reading difficulties. *Scientific Studies of Reading, 3*(1), 69–94.

Stahl, S. A., Duffy-Hester, A. M., & Stahl, K. A. D. (1998). Everything you wanted to know about phonics (but were afraid to ask). *Reading Research Quarterly, 33,* 338–355.

Storch, S. A., & Whitehurst, G. J. (2002). Oral language and code-related precursors to reading: Evidence from a longitudinal structural model. *Developmental Psychology, 38*(6), 934–947.

Strickland, D. S. (2000). Classroom intervention strategies: Supporting the literacy development of young learners at risk. In D. S. Strickland & L. M. Morrow (Eds.), *Beginning reading and writing* (pp. 99–110). New York, NY: Teachers College Columbia University.

Tierney, R., & Readence, J. E. (2000). Teaching reading as a language experience. In *Reading strategies and practices: A compendium* (5th ed., pp. 198–228). Boston, MA: Allyn & Bacon.

Tompkins, G. E. (2005). *Language arts: Patterns of practice* (6th ed.). Upper Saddle River, NJ: Pearson Prentice-Hall.

Tompkins, G. E. (2012). *Teaching writing: Balancing process and product* (6th ed.). Boston, MA: Allyn & Bacon.

Ukrainetz, T. A., Ross, C. L., & Harm, H. M. (2009). An investigation of treatment scheduling for phonemic awareness with kindergartners who are at risk for reading difficulties. *Language, Speech, and Hearing Services in Schools, 40*, 86–100.

Walsh, G., Sproule, L., McGuinness, C., & Trew, K. (2011). Playful structure: A novel image of early years pedagogy for primary school classrooms. *Early Years, 31*(2), 107–119. doi:10.1080/09575146.2011.579070

Zucker, T. A., Justice, L. M., & Piasta, S. B. (2009, October). Prekindergarten teachers' verbal references to print during classroom-based, large-group shared reading. *Language, Speech, and Hearing Services in Schools, 40*, 376–392. doi:10.1044/0161-146(2009/08-0059)

Children's Books

Carney, E. (2012). *Bats*. Washington, DC: National Geographic Kids.

Iorio, N. (2005). *Bats*. New York, NY: HarperCollins Children's Books.

Karlin, N. (1996). *The fat cat sat on the mat*. New York, NY: Sandy Creek.

Spann, M. B. (n.d.). *Bees' tea party*. Vernon Hills, IL: Learning Resources.

Spann, M. B. (n.d.). *The mix*. Vernon Hills, IL: Learning Resources.

Wood, L. (2010). *Bats*. New York, NY: Scholastic.

Examples have been adapted including elements of the following lessons available on the Project SEEL database (http://education .byu.edu/seel/database/search):

A Big Enough Pig

A Big Enough Kid

A Cluttered Classroom Closet

Bb Bus

Big Enough to Skip

Buzz the Bear

Cook an Egg: Drop, Pop, Top, and Slop

The Fat Cat Went Splat

Hop to a Shop to Buy Pop

Making Pizza

My Cow Knows How to Bow

Rag Bag

Scrub the Cub

Flip, Tip, and Rip to Make a Pizza

An Overview of a Kindergarten Curriculum

Sequence of Skill Presentation	*Example Instructional Activities*
Introduce a small core of letter-sound associations, one at a time, in meaningful contexts (e.g., B, M, T, and short A); associate the sound with the letter and call attention to it in alliteration phrases; "read" target letters in initial position in words or write target letters to signal meanings within a context or text	Put Bs on a big, broken box—a/k/a a bus; "ride" the bus holding onto the sides; bounce and bump into branches; brake at a big *B* for bakery; trade Bs for bread and buns; write about the experience of taking the big broken bus to the bakery; and identify Bs in words that make the /b/ sound
Contrast familiar letter sounds with new ones; as new letters and their sounds are introduced, arrange for children to make choices between a new target letter and previously introduced ones	Pick *M* to march or *T* to tip toe; make animal costume parts by putting Ms, *M* words, and *M* items on a monkey mask and Ts, *T* words, and *T* items on a tiger's *T* tail.
Introduce one short *a* (ă) word family (e.g., *ag*) in meaningful contexts; highlight the ending	Make a rag bag with scraps of cloth; make a tag for the rag bag; write "bag" on the bag and tag; perform actions with the rag and bag: wag the rag or bag like a flag and drag and wag a rag to clean.
Engage in follow-up activities that contrast familiar letter-sounds with new ones; read word family words in contexts and in texts; blend target onsets and rimes; manipulate the individual sounds, build new words by changing the onset; write familiar words to dictation and segment at the sound level (e.g., *t-a-g* and *b-a-g*).	Read a text about making rags and a rag bag and tags for the bag; find the –*ag* in words in a target text; segment and blend –*ag* words auditorially (r–ag = rag); stretch a rag with –*ag* words written on it and say the words with elongated vowel

Sequence of Skill Presentation	Example Instructional Activities
Introduce new targets; gradually add more letter-sounds to the core (e.g., p, f, c) and other short *a* (*ă*) word family endings (e.g., *-ap*, *-ack*, *-am*, *-an*); highlight the new target patterns and letter-sounds in context and provide meaningful reasons to read	Tap, slap and snap bottle caps to make music; follow a map to find caps; make a cap out of scraps by snapping on straps and flaps and snaps (the children read the initial *f*, *s*, *c*, and the teacher reads the rest of the blends); follow a map to find bottle caps and *-ap* things, put *-ap* things in a cap, place the cap on a lap, and pretend to take a nap (teacher would "read" *l* and *n* if not previously introduced)
Build and spell words encountered in target experiences; contrive an event that highlights target words and guide children in dictating ideas about their experience; in each case, engage in follow-up analysis and synthesis activities at the onset + rime and phoneme levels; call attention to the final consonant and medial vowel in CVC words	Write about making a cap; create an "*-ap rap*" (tap a cap, slap a cap, snap a cap, clap a cap, flap a cap); list *-ap* words; write *-ap* street names on a map and on signs around the room; identify the medial vowel and final consonant in *map*, *tap*, *bat*, *mat*; blend and segment *-ap* words at the onset-rime and phoneme levels; build words by changing initial and final consonants.
Intermix word families; review simple CVC short *a* (*ă*) words (with different final consonants); build words by varying the initial and final consonants	Intersperse short *a* (*ă*) words in the same activity and text (e.g., put on a cap; pack a back pack with snacks and snack packs, snap the pack; follow a map along tracks tapping tracks and snapping fingers; take a nap by a shack, follow a map back along the tracks.
Introduce a new medial short vowel in word families; use familiar and new letters as onsets (e.g., introduce *-ip*)	Show ways to sip and drip: tip, dip, snip (a paper cup); snip the tip (of a straw), dip the tip and drip, sip from the tip; tip (a cup) and drip; drip and sip; dip and drip; tip and sip; put a drip on your lip.

continues

191

Sequence of Skill Presentation	Example Instructional Activities
Contrast previously introduced words with different medial vowels; intersperse newly introduced word family with previously introduced ones (e.g., contrast -*ip* and -*op*).	Engage in an activity where children drip and drop drops (of water); rip the tip of a paper strip, dip and drop (on tissue or construction paper to make spots and drops, drip drops of water to make spots and dots. Read or write about the activity: Drip! Drop! Drip. Drop. Drip. Drip some drops to make a spot. Drip some drops to make a dot. Drip some drops. Drop some drips. Drip! Drop! Drip and drop.
Decode and spell words out of context at the phoneme level; write from dictation; create words by selecting and blending letters that represent sounds; build new CVC words by varying the vowel and final consonant in familiar words; after each vowel and word family is introduced, manipulate target words at the onset-rime and phoneme levels	Read and write the words *bat, bit, mat, sat,* and *sit* out of context; change the *ă* to an *ĭ* to make a new word; write to dictation or manipulate letters to create the words; vary final consonants (e.g., *bat-bag, mat-map, pit-pig*) and contrast examples (e.g., *tap* vs. *pat*–decide to tap a bat or cat with a finger or gently pat a bat or cat with a hand); vary the medial vowel (e.g., *tip-tap, pat-pit, sit-sat*).
Continue to introduce new sets of targets; toward the end of the year teach additional consonants (moving to less common letters and their sounds) and short vowel word families (short *e* and short *u*) and teach the *sh* digraph in the initial and final positions in words (ship, bash, smash, wish, dish, fish, shush, etc.)	Wish for a fish, wish for a fish in a dish, swish and squish the fish; let a girl puppet (she) smash and bash trash, stash trash, stash trash, clash as she smashes trash in a trash can, Take a ship trip to a shack or shed

Sequence of Skill Presentation	Example Instructional Activities
Support children in reading simple blends; let children read the first consonant in blends while the teacher "reads" the other consonant and models producing a blend in initial position in words; toward the end of kindergarten introduce one common blend (sp); provide high levels of support when children encounter blends	Highlight /sp/ in an activity and then read about it; spill /sp/ objects (spools, sparkles, sprinkles) from a spoon; spin spools on a spot; spill to see if an object or /sp/ card lands on a spot; spill items or "sp" out of a spout created by cutting off the top part of a water bottle
Engage in reading of leveled texts and writing with short vowel words; let children engage in more independent reading and writing activities as they review all that was taught; support children as they "read" words with emphasis on decoding or encoding words at the phoneme level	Engage in guided reading of short vowel texts where children practice reading short vowels and consonants introduced along with /sh/ digraph, /sp/ blend, and /ck/ final double consonant.

Chapter 7

Using Sounds and Letters to Form Words: Developmental Spelling

Kendra M. Hall-Kenyon, Ann C. Sharp, and Brenda L. Sabey

Teachers and researchers have long debated spelling "best practices" (Schlagal, 2002). The majority of the debate has centered around a comparison between more traditional spelling programs, which emphasize single spelling lists, and developmental spelling programs, which emphasize differentiated instruction and teach a variety of spelling strategies. The goals are the same, accurate application of conventional spelling; however, the approaches are vastly different.

Perhaps the most significant difference between these two approaches relates to the way a teacher handles a student's spelling errors. A traditional approach places primary emphasis on correct spelling, and children's spelling progress is tracked according to the number of words spelled correctly on a weekly list. A developmental spelling approach has the same goal of conventional spelling, but it places additional emphasis on children's inductive reasoning as they work out logical relationships between sounds and letters in attempting to represent sounds in words.

With a developmental spelling approach, teachers and SLPs pay close attention to the ways children make decisions about how to represent sounds in forming words. For example, when a kindergartener writes *mi* to represent the word *my*, the instructor recognizes this as the child's ability to correctly represent the /ī/ sound in a word, even if the word is spelled incorrectly. The instructor does not worry about the misspelling of the word at this point because she understands that as the child has more experience with the letter *y* in conventional reading and writing, he will understand more about the multiple sounds that one letter or combination of letters can make. For example, as a first grader the child may know that the letter *y* makes the /ī/ sound at the end of a word (e.g., *my*, *by*, *why*) because he encounters these words in his reading. As he becomes a better reader and gains more and more exposure to words in both reading and writing, he will likely also come to understand that the letter *y* can make more than just the /ī/ in words (e.g., the /ē/ sound, as in *happy*, *baby*, and *sunny*). This example illustrates how teachers who are taking into account the developmental nature of spelling might think differently about the words children misspell and their connection to reading and writing development.

The developmental approach to spelling emphasizes the relationship between children's reading and spelling skills (Al Otaiba, Puranik, Rouby, Greulich, Sidler, & Lee, 2010; Christo & Davis, 2008; Ehri, 2000; Hammill, 2004; Mehta, Foorman, Branum-Martin, & Taylor, 2005; Weiser & Mathes, 2011). This relationship is not surprising when one considers the connection between phonics (or decoding) and early spelling acquisition; they are mirror-like processes and are thus defined similarly. *Phonics* is defined as a system of understanding letter-to-sound correspondences that aid children in word recognition. *Spelling* is defined as the ability to understand sound-to-letter correspondences that aid children in spelling conventionally. Phonics and spelling develop together in a side-by-side synchronized fashion (Ehri, 1997; 2000). However, spelling (encoding) can be more difficult than phonics (decoding) because it requires producing the orthographic patterns from memory, while decoding only requires recognition of those patterns.

While the topics in this chapter are closely related to those discussed in the phonics chapter of this book, this chapter focuses on encoding rather than decoding. It describes the stages of spelling development, important principles that comprise the foundation of spelling instruction, and instructional concepts related to the developmental stages that should be addressed when creating spelling instruction for young children.

Spelling Development

Children progress in a predictable sequence as they acquire knowledge about words, sometimes summarized in a sequence of three words: "alphabet, patterns, and meaning" (Invernizzi & Hayes, 2004, p. 221). In the alphabet phase children first come to understand that individual sounds can be represented by symbols and written down. As they learn the alphabet, they learn which sounds go with which symbols. Then as they transition to the pattern phase, they start to recognize letter patterns, such as vowel digraphs that are consistent across words (e.g., *oa*, *ee*, and *ai*) or complex consonant clusters (e.g., *spr*, *squ*, and *tch*). Finally they move to the meaning phase in which they see the value of knowing that spelling and meaning are connected: that words that are similar in sound and meaning will likely share similarities in spelling (e.g., *nation* and *national*). This understanding leads logically to knowledge of prefixes and suffixes, roots and derivations (Invernizzi & Hayes, 2004).

Multiple researchers (Beers & Henderson, 1977; Ehri, 1986; Henderson, 1990; Bear, Invernizzi, Templeton, & Johnston, 2008, 2012) have moved from this general progression to codify specific stages of development in order to provide specific guidance for instruction. Although the numbers of and labels for the stages vary, further examination reveals that the individual concepts and general sequence of progression are basically the same. This chapter will consider the stages suggested by Henderson (1990) and refined by Bear et al. (2008, 2012), as they are perhaps the best known and are based on a body of research (Bear, 1982; Morris, 1993; Templeton, 1979; Templeton & Bear, 1992; Templeton & Scarborough-Franks, 1985; Zutell, 1979). Each stage is described below.

Emergent Stage

The first stage of spelling development is the emergent stage. At this stage, spellers know only some of the letters of the alphabet, and there is considerable variability in the letters children know. They also do not yet understand sound-symbol relationships. Scribbles and drawings often characterize children's writing early on in this stage. However, as children develop within this stage, they begin to use letters to represent sounds in their writing (e.g., they may write the letter *M* to represent the word *mom)*. As children's knowledge of letter-sound correspondences increases, they move towards the next stage of development (Bear et al., 2012).

Letter-Name Alphabetic Stage

Children's strategy for spelling and understanding of letter-sound relationships is revealed in the name of this stage, the Letter-Name Alphabetic Stage, since children use names of letters to spell words (Sabey, 1999). For example, the word *elephant* could be spelled *lfn*. At this stage children's spelling also tends to emphasize the initial and final sounds — *cat* might be spelled *kt*. As children progress through this stage, they begin to include the medial vowel in familiar CVC words (e.g., *kt* becomes *kat*). They also know a larger number of high frequency words that they can readily use in their writing (Bear et al., 2012). Toward the end of this stage children begin to represent two initial consonants, such as *bl*, with both letters (a consonant blend) and some single sounds, such as *sh* in *ship*, with two letters (the *sh* digraph) (Bear et al., 2012).

Within-Word Pattern Stage

The Within-Word-Pattern stage is characterized by the use of more complex spelling patterns. Spellers distinguish among vowel sounds, long and short, and recognize that combinations of letters can be used to represent particular sounds (e.g., *ee* represents the long vowel sound in *feet*). Children at this stage experiment with the use of different patterns in their writing although they often do not correctly apply their knowledge of different spelling patterns in their writing (Bear et al., 2012). They may overuse the vowel-consonant-silent-*e* pattern or misuse the double-vowel pattern, for example.

Syllables and Affixes Stage

At this fourth stage, Syllables and Affixes, spellers are ready to study polysyllabic words, and they begin to apply some of the spelling patterns they learned previously to words with more than one syllable (Sabey, 1999). Children in this stage learn that they should double consonants when making a single syllable word into a multisyllable word (e.g., change *run* to *running*), an indication that they are ready for this stage (Henderson, 1990). Word study activities also should address similarities and differences in meaning and pronunciation based on spelling (e.g., open and closed syllables [be/gin = first syllable open and second syllable closed]; common prefixes [pre-, mis-, non-] homophones [bear and bare]; and the schwa sound in unaccented syllables [a/bout, doz/en]) (Bear et al., 2012).

Derivational Relations Stage

The derivational relations stage is the most sophisticated stage of spelling development. Students at this stage have mastered high frequency words and are secure in their understanding that changes in spelling impact meaning and that different meanings can be conveyed in words that are spelled the same. "The spelling/meaning connection is the foundation for an in-depth exploration of Greek and Latin roots, bases, and affixes" (Sabey, 1999, p. 419), which is the focus for instruction at this stage (Bear et al., 2012).

Instructional Considerations

Once teachers and SLPs have recognized the basic stages through which spellers develop, additional considerations must be involved in actually choosing spelling curriculum and designing specific instruction. Individual students will move through developmental stages at different rates and according to different patterns. Teachers and SLPs need to consider the students' current skill levels and differing instructional needs so that they can customize their spelling instruction according to the individual needs of the children in their classroom. After discussion of such considerations, the remainder of this chapter provides guidance for specific instructional practices and applications.

Beyond Traditional Spelling Instruction

As teachers and SLPs consider specific student needs along with the developmental stages, they will recognize weaknesses common in the ways spelling has traditionally been taught and will discern corrections that must be made. First, instruction should go beyond mere word memorization to include all aspects of word knowledge that impact spelling. Second, in order to develop strategic and independent spellers, instruction must go beyond merely drilling sequences of letters in lists of words through repetition. Third, instruction must be based on assessment that includes more than a percentage indicating how many words a student spelled correctly.

Beyond Memorization

Spelling curriculum in the past has consisted largely of periodically distributing lists of words that gradually increase in difficulty. The intent was for these lists to be memorized for later use in reading and writing. However, for many students the memorization-use connection does not happen. Teachers frequently lament that students get the words right on the test on Friday morning, but misspell the same words writing in their journals on Friday afternoon (Schlagal, 2002).

Current understanding of what it means to really know how to spell demonstrates that spelling curriculum must include more than just memorizing weekly lists. Spelling instruction needs to include all knowledge that children of a particular level could possibly use to spell a word. The developmental continuum of spelling acquisition clearly demonstrates cumulative knowledge of the alphabet, oral vocabulary, phonemic awareness, phonics, structural analysis, affixes, Latin and Greek roots, word origins, derivations, and so forth; all need attention at the appropriate developmental level in the spelling curriculum (Berninger et al., 2010). Based on this broader view of spelling instruction, many prefer to refer to it as *word study*, a more inclusive and appropriate term. Regardless of terminology, this more inclusive perspective obviously changes the content of spelling curriculum, leading to the second consideration.

Beyond Lists

Anyone watching the National Spelling Bee championships analytically enough to reflect on what these "good" spellers do can see that they are using more than their memories of past spelling lists to spell words. They are accessing multiple knowledge bases and strategies in order to spell words far beyond their lexicon. A strong memory and some "sounding out" techniques can be helpful (Mann, Bushell, & Morris, 2010) but are not enough. Though all students will not reach the national championship level of competency and skill, all can learn to draw from multiple strategies to spell words. For example, children who learn to examine the orthographic features of words are better equipped to make generalizations to other words (Bear et al., 2008; Invernizzi & Hayes, 2004). Spelling instruction should provide students with multiple tools for spelling words and then teach them when and how to use those tools as they learn new words.

Beyond Percentage Scores

As in all other areas of curriculum, adequate and appropriate assessment is critical to effective spelling instruction. It has to go beyond measuring the percentage of words a student spelled correctly (Apel, Masterson, & Niessen, 2004) and should include an "error-correction procedure" (Mann et al., 2010, p. 89). Spelling assessment must provide information regarding all aspects of word knowledge so that it can inform instruction beyond simple word memorization. Screening strategies should indicate the current status of a child's spelling knowledge, provide a way to document a child's acquisition of spelling concepts and strategies, and monitor each child's learning, showing teachers where to intervene when learning has stalled.

Both qualitative and quantitative assessments should be used in making decisions about spelling instruction. Quantitative assessments can document learning, while qualitative assessments can provide in-depth understanding of a child's current knowledge along with insight as to why students are having difficulty spelling. Discovering these insights is critical in making actual adjustments to spelling instruction in order to most effectively meet children's needs (Masterson & Apel, 2010). Table 7–1 provides two examples of spelling assessments that go beyond percentage scores to include both qualitative and quantitative components.

The Primary Spelling Inventory (Bear et al., 2012) and the PALS assessment (Invernizzi, Sullivan, & Meier, 2001) provide good quality comprehensive assessments of a child's knowledge about how words work, with a helpful focus on the stages of development most appropriate for preK to 2nd grade. Additional assessments measure individual aspects of word knowledge: for example, the Yopp-Singer Test of Phonemic Segmentation (Yopp, 1995) and the Roswell-Chall Blending Test (Roswell & Chall, 1997). Teachers can consider these assessments as part of the comprehensive spelling assessment to provide data to inform and differentiate instruction as needed.

Differentiation

In many classrooms, teachers are careful to provide differentiated reading instruction through small group reading sessions, such as guided reading, in an effort to provide children with individualized instruction based on their specific needs. However, teachers often do not treat spelling in the same way, even though this type of differentiated instruction would likely improve children's spelling and decoding skills (Templeton, 2011). Teachers and SLPs can and should rely on appropriate assessments, such as those described in the section above, to determine children's spelling abilities and then group children for instruction according to their areas of need. Additionally, students who are learning English as another language will have variability in spelling development, some of which SLPs and teachers may be able to anticipate. For example, students from other language backgrounds may have difficulty recognizing or discriminating sounds that are not common in their

Table 7–1. Spelling Assessments Including Both Quantitative and Qualitative Procedures

Spelling Assessment	Quantitative Data	Qualitative
Primary Spelling Inventory[a]—PSI (Bear et al., 2012) Children spell a list of words that include a range of spelling features that span all or part of the developmental spelling continuum.	Children receive basic score for words spelled correctly and features used correctly.	Teacher examines the quality of the spellings or misspellings and takes inventory noting: • features used consistently and correctly, • features children "use but confuse" (Bear et al., 2008), and • features for which children show no knowledge. The teacher then uses that information to identify the instructional level.
PALS K (Invernizzi, Sullivan, & Meier, 2001)[b] Children complete tasks in • beginning sound identification, • rhyme, • alphabet recognition, • spelling of CVC words, • concept of word, and • word recognition.	Children receive a basic score for each of the subtests. The PALSK spelling subtest requires children to spell simple CVC words with common rime endings.	The PALS assessment provides teachers with explicit information about what their students know regarding fundamental word concepts to help guide their teaching.

[a]The Primary Spelling Inventory focuses on the first two stages of spelling development: Letter-Name and Within Word Pattern.

[b]The PALS 1-3 assessment has a few different subtests and includes a more traditional spelling inventory that is similar to the PQSI (Bear et al., 2008).

native language (e.g., kindergarten children from Spanish-speaking backgrounds may have greater difficulty differentiating between the short a and short e vowels; these vowel sounds don't exist in the Spanish language). More specific information about spelling instruction for second language learners follows in the section below. Teachers and SLPs should also remember that in spelling, as with most developmental theories, a student does not necessarily step over a specific line as he progresses from one stage to another. Some overlap of behaviors is likely as a child progresses along the continuum of spelling development. Ultimately, appropriate instruction means differentiated instruction.

Varied Needs

Traditionally, "differentiated" spelling instruction meant the good spellers got more words to learn and the struggling spellers got fewer words each week. However, we argue that this is not "different" instruction or practice. In fact, with this model students who actually need more support and practice get less. Appropriate differentiated spelling instruction begins with determining what each student knows about spelling words and what each still needs to learn. Then children are grouped according to similar needs, and instruction is provided for each group of students—not less, just different. For example, in a kindergarten classroom, a teacher may have a group of children who are able to spell basic CVC words, a common curricular goal for kindergarten, and are ready to move to more challenging words such as CVC words that begin with a blend (e.g., *flip, flap, flop*). The same teacher or SLP may also have a group of children who are able to spell some basic CVC words but are still struggling to differentiate the medial sounds in these words (e.g., spelling *pit* as *pet* because they are struggling to differentiate the /ĕ/ and /ĭ/ sounds). In addition, she may have a third group of children who are still struggling to hear and record each of the individual phonemes in basic CVC words and therefore "spell" those words with only the first and/or last letter (writing *mt* for *mat*). Once the teacher or SLP has identified some of the common needs, she can plan whole class and small group instruction that will meet all of the children's specific needs.

English Language Learners

The developmental stages of spelling must also be considered when individualizing spelling instruction for English language learners (Bear et al., 2012). All language and literacy instruction, including spelling, should take a child's knowledge of her first language into account (Dickinson, McCabe, Clark-Chiarelli, & Wolf, 2004; Lopez & Greenfield, 2004; Proctor, August, Carlo, & Snow, 2006), recognizing the benefits and the challenges she will face because of the similarities and differences between the first language and English. If she is fluent in her first language, she will have a sense of how words function and how words are composed of sounds. If she has begun reading and writing in her first language, transferable awareness and capabilities may be present.

Depending on the first language, a range of sounds will be unknown, along with a range that are known because they are similar to those of the child's first language. Some languages use the same alphabet as English; others do not. As she learns new words and sounds and fits them into her schema for language, she will develop cognitive flexibility that will eventually be an advantage in her literacy development. However, if she is early in her English development or if her first language is very dissimilar (e.g., Russian, Arabic, or Xhosa), individual help from an SLP or an individual fluent in her first language may be necessary.

Most if not all of the spelling strategies that can be used with monolingual students can also be used with bilingual students who are progressing in their English development. Bear et al. (2008) suggested that teachers make sure that instruction "highlights connections" (p. 53): for example, words with common letter-sound patterns or words with common roots and/or affixes. Many languages have words with sounds and meanings very similar to those of English (e.g., the Spanish word *ensalada* and the English word *salad*). Recognizing these relationships emphasizes the "spelling-meaning" connection in English; thus ELL students can be taught to look not only for "groups of letters within words that may represent chunks of sound but also [for] those that represent chunks of meaning" (Templeton, 2009, p. 199). Bear et al. (2012) also emphasized that instruction should be adapted to personally meaningful to each individual based on her background experience and knowledge.

With these considerations in mind, SLPs and teachers are ready to address concepts necessary for effective spelling instruction and ways these concepts can be applied. For the purposes of this chapter, we have separated the instructional concepts into two major categories: alphabet concepts and letter/sound pattern concepts. Within each of these categories we define important terms and illustrate them with instructional examples.

Instruction Based on Alphabet Concepts

Basic alphabet concepts, which consist of knowledge of letters (consonants and vowels) and their corresponding sounds, also include foundational skills, which are prerequisites for understanding the more advanced letter-sound and spelling skills. For example, spelling performance is impacted by children's phonological awareness skills (Lombardino, Bedford, Fortier, Carter, & Brandi, 1997), concept of word (Niessen, Strattman, & Scutter, 2011; Roberts, 1996), and oral language abilities (Roskos, Tabors, & Lenhart, 2009). Thus, when children are not meeting instructional goals in spelling, the teacher or SLP must ensure that these and other foundational skills are assessed, revisited, and reinforced.

Foundational Skills

Several foundational skills impact children's spelling, including concept of word, phonological awareness, and oral vocabulary development. Although these are not always considered part of formal spelling instruction, they lay an important foundation from which children can build strong spelling skills (Weiser & Mathes, 2011).

Children become aware of printed words as they notice the spaces that group letters together on the page, then begin to attend to the letter sounds within the grouped units. What we refer to as *concept of word* develops as this awareness progresses to understanding that words they speak are represented by specific printed words they can learn to recognize (Morris, Bloodgood, Lomax, & Perney, 2003). Phonological awareness develops as they become acutely aware of the sound system of language that is separate from but interdependent with meaning. As children gain greater facility in hearing the phonemes (individual sounds in language), they are learning to convert their knowledge of sounds into letters and eventually into words on a page. Oral vocabulary, the words a child knows (i.e., understands and uses) in conversation, becomes the reservoir from which words are drawn into reading-writing vocabulary.

These foundational skills, which are addressed during traditional reading and writing instruction, are also key in developing children's early spelling skills. For example, concept of word can be taught during a shared writing activity in which the teacher or SLP draws attention to the beginnings and endings of words she writes on chart paper or a white board from the children's dictation. Letter-sound correspondences are strengthened during the same activity as she pronounces the words slowly while including them in the shared texts: for example, "I'm glad Suzie used the word *can. C-a-n — can.* That's such a good word to know." When children are able to write some of the words themselves, she moves on to interactive writing, during which she shares the marker with them, encouraging them to write some of the letters, words, or even phrases as they are able (Figure 7–1).

Phonological awareness skills can be practiced during a picture sort, which is a common word study activity (Bear et al., 2012) in which children sort pictures of words with the same onset (e.g., *bat, bear, boat*; *mouse, man, map*; *train, truck, turtle*) or engage in a playful sorting activity in which they pack "Sally's silly suitcase" with /s/ items. Children enjoy playful sorting activities in which

Figure 7–1. During an interactive writing activity, this child uses basic vowel and consonant patterns to form one-syllable words. The teacher supports as necessary.

they manipulate real and pretend objects in meaningful contexts. For example, in the Silly Sally's Suitcase /s/ sorting activity, children pack socks and sweaters (items typically packed in a suitcase) along with "silly" items such as a sandwich, soup, or a snowman. Teachers and SLPs emphasize and exaggerate the beginning /s/ sound in each word as they pack the items for silly Sally.

Oral vocabulary is increased as teachers promote discussion and provide opportunities for children to talk. Teachers and SLPs should allow for discussion of books and themes they are studying. New words or particularly interesting words should be pointed out and discussed. Instructors can help extend children's vocabulary knowledge by using challenging yet appropriate vocabulary during classroom discussions. The more words a child has in her oral language reservoir, the more words will likely become part of her written vocabulary as well.

Consonants

After children have learned an adequate number of letter names and sounds, they are ready to apply that knowledge to decode and encode simple CVC words (e.g., *cat, hop, sit*). It is important to note that studies have shown that children who can name the letters of the alphabet have more facility at matching letters with their sounds than children who cannot, and thus they likely have an advantage in acquiring the ability to decode (Lonigan, 2006; Treiman, 2008) and similarly to encode words.

When children begin spelling simple CVC words, they can typically hear and record the beginning sound (e.g., writing *d* for *dog*). The ending sound typically comes next (e.g., writing *dg* for *dog*). The medial (vowel) sound is generally the most difficult for children to hear and identify. When teachers and SLPs teach consonants, they will likely start with the most commonly used consonants (e.g., *M, S, T, B*) and continue with those that carry the sound in the name of the letter (e.g., *B, D, J, K, F, L, M, N*). These consonants enable a beginning reader to remember and associate the letter with its sound. Letters that do not carry the sound in their name are harder to remember: for example, *C, G, H,* and Y (Kim et al., 2010).

Beginning consonant instruction might include using letters to signal in context some of the words the students might use to communicate. For example, during a cooking activity, children write *B* or *S* on a piece of paper to distinguish between big and small amounts of each ingredient (e.g., flour, sugar, salt, baking powder), or they can write the beginning consonant of each ingredient. Also children can use letters to categorize, sort, and make choices. For example, at snack time they might select or write a *C* to request another cracker or a *D* to ask for more of a drink. These activities, like others reported in this chapter, highlight the need for children to learn spelling in the context of meaningful experiences rather than in isolation (Alderman & Green, 2011).

Children can also be encouraged to listen for the beginning and ending sounds in words involved in shared reading. ("This word begins with *p*. What sound can you hear at the beginning of this word?") Shared writing is also a good context. ("You want me to write *sat*. What does *sat* begin with? What does *sat* end with?" So we have *s* - *t*. Now to complete the word, I would write *s* - *a* - *t* for /s/ /ă/ /t/.") The familiar Making Words game (Cunningham & Cunningham, 1992) can also be used as a technique, using letter trays and letter tiles to manipulate and change beginning and ending sounds in simple CVC words to create new words (e.g., *pot* to *hot* or *bat* to *cat,* or *hip* to *hit)* (Figure 7–2). Picture sorts, as described above, can also be used and extended by including the letters along with the pictures.

Short Vowels

As in learning consonants, children learn short vowel names and sounds and then they apply that knowledge in decoding and encoding simple CVC words (e.g., *cat, hop, sit*). Children can first learn short vowel rime endings as chunks (e.g., *-ap, -at, -ack*) and then move to blending and segmenting these chunks into individual phonemes. To reinforce these rime endings, the teacher can furnish games and activities in which sounds are repeated and then provide opportunities for practicing the target spelling patterns. For example, large "footprints" on the floor might be the setting for children to "track back for a snack," which they repeat as they go to

Figure 7–2. Children can use letter tiles during small group or independent center activities to change and manipulate beginning and ending sounds in simple CVC words to create new words.

the snack table, and then during snack they can unpack their snack (e.g., pretzels or crackers) and crack (break in ½) or stack their snack. Once children have engaged in this experience, they can write about it during a shared writing activity during which the teacher can draw attention to the *-ack* rime ending. These kinds of playful and engaging activities help the class move beyond traditional memorization tactics and learn words, including spelling patterns, by highlighting particular patterns within meaningful contexts.

Instructional activities that emphasize rime endings can also be used to help children in the early letter-name alphabetic stage recognize the medial vowel sound. For example, when teaching the /ŭ/ sound, the teacher may engage in an activity focused on the *-uck* rime ending, having children "rescue" letters that are "stuck in the muck" by sucking through a straw to pick up the letter cards and then placing them in the correct position (initial, medial or final) within a partially spelled word (Figure 7–3). Children then begin to recognize individual phonemes by fully analyzing these words, examining their beginning, middle, and ending sounds. These skills can be extended during a follow-up activity using an "I Can Spell Chart" (Gaskins, 1997) that requires children to answer questions about one of the target *-uck* words. ("How many sounds

Figure 7–3. Children can analyze words they learned during the "stuck in the muck" activity using the "I Can Spell" chart.

are heard? How many letters can be seen? Why are there so many letters and so many sounds? What is the first sound? The last sound? The middle sound? What pattern do you see in each word?")

Analyzing words focuses children's awareness at the phoneme level and prepares them to spell and decode simple CVC words quickly and accurately. Spelling by analogy is a similarly useful strategy, as the teacher and SLP can draw children's attention to the similarities and patterns in the words. For example, "Let's look at *hat, cat, mat,* and *rat.* What is the same in these words? How could looking at these words help me spell *sat?* How about *pat?*" This strategy is equally effective in the more advanced stages, such as derivational relations by which a child may use a root or a base word to spell a derivation of it: for example, using *music* to spell *musician.* Such strategies mark the beginning of helping children to learn to be strategic spellers, using what they already know about familiar words to help them spell new words.

Dictation activities, when done systematically, can also improve students' ability to distinguish individual sounds in words, which in turn can increase their phonemic awareness (Ehri, 1997) and help teachers emphasize particular spelling patterns and individual letter-sound correspondences. Similar to other supported and unsupported reading and writing opportunities (e.g., shared reading/ writing, interactive writing), dictation may be most effective after children have participated in other activities that address retrieving or recognizing letter-sound patterns: sorting words, decoding by analogy activities, or spelling games that emphasize the target spelling pattern. For example, after playing a game in which students made frogs jump to a log in the fog and found the similarities and differences in the target -*og* words, teachers could then dictate key words in a Cloze sentence to students in the early letter-name alphabetic stage. The teacher would read the sentence and children would fill in the target -og words ("The ____ sat on the ____."); care would be given to producing each sound when students needed additional support. To students who are in the middle letter-name alphabetic stage, the entire sentence would be dictated (e.g., "The frog sat on the log") and the teacher would provide necessary support for words that do not include the -*og* rime ending and for those sight words that were not previously learned. Referring to a word wall for the sight words would also be helpful. During either sentence dictation activity, the teacher would emphasize the target sounds and spelling patterns and draw upon different types of support (e.g., segment words by onset-rime instead of phoneme, provide rime ending or medial sound, or ask child to write the target word by looking at word with similar rime ending).

Instruction Based on Pattern Concepts

The term *pattern concepts* refers to clusters of letters that consistently act the same across words and positions within words. For example, *sh* will sound the same whether it is located at the beginning, the middle, or the end of a word. Included in this category are consonant patterns, such as blends, digraphs, and other consonant groupings, as well as vowel patterns, such as digraphs, silent *e* pattern, diphthongs, and *r*-controlled vowels. In addition, syllable/word patterns, such as CVC, CVVC, onset/rime, and spelling by analogy, are explored instructionally. Important aspects of effective spelling instruction are built around these and other patterns (see Apel & Masterson, 2001).

Consonant Patterns

Consonant patterns include blends (e.g., *bl, fr, st*), consonant digraphs (e.g., *sh, th, ch*), and other common clusters (e.g., *-tch, -dge, -ge*). Learning about simple consonant patterns takes children beyond simple one-sound-one-letter matching and introduces the fact that a single sound can be represented by multiple letters acting together. The blend requires a slightly more complex procedure of "sounding out," as both letter sounds can be heard but are blended together. Digraphs require children to learn a single sound and a matching visual representation, just like they did with the initial alphabet, but this symbol includes multiple letters. Learning these patterns expands children's repertoire of words they can successfully spell and allows them to use those patterns to spell new unknown words.

Instructional strategies that help children learn simple consonant patterns are similar to those used when learning individual letters and sounds; however, when learning these patterns the children learn to consider the clusters as chunks, not as separate letters. For example, word sorts can be extended to compare the consonant digraph with each individual letter (Bear et al., 2012). Children might sort words that start with *sh* from those that start with *s* or *h* separately (e.g., *ship* as different from *sip* and *hip*). This helps them begin to understand that a digraph functions differently than the individual letters that make up the digraph. A similar activity can also be done with blends (e.g., sorting words into three categories: *bl* words, *b* words, and *l* words—*black, back,* and *lack*). Children might enjoy learning these consonant patterns by a word-making activity in which they sail a *sh*-ship through the sea picking up cards with endings written on them that combine with the initial digraph to make words (e.g., *sh-irt, sh-ort, sh-ark, sh-oe*). The ship can be a small paper ship with the *sh* digraph written on it that children hold and move around a poster board with the sea drawn on it and word ending cards scattered over it. Or the children can act as the ships (holding a card with the *sh* digraph written on it) and move around an area of the room (which becomes the sea) to locate the word ending cards to make words. In either case, the children practice making words with the *sh* digraph in the context of an engaging activity.

Vowel Patterns

Vowel patterns include vowel digraphs (e.g., *oa*, *ea*, *ie*), dipthongs (e.g., *oi*, *ow*), long vowel patterns (e.g., *VCe*, -*ay*, -*ow*), and *r*-controlled vowels (e.g., *ar*, *er*, *ir*). Understanding the complexity of long vowels is an important step in spelling acquisition. When children acquire long vowel patterns, they are able to develop another strategy for spelling new words: trying multiple patterns, starting with the most common or most familiar, and seeing what "looks right." If the first pattern seems wrong, they can try another. This spelling strategy is sometimes informally referred to as Las Vegas spelling, or spelling by the odds. Additionally, as students become more proficient they look for patterns that are consistent across words. They do not automatically just sound out a new word to spell it. When they hear a long vowel, they think in patterns, not single letters.

When children are ready to learn these patterns, they can begin to analyze words in more complex ways. For example, during the week a small group of children can collect words that all have the same long vowel sound. Once the words are collected, the children then make a frequency bar graph and determine the most common pattern and the least common. Children can also analyze words in their writing, their peers' writing, or co-constructed writing they have done with the teacher (i.e., shared or interactive). When a child misuses a vowel pattern, the teacher can alert him to the misspelling and encourage him to consider another pattern that creates that same sound. For example, if a child writes *bote*, the teacher may tell the child that although this is not the correct way to spell the word, it does have the /ō/ sound. The teacher then encourages the child to think of another way he can create the /ō/

sound (e.g., *oa*) and to try that combination in order to get the conventional spelling.

Vowel patterns can also be compared in order to highlight the different letter combinations used to spell the same sound. For example, in one activity children can read and spell two long *e* patterns (*ee* and *ea*) as they "meet to take a seat and have a treat." During the activity the children pretend go on a picnic. ("We'll follow a street and meet at a picnic spot. We'll spread out a sheet for our picnic. We'll meet for a treat, a treat made out of wheat [cereal]. We'll eat our treat on the sheet. How neat!!!") The teacher can use word cards or sentence strips to highlight the *ee* and *ea* words throughout the activity. ("*Treat* and *sheet* have the long *e* sound, but look how they are spelled differently. One has the *ee* vowel pattern and the other has the *ea* vowel pattern.") After the activity, the children can participate in an interactive writing session where they record their experience. ("We followed the street so we could meet and have our treat. We took a seat on a sheet to eat our treat made out of wheat. How neat!!") During the writing experience, the teacher would emphasize the target words and help the children to differentiate between the words that have the *ee* pattern and those with the *ea* pattern.

Syllable/Word Patterns

Children can also be taught to recognize the five simple spelling patterns that dictate the long or short sound of the vowels. Five fundamental patterns lay the foundation for most words: the CVC pattern and the CVCC pattern, in which the vowel pronunciation is short, also the open vowel pattern (CV), the silent *e* pattern (CVCe), and the adjacent vowel pattern (CVVC), in which the vowel pronunciation is long. Then when a child has misspelled a word like *bote,* the teacher can ask him to think of another pattern that also supports a long vowel sound. This narrows the child's cognitive search and allows him to see the consistencies in spelling. When taught these five patterns of the writing system, children come to recognize that there are only a few patterns to draw from, and they can better strategize in determining which pattern to use. They rely less on guessing and more on pattern detecting. The power of these five common patterns is they lay the foundation for later adding multisyllabic words to children's repertoire. Children also learn basic syllable rules, such as open and closed syllable patterns.

As children begin to learn basic syllable and word patterns, they can spell by analogy: using what they know about familiar patterns to help them spell unknown words that have similar sounds. This is a powerful strategy because it works with all patterns. Working from the known to the unknown also helps children think more deeply about the word patterns they know: recognizing why words may or may not be spelled correctly based on simple spelling rules/patterns. For example, the activity "YES or NO" has children take a word card from an envelope and decide whether the word is spelled correctly and goes on the YES side or incorrectly and belongs on the NO side (Figure 7–4). Then the child is asked to explain why. For high performing groups, word cards can represent any number of common errors (e.g., *bg* doesn't have a vowel, *yix* isn't a real word, *ckat* can't be correct because *ck* never comes at the beginning of a word, etc.). For a lower performing group, the word cards represent only one type of error (e.g., *mvt*, *pbn*, and *lkg* need medial vowels instead of medial consonants).

Figure 7–4. Children can differentiate between "real" words and nonsense words during the YES-NO activity. See the SEEL Web site for more information (http://education.byu .edu/seel/).

Conclusion

The development children go through as they progress from forming a few random letters to using written words to express themselves is miraculous in nature, but not in timing, regularity, or predictability. Children go through a series of approximate stages (often overlapping and recursive) (Rittle-Johnson & Siegler, 1999) at their own rates, according to their own learning styles, influenced by their previous literacy experiences (often including a different first language). Learning what words are, how they function, how to use them, and how to use the sounds and symbols of language to spell them are complex developmental experiences.

This chapter has dealt with many facets of that process, beginning with random scribbles on a piece of paper and continuing to complex understanding of morphemes. Teachers and SLPs who know how to recognize the developmental stages of spelling can understand and appreciate both similarities and differences in children's learning. They realize that simply shortening the weekly spelling list will not differentiate to meet students' needs; they note where each student is in the process of learning the nature and functions of language as well as the processes involved in spelling. Thus many refer to spelling instruction as *word study*, considering the inclusive term to be more accurate. Students are grouped and instructed according to what they need, not according to testing percentages.

Word study activities use phonological awareness and letter knowledge as a foundation, leading students to comprehend the alphabetic code. Children come to understand that speech sounds are represented by letter symbols. From there they gain knowledge of orthographic patterns, which enable them to map larger strings of letters together. In the process, spelling behaviors such as using rules, sounding words out, and retrieving accurately from memory may dovetail into what children understand and know; their spelling behaviors reflect their development. An instructional method that guides children through this process and solidifies knowledge and skills in their memories will eventually produce better readers and writers (Sharp, Sinatra, & Reynolds, 2008).

The processes of encoding and decoding are acts of translation from sounds to symbols and symbols to sounds in order to produce a recognizable pronunciation or spelling of a printed word.

At first this process is very deliberate and labor intensive. Whether segmenting to spell a word or blending to decode one, beginners sound out letter by letter, then word by word—often in a slow and halting manner. Eventually, after lots of practice writing and reading, the process evolves into a smooth expressive progression of phrases and sentences. Over time and with lots of exposure, the important beginning skill sets required for the tasks become unconscious and no longer require deliberate thought. This give and take between deliberate decoding and encoding and automatic word recognition continues as the child progresses through higher and higher levels of sophisticated text. For the experienced writer and reader, identifying and producing words becomes an accurate and unlabored process, although inaccuracy and labor have been among its early necessities.

Thus spelling instruction must be approached differently in today's classrooms. The traditional pattern of passing out a spelling list on Monday, assigning children to drill the words at home, and having them reproduce the words on Friday is not sufficient to teach the multifaceted processes involved with spelling. Spelling is no longer viewed as a simplistic need with simplistic solutions. Teachers have to understand it and approach it for what it is: an important aspect of language/literacy development that requires an extensive variety of skills and practices. Templeton (2011) reminded us,

> [T]he primary purpose of spelling instruction is to guide and support children's exploration of the structure of written words so that they will process deeply and understand more clearly the relationships between print and language at the alphabetic, pattern, and meaning levels. (p. 251)

This definition requires a broader conception of how we approach and what we include as spelling instruction while still emphasizing the "traditional objective of spelling instruction: Helping students learn the conventional spelling of words" (Templeton, p. 251).

References

Alderman, G. L., & Green, S. K. (2011). Fostering lifelong spellers through meaningful experiences. *Reading Teacher, 64*(8), 599–605. doi:10.15 98/RT.64.8.5

Al Otaiba, S., Puranik, C. S., Rouby, D. A., Greulich, L., Sidler, J.F., & Lee, J. (2010). Predicting kindergarteners' end-of-year spelling ability based on their reading, alphabetic, vocabulary, and phonological awareness skills, as well as prior literacy experiences. *Learning Disability Quarterly*, *33*(3), 171–183.

Apel, K., & Masterson, J. J. (2001). Theory-guided spelling assessment and intervention: A case study. *Language, Speech, and Hearing Services in Schools*, *32*, 182–195.

Apel, K., Masterson, J. J., & Niessen, N. L. (2004). Spelling assessment frameworks. In C. A. Stone (Ed.), *Handbook of language and literacy: Development and disorders* (pp. 644–660). New York. NY: Guilford Press.

Bear, D. R. (1982). *Patterns of oral reading across stages of word knowledge.* Unpublished doctoral dissertation. University of Virginia, Charlottesville.

Bear, D. R., Invernizzi, M., Templeton, S., & Johnson, F. (2012). *Words their way* (5th ed.). Upper Saddle River, NJ: Pearson.

Beers, J. W., & Henderson, E. (1977). A study of developing orthographic concepts among first graders. *Research in the Teaching of English*, *11*, 133–148.

Berninger, V. W., Abbott, R. D., Nagy, W., & Carlisle, J (2010). Growth in phonological, orthographic, and morphological awareness in grades 1 to 6. *Journal of Psycholinguistic Research*, *39*(2), 141–163.

Christo, C., & Davis, J. (2008). Rapid naming and phonological processing as predictors of reading and spelling. *California School Psychologist*, *13*, 7–18.

Cunningham, P. M., & Cunningham, J. W. (1992). Making words: Enhancing the invented spelling-decoding connection. *Reading Teacher*, *46*(2), 106–115.

Dickinson, D. K., McCabe, A., Clark-Chiarelli, N., & Worlf, A. (2004). Cross-language transfer of phonological awareness in low-income Spanish and English bilingual preschool children. *Applied Psycholinguistics*, *25*, 323–347.

Ehri, L. C. (1986). Sources of difficulty in learning to spell and read. In M. L. Wolraich & D. Routh (Eds.), *Advances in developmental and behavioral pediatrics* (pp. 121–195). Greenwich, CT: JAI Press.

Ehri, L. C. (1997). Learning to read and learning to spell are one and the same, almost. In C. A. Perfetti, L. Rieban, & M. Fayol (Eds.), *Learning to spell: Research, theory, and practice across languages* (pp. 237–270). Mahwah, NJ: Erlbaum.

Ehri, L. C. (2000). Learning to read and learning to spell: Two sides of a coin. *Topics in Language Disorders*, *20*, 19–36.

Foorman, B. R., Francis, D. J., Fletcher, J. M. Schatschneider, C., & Mehta, P. (1998). The role of instruction in learning to read: Preventing reading failure in at-risk children. *Journal of Educational Psychology*, *90*(1), 37–55.

Gaskins, I. W. (with Downer, M., Cress, C., O'Hara, C., & Donnelly, K.) (1997). *Revised beginning program.* Media, PA: Benchmark Press.

Hammill, D. D. (2004). What we know about correlates of reading. *Exceptional Children, 70,* 453–468.

Henderson, E. (1990). *Teaching spelling* (2nd ed.). Boston, MA: Houghton Mifflin.

Invernizzi, M., & Hayes, L. (2004). Developmental-spelling research: A systematic imperative. *Reading Research Quarterly, 39,* 2–15.

Invernizzi, M., Sullivan, A., & Meier, J. (2001). *PALS-PreK phonological awareness literacy screening.* Charlottesville, VA: University of Virginia.

Kim, Y., Petscher, Y., Foorman, B., & Zhou, C. (2010). The contribution of phonological awareness and letter name knowledge to letter-sound acquisition—A cross-classified multilevel model approach. *Journal of Educational Psychology, 102,* 313–326.

Lombardino, L. J., Bedford, T., Fortier, C., Carter, J., & Brandi, J. (1997). Invented spelling: Developmental patterns in kindergarten children and guidelines for early literacy intervention. *Language, Speech, and Hearing Services in Schools, 28,* 333–342.

Lonigan, C. J. (2006). Development, assessment, and promotion of preliteracy skills. *Early Education and Development, 17*(1), 91–114.

Lopez, L. M., & Greenfield, D. B. (2004). The cross-language transfer of phonological skills of Hispanic Headstart children. *Bilingual Research Journal, 28*(1), 1–18.

Mann, T. B., Bushell, D., & Morris, E. K. (2010). Use of sounding out to improve spelling in young children. *Journal of Applied Behavior Analysis, 43,* 89–93.

Masterson, J., & Apel, K. (2010). Linking characteristics discovered in spelling assessment to intervention goals and methods. *Learning Disabilities Quarterly, 33*(3), 185–198.

Mehta, P. D., Foorman, B. R., Branum-Martin, L., & Taylor, W. P. (2005). Literacy as a unidimensional multilevel construct: Validation, sources of influence, and implications in a longitudinal study in grades 1 to 4. *Scientific Studies of Reading, 9*(2), 85–116.

Morris, D. (1993). The relationship between children's concept of word in text and phoneme awareness in learning to read: A longitudinal study. *Research in the Teaching of English, 27,* 133–154.

Morris, D., Bloodgood, J. W., Lomax, R. G., & Perney, J. (2003). Developmental steps in learning to read: A longitudinal study in kindergarten and first grade. *Reading Research Quarterly, 38*(3), 302–325.

Niessen, N. L., Strattman, K., & Scudder, R. (2011). The influence of three emergent literacy skills on the invented spellings of 4-year-olds. *Communication Disorders Quarterly, 32*(2), 93–102.

Proctor, C. P., August, D., Carlo, M. S., & Snow, C. (2006). The intriguing role of Spanish language vocabulary knowledge in predicting English reading comprehension. *Journal of Educational Psychology, 98*(1), 159–169.

Rittle-Johnson, B., & Siegler, R. S. (1999). Learning to spell: Variability, choice, and change in children's strategy use. *Child Development, 70*(2), 332–348.

Roberts, B. (1996). Spelling and the growth of concept of word as first graders write. *Reading Psychology, 17*(3), 229–252.

Roskos, K. A., Tabors, P. O., & Lenhart, L. A. (2009). Joining oral language and early literacy. In *Oral language and early literacy in preschool* (pp. 1–6). Newark, DE: International Reading Association.

Roswell, F., & Chall, J. (1997). *Roswell-Chall auditory blending test.* New York, NY: Essay Press.

Sabey, B. (1999). Megacognitive responses of an intermediate speller while performing three literacy tasks. *Journal of Literacy Research, 31*(4), 415–455.

Schlagal, R. (2002). Classroom spelling instruction: History, research, and practice. *Reading Research and Instruction, 42*, 44–57.

Sharp, A. C., Sinatra, G. M. & Reynolds, R. E. (2008). The development of children's orthographic knowledge: A microgenetic perspective. *Reading Research Quarterly, 43*(3), 206–226.

Templeton, S. (1979). Spelling first, sound later: The relationship between orthography and higher order phonological knowledge in older students. *Research in the Teaching of English, 13*, 255–264.

Templeton, S. (2009). Spelling-meaning relationships among languages. In L. Helman (Ed.), *Literacy development with English learners: Research-based instruction in grades K–6* (pp. 196–212). New York, NY: Guilford Press.

Templeton, S. (2011). Teaching spelling in the English language arts classroom. In D. Lapp, D. Fisher, J. Flood, J. Jensen, & J. R. Squire (Eds.), *The handbook of research on teaching the English language arts* (pp. 247–251). New York, NY: Routledge.

Templeton, S., & Bear, D. R. (Eds.). (1992). *Development of orthographic knowledge and the foundations of literacy: A memorial festschrift for Edmund H. Henderson.* Hillsdale, NJ: Erlbaum.

Templeton, S., & Scarborough-Franks, L. (1985). The spelling's the thing: Knowledge of derivational morphology in orthography and phonology among older students. *Applied Psycolinguistics, 6*, 371–390.

Treiman, R. (2008, Oct.). *Spelling development in typical and dyslexic children.* Keynote address at the Illinois Branch of the International Dyslexia Society, Oakbrook Terrace, Illinois.

Weiser, B., & Mathes, P. (2011). Using encoding instruction to improve the reading and spelling performance of elementary students at risk for literacy difficulties: A best-evidence synthesis. *Review of Educational Research, 81*(2), 170–200.

Yopp, H. K. (1995). A test for assessing phonemic awareness in young children. *The Reading Teacher*, 49(1), 20–29.

Zutell, J. (1979). Spelling strategies of primary school children and their relation-ship to Piaget's concept of development. *Research in the Teaching of English*, *13*, 69–80.

SEEL Lessons Mentioned

Frog on a Log

Stuck in the Muck

Chapter 8

Bringing Stories to Life: Approaches to Understanding and Enjoying Narratives

Barbara Culatta, Kendra M. Hall-Kenyon, and Sharon Black

Stories have natural appeal for young children, as well as significant potential for developing and refining comprehension skills. Teachers and SLPs can work in a number of instructional contexts to facilitate skills related to understanding and creating narratives. This chapter presents instructional methods related to developing literacy through stories: introductory preteaching, dramatic storytelling, shared reading, individual or scaffolded retelling, graphically representing, and group enacting. Although certain strategies apply to particular tasks, most can be easily applied to the other instructional contexts as well.

To illustrate specific interventions, the trade book *Lost* by David McPhail (1990) will be incorporated throughout the chapter. *Lost* is the story of a bear that climbs into a snack truck, falls asleep, and wakes up in a city. The bear feels sad and frightened until he meets a boy who tries a number of clever and humorous strategies to help him find his way back to the forest.

Introduce the Story

Regardless of the specific strategies or activities that will be used in exploring the story, the teacher or SLP can do much to support narrative skills and story comprehension by introducing and pre-teaching important ideas. Activities used to introduce and preteach can attract interest as well as prepare students to comprehend a text in any of the following instructional contexts: telling stories dramatically, engaging in shared reading and discussion, representing stories graphically and/or retelling them, or enacting them as groups with varying levels of teacher support.

Activate Prior Knowledge and Interest

To draw children into a story, the teller or reader can begin by drawing parallels between the text and the children's experiences (e.g., "When have you felt alone or afraid?" "How did you feel when someone offered to help you?") As children relate events and characters' feelings to their own personal experiences, they are "finding themselves" in the text (Barton, 1995). With that identification, they can use their prior knowledge and feelings as background to help them understand a story (Donahue & Foster, 2004; Keene & Zimmerman, 1997; Ketch, 2005; Raphael, Highfield, & Au, 2006).

The instructor may model this identification by describing an experience of her own: perhaps a time when she was lost in an unfamiliar city, was awkward in a different culture, or had an opportunity to help someone in need. She might also ask questions leading into the background or main ideas of a story: for example, "What do you know about forests where bears live?" "How is a forest different from the city?" "Have you ever been in a strange place where you did not know where to find things or how to act?" In this way, the instructor's goal is to help children think about and share their personal experiences that connect with the story (e.g., being lost, not knowing how to act in a certain situation/environment, and helping those who are lost).

Once children can identify with the characters, stories can provide a framework for connecting new ideas with children's knowledge and experience. In supporting comprehension of *Lost*, a teacher or SLP might want to begin by having the children express their existing knowledge of bears, cities, forests, and maps; recalling what they know about bears and forests prepares children to explore new information about the necessary fit between an animal's needs and the place it lives. These ideas may also be extended to consider human needs and environments if the instructor encourages children to talk about their feelings and experiences concerning familiarity, fears, and friendship and about ways that help can be needed and given.

Provide an Experience

In addition to bringing out information from children's own lives, the teacher can simulate a situation or evoke a feeling that can be related to a story's theme (Ukranitz, 2006). Arranging an experience is particularly important if the content of a story is distant from or inconsistent with children's own lives. In preparing children for the story *Lost*, the teacher and children could pretend that a stuffed animal is a lost pet and role-play ways they might figure out how to find its owner and get it back where it belongs.

Role play involves the imagination in exploring experience: Perhaps one child could be a lost boy and another be a park ranger giving him ideas about how to get from the forest to the city (look at a compass, follow a trail, use a map). Role-played or simulated experiences can give children a framework for relating the story.

In addition to understanding characters and feelings, simulated experiences can provide a context for explaining or introducing concepts and vocabulary that are important to the story. Unfamiliar vocabulary that is significant to the story and appropriate to the students' developmental levels can be pretaught with examples of the word's meaning or through talking about the shared experience (Nelson & Van Meter, 2006).

Give Reasons to Listen or Read

Children can focus on story events more easily if they have something to look for or anticipate (Westby, 2005). The instructor may give the children something interesting to look for in the story:

perhaps to see how a character solves a particular problem. The children may make their own predictions and then read or listen to the story to find out if they were right.

> Teacher: How do you think the boy will get the bear home?
>
> Child 1: I think a policeman's going to take him home.
>
> Child 2: Maybe they'll get on an airplane.
>
> Teacher: "Let's read and see."

Or one of the children may have had a related experience to share. For example, the instructor might ask a student whose family got lost during a recent road trip what she thinks the boy might do to help the bear find his way home (e.g., look at a map, ask for directions, use phone to find directions).

Another way to provide a purpose is to tell the children to listen for a specific piece of information. They may want to know what the boy and the bear do in the story to try to get the bear back to his home in the forest. Children may also pay attention to find out what it is like for an animal to be lost in a city and what a person might do to help.

Preview the Story Content and Organization

The instructor can orient the children to the story by giving a preview of the story content and organization: highlighting the theme, important ideas, and story elements. Inferences might be guided as well (Wallach, 2008). A content preview for *Lost* might go something like this:

> This story is about a bear that wakes up after a nap in the back of a truck and finds himself in a city with lots of big buildings. He is afraid because he has never been in a city before, and he wants to go home. A boy finds the bear and offers to help. They become friends and try all kinds of different ways to get the bear back to his home in the forest. As we read [or hear] the story, we'll find out how the boy gets the bear back home.

Some previews are extended to include more details on the characters' problems, feelings and desires, attempts, and consequences.

The SLP in particular may want to do some extra preteaching with a group of students who are struggling with the language demands of stories.

Once the teacher or SLP has introduced the story and engaged children's interest and curiosity, she can present the story in the manner and context that she considers most appropriate to the particular narrative and most enjoyable and meaningful to the children. Some popular methods that are particularly engaging for young children are telling the story dramatically, engaging in shared reading, representing the story graphically and/or retelling it, and enacting the story as a group.

Tell Dramatically

Oral storytelling is one of the oldest and most effective ways of involving young children in literacy. For dramatic storytelling, most often presented in large group settings, tellers recount stories in their own words, using exaggerated vocal techniques, character voices, gestures, and audience participation.

After introducing and activating interest in a story, the teacher or SLP may want to tell it in an animated, dramatic way during which she gives children opportunities to be actively involved (Trostle, 2007; Trostle & Donato, 2001). Certain techniques can be used when telling stories both to enhance interest and to support comprehension.

Adjust Complexity and Input

While narrating the story, the teller adjusts its complexity, including the content, story structure, and syntax (Blank, 2002; Gilliam & Ukranitz, 2006). Doing so alters the demands on children's language and conceptual levels.

The complexity of some stories can be adjusted by recasting utterances: saying the same thing in different ways so that children with language difficulties benefit from both the repetition and the variety of language. The teller should consider particular children's language levels, being continually responsive to their comments and conscious of other indicators of comprehension (facial expressions, level of attention, etc.). In *Lost* most of the children enjoy hearing the boy tell the bear, "Don't worry, the buildings won't hurt you." However, a child who is not used to nonliteral statements may be a little confused, especially if he struggles with processing and using language. Seeing a look of confusion on the child's face, the teller may quickly recast: "Tall buildings are so strange to a bear because he's never seen buildings. So the boy has to tell him that buildings won't do anything mean to him."

Conceptual demands must also be carefully considered. The teller must decide what content to highlight: focusing the children's attention on major story components, commenting on critical elements, or filling in assumed information to support comprehension (McGuinness, 2004) (e.g., "The bear is depending on his new friend. The boy is not going to let him down.") However, too much new knowledge or highly complex content may require too much effort for the children, making the story difficult to relate to or understand.

Part of clarifying content for children is to avoid calling attention to irrelevant distracting details. In trying to find the bear's home, the boy takes the bear to a park because he sees the trees and thinks the park may be a forest. At the park the boy and bear get distracted with eating hot dogs, riding on a boat, and playing on swings. These specific activities are not as relevant to the rest of the story as the fact that the park is not the bear's home. Thus it is not necessary for the instructor to draw attention to the park activities. Rather, the instructor should focus the discussion on the most important actions in order to help children understand the main ideas or story structure elements.

Organize the Telling Clearly and Logically

Narratives tend to have a standard organizational structure tied to a predictable action sequence with definable relationships between motives and actions, sometimes referred to as the *macrostructure* or *story schema*, which readers or listeners have learned to anticipate (Mandler & Johnson, 1977). These expectations can be expressed as an interrelated set of story grammar elements (Stein & Glenn, 1979). The story grammar elements control the higher level ideas that are most relevant to the plot structure (Table 8–1).

Table 8–1. Description of Story Grammar Elements in *Lost*

Element	*Description*	*Example from* Lost
Setting	The situation (time, location, context) that exists when the story starts	A bear in the forest sees a snack truck, crawls in, and falls asleep.
Initiating event	A happening, event, or change that occurs— possibly an environmental occurrence, a problem, or a thought or feeling that a character has	Bear: Wakes up to find himself in a city Boy: Finds the bear
Reaction: goal and plan	The way the character responds to the initiating event, including the goal and plan that are devised	The bear is sad and frightened. The boy is sympathetic. The bear and the boy want to find their way to the forest. They decide to look for trees.
Attempts	The actions the character undertakes to try to carry out the plan	The bear and boy find trees in several places, but not enough to be a forest. The boy then takes the bear to the library to find a map and information on how to get to the forest.
Consequence	The result of the attempts, whether or not the character meets with success or failure	Attempts to find trees in the city are not successful. But the trip to the library leads the bear and boy to know what bus to take to get to the forest.
Reaction/ resolution	The character's emotional or behavioral response to what has occurred	The bear is happy to be back home, but the boy discovers he is lost. The bear begins to take the boy back to the city.

In telling a story, the narrator can highlight the organization and connect the events in the story to the overall structure: for example, how an initiating event can lead to a goal that leads to a plan and attempts, and how attempts have consequences that either meet or fail to meet the desired outcome (Ukrainitz, 2006). With guidance children can learn to look for these relationships.

The book *Lost* is a complete narrative that includes multiple attempts to achieve the goal. The initiating event in the book, which occurs when the bear wakes up to find himself in the city, presents an obvious problem that generates feelings of confusion and fear. The goal and plan are implied by the boy as he promises to help the bear (inference—find its way home). Attempts and consequences follow: the fountain in the public square (incorrect guess), the park (more trees but still not a forest), the public library (some useful resources and a direction to go), and a bus ride (which eventually achieves the goal). Even in good children's stories, the inferences are not always easy to make, and the SLP or teacher may want to provide extra guidance for students who struggle with interpreting language. Children can be guided to use background knowledge as well as information in the text to make inferences (Wallach, 2008).

Since the style of the story flows naturally as the boy's account of the experience, the goal and attempts aren't signaled by such explicit words as *wanted to* or *tried to,* etc. The rhythm of the story simply moves from attempt to attempt: When the boy leads the bear in a new direction, the coming of a new attempt must be inferred. The overall consequence, of course, occurs as the bear is back in a forest and the boy realizes that *he* is lost. The reaction is that the bear promises to help the boy (inference—the bear now cares about the boy as much as the boy cares about the bear). In the final illustration the two are walking toward a city. Thus although the goal and plan are not explicitly identified in the *Lost* story, they can be inferred; and the instructor can highlight the key story elements during instruction (Merritt, Culatta, & Trostle, 1998).

Comments, stress, repetition, recasting, and intonation can be used to emphasize story elements (Blank, 2002). In the book *Lost*, signal words and redundancy are not involved because of the simplicity of the story, but an SLP working with children who have language challenges or a preschool teacher of very young children could call attention to the story's initiating problem by making a statement such as "The bear has a *problem*. When he wakes up he finds himself in a *city instead of his forest*." A statement such as "He *needs to get back* to the forest where he lives" would call attention to the goal. "They *tried* to find the forest by looking for trees, *but* this wasn't enough" demonstrates the failed attempt for solution.

Highlight Grammatical Connections

In stories, grammatical forms such as conjunctions and pronouns signal relationships between ideas across sentences (Halliday & Hasan, 1976). Children's understanding of these grammatical forms, sometimes referred to as cohesive devices, permits them to build an understanding of the story as a connected whole. The use of conjunctions in storytelling is treated here because of their importance in creating coherence or continuity in a text.

Conjunctions are particularly useful for tying story grammar elements together. In stories, *disjunctive conjunctions* (*but, although, either*) often express problems, alternative plans, obstacles, or failed attempts. For example, in *Lost* the boy thought the park was the forest BUT the park didn't have enough trees. A problem also occurred at the end of the story: The boy got the bear back to the forest BUT the boy didn't know how to get back to the city. *Causal conjunctions* connect goal-oriented attempts in stories to their consequences. Story characters encounter external problems or internal thoughts or feelings that influence or "cause" their plans and goals, and then their actions lead to outcomes or consequences; thus characters encounter motivations that lead to actions as well as actions that lead to outcomes. An example of implied causation in *Lost* is when the bear arrives in the city and is afraid BECAUSE he has never seen tall buildings or large crowds of people before.

The storyteller should highlight conjunctions to help students weave information together. Conjunctions can be stressed or filled in (if they must be inferred) when characters' emotions or thoughts lead to goals or plans, when obstacles or failed attempts lead to a change in plans, and when attempts lead to consequences. ("The boy and the bear have been having fun in the park, BUT they have lost a lot of time. BECAUSE it is getting late, they will have to hurry now.")

The teacher or SLP can model, highlight, and fill in connections in telling the story, along with explaining or elaborating on relationships. With exposure children can learn to anticipate and express cause/effect relationships (Hayward, Gillam, & Lien, 2007; van Kleeck, Vander Woude, & Hammett, 2006). Even if conjunctions are not signaled in the story as it is written, the teller can make the connections clear (add the words, emphasize them with stress or pauses, restate the relationship) while telling the story. (Additional supports for cause/effect connections will be dealt with in the section on engaging children in shared book reading.)

Provide Contextual Supports

Most stories include some information that is presented in language only, taking children's minds into places or situations they have not experienced. Understanding some stories depends heavily on language with little situational or contextual support, sometimes referred to as *decontextualized use of language* (De Temple, 2001; Dickinson & Tabors, 2001; French, 1988; Lucariello, 1990; Pelligrini & Galda, 1990, 2000) — literally language used *outside a specific context.*

One way to bridge to or to support decontextualized language is to talk about how information and events that are present and noticeable (thus contextualized) relate to information that is remote, abstract, or difficult to represent visually (Blank, Marquis, & Klimovitch; 1994, 1995; Cummins, 1984; De Temple, 2001; Hedberg & Westby, 1994; Hicks, 1990; Mlilosky, 1987). In dramatic storytelling the teacher or SLP provides contextual cues to support comprehension and help to convey meaning, as well as engage the children in the telling: for example, props, intonation, gestures, facial expressions, and character voices.

Vary Intonation and Facial Expressions

Animated facial and vocal expressions can convey meaning beyond the words alone (e.g., a deep, gravelly bear voice with just a tinge of panic and a perplexed facial expression). Variety in intonation, pitch, volume, and vocal quality can signal different meanings as well as keep children engaged and actively processing language. Pauses and stresses convey both importance and emotion. Expression and tone can also be used to enhance implications such as the confidence the boy feels when he realizes he can get information from the library or the disappointment he feels when he discovers that the clump of trees near an office building isn't a forest.

Include Actions, Gestures, Movements

In addition to vocal and facial expressions, the teller can use expressive gestures and movements to enhance oral language. Words and phrases may be demonstrated visually as the teller describes and comments on events and characters' actions. Gestures for *Lost* might include reaching for the bear's paw to help him out of the truck, pushing the elevator button to go to the top of the tall building (where the boy and bear go to look for trees), or turning pages in books in the library as they search for a map to take them to the forest.

The narrator can re-create the actions of the characters or ask the children to do such actions. Information represented in language is more recognizable paired with supports, even though the information in the language and contextual cues may not be completely redundant. The storyteller can illustrate the narration with props and can even invite children to represent characters by mimicking character actions: for example, the boy touching his head when he has a good idea or the bear using a push-back gesture when they get to a place that is not a forest.

Refer to Pictures and Objects

Various types of props, pictures, and costumes can enhance storytelling. The teller can set the scene with simple props: for *Lost,* a line drawing of city buildings might represent the city that is so puzzling to the bear. Simple pictures and object props provide concrete representations of story events: an empty paper towel roll for the spyglass through which the boy and bear look, a map for the search for forests in the library. Puppets, easily made from paper bags, socks, or even envelopes, can act out events, carry out conversations, and otherwise animate story events. Paper headbands or picture name tags can be used to represent characters and encourage children to take character parts (e.g., child wearing a picture of a bear on a lanyard around his neck to play the part of the bear).

Use Character Voices

Many storytellers assume the role of narrator, telling the story from the perspective of an uninvolved observer. As narrator, the teller can insert character depictions or character dialogue, using a different voice for each character and giving each a distinctive personality. He can shift into telling or commenting on the story from the character's perspective, conveying and elaborating story information in that character's voice from the character's point of view. For example, *Lost* is told from the child's point of view, but a teller could insert comments from the bear. Another option during the telling is to pretend to talk to a character and then switch to answering in the character's voice.

Draw Upon Context to Teach Words

Important words can be exemplified and clarified as a story is told (De Temple & Snow, 2003). The instructor can use contextual supports to help illustrate word meanings, drawing on gestures, actions on objects, facial expressions, and intonations. Facial expressions should be used to exemplify feeling words, since most emotions can be reflected in facial expressions. A teller can use and emphasize words that fit important ideas in the *Lost* story, even though they may not appear in the book (e.g., *disappointed, puzzled, confused,* and *distracted*).

Props, intonation, and actions are not the only contextual supports that help teach word meaning. A story itself can provide a situation that contextualizes words (Beck, McKeown, & Kucan, 2002; Nelson & Van Meter, 2006). For example, when the bear realizes that a clump of trees in the city isn't his forest he becomes *disappointed*. Although the word *disappointed* doesn't actually appear in the book, it is an important underlying concept that is part of the bear's experience, and an adult paraphrasing the story would be likely to use it. If very young children or a child struggling with language would be likely to be puzzled by this word, the context of the bear not finding what he expects would effectively exemplify or illustrate the meaning. The adult could briefly call attention to the connection.

Teaching important vocabulary during a dramatic storytelling experience involves associating words with contexts that are familiar to the children, situations they have actually experienced. Child-friendly explanations can be provided as words are encountered in the story, referring to ways that a targeted word relates to experiences or situations that are familiar to the children (Beck, McKeown, & Kucan, 2002). For example, an adult telling the story of *Lost* in his own words might use the word *frustrated* when telling how the boy feels when his first three attempts to help the bear don't come even close. While relating the word meaning to experiences in children's lives, the SLP might pair the word with simpler, familiar synonyms ("confused and upset"); explain the meanings of the word or expression ("when you can't understand why you keep getting things wrong"); provide familiar examples ("like never getting the basketball in the net"); or talk about how the word is used or what it means when children encounter it in everyday situations ("how you feel when you are trying to do something and you can't") (see McGuinness, 2004; Nelson & Van Meter, 2006).

Involve Students

Young children love to participate in storytelling. The teller can use a particular gesture to cue the audience to join in with a specific phrase, a responding gesture, or a quick action on a prop (Merritt, Culatta, & Trostle, 1998; Trostle & Donato, 2001). Some authors recommend weaving in a form of audience response, verbal or nonverbal, at frequent intervals.

Gestures and Expressions

At frequent or occasional intervals in a story, the audience can produce a relevant gesture (e.g., wave, clap) or chant a phrase or expression that is spoken or read (e.g., "Thank goodness"). The teller might need to edit the story to include a repetitive element. For instance, when telling *Lost* the teller might emphasize the characters' growing discouragement with each failed attempt by asking, "Is this the bear's home?" The children could respond in unison, "No, there's not enough trees."

The children might act as bystanders, watching the boy and the bear try to figure out how to get the bear home.

Teller: Would this be a good place for the bear?

Group: No! Bears belong in a forest.

Props

Giving children quick turns to act on a prop also involves them as active audience members (Figure 8–1). Each child may hold a prop if the teacher has enough multiples, or each child can be given a short turn with the same prop. Audience members stay involved during others' turns if the teller-child interaction is compelling and worth watching. If children make comments during their turns, the teller should respond to their inputs, carrying on a short conversation if appropriate. For example, during *Lost* the bear and boy look through a telescope from the top of a high building. If the teacher, SLP, and several parents have saved paper towel tubes, each child might look through a "telescope" to search for a forest. Each child can take a turn putting a green Post-it note on the same map to mark the place he or she might look for the bear's forest.

Figure 8–1. The bear and the boy look for the forest from the top of a building in the city.

Engage in Shared Book Reading

Story comprehension can be facilitated as adults read stories to and with children (McKeowan & Beck, 2006; Reese, Cox, Harte, & McAnally, 2003; van Kleeck, Stahl, & Bauer, 2003). Shared book reading is a relevant context for supporting comprehension as well as facilitating attention to print (Cunningham & Zibulsky, 2011; Gilliam & Ukranitz, 2006; Justice & Ezell, 2004). This section deals with ways to model and scaffold comprehension, involves children in interactions around texts, and supports decoding.

Model and Scaffold Comprehension Strategies

To support comprehension during shared book reading, a teacher or SLP may periodically stop reading to model and stimulate thinking. She may share and elaborate her thinking and connect ideas (Cunningham & Zibulsky, 2011; Gilliam & Ukrainitz, 2006; McKeown, & Beck, 2006; van Kleeck & Vander Woude, 2003). In modeling comprehension strategies, the adult verbalizes how she processes the story. She may use phrases like, "I remember," "I wonder," "I'm guessing," "I'm interested in knowing," "because of," or "I predict that." Assumptions can be made into a transparent thinking process with phrases like "I am guessing that," "When I read _____, I assume that," or "I'm pretty sure that." When reading the story *Lost*, the teacher might think aloud during the scene in which the boy and bear are playing in the park: "I wonder if the boy and the bear have forgotten about getting the bear home" or "I'm thinking that playing in the park isn't as important as finding a way back to the forest—I hope they don't spend too much time playing."

Identify the Plot Structure

The teacher can think aloud to help children identify the plot structure, or she may impose a clear organization onto the story while modeling her thinking. ("If I were _____, I would really be having a *problem* with this—wouldn't you? I wonder what he's going to do to try to solve the problem.") If elements of the plot must be inferred, they can be labeled as *plans, goals, attempts*, and *consequences*. The adult may ask and answer her own questions to demonstrate how to reflect on what is known and not known: for example, "Why is the boy lost now? The picture shows he fell asleep on the bus. Can getting lost be a consequence of not knowing where you are going?"

Fill In and Elaborate Ideas

Closely related to clarifying structural elements in a story is the process of elaborating story ideas: providing relevant background information, calling attention to different characters' perspectives, filling in missing but assumed information, and relating familiar to unfamiliar content (Blank, 2002). As the instructor or children read what is explicitly stated in the story, the adult can weave in comments and insert implied information (Blank, 2002; Wallach, 2008).

On the surface, *Lost* is a story of an adventure in which a boy and a bear make some mistakes and finally solve their problem. On a concrete level, a character (albeit a bear) is lost and unhappy, and a fairly clear inference is that a "street savvy" boy (who knows his way around observation decks and libraries) should help. The boy tries to help the bear find his way back to the forest, but the boy doesn't really know what a forest is like or what a bear needs to survive. While children may be able to infer that wild animals don't survive well in cities, the adult could elaborate by explaining that bears naturally want to find a cave or hiding place where they can feel safe or that the kind of food bears like is found in forests, not pet stores.

A teacher or SLP can enhance children's ability to deal with higher level language by expanding concrete story information to convey abstract and remote content in ways children can understand (Blank, Marquis, & Klimovitch, 1994; Cummins, 1984; Dickson & Tabors, 2001; Pellegrini, & Galda, 1990)—using familiar and concrete events as bridges to talking about remote and abstract ideas (Blank, 2002; Wallach, 2008). Instructor elaborations can help the children go beyond the concrete storyline to find within the incidents more abstract meaning: for example, a pattern of developing friendship. The boy's ideas, although clever, aren't always terribly sensible. Nevertheless, as they struggle and play together, the boy and the bear develop the mutual caring that is characteristic of true friendship. Friends try to help each other; they stick together; and they don't blame or complain when something doesn't quite work out. Calling attention to or asking children what they do to help friends or take care of friends will help them make those deeper inferences and connections.

Make Predictions

Predicting what might happen next is a form of inferencing that requires reasoning through events or situations to guess what is not yet stated. When the boy's first few attempts to find the bear's home include a hotel (with trees in front), a city square with a fountain, and a park with a lake, children can infer (with teacher guidance if necessary) that the boy has little or no experience with the natural habitat of bears. The teacher or SLP may also model how she is making her predictions about further events in the story. She may call attention to information needed to make an inference or prediction, including pictured information, facts or relationships the children know from experience, or ideas or events stated in the book (McKeowan & Beck, 2006; van Kleeck, Vander Woude, & Hammett, 2006; Wallach, 2008). For example, in the failed attempts in *Lost*, the boy has been trying to find a forest in the city: the building with trees in front, the public fountain, the park. The adult might point this out and ask the children if they predict that the boy and the bear will find the bear's home somewhere in the city. Through such modeling, the children learn to make predictions based on their ability to connect information and/or events in the story.

Support Connections

In addition to finding connections between story events and details as they make predictions, students can acquire a deeper understanding of the story by relating story ideas to what they have experienced and observed in their own world (McKeowan & Beck, 2006). For example, a teacher or SLP may need to guide students in recognizing emotions and noticing the role they play as problems, actions, intents, and motives develop in the story. This can be done by helping children relate characters' emotions to their own. In *Lost*, emotions are not stated in words. The bear's emotions are portrayed vividly in the illustrations. But the boy's face is small in comparison to the greater bulk of the bear, and his expressions do not become prominent until the end when he discovers that he himself is lost. Children need to find clues to the boy's feelings in his actions or goals, thinking about ways they would feel in the story circumstances as well as feelings that would make them behave as the boy did. Making these inferences requires manipulating ideas in language and thus gives students more practice with decontextualized language skills.

During shared book reading children can better comprehend story circumstances by relating them to what they know about events in their world (van Kleeck, 2007) and thus make inferences intended by the author. For example, narratives may introduce a wide range of conflicts and resolutions, along with new perspectives (Wolf & Hicks, 1989). Children who have lived all their lives in cities may learn how strange their environment might seem to someone who is not accustomed to it: looking at everyday things like libraries and busses through the eyes of someone who is experiencing them for the first time.

Children can better comprehend relationships of goals to actions and of actions to consequences by drawing inferences from causes and effects they understand. For example, the plot of _Lost_ is built around implied causes and effects. The bear ends up lost in a city _because_ he falls asleep in a truck. Attempts to find the bear's home fail _because_ the boy doesn't understand forests any better than the bear understands cities. (He assumes that trees + water = forest.) Later the boy ends up lost in a forest _because_ he falls asleep on a bus. The word _because_ isn't used in the book, but the interest and humor of the story are in the causes and effects that are inferred.

Stimulate Children's Interactions Around the Text

Specific types of interactions with children during the reading process can actively involve the children in interactions around a text and thus facilitate comprehension (Cunningham & Zibulsky, 2011). To involve and support children, the adult may ask questions about the more concrete and contextualized parts of the story and then use those reminders of basic story ideas as jumping-off points to support children in making inferences and noticing connections to and between ideas.

Balanced interactions during and after shared reading permit the teacher and children to create meaning together and deepen their understanding of story ideas (Cazden, 1988; McKeown & Beck, 2006; Merritt, Culatta, & Barton, 1998; Raphael, Highfield, & Au, 2006; Wells, 1986). Comments, elaborations, and modeled thinking (as discussed) help children experience inferences, and other forms of critical and creative thinking. Purposefully structured questions and thoughtful responses to children's responses can more actively involve children in the process (McKeown & Beck, 2006).

Ask Different Question Types

During shared reading, the teacher involves children in conversations by purposefully asking different types of questions to draw out specific kinds of information and stimulate different kinds of thinking (Blank, 2002; McKeown & Beck, 2006; Merritt, Barton, & Culatta, 1998; Raphael, Highfield, & Au, 2006; van Kleeck, Vander Woude, & Hammett, 2006). Table 8–2 explains the form and purpose of various question types.

Acknowledge and Expand on Children's Contributions

As the children respond to the various types of questions, the teacher should acknowledge their contributions and build on what they say (McKeown & Beck, 2006). Nonverbal responses and encouragement include accepting and inviting body language or facial expressions and/or eye contact; verbal responses should include sincere acknowledgment and/or a comment that further extends the exchange (Rosenfeld, Hardy, Crace, & Wilder, 1990). To interpret students' responses, teachers should not merely listen to their words, but also attend to behaviors and expressions that convey their thoughts and emotions (Bretherton, Ritz, Zahn, Waxler, & Ridgeway, 1986), including body language, facial expression, and tone of voice.

Commenting on students' responses reinforces their efforts and permits the instructor to highlight or repeat ideas that need reiteration. To enhance comprehension, teachers and SLPs may respond to children's contributions by rephrasing, highlighting, summarizing, or elaborating (expanding, emphasizing). Expanding children's

Table 8–2. Types of Questions Recommended for Shared Reading, with Definitions and Purposes

Type of Question	Definition	Purpose
Prior experience and background knowledge (Have you ever been lost? What do you know about forests?)	Recall something they know or have experienced related to the story	"Set stage." Call up knowledge and experience children have related to the story
Factual questions (What did the boy and the bear find in the library?)	Recall something actually stated in the story	Stimulate recall and review facts to be applied in inferences, etc
Inference questions (How do you think the bear felt when he realized that the tress in the city and the park were not his forest? Why?)	Answer "Why" questions; Draw conclusions; connect ideas from different parts of the text (e.g., how one character's actions influenced another's, how events changed over time)	Require students to infer: e.g., make connections, discover causes, weigh alternatives, use clues from the text to answer questions about information not directly stated
Application (transfer) questions (What did boy and bear learn in the story that can help them get the boy home?)	Apply something in the story to a new situation	Make predictions, anticipate reactions and consequences

contributions into a conversation with questions and comments to keep up an interactive exchange gives shape and structure to the experience and supports comprehension (Gilliam & Ukranitz, 2006; McKeown & Beck, 2006).

Support Decoding

Shared reading routines often involve strategies or procedures for supporting print awareness or decoding (Justice & Ezell, 2004). In addition to sharing the ideas in the book, the adult supports the children as they engage in reading the text. In order to support decoding in a shared book reading experience, the adult needs to ensure that the children are able to clearly see the text and can easily follow the words (e.g., large text with adult using a pointer, individual students with their own copy of the text, one-on-one reading of the text with adult and child looking at the text side-by-side). The adult reads the text aloud, pointing to the words while pronouncing them. Depending on the number of children in the group and their age and reading level, subsequent readings may involve the group reading the text in unison as the teacher points to the words, filling in familiar words as the teacher reads the text and pauses, decoding specific words as the teacher pauses etc.

The adult should select a text at the children's instructional level so that they are able to be successful in decoding the words with some supports. Some strategies to support decoding include the following:

◆ Engage in simultaneous reading. The adult and children read aloud together. However, the level and amount of support changes based on the readers' skill level.
◆ With younger readers, re-read the story or sections of it, having children supply particular words. The adult may pause at certain words and either have the children read them in unison or point to a different child to supply each word.
◆ Guide older readers in attempting multisyllable words. The adult may pause to point out word parts or letter combinations that children can recognize and demonstrate how they come together to form the word.
◆ Pre-teach a particular targeted phonic pattern with example words so that children will be prepared to read such words while reading the story.
◆ Avoid letting the child(ren) struggle, as focusing too hard on decoding may interfere with comprehension.

Represent and Retell Stories

Shared stories, told and read, can serve a number of different purposes: sharing enjoyment, motivating reading, enhancing language use, embedding phonics, understanding story grammar elements, relating story ideas to personal experience, and learning to draw inferences, among others discussed in this chapter. If the purpose of sharing a story is to help children understand aspects such as story grammar, sequence, and inferences, then visual representations and retelling can be valuable activities, particularly if a teacher or SLP pairs a simple graphic with a paraphrased version of the story.

Use Graphic Representations to Clarify Structure and Relationships

Children initially process information more effectively when seeing is added to hearing, particularly with abstract concepts, decontextualized language, and story structure. Teachers can use visual representations to highlight main ideas and important relationships and to involve the children in remembering story events. Graphing can also guide and scaffold students during the retrieval process.

Graphically Depict the Story's Structure

A story map represents a particular story in relation to the generic structure typical of stories (Idol, 1987; Marzano, Pickering, & Pollock, 2001; Reutzel, 1984). In using a graphic representation to highlight main ideas, he calls attention to and even exaggerates main ideas and organizational components, building in redundancy that is especially helpful for students with language difficulties. Main story ideas and their relationships (story grammar or story structure) can be represented with a flow chart or tree diagram, with events represented by words and/or pictures in cells that are linked with lines or arrows on which cause-effect or temporal relationships can be signaled with key words, as illustrated in Figure 8–2. As the teacher refers to the map while telling or reading, he can illustrate the representation or add to the map as the story evolves.

Use Pictures to Represent Main Events

A picture sequence or series of quickly sketched pictographs can be placed in a logical order to illustrate a story's main events (Ukranitz, 1998). The sequence can also be presented in a story web: a sequence of pictures placed clockwise around a picture of the story's main event, initiating event, or main character, illustrating the important happenings initiated by the event or involving the character.

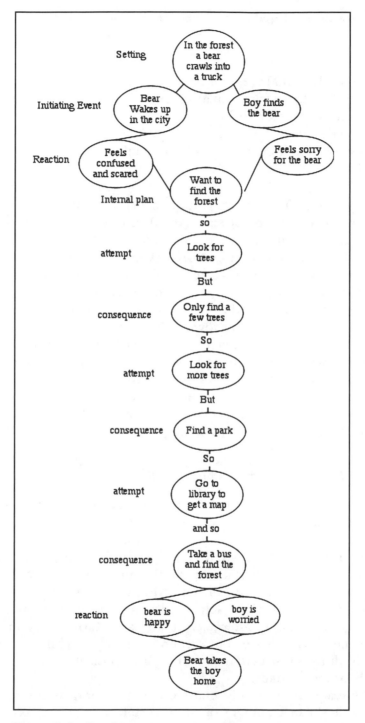

Figure 8–2. Graphic representation of the story *Lost*.

Use Charts to Connect Inferences

Several kinds of matrices can be used to connect implied information to stated story events. Charting explicit and implicit information allows the instructor to highlight important ideas and relationships needed to understand the story. The following very similar charts work well at helping children visualize relationships among story ideas.

- ◆ *Inference chart:* A two-column chart that lists story events (character actions or statements) in one column and provides space in the other column for children and teachers to fill in inferences about each event.
- ◆ *Emotion chart:* A two-column chart that lists events in one column and provides space in the second column for students to fill in how the characters felt or what they thought about each event, as shown in Table 8–3.
- ◆ *Perspective chart:* A chart that lists events in a center column, with side columns in which the teacher or students write different characters' perspectives of the same event, a column for each character being compared, as shown in Table 8–4 (generally used with 2nd and 3rd grade children with high levels of support).

Co-Construct the Representation and Talk It Through

There are several ways that children can become involved in graphically representing stories (Davis & McPherson, 1989; Gilliam & Ukranitz, 2006; Idol & Croll, 1987; Macon, Bewell, & Vogt, 1989). A simple but beneficial strategy is for children to provide information orally as the teacher or SLP fills in information on a map, chart, or diagram written on chart paper, the whiteboard, or a projected overhead. The teacher can guide the students with purposeful questions. An alternative is to use a Cloze story map, on which the teacher leaves out certain elements so children can fill them in during instruction as a large group or afterward in small groups or individually.

As teachers explicitly chart out main characters and story events, they can comment on how certain events are associated with feelings and thoughts of characters or how characters felt at certain points of the narrative. This strategy gives children clues

Table 8–3. An Emotion Chart

Event (Action or Happening)	Bear Feels
Bear wakes up in the city	Frightened, confused
Boy says he will help	Comforted, less worried
Boy takes bear to some trees in the city	Disappointed, puzzled
Boy looks for trees from a tall building and takes the bear to the park	Disappointed, glad to play in the park
Boy and bear go to the library to find a map	Sees the forest on the map and feels relaxed
Boy and bear take a bus to the forest	Happy to be home
Boy says he is worried about getting home	Eager to help the boy

Table 8–4. A Perspective Chart

Boy Feels and Thinks	Event	Bear Feels and Thinks
Surprised, sorry for the bear	Bear wakes up in city	Scared, confused
Disappointed (didn't find the forest)	Finds a tree near hotel	Sad (isn't a forest)
Disappointed that the park isn't the forest; BUT enjoys being in the park	Finds trees in park	Disappointed BUT likes the park
Happy to get bear home	Takes the bus to the forest	Happy to be home
Confused, worried	Boy is far away from the city	Eager to help the boy

to important implicit information. Providing a summary of a story that is supported by a graphic representation also serves as another opportunity to hear the story with main ideas highlighted.

Once the story has been represented visually, the teacher can use the representation to connect characters' motives and plans with their attempts to reach their goals and to connect the attempts with their resulting consequences. The most important guiding principle for graphic representations is to "talk through" the connections (Stahl & Vancil, 1986). As teachers and students gain experience, the children can become responsible for reflecting on and talking about the story grammar elements as the story is mapped or charted. Children can even be guided in small groups to create or fill in a graphic to refer to during further treatment of the narrative. Once the map or chart is constructed, children can use it to help them in retelling the story.

Retell the Story

Having students retell the story is often a follow-up activity from graphic representation, although it can be an independent activity based on some of the same patterns of thinking and analyzing involved in a graphing process. The experience of retelling a story can deepen and reinforce children's comprehension and strengthen their narrative skills. Supported retellings can be socially constructed when the teacher or SLP scaffolds the process; a variety of ways have been suggested.

Motivate the Retelling

Effective retelling requires retrieval and organization of components similar to those involved with visual representation; but language without reliance on visual supports is more abstract and more difficult for many children to handle. Thus students must be sufficiently motivated as well as adequately supported (with or without visuals) if they are to engage actively in it. The teacher or SLP can provide a reason to retell, such as creating and illustrating the retold version with drawings or pictographs (Ukrainetz, 2006), using the computer or iPad to turn the story into a personal book with simple but creative interactive options (e.g., Pictello story making application for the iPad), making a "big book" from chart paper, or telling the story to non-classmate peers or younger children.

Co-construct and Support the Retelling

As with graphic representations, a skillful instructor can aid children's retrieval and increase their level of confidence by making the retelling task a co-construction. Preschool or early grade children with limited language skills can retell in small groups supported by the teacher or SLP according to individual needs. In place of a graphic representation, the instructor may fill in story information, supply Cloze or sentence completion prompts, or ask a mixture of open-ended and specific closed questions that frame the story according to organized story grammar elements (Pelligrini & Galda, 1990; Wallach, 2008), as shown in Table 8–5. Or the instructor might give the setting and ask the student to complete the story. Teachers can initially provide a high level of visual or verbal support if necessary, but gradually release more and more responsibility to the student.

Showing or acting on props or using a picture sequence can provide variety as well as reminding children of the various events. Additionally, manipulatives such as paper cut-out props or miniature objects act as reminders of story characters and events.

Table 8–5. Story Grammar Prompts to Support Organized Retelling

Setting	What was happening when the story began? (Who was there?) Who were the characters and what were they doing when the story started?
Initiating Event	What big (interesting, new) thing happened? What happened to the character when he _____? What happened to surprise (excite, upset) the character? So the character was (state what was happening when the story started), and then what happened? (Put stress on *happened*.) What problem did the character encounter?
Goal	What did the character want to do? Want to get or to see?
Plan	What must the character do to achieve his goal? What will the character try to do to get what he wants?
Internal Response	How did the character feel when _____?
Attempt	What did the character try to do to _____?
Consequence	When he tried to _____, did it work? Did he get what he wanted?
Reaction	How did the character feel when _____?

As children become more skillful with retelling or co-constructing and teacher input is reduced, the instructor can determine how much of the story structure and content the children have integrated. When a new narrative is introduced, support may need to increase again if the content is unfamiliar or more difficult.

Vary the Task

Repeated retelling of stories strengthens children's comprehension of and ability to produce narratives, as well as their general sense of story structure (Dennis & Walter, 1995). To maintain student interest through multiple retellings, the teacher or SLP may change the nature of the task: using different props, creating a digital version with a story-making iPad application, or involving puppets. Children can dictate their retelling to an adult who types it into a computer, tell the story into an audio recorder, or create a version of the story to be reread from the "author's chair." Or the instructor and children can write a parallel story altering some component or elaborating or changing the ending (Gilliam & Ukranitz, 2006). As the task varies and children get repeated opportunities to tell the story, the instructor can continue to fade support.

Enact the Story

Enacting a story can be an appealing activity for enhancing narrative skills, as children take on character roles and act out the events in stories they have heard or read (Culatta, 1994; Martinez, 1993). Generally more loosely structured than storytelling sessions, enactments work well in small group settings where children can be spontaneous as they ad lib their character parts.

Set Up the Activity Carefully

The instructor mediates the enactment process, guiding the children through procedures to help them re-create the story. A number of basic steps are involved in the process.

Negotiate Roles

Negotiation and communication abilities can be developed as children and instructor decide who will assume various roles. With repeated enactments, roles can be rotated so more children can play major parts. If enactments take place in multiple small groups or at a station, more than one child can take the same role at the same time. Small group enactment would be especially effective with *Lost*, which has only two book characters; however other logical parts, like the truck driver or bus driver, can be added in the enactment.

Sometimes the instructor may want to assign rather than negotiate roles — placing verbally competent children in the main roles for the first enactment and having children with language differences or disabilities begin as minor characters. A minor role can be more attractive if the teacher or SLP creates a reason for the child to find the role special. For example, the child playing the truck driver (pictured but not mentioned in the text) in *Lost* might get to drive a big-box snack truck and/or use tools to fix the flat tire. As the children with language needs observe what the more verbal characters say and do, they can move into more dominant roles when they understand what is expected and develop confidence in their ability to do it.

In the process of assigning or negotiating roles, the instructor can make comments that remind the children what the characters will do. ("The bear is worried, so the boy will comfort him — maybe even touch his shoulder or pat his paw.") When roles are assigned, the instructor can help the children label their characters with a nametag or a very simple costume prop: possibly a headband with ears for the bear or a cap and set of keys for the truck driver.

Convey Story Information While Setting the Scene

Important information about a story can be represented while setting the scene for the enactment. For *Lost* the instructor could explain that simple murals or drawings, one with tall buildings to represent the city and one with trees to represent the forest, should be placed at opposite ends of the drama area because the city and the forest are far apart and very different. Children can make choices on how to set the scene, with suggestions or prompts from the teacher, including conversation that reminds them of the story events that will take place in the settings.

Develop Characters, Character Interactions, and Dialogue

Creating conversations between characters in a story enactment can benefit children's narrative skills. In addition to conveying important story information, dialogue helps children learn to maintain topical threads as they practice connecting ideas across turns.

Help Children Understand When and How to Create Dialogue

Where conversation is implied rather than expressed in the story or is quite one-sided (as in *Lost*), the instructor can guide the children in creating interchange and possibly creating characters. For example, although a librarian is not explicitly represented in *Lost,* libraries always have librarians, and the boy might need to explain the bear's presence and ask where to find useful books and maps. Similarly, the boy might interact with other passengers on the bus. A bear on a bus seat is hardly an everyday sight, and it wouldn't be difficult for several children to think of something to say.

The instructor may guide the exchange by finding reasons for conversing: For example, characters commonly interact as they set common goals, solve problems, and share feelings (Shugar & Kmita, 1990). Although the bear doesn't speak much in the book *Lost*, it is not much additional stretch of the imagination for a bear who swings, slides, rides a boat, and eats hot dogs in a park to talk about his problems and react to the boy's creative solutions, while the instructor guides the children in connecting and elaborating information (French, 1988; Wells, 1986). "What if" brainstorming may help in deciding why characters talk and what they might say. ("What if the bear was scared in the elevator? How would he feel moving upward so fast in such a cramped space?—it's hardly like climbing trees to look around in a forest. What would he say to the boy? What would the other people in the elevator say when they found themselves standing inches away from a large bear—with no place to run?")

The teacher or SLP might pretend to be the bear and role play with the boy to model how a conversation might go, letting others join in for brief comments as people on the elevator. The instructor can keep the exchange going by being responsive to each child's initiations or contributions (Shugar & Kmita, 1990): acknowledging what the child says, repeating and elaborating the content, and matching or expressing the emotion. In these ways the instructor both elaborates story content and shows that she values the child's contributions (Wallach, 2008).

One way to encourage children to take part in creating dialogue is to phrase questions that request information the character wants and presumably doesn't already know (Culatta, 1984): "Why is this little room going up so fast?" "Are we going to fall?" Another way to pass the turn to a child is to provide a choice or decision: "Should we take another turn on the swings, or is it time to move on?" Or the instructor might give information the child needs to refute: "It's getting late, Bear. Maybe you could sleep in this parking lot—just for tonight." In addition to verbal questions and comments, the instructor can cue a child to take a turn by nonverbal strategies: silence, proximity, and/or gaze.

Guide Character Actions and Dialogue with Narrative Voices

To guide the enactment in an organized, coherent fashion, the teacher or SLP can assume different narrative voices to structure the sequence, highlight the main ideas, and guide children in action and dialogue: narrator, focal character, and stage manager (Pellegrini & Galda, 1990; Wolf & Hicks, 1989). The narrative voices become the medium by which the instructor coaches character exchanges with prompts, assertions, and supports. Additionally, these narrative voices can be used to build in redundancy, further highlight important information, and coach character actions and exchanges.

The impartial narrator is a role instructors commonly assume as the children carry out their parts in an enactment (Pellegrini & Galda, 1990; Wolf & Hicks, 1989). The narrator tells the story impartially, comments on the characters' actions, fills in information such as relevant feelings and thoughts of the characters and other inferences, clarifies main ideas and connections, and comments on story events: showing pictures from the book if appropriate. For example, the narrator might show the pictures of the boy and bear playing in the park and say, "Parks can be so much fun. They enjoyed a boat ride, had some lunch, and played on swings and slides. They had so much fun they almost forgot about getting the bear home—and they lost track of the time." (This can avoid having to portray these actions in the drama corner or makeshift stage, especially if the SLP or teacher regards them as not being relevant to the characters' goal, plan, or attempts.)

Since narrators can see into characters' minds and memories, the narrator role can prompt children to incorporate ideas and specific behaviors into their character roles and to improvise dialogue as well. The narrator for *Lost* might state, "The boy knows he can find out about anything he wants to know by looking for books in the library; libraries even have maps and books about forests." This scaffolding prepares the child who is playing the boy to explain to the librarian what he needs and why (Figure 8–3). Children with language differences or deficits will probably need this kind of support in their character roles. If the teacher is narrating, the SLP can add more coaching.

The role of a major character enables the instructor to incorporate guiding and prompting through the character's actions and dialogue, including the feelings, assumptions, and intents that frame story development. For example, while portraying the bear in *Lost*, the instructor could express the bear's fears about spending the night in the city. If the bear makes humorous comments showing how he perceives the fountain (cold shower), the elevator (flying

Figure 8–3. The "bear" and the "boy" follow the librarian's suggestion to look for a place on the map where there are lots of trees, as an interested audience member looks on.

box), the observation deck (mountain with magic spectacles), the park, the library, the bus, and so forth, students portraying aspects of those scenes are cued as to what they could say and when.

Using a character's voice, the instructor can examine story events from that character's point of view, emphasizing reactions that could easily be obscured by vivid action and description. For example, at the beginning of *Lost* the boy questions the bear about how he got lost and what his home is like, and the bear responds to each query. The instructor (as either boy or bear) can manipulate the conversation to emphasize the difference between the bear's confusion and the boy's confidence and thus prepare to gradually show the relationship developing between them. The teacher doesn't necessarily feed the child lines, but facilitates the child's responses by structuring the general flow of the conversation (Shugar & Kmita, 1990). The teacher-character can also prompt conversation by making an inaccurate statement. If playing the boy in *Lost*, he might insist the park must be the bear's home because he sees trees and enough open space for a bear to run and play. This prompts the bear to explain what the forest really looks like and why a bear couldn't live comfortably in a park.

Stage manager is a role in which the instructor stands outside of the play to direct its development, telling the actors explicitly what they should do in their character roles. ("Now boy, where do you go when you need information? There's even a table to hold the books while you're looking at them.") In the course of directing or "stage managing," the teacher can remind the children of the story sequence, possibly referring to a story map, cue cards, a picture sequence, or pictures from the book. ("Wondering where to go next? My story map says . . . ") Information about characters or underlying themes and ideas can also be worked in. The stage manager may even remind a child what information the character needs to convey. ("Bears don't know much about finding information. You may want to tell the bear why you are taking him to the library.")

Use Props to Illustrate the Story and Make It More Concrete

In almost any story enactment, real objects can be combined with less concrete props to illustrate story events (Culatta, 1994). Westby (1988) has suggested a continuum for the amount of contextual information provided in props for play and story enactment: moving from real objects to replicas, to object transformations (a box becoming a truck), to construction materials (masking tape or a chalk line indicating a road), to pretend gestures (the action of pushing a button representing an elevator), to language alone (e.g., "The forest is way over there") (Figure 8–4).

The extent to which abstract props are used in story enactments depends on the children's capacity to move beyond the use of concrete objects to set scenes, situations, and roles. Some pretend props or absent objects should be included to stimulate and engage children in decontextualized language use. But even when language is the primary mode of representation, at least a few real objects should still be used to engage children and motivate their interest (Pellegrini & Galda, 1990). A child holding a paper towel tube can still use words to describe how the real instrument functions (and will probably be more motivated to do so). Actions, gestures, facial expressions, or prominent intonations can sometimes be used in place of props to give a concrete aspect to decontextualized language use (Blank, 2002; Dickinson, 2001): for example, the boy and the bear grinning, shouting, and "high fiving" each other when they arrive in the forest.

Make Props Available for Additional Enactments

Since multiple exposures to stories support comprehension (Dennis & Walter, 1995; Sell, Ray, & Lovelace, 1995), children can benefit

Figure 8–4. The bear wakes up in a snack truck (represented by a box) and finds himself in a strange city (represented by a line drawing of tall buildings).

from opportunities to enact a story more than once. They can re-enact a story in cooperative groups, at centers, or in free-choice time with less support. Motivating props can be made available, along with the book and perhaps a graphic representation (picture sequence or story web) in a corner of the classroom or in a dramatic play area. Volunteers and parents can mediate story re-enactments. Sometimes after a mediated re-enactment, children can carry out a second or third re-enactment of the story directed by classmates who are older or more competent with language.

Props, roles, and purpose may be changed as well as support level. As experience is gained, the instructor may fade supports that are no longer needed and gradually release teacher-mediated supports to the children themselves. The re-enactments permit students to more spontaneously and confidently represent stories since they have had some experience with the story previously during the telling and guided enactment. The story could be told with paper cutout props, a child might act as the narrator, or the story could be rewritten to include different characters or perspectives.

Similarly, when the kind and function of props and the manner of presentation are shifted, a story enactment can be turned into a play or reader's theatre production, with children assuming roles which can be self-selected or assigned by the adult and rehearsed in groups (Culatta & Trostle, 1998). After the leader reviews the story, characters, and sequence, the children can refer to a chart or graphic representation illustrating the story grammar elements and the sequence of events to write the parts. Such an approach encourages children to utilize meta-linguistic elements and to reflect on the elements of a story in a metalinguistic, analytic way.

Summary

Narratives are among the first literacy experiences children encounter and among the most lasting sources of literacy enthusiasm. A considerable range of skills and capabilities can be developed through narrative study, with processes that children can enjoy as they benefit. If teachers and SLPs understand the nature, structure, and components of the narrative, as well as the cognitive and linguistic demands of narrative comprehension, they can employ a number of strategic and enjoyable learning contexts. Instructors and children can interact with and enjoy narratives through dramatic telling, shared reading, purposeful charting and retelling, and enacting/re-enacting. Individual needs and learning characteristics, including those of students with language difficulties and delays, can be considered, adapted to, and effectively met.

References

Barton, J. (1995). Conducting effective classroom discussions. *Journal of Reading, 38,* 346–350.

Beck, I., McKeown, M., & Kucan, L. (2002). *Bringing words to life: Robust vocabulary instruction.* New York, NY: Guilford Press.

Blank, M. (2002). Classroom discourse: A key to literacy. In K. Butler & E. Silliman (Eds.), *Speaking, reading, and writing in children with language learning disabilities: New paradigms in research and practice* (pp. 151–173). Mahwah: NJ: Lawrence Erlbaum Associates.

Blank, M., Marquis, M. A., & Klimovitch, M. O. (1994). *Directing school discourse.* Tucson, AZ: Communication Skill Builders.

Blank, M., Marquis, M. A., & Klimovich, M. O. (1995). *Directing early discourse.* Tucson, AZ: Communication Skill Builders.

Bretherton, I., Fitz, J., Zahn-Waxler, C., & Ridgeway, D. (1986). Learning to talk about emotions: A functionalist perspective. *Child Development, 57,* 529–548.

Cazden, C. (1988). *Classroom discourse: The language of teaching and learning.* Portsmouth, NH: Heinemann.

Culatta, B. (1994). Representational play and story enactments: Formats for language intervention. In J. F. Duchan, L. E. Hewitt, & R. M. Sorinmzi-ieier (Eds.), *Front theory to practice.* Englewood Cliffs: NJ: Prentice-Hall.

Cummins, J. (1984). *Bilingualism and special education: Issues in assessment and pedagogy.* Austin, TX: Pro-Ed.

Cunningham, A., & Zibulsky, J. (2011). Tell me a story: Examining the benefits of shared reading. In D. Dickinson & S. Neuman (Eds.), *Handbook of early literacy* (Vol. 3, pp. 396–411). New York, NY: Guilford Press.

Davis, Z. T., & McPherson, M. (1989, December). Story map instruction: A road map for reading comprehension. *Reading Teacher, 42,* 232–240.

De Temple, J. M. (2001). Parents and children reading books together. In D. K. Dickinson & P. O. Tabors (Eds.), *Beginning literacy with language* (pp. 31–51). Baltimore, MD: Paul H. Brookes.

De Temple, J., & Snow, C. (2003). Learning words from books. In A. van Kleeck, S. Stahl, & E. Bauer (Eds.), *On reading books to children* (pp.16–36). Mahwah, NJ: Lawrence Erlbaum Associates.

Dennis, G., & Walter, E. (1995). The effects of repeated read-alouds on story comprehension assessed through story retellings. *Reading Improvement*, *32*(3), 140–153.

Dickinson, D. K., & Sprague, K. E. (2001). The nature and impact of early childhood care environments on the language and early literacy development of children from low-income families. In S. B. Neuman & D. K. (Eds.), *Handbook of early literacy research* (pp. 263–280). New York, NY: Guilford Press.

Dickinson, D. K., & Tabors, P. O. (Eds.). (2001). *Beginning literacy with language: Young children learning at home and in school*. Baltimore, MD: Brookes.

Donahue, M. L., & Foster, S. K. (2004). Integration of language and discourse components with reading comprehension: It's all about relationships. In E. R. Silliman & L. C. Wilkinson (Eds.), *Language and literacy learning in schools* (pp. 175–198). New York, NY: Guilford Press.

French, M. M. (1988). Story retelling for assessment and instruction. *Perspectives for Teachers of the Hearing Impaired*, *7*(2), 20–22.

Gillam, R., & Ukrainetz, T. (2006). Language intervention through literature-based units. In T. Ukrainetz, (Ed.), *Contextualized language intervention: Scaffolding preK–12 literacy achievement* (pp. 59–94). Eau Claire, WI: Thinking Publications.

Halliday, M. A. K., & Hasan, R. (1976). *Cohesion in English*. London, UK: Longman.

Hayward, D. V., Gillam, R.B., & Lien, P. (2007). Retelling a script-based story: Do children with and without language impairments focus on script and story elements? *American Journal of Speech-Language Pathology*, *16*, 235–245.

Hedberg, N. L., & Westby, C. E. (1993). *Analyzing storytelling skills*. Tucson, AZ: Communication Skill Builders.

Hicks, D. *(1990)*. Narrative skills and genre knowledge of story retelling in the primary school grades. *Applied Psycholinguistics*, *11*(1), 83–104.

Idol, L. *(1987)*. Group story mapping: A comprehension strategy for both skilled and unskilled readers. *Journal of Learning Disabilities*, *20*(4), 196–205.

Idol, L., & Croll, V. J. *(1987)*. Story-mapping training as a means of improving reading comprehension. *Learning Disability Quarterly*, *10*, 214–229.

Justice, L., & Ezell, H. (2004, April). Print referencing: An emergent literacy enhancement strategy and its clinical applications. *Language, Speech, and Hearing Services in Schools*, *35*, 185–193.

Keene, E. O., & Zimmerman, S. (1997). *Mosaic of thought: Teaching comprehension in a reader's workshop.* Portsmouth, NH: Heinemann.

Ketch, A. (2005). Conversation: The comprehension connection. *Reading Teacher, 59*(1), 8–13.

Lucariello, J. (1990). Freeing talk from the here-and-now: The role of event knowledge and maternal scaffolds. *Topics in Language Disorders, 10,* 14–29.

Macon, J. M., Bewell, D., & Vogt, M. (1989). *Responses to literature—grades K–8.* Newark, DE: International Reading Association.

Mandler J. M., & Johnson, N. S. (1977). Remembrance of things parsed: Story structure and recall. *Cognitive Psychology, 9,* 111–151.

Martinez, M. *(1993).* Motivating dramatic story reenactments. *Reading Teacher, 46*(8), 682–688.

Marzano, R. J., Pickering, D. J., & Pollock, J. E. (2001). *Classroom instruction that works: Research-based strategies for increasing student achievement* (pp. 72–83). Alexandria, VA: Association for Supervision and Curriculum Development.

McGuinness, D. (2004). *Early reading instruction: What science really tells us about how to teach reading.* Cambridge, MA: MIT Press.

McKeown, M., & Beck, I. (2006). Encouraging young children's language interactions with stories. In D. K. Dickinson & S. B. Neuman (Eds.), *Handbook of early literacy research,* (Vol. 2, pp. 281–294). New York: NY: Guilford Press.

McPhail, D. (1990). *Lost.* Boston, MA: Little Brown and Company.

Merritt, D., Culatta, B., & Trostle, S. (1998). Narratives: Implementing a discourse framework. In D. Merritt & B. Culatta (Eds.), *Language intervention in the classroom* (pp. 277–330). Clifton Park, NY: Thomson Delmar Learning.

Milosky L. M. (1987). Narratives in the classroom. *Seminars in Speech and Language, 8*(4), 329–343.

Nelson, N., & Van Meter, A. (2006). Finding the words: Vocabulary development for young authors. In T. Ukranitz (Ed.), *Contextualized language intervention: Scaffolding preK–12 literacy achievement* (pp. 95–144). Eau Claire, WI: Thinking Publications.

Pellegrini, A. D., & Galda, L. (1990). Children's play, language, and early literacy. *Topics in Language Disorders, 10,* 76–88.

Pellegrini, A. D., & Galda, L. (2000). Cognitive development, play, and literacy: Issues of definition and developmental function. In K. Roskos & J. Christie (Eds.), *Play and literacy in early childhood* (pp. 63–74). Mahwah, NJ: Erlbaum.

Raphael, T., Highfield, K., & Au, K. (2006). *QAR now: A powerful and practical framework that develops comprehension and higher level thinking in all students.* New York, NY: Scholastic.

Reese, E., Cox, A., Harte, D., & McAnally, H. (2003). Diversity in adults' styles of reading books to children. In A. van Kleeck, S. Stahl, & E. Bauer (Eds.), *On reading books to children* (pp. 37–57). Mahwah, NJ: Lawrence Erlbaum Associates.

Reutzel, D. R. (1984, December). Story mapping: An alternative approach to comprehension. *Reading World, 24*(2), 16–25.

Rosenfeld, L., Hardy, C., Crace, R., & Wilder, L. (1990). Active listening. *Soccer Journal, 4*, 45–49.

Sell, M., Ray, G., & Lovelace, L. (1995) Preschool children's comprehension of a 'Sesame Street' video tape: The effects of repeated viewing and previewing. *Educational Technology Research and Development, 43*(3), 49–60.

Shugar, G. W., & Kmita, G. (1990). The pragmatics of collaboration: Participant structure and the structures of participation. In G. Conti-Ramsden & C. Snow (Eds.), *Children's language* (Vol. 7, pp. 273–303). Hillsdale NJ: Lawrence Erlbaum Associates.

Stahl, S. A., & Vancil, S. J. (1986). Discussion is what makes semantic maps work in vocabulary instruction. *Reading Teacher, 40*, 62–67.

Stein, N. L., & Glenn, C. G. (1979). An analysis of story comprehension in elementary school children. In R. O. Freedle (Ed.), *New directions in discourse processing* (pp. 53–120*)*. Norwood, NJ: Ablex.

Trostle, S. (2007). Facilitating emergent literacy skills: A literature-based, multiple intelligence approach. *Journal of Research in Childhood Education, 21*(2), 133–148.

Trostle, S., & Donato, J. (2001). *Storytelling in emergent literacy: Fostering multiple intelligence.* Albany, NY: Delmar Cengage Learning.

Ukrainetz, T. (2006a). Assessment and intervention within a contextualized skill framework. In T. Ukranitz, (Ed.), *Contextualized language intervention: Scaffolding preK–12 literacy achievement* (pp. 7–58). Eau Claire, WI: Thinking Publications.

Ukrainetz, T. (2006b). Teaching narrative structure: Coherence, cohesion, and captivation. In T. Ukranitz (Ed.), *Contextualized language intervention: Scaffolding preK–12 literacy achievement* (pp. 195–246). Eau Claire, WI: Thinking Publications.

van Kleeck, A., Stahl, S., & Bauer, E. (2003). *On reading books to children.* Mahwah, NJ: Lawrence Erlbaum Associates.

van Kleeck, A., & Vander Woude, J. (2003). Book sharing with preschoolers with language delays. In A. van Kleeck, S. Stahl, & E. Bauer (Eds.), *On reading books to children* (pp. 58–94). Mahwah, NJ: Lawrence Erlbaum Associates.

van Kleeck, A., Vander Woude, J., & Hammett, L. (2006). Fostering literal and inferential language skills in Head Start preschoolers with language impairment using scripted book-sharing discussions. *American Journal of Speech-Language Pathology, 15*, 85–95.

Wallach, G. (2008). *Language intervention for school-age children.* St. Louis, MO: Mosby Elsevier.

Wells, G. (1986). *The meaning makers: Children learning language and using language to learn.* Portsmouth, NH: Heinemann.

Westby, C. E. (1988). Children's play: Reflections of social competence. *Seminars in Speech and Language, 9*(1),1–14.

Westby, C. E. (2005). Assessing and remediating text comprehension problems. In H. W. Catts & A. G. Kamhi (Eds.), *Language and reading disabilities* (2nd ed., pp. 157–232). Boston, MA: Allyn & Bacon.

Wolf, D., & Hicks, D. *(1989).* The voices within narratives. The development of intertextuality in young children's stories. *Discourse Processes, 12,* 329–351.

Chapter 9

Learning About the World: Exploring and Comprehending Expository Texts

Sharon Black, Kendra M. Hall-Kenyon,
and Barbara Culatta

The kindergarten teacher reads from the book *Frogs* by Chris Henwood (1988, p. 12), from the series *Keeping Minibeasts*:

> As frogs are short and fat and very slippery, they are very difficult to handle. When handling frogs use wet hands, as hot hands can harm their delicate skin. You can use a strainer or a damp towel or cloth held very gently around the body.

She shows the picture accompanying this text: on one page a photograph of a small frog sitting in a kitchen strainer, on the opposite page a tiny frog held in a person's cupped hand. She shows a strainer she has brought from home, places a small ceramic frog in it, and passes it among the children (Figure 9–1).

The book also gives a brief explanation with large, attractive photographs of what a frog's tank should include. Children who

Figure 9–1. Children examine a model frog being carried "safely" in a kitchen strainer.

have had experience with "pet" frogs are invited to share, and the teacher guides the discussion to draw attention to ways that the frog owners have met the needs of their pet. Contributions and ideas are welcomed. Children then examine a real frog tank that the teacher has brought, along with some of the supplies recommended by the book. Later during small group time each cluster of children will be given some small boxes and containers to create their own frog tanks.

During a lesson the following day, the teacher will show some pictures of frogs in their natural pond habitat. As the teacher shows pictures of what these pond frogs eat and how they get their food, she will ask the children how this compares with what and how the pet frog will eat. They also can think about needs such as water and light. As they discuss differences and also similarities between "pond frogs" and "pet frogs," the children will sit on the rug with a large two-column chart lying in the center. They will place pictures or small objects in the columns to represent the items as they compare them: for example, a picture or a few pieces of commercial frog food on one side and pictures of flies and mosquitos (real ones not recommended) on the other. The teacher can point out that the needs of the frogs are the same, but when they are living in different circumstances these needs must be met in different ways.

As they are learning about frogs, the children are also being prepared with some of the vocabulary and skills that they will need to work with expository texts. They are learning to talk about and understand similarities and differences related to particular dimensions (e.g., adapting to habitats, obtaining food, meeting needs) as they compare the lives of pet frogs and pond frogs. They are noticing and thinking about relationships in what they learn. They are processing information delivered by the teacher (oral expository text) along with the printed expository text in the book. Their prior interests, knowledge, and experience have been asked for and treated respectfully—enhancing their engagement with and ability to relate to expository text.

These benefits, along with others, are discussed in this chapter, in addition to some specific teaching strategies and lesson ideas. Both content and structural issues will be treated. The frog sequence is part of a two-week unit introducing children to expository texts (written and oral), along with activities related to pond animals: frogs, turtles, snails, fish, and ducks.

Use of Expository Texts With Young Children

Traditionally most teachers of preschool, kindergarten, and first grade children have used very little expository material in their classrooms (Duke, 2000). But research is demonstrating that expository texts are critical in helping children acquire and share information and are thus vital to children's success in school (Pearson & Duke, 2002). Thus, more and more teachers are using a variety of expository texts when teaching both literacy and content knowledge.

Nature and Forms of Expository Texts

Expository writing can be considered in terms of its prefix *ex*: It explains, explores, exhibits, explicates, exemplifies. In its simplest terms, expository text gives the facts—teaches truths about the world in which we live (see Tompkins, 2012). Using the comparable term *nonfiction*, Duthie (1994, p. 588) recorded her first graders' ideas:

> "It gives information about things around us . . . like, if you have a farm, you can get information about it."

> "If you have a sick cat and you can't call a vet, you could look in nonfiction."

> "It can teach you about fruits and vegetables."

> "You can find out what's inside your body."

> "[It] can tell you about space, planets, and stuff like that."

Even first graders have a basic sense of what expository (nonfiction) text is (Duthie, 1994; Pappas, 1991, 1993) and how it can relate to their interests and needs. Whether they are concerned with frogs, farms, or sick cats, they know that there are written texts where they can go to learn.

Preschool teachers may begin with attractive posters and with simple factual books that include vivid pictures and a sentence or two of text per page. On the kindergarten level simple science books, biographies, guidebooks, and photo essays can be found (see Tompkins, 2012), teaching children how tadpoles swim, how to select healthy breakfast food, or how crayons are made. Older, more experienced children (particularly advanced readers) can learn to read newspapers, children's magazines, and how-to books.

As children become more experienced with expository texts, teachers and SLPs can begin pointing out ways they are structured in order to treat different kinds of subjects. For example, most biographies are organized in a sequence that allows readers to follow the passage of time. Healthy breakfast food may be compared to unhealthy options so that readers can easily understand changes that would improve their health. Different aspects of physical features and habitats of tadpoles might be treated for a descriptive structure. Later in the chapter some ways for teaching about these and other structures are discussed in detail.

Purposes for Using Expository Texts

When children develop interest in and ability to work with expository texts, they are preparing for success that will extend throughout their school experience. Despite traditional teacher apprehension that expository texts will be too difficult, research has shown that young children are capable of comprehending and learning from expository texts (Duke, 2000; Pearson & Duke, 2002; Williams, Hall, & Lauer, 2004) and of developing enhanced abilities through using them. Expository texts are designed to support children's content knowledge and to allow for opportunities to extend comprehension skills, even at an early age (Culatta, Hall-Kenyon, & Black, 2010).

Supporting Children's Content Knowledge

Children's natural curiosity about their world makes it easy to stimulate their interest in reading and talking about subjects that interest them (Neuman & Dickinson, 2001). Expository texts can be used to introduce children to new subject matter or to expand what they already know from prior experience. For example, some children may have seen frogs (or pictures of frogs) living on land or in the water, and teachers can find simply written but exciting, colorful expository books giving additional information about frogs: for example *Frogs*, one of the National Geographic early readers (Carney, 2009).

As children become interested in finding information, they can also become aware that different authors treat subjects in different ways. When her first graders were excited about what they had learned about *Whales* from the book with that title by Gail Gibbons (1991), Duthie (1994) read to them a book also titled *Whales* by Simon (1989) and another by Martin (1988). These young children surprised the teacher by how quickly they noticed facts and features that were the same and different in these books. As they become older, children will learn to locate information in several sources and further develop their abilities to add and blend new information with their existing knowledge. *Frogs* is also a popular title for books on a kindergarten–first grade level, with lively, beautifully illustrated *Frogs* titles by Time for Kids Science Scoops (Satterfield, 2006) and Scholastic (MacLulich, 1996), among many.

Even in learning that occurs from observation or hands-on experience, such as preparing a "home" for a classroom frog, information students gain from expository texts can prepare them for further experiential learning. If the classroom frog is to be observed as a science project, the teacher or SLP might help the children make a list of questions they would like to learn about and anticipate what they think they will observe. After the observation, the class may discuss what they observed and talk about the things they still wonder about. Written expository texts may be created by having children dictate (preschool) or write (early grade) science "logs" or journals. In addition to comparing what they see to what they have read, they may compare class observations to their personal experiences on topics like caring for pets. Group logs can be compiled as a shared or interactive writing experience.

Extending Comprehension Skills

Children who do not begin to receive instruction in text comprehension at the preschool level may struggle with comprehension tasks later in school (Catts, 1997) when information density is increased (Gajria, Jitendra, Sood, & Sacks, 2007) and text structure is more complex. Even young children sense differences between narrative and expository texts. Pappas (1991, 1993) found that kindergarten children who pretended to read both storybooks and informational books did so differently. Children in Christine Duthie's first grade class concluded during a discussion that "nonfiction teaches us" (1994, p. 588). By first and second grades children are exposed to increasing numbers of expository texts, including content area books related to the curriculum, informational trade books, and children's current events newsletters (Culatta, Horn, & Merritt, 1998). To work effectively with these materials, they need to be able to recognize different ways texts can be organized and to notice relationships and arrangements of ideas.

Many children who do not have strong language skills and adequate text comprehension strategies encounter what some educators refer to as "the fourth grade slump," when the emphasis shifts from learning to read to reading to learn (Otto & White, 1982; Westby, 1985), and expository texts become a dominant aspect of curricula (Alvermann & Moore, 1991; Chall, 1983). By this time most children have had plenty of experience with narrative texts and have developed skill sets for comprehending them. But if they have not had adequate experience with expository texts, they do not have the complex skill sets necessary to handle striking differences in structure and vocabulary as well as cognitive complexity (Gajria et al., 2007; Ogle & Blachowicz, 2002) when informational materials supersede narratives in much of their school experience.

To develop skill sets for expository reading, children need continual exposure to and instruction for dealing with expository text demands (Pappas, 1991). Knowledge of a genre requires substantial experience with it (Dreher & Gray, 2009; Duke, 2000). Students need instruction and shared experiences with quality texts, including opportunities for reading, writing, and discussion (Duke & Pearson, 2002). Additionally, if expository materials are made available in reading corners and classroom libraries, children can increase their exposure by the choices they make when time is available to them for free reading. Choices from a variety of expository materials (including children's dictionaries, visual reference books, brochures etc.) are particularly useful, as children need to recognize and use different types of expository texts (Alvermann & Moore, 1991; Pearson & Duke, 2002) (Figure 9–2).

Oral Exposition as a Bridge

Generally exposition is taught in terms of written text. However, "oral productions can be functionally equivalent to written productions, allowing skill transfer" (Ukrainetz, 2006b). In giving explanations [and other forms of expository information], young children

Figure 9–2. Expository books need to be made available with others in a classroom library so that children will have exposure by choice as well as by teacher plan.

depend heavily on supported conversation because they lack extensive knowledge on many topics (Ninio & Snow, 1996). But they do explore expository topics in tandem with supportive adults. For example, Snow and Kurland (1995) found that of 68 mother and five-year-old dyads who were given magnets and varied objects to play with, 62 "engaged in some interactive 'science process talk'" (as cited in Ninio & Snow, 1996, p. 188). Children commonly use "primitive explanations" in their early speech that develop through supported conversation; however, these do not become effective in a practical sense until conversational practice has honed students' skills (Ninio & Snow, 1996, p. 189).

Supported oral exposition, although helpful to all children, is of particular value to those with language difficulties. Ukrainetz (2006b) recommended that SLPs begin expository work with pre-schoolers by using conversation to scaffold a child into supplying details to develop an expository topic (e.g., "Why is your turtle a good pet for you?" "What do you feed it?" "Is it hard to keep its tank clean?"). Ukrainetz added that in a small group peers may suggest details as well ("Turtles don't jump around like frogs"). Ukrainetz suggested that the SLP model connected discourse by supplying connectives and adapting sequence. ("You say turtles are good pets *because* they don't jump around too much *and* they eat almost anything. *Also*, turtles make good pets because it's easy to keep the tank clean.")

In the process of exposing children to factual books and other written expository texts, teachers should blend their own oral expository content with written text that is read or told. Explanations and additions to texts read, class experiments, and other shared experiences are some ways this may be done.

Strategies for Dealing with Expository Content

Processes and strategies involved in young children's exposure to and instruction for expository texts vary greatly. Some experiences may be designed primarily to teach content, so content will be the first consideration in selecting texts, planning lessons, preparing materials, and delivering instruction. Other experiences may center on processes of thinking, reasoning, or problem solving; thus, the teacher will give particular consideration to pattern(s) of organization or thought and will teach these patterns explicitly, demonstrating how they guide content. For the purposes of this chapter, content and structure are handled separately, although these considerations are in reality variable and interactive. Content issues are considered first, followed by structural/organizational matters.

The content of a text—its themes, ideas, facts, and development—must be comprehensible to students. The more familiar the content is and the more closely it aligns with children's prior knowledge, the more appropriate it will be for engaging student interest and developing both content knowledge and expository text skills. If the children cannot find personal connections to the material, they may lack interest in the text. If a text contains too much new content and unfamiliar language, they may have difficulty with comprehension.

Children's Prior Interest, Knowledge, and Experience

The context for an experience with expository text begins with students' prior interest and knowledge concerning the topic. Children's natural curiosity is enhanced when personal connections can be made.

Some expository texts introduce the sort of information for which the class will have little background knowledge to which a teacher can directly relate new content. If a text contains too much new content or content too abstract or too far outside most of the children's experience, the teacher may need to use a variety of strategies to allow for the unfamiliarity and/or abstract nature of the information.

Connecting to Common Experiences

Relating information in expository texts to children's own experiences gives them a concrete basis for making meaning. Many of the children will have seen common animals like frogs or turtles (or pictures or movies of them), and a few might have had these animals as pets of their own. They need opportunities to call up their experiences (including stories and documentary videos) and share them. If a turtle is being added to the science table, the teacher can encourage children to tell where and when they have seen turtles and describe them. Children with older siblings who have observed or learned about turtles in their school classes might be eager to share some of knowledge they have picked up in advance. The teacher should emphasize experiences that a large number of children have had or have likely had in order to help all children participate in the discussion and gain new understanding by extending their prior knowledge and experiences.

Providing Experiences

When practical, teachers should attempt to arrange for shared experiences as they prepare the children for expository texts on a topic. A relevant nature walk is a valuable experience if children are properly prepared and are asked to reflect on their observations afterward. If circumstances and resources allow, a field trip to a pond or lake, a nature preserve, a sea life display, a zoo, or a museum can sometimes be arranged. A television documentary on DVD may be used to show turtles in a variety of environments, and YouTube includes many interesting clips showing turtles. A live turtle can make its appearance in the science area before the turtle texts become part of the unit (if "hands on" includes only gentle hands — a few at a time). In small groups children can observe and talk about the way the animal moves, eats, goes into and out of its shell etc. After such multisensory experiences, children are ready to listen with greater interest to picture books describing lives or habitats of turtles. Some additional experiences that may be shared are included in Table 9–1.

Kindergarten and first grade students can draw and write about what they observe (Figure 9–3), or they can engage in composing a shared group expository writing on chart paper. Younger children should have opportunities to create oral expository texts by discussing what they have seen and felt.

Ways to Clarify Content

Expository texts are by nature more abstract than stories, as they deal with general facts rather than specific events (Ukrainetz, 2006b). Thus, they depend more on language to convey a wider variety of information, putting higher cognitive and linguistic demands on preschool and primary grade children. Many will have difficulty understanding and talking about situations and events

Table 9–1. Experiences Teachers Can Provide to Help Children Relate to Expository Information: An Example from Science

Strategy	Purpose	Sample Applications
Active experience	Produces shared knowledge; generates shared enthusiasm	Provide field trips, science table, classroom pets, visitors, artifacts from other cultures, documentaries (public television, etc.), role plays, hands-on materials related to a unit theme, materials to create props for instructional activities.
Photographs	Allows children to *see* what exists in nature and through special effects to examine particular aspects	Provide natural photographs, abundantly available in books and magazines (e.g., *National Geographic*) and on the Internet. Allow children to see animals (and other phenomena) in motion through video footage, which can be paused frequently for children to talk about their impressions and teachers to link what children are seeing with what they have read and are reading in expository texts. Internet materials can be zoomed in and out to examine and emphasize small details.
Simulation	Helps children experience something comparable with their senses	Arrange for children to sit in big chairs as they work on small desks so they can feel how it is to be out of their usual environment; play a game where some children represent frogs' enemies (e.g., birds, fish, reptiles) and other children represent frogs that try to protect themselves with camouflage to "hide" or with "poison" on their brightly colored "skin" to prevent from being touched; use Internet simulations to enable students to vicariously participate in experiments.
Personal Narrative	Portrays expository content in real-world settings	Teachers, SLPs, parents, or other special guests relate their own experiences with content children have been learning: may range from being bit by a snapping turtle to camping or fishing expeditions where several target animals were observed, to having worked with wildlife exhibits at a museum.

Figure 9–3. A child shares what she has drawn and written about a nature walk.

that are removed in time and space or are difficult to visualize. The capacity to acquire information only through language, referred to as *decontextualized language ability*, is important to capabilities children need to develop with academic language (Blank, Rose, & Berlin, 1978). Specific instruction and practice should be provided for young children in dealing with both the kinds of information they will find in expository texts and the language they need to explore and express it.

Providing Analogies to Everyday Objects and Experiences

For children who have never watched a frog move, a frog's swimming process may be difficult to understand. The book *Frogs and Toads* (Petty, 1985) explains, "Its powerful back legs with webbed feet are also good for swimming" (p. 14). The SLP or teacher might show swim fins to compare to these weblike feet in the way they enable a swimmer to move fast in the water.

Scaffolding

As they learn to deal with the varied content of expository texts, students will require some scaffolding from the teacher and SLP. Differences in students' backgrounds and experiences, as well as vocabulary and basic language processing skills, affect their ability to follow and understand factual information more than their ability to deal with narratives, with which they are more familiar. In some classes small group scaffolding is necessary before and/ or after an expository text is treated by the class.

Scaffolding involves a combination of "strategic support" provided by the SLP or teacher and "active involvement" in the responses of the student(s) (Ukrainetz, 2006a, p.18). Ideally the students' active involvement develops into an ability to gradually assume more control of the cognitive process, a goal sometimes represented by an image of "handing over" the skill (Ukrainetz, 2006a, p. 18). Varying levels of scaffolding for expository materials can be provided during large group, small group or one-on-one instruction (Friend, Cook, Hurley-Chamberlain, & Shamberger, 2010; Scruggs, Mastropieri, & McDuffie, 2007; Sileo, 2011).

Modeling Ways to Think About Expository Content

Ukrainetz and Ross (2006) have pointed out that "SLPs are particularly adept at finding ways to bypass limited reading to allow for high-level language exchanges" (p. 520). If some children have difficulty following language-based modeling of a reasoning sequence, the SLP might want to provide an experience sometimes referred to as "mental modeling" (Nettles, 2006, p. 226), working in tandem with the students at putting their thoughts and thought processes into words (Gillam, Fargo, & Robertson, 2009). For example, for children who are not accustomed to thinking with analogies, the teacher might demonstrate how to reason through the frog foot–swim fin comparison:

A frog's foot isn't really a swim fin. You can't take it off the frog and strap it on your own foot. But when I look at the picture of the frog's foot, I can see that it's long compared to the rest of the frog, and it gradually gets wider. There are flat pieces of skin between the frog's toes [shows picture—e.g., Satterfield, 2006, pp. 8–9; Zoehfeld, 2010, p. 25]. When I look at the swim fin, I can see that it makes the swimmer's foot longer, and it gradually gets wider too. This one has ridges between flatter pieces like the skin between the frog's toes [shows swim fin and lets children run their fingers over it]. I know that swim fins help me move faster in the water. So since frogs' feet are built like swim fins, I can tell that their feet help them move faster in the water too.

When teachers take children through the processes that fill in implied information, they use modeling to work with students' weaknesses in inferencing as well as overall comprehension (Silliman, Bahr, Beasman, & Wilkinson, 2000). They may model inferencing through the process of thinking aloud. Also, as students experience the process and participate in the conversations, the teacher may ask them how they figured something out (Gunning, 2000) or urge them to explain their idea further.

Guiding with Questions

Questions with accompanying instructional conversation can be adapted to a wide variety of student contexts, including large groups, small groups, or individuals. Though we may tend to associate question asking with evaluating students' understanding, questioning is also a valuable way to facilitate learning (Nettles, 2006), particularly where expository texts are concerned.

Young children often have difficulty distinguishing and remembering the main ideas in an expository selection, and careful small group questioning can help them in doing this (Gunning, 2000). Such questions take place during the reading process and are compatible with it, and they focus children's thinking onto the text (Nettles, 2006). For example, *From Tadpole to Frog* (Zoehfled, 2011) recounts with simple text and vivid pictures the life cycle of the frog, from egg to adult. Simple questions can be used to guide the children through the developmental cycle: "What does the picture show us?" "In this next stage, what do you see that is different?" "How is the tadpole changing now?" The questions keep students' minds on changes and progression so they can provide answers. Children also learn to anticipate that some factual books tell how things and events change over time.

A book titled *Frogs* (Maclulich, 1996), produced by the Australian Museum, introduces young children to a wide variety of frogs. In the section of the book showing different frog habitats, the teacher or SLP can use questions to help the children to interpret the pictures and figure out the extent of the differences in places frogs live: "We just saw a frog in a pond. Well, this certainly isn't a pond. Where does this frog live?" "This frog is sitting in a hole surrounded by brown dirt, with no water in sight. Where do you think it lives?" "The desert frog is brown, and the forest and pond frogs shown here are green. How would the color help to protect the frog from its enemies?"

Inferential questions scaffold children through the process of making inferences, teaching children to "read between the lines" (Nettles, 2006). Generally this requires relating the text to past knowledge and experiences in order to figure out what has been left out (Ukrainetz, 2006b). Many children with language problems have particular difficulty with inferencing and will need specific practice with the process, including concrete, visual references. For example, the simple but appealing book *Sturdy Turtles* (Martin-James, 2000) informs the children that turtles have no teeth but must tear their food with their sharp beaks. It mentions that the mouth has hard edges, but says no more about the eating process. There is a photograph in the book that shows a turtle with a large worm half way out of its mouth. The book doesn't mention how food is further broken down. By asking careful questions and perhaps adding a demonstration, the instructor can lead the children to infer what happens. "What does the book say the turtle's mouth is like?" "Would the worm be hard or soft?" If I were to pull something soft between two hard edges, like the top and the bottom of the turtle's jaw, what might happen? The instructor shows a large shell or other object with two hard surfaces and invites the children to share their ideas. If children do not infer the answer at this point, the instructor can pull a piece of soft lunchmeat between the surfaces or use the objects to "chomp" down on the meat. "What is happening to this soft piece of meat?" "Could a turtle swallow it now?"

Adjustments for Linguistic Complexity

On preschool through first grade levels, narrative language is basically quite familiar. Stories, either written or strictly oral, involve concrete nouns and active verbs, with an occasional foray into feelings and emotions. However, many expository texts require language that is more complex in structure and vocabulary. Although the amount of text may be limited, expository concepts tend to require sentence structures that children are not accustomed to processing within a text, and the teacher may need to repeat and reword difficult passages. Vocabulary is more advanced, and exploring words together can be an interesting as well as thoughtful process.

Introducing Language Differences

With preschool children, SLPs and teachers do a lot of paraphrasing and summarizing rather than extensive direct reading of expository texts. But classes of kindergarten and first grade children may be ready to deal with some of the differences in language used in different types of texts, particularly as they are beginning to write some factual pieces themselves (science or math journals, procedural texts, etc.).

A teacher or SLP can create lists, charts, and big books using expository content and language to be presented and discussed, particularly in small groups. Having the children do a group composition of a similar chart or a big book or "report" completes the pattern of "modeling plus evoked production strategies" that some researchers (e.g., Cirrin & Gillam 2008) have found effective for helping children get a feel for language structures. Children learn language structures by experiencing them. Additionally, as the SLP (or other member of the instructional team) reads texts with students who are struggling, he may want to stop frequently on individual words to talk about them (Justice & Ezell, 2004; Justice, Kaderavek, Fan, Sofka, & Hunt, 2009) and comment on ways they are used.

Paraphrasing

Linguistic complexity can be adapted by paraphrasing parts of a text, either in a large or small group context. In addition to simplifying the syntax (and often the content), teachers can construct a paraphrase to provide redundancy—repetition that gives children a second chance to understand a concept or relationship between ideas more completely. The SLP or teacher may add brief explanations, stop to define a word, or fill in missing information.

For example, the big book *Keeping Warm, Keeping Cool* (Cutting & Cutting, 1993) explains how snails stay warm: "Snails find cracks and crevices in rocks to hide in. They draw their bodies into their shells and close up the opening with slime" (p. 11). An SLP might paraphrase in simpler language: "To keep themselves warm, snails climb into small openings in rocks. Then they pull themselves into their shells. They use slime to cover up the small space that is still open." If she wanted to help the children interpret *crevices*, she might say, " . . . climb into cracks and slightly bigger openings called *crevices*." Additional information might be included: "Snail shells cannot close up completely enough to protect the snail. So snails have to cover up to keep cold out as well as protect themselves from their enemies." As children tend to enjoy elaborating words like *slime*, the teacher or SLP might want to add words like *slippery* and *gooey*—to help them remember, of course.

Vocabulary Development

The size and variety of a student's vocabulary is important to success with almost any curricular content or activity (Nelson & Van Meter, 2006, p. 97). Children are, of course, much more likely to learn and retain things they value. In a classroom culture that values words, the classmates and instructors provide an authentic appreciative audience for interesting new words students understand and are able to use (Nelson & Van Meter, 2006). This can be particularly important for the words students are learning in conjunction with expository texts. Not only are these words less familiar, longer, and harder to read (Nettles, (2007), sometimes they just look different from the words children encounter in storybooks. If learning these words is treated as an accomplishment that students want to share, then students are more likely to put forth the greater effort that may be required to learn them.

Learning words found in expository texts has important benefits for and beyond comprehension of specific texts. Neuman and

Dwyer (2009, p. 384) acknowledged that "a rich foundation of vocabulary knowledge" is critical to children's reading comprehension. The use of the word *knowledge* is significant; the authors continued, "[V]ocabulary is more than words. It is knowledge. To know a word's meaning is to know what a word represents" (p. 384). These authors further noted that as children learn word meanings they become aware of the "network of concepts," the "rich interconnection of knowledge" that makes text meaningful. Thus teachers and SLPs need to guide children in making these connections and to introduce varied contexts and applications for the words (Kindle, 2010). Without the richness of contexts and applications, students do not gain the deep conceptual knowledge that should be associated with words (Beck, McKeown, & Kucan, 2002). They are merely learning *labels* (Gunning, 2000), not language. These rich associations make students more aware of new words and thus more able to discern their features, use them, and relate them to other words they encounter (Nelson & Van Meter, 2006).

Simple child-friendly definitions and explanations are essential (Beck, McKeown, & Kucan (2002). For example, page 15 of *Frogs and Toads* (Petty, 1985) says that a frog needs to keep its skin *moist*: a new word to many preschool children. "*Moist* means just a very little bit wet" may not be a very scientific or poetic definition, but it uses common child language to get an idea across. Concrete experiences can be added. If the teacher uses a spray bottle that creates a very fine mist, the children can experience a "moist hand." A cloth that has been wet and is almost dry will also use sensory involvement to make the concept quite clear. Table 9–2 shows some additional ways that new words can be explained to help children form associations and make applications relevant to other content they will encounter.

Multiple exposures to words in a variety of contexts help children to have a better understanding of meaning and usage; some authors recommend at least five usages in a week (Nelson & Van Meter, 2006). Thus teachers and SLPs should find other opportunities to use the word *moist* in their classroom.

Vocabulary words should be taught in meaningful contexts (Nelson & Van Meter, 2006) in relation to students' learning, not from isolated lists. After discussing the frog's "moist" skin, students might look at other moist pond creatures; they might also feel with their hands the moist ground in which plants in the pond habi-

Table 9–2. Ways of Helping Children with Vocabulary Encountered in Expository Instruction

Method	Examples
Comparison/ contrast	To explain *moist* by comparison/contrast, the SLP or teacher may pass around three pieces of fabric: one that is *wet*, one that is *dry*, and one that is *moist*, encouraging the children to describe how each one feels to them.
Associations	The SLP or teacher may show and discuss objects and pictures representing things the children are familiar with that are typically moist: e.g., a damp sponge, a piece of cheese, freshly washed berries. They may recall that frogs usually live by ponds, swamps, or lakes, where their skin is naturally moist.
Multiple examples	The children may recall times that their own skin is moist: e.g., after they have mostly dried off after a bath, when they have spilled a drink and their mom can't get their shirt quite completely dry, when they have been sweaty after sitting in the hot sun.
Words or phrases in context.	If there is a frog in the class science area, the teacher can show the frog in its tank and explain how she has provided for it to keep its skin moist. The group may look at pictures of frogs in natural habitats where it is easy for them to keep their skin moist or desert habitats where they go underground for moisture.

tat grow and thrive. In a completely different context, a member of the instructional team might ask a child to "please bring me a moist paper towel to clean the turtle's tank," and the students could brainstorm other moist things that they can find in their classroom or in their homes.

Children with language difficulties need more exposure to new vocabulary in order to learn the words and use them easily. Bunce (2006) recommended ten exposures in contrast to the four or five needed for typically developing peers. But merely increasing numbers is not sufficient. Researchers praise naturalistic classroom settings with an environment that stimulates language use (Bunce, 2008; Bunce & Watkins, 1995). Evidence has shown that when

SLPs collaborate with teachers in planning large group instruction, activities can be adjusted to ensure that vocabulary development of children with language difficulties can be improved, even as the class remains together. Additionally, the SLP may give small groups of children with language problems additional exposure and practice with the words at stations or in small groups without removing them from the classroom. Peers can provide some of the needed exposure and practice (Nelson & Van Meter, 2006). Some vocabulary games, especially playful ones, provide learning reinforcement as well as making words fun. Dramatic play can also be set up to provide opportunities for the use of targets (Bunce, 2008): For example, a pretend pet store gives peers plenty of opportunities to use words they have learned from expository texts about animals.

Strategies for Dealing with Organization/Structure

The structure of a text refers to its overall pattern of organization: the highest or broadest level of connection among main ideas (Meyer & Rice, 1984). After children become familiar with various relationships common among ideas in expository texts, they can begin noticing how those ideas become patterns by which text is organized and sequenced (Hall, Sabey, & McClellan, 2005; Williams, Hall, Lauer, Stafford, DeSisto, & deCani, 2005). Becoming aware of text structure is an important component of children's instruction in expository text comprehension (Englert & Thomas, 1987; Meyer, 1975; Meyer & Freedle, 1984) and information retrieval.

   Five structural patterns are commonly found among texts used in schools: sequence, problem-solution, compare-contrast, cause-effect, and description. Some texts combine patterns. Being able to identify the structure of a piece can also be very important in helping children to recognize the options available when they begin organizing expository writing of their own.

   Understanding and recognizing text signals, such as headings and particular words that signal the organization of the text, are also important when teaching children to comprehend expository text. Children who are not familiar with these features may skip over them or not know how to use them to improve their understanding of the text. Ukrainetz and Ross (2006) noted that the literature specifies that teachers should use "[e]xplicit, systematic attention to text structure and features that indicate how ideas are related to one another" (p. 517).

Signs and Signals

Headings and signal words/phrases provide cues and scaffolds that can be discerned by many children of kindergarten age and above. Teachers and SLPs need to consider children's individual levels in selecting whether and how these strategies should be used.

Using Headings as a Guide

Children can look for visual signals to help them in understanding what they read. An expository text with a clear structure may provide visual clues to the relationship and the logical structure/ sequence of the content. The most common of these visual aids, headings, are signalizing devices that early grade children can easily notice (Ukrainetz, 2006b) and use. Particularly with computer presence and Internet access in so many homes, a large number of children are accustomed to seeing headings along with other visual symbols and indicators: Headings for them are part of the "look" common for written texts. They are capable of learning that headings are also part of the way texts should be read. Headings that have been set up correctly can help them locate information they need and sometimes even provide a guide to understanding the overall text structure.

Locating Specific Information. If children are interested in specific information, headings can help them locate it more easily. In introducing the headings, the teacher might ask the children what they would like to learn about and show them how the headings can help them locate that information. For example, *Discovering Frogs and Toads*, by Mike Linley (1986), from the *Discovering Nature* series for young children, has headings that accurately indicate groupings of information: "Where Frogs and Toads Live," "The Life History of Frogs and Toads," "Food and Feeding," "Enemies and Defense," and "How to Keep Frogs and Toads." If the children are wondering what to feed the frog on the science table, the headings for the third and fifth sections can help them find what they need. Information within these sections is simple and easy to follow. However teachers and SLPs need to be familiar with the book to be sure that the headings are not deceptive in indicating what each section will cover.

Discerning Structure. In some big books or other large texts the teacher can read through headings with the children in advance to help them get a feeling for what the structure will be and then can pause to point out the structure as they read together. But since some authors and publishers of children's books are not careful with headings, teachers need to preview headings carefully, focusing on structure, before relying on a particular book for this kind of lesson.

For example, if a text exemplifies problems that may cause frogs to become extinct (loss of wetlands, pesticides killing the bugs frogs eat) and solutions for these problems (designating protected areas, preventing development in certain natural habitats) and the headings clearly signal the problem/solution organization, a teacher or SLP can use the headings to call attention to this organizational pattern. However, if the headings preview content without any reference to relationships, then an instructor should not use them in teaching organization unless he breaks the text down into smaller sections or superimposes a structure on the whole. For example, *The Life Cycle of a Frog* (Kalman, Smithyman, & Rouse, 2002) is a mixed text structure, in which one section has a fairly clear sequential organization ("What Is a Life Cycle"), and other sections have different patterns: description ("Facinating Frogs") and problem/solution ("Surviving Winter"). Some sections have organizations that are difficult to detect (e.g., "Floating Eggs"). If using this book the SLP or teacher would likely want to map the sections with the clear organizational patterns separately, especially when children are first learning to identify text structure.

If an SLP or teacher has difficulty finding a simple book with satisfactory headings for his purposes that is large enough to be easily seen by the target group of children, he can create a big book or newsletter article with headings to show the children. Some children's magazines have headings that can be used for illustration as well. Or the SLP or teacher can create headings to outline the organization of a poorly headed text that is being discussed.

Recognizing and Using Signal Words and Phrases

Signal words and phrases do not stand out in large, varied, or colored print as headings do, but they also indicate what kind of information is coming up and how it is related to what went before (Ukrainetz, 2006b). For example, words such as *same, different, alike,* and *in comparison* signal a compare/contrast structure; similarly, words such as *first, second, third, next,* or *then* signal a sequence. Children can learn to recognize and use these words and phrases in their own early writing (Meyer & Poon, 2001; Williams et al., 2005). Table 9–3 gives some signal words that are common in expository structures.

Gail Tompkins (2012) has suggested that teachers tell children that "authors use cue words as a 'secret code' to signal the structures" (p. 204). Thus a teacher or SLP might use a treasure hunt or a detective game to involve students in finding the words that relate sections of an organizational pattern, letting the reader know

Table 9–3. Some Common Signal Words

Clue	Words and Phrases
Description: A new idea or even a new subject is coming.	*Also, another, in addition, for example*
Sequence: Another event or step in a process is coming.	*Before, after, later, then, meanwhile, first (second, third,* etc.*), then*
Problem-solution: Something coming will take care of the problem.	*Problem, difficulty, challenge, solve, solution, ask, find, figure out, why, so*
Compare-contrast: Something is like or different from something else.	*Like, alike, same as, different, contrast, opposite, but, on the other hand*
Cause-effect: Something made something else happen.	*Because, reason why, therefore, then, effect, cause, result, so*

where to go and what to anticipate. An analogy using traffic signals might also be used. The goal is to help children become aware of how signal words and phrases work, what some of the most common ones are, and how signals can make something easier to read by showing its structure and indicating relationships among the major ideas.

An easy and obvious text can be a good beginning. During the unit on pond animals, a teacher of young children might introduce her students to signal words with *Turtle Day* by Douglas Florian (1989), a simple picture book on a pre-reading level with a very clear problem-solution relationship. The book begins, "Early in the morning Turtle woke up. It was dark inside his shell so he stuck his head out." There is a problem (darkness) and a solution (putting his head out). The word *so* signals the relationship. The book continues, "Turtle was cold, *so* he sunned on a log. Turtle was hungry *so* he ate a large leaf." The book is a series of problems followed by solutions. After the first page, the top part of each page has a solution for the last problem, and the bottom of the page presents a new problem—opposite a large drawing of a turtle emerging from his solved problem. The repetition of the pattern emphasizes it and the word that clues it, and the attractive illustrations encourage the children to predict how each problem will be solved on the following page.

Follow-up activities are sometimes necessary in helping young children recognize relationships. For example, a problem-solution game might follow *Turtle Day* in which the teacher repeats each problem (i.e., "Turtle saw a big fish SO") and the children act out the solution (scrambling out of the water). The teacher may reiterate or emphasize the solution if desired. Thus children internalize the problem/solution pattern and the linking word. Visual representations of organization can be very useful in helping children sense that there is a pattern and there is probably a reason for it. Figure 9–4 represents the first few problem-solution situations from *Turtle Day.*

Though not all problem/solution patterns are this simple and explicit, children learn from *Turtle Day* and its chart that when a problem is expressed, they can anticipate that a solution will come, and that words like *so* are a cue to help them to identify what it is.

With a little more practice children can learn to recognize cues that are not so obvious or so repetitive. *Frogs and Toads* (Schultz,

1999) is developed with a sequence, another common pattern in expository texts for children. The items involved in the sequence are shown in Figure 9–5 along with some signal words that might be used in discussing it.

The concept of signals may be easy for some children to understand, less easy for others. Comparing simple signal words to signals common in the children's experience may be a helpful memory device. For example, yellow diamond-shaped signs are often placed preceding road conditions that require extra care: a tricky curve, a moose crossing, etc. They help us anticipate conditions/situations that are coming up. Signal words also tell us of how things are

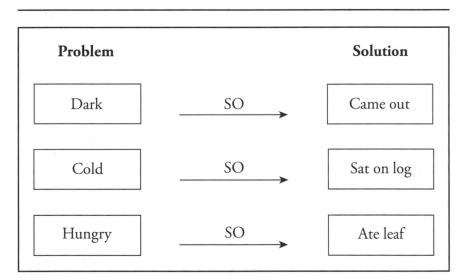

Figure 9–4. A simple chart to help young children understand how problem-solution relationships are developed in *Turtle Day* (Florian, 1989). The book and chart are on preschool level.

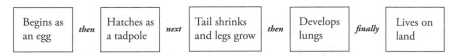

Figure 9–5. A graphic showing how "signals" are used to link happenings in time sequences in *Frogs and Toads* (Schultz, 1999). The book and graphic are on kindergarten level.

going to come together and what kinds of relationships we will find. Diamond-shaped yellow signs or word cards can be cut from sturdy paper so they can be held up. If there is a sign with *so* while the teacher is reading *Turtle Day*, young children can take turns holding up *so* when it comes up in the story. Similarly, if the teacher is reading or paraphrasing a text with a lot of comparison, like *Frogs and Toads* (Petty, 1985), signs might feature *same, different, both*, and *but*. If the target text has few signal words, the teacher can add some when commenting on or recasting the content. For example, if a text states that frogs have large ears that help them search for food, the teacher would probably add, "This is *because* their ears hear the flies and insects they catch to eat."

Some children's expository texts do not include the signal words that teachers or SLPs want the children to learn. So adaptations may have to be made. The adult may paraphrase or recast some of the sentences, using the target words loudly and clearly. If she wishes to extend the text with oral exposition, she can identify relationships among ideas in a text, such as cause/effect or problem/solution, that require the use of specific signal words she wants to teach. Or she can compose a teacher-made big book on a topic relevant to the current unit, featuring the target organizational structure and the specific words she has planned to teach. She can also map information onto a visual organizer representing sequence, compare/contrast, problem/solution, etc., and while reviewing the chart she may emphasize the target words and pause to explain why she is using them (see Figures 9–4 and 9–5). As children become accustomed to and comfortable with signal words, the teacher or SLP can guide them and encourage them in using these words in their own emergent writing (Vukelich, Evans, & Albertson, 2003)—beginning with shared writing and gradually working toward independent expression.

Representing the Organization Graphically

Texts can be diagrammed and discussed in ways that help even young children become aware of patterns. Graphic representations make the organization of a text visual, which improves students' understanding and recall of text content (Duke & Pearson, 2002). As the graphic representation depicts relationships (Moore & Readence, 1984), it gives students a way to "map out" the text so "thinking becomes external" (Hall-Kenyon & Black, 2010, p. 342; see also Calfee & Patrick, 1995; Graves, Juel, & Graves, 2011) and concrete. The process of co-constructing the charts gets the children actively involved in both the content of the books and the reasoning process. Some teachers prefer to leave cause-effect and combined structures, along with formal argumentation, until children have had more experience. Thus examples of graphic representations for the simpler structures (sequence, problem-solution, description, and comparison-contrast) will be treated in the following section.

Some Specific Structures and Suggestions for Addressing Them

Because expository texts can have so many different purposes, they use many different structures for representing the relationships among ideas. Five structural patterns are commonly found among texts used in schools: sequence, problem-solution, compare/contrast, cause-effect, and description. Some texts combine patterns. Recognizing structure, thus discerning the relationship and sometimes predicting the sequence of high-level ideas, is important to comprehending, remembering, and retrieving information encountered in expository texts.

Representing a Sequential Organization

Examining sequential organization is easy. For example, a teacher working with a process text, such as an explanation of how to build a pond, might provide a context with the need (i.e., to provide a habitat for insects, small pond animals, and fish) and then read and/or talk about the stages involved in development. While doing this, she could write a key word or brief phrase representing each step on a card and engage children in drawing simple illustrations. Lining up the cards in the correct order, she would guide the class in reviewing the sequence: for example, (1) find water source (2) dig hole, (3) fill hole with water, (4) add gravel, (5) check water movement, (6) check and add plants, (7) watch insects and animals come, and (8) add fish. Indicating the line of cards the teacher might comment that this information is put together like a line (cf. Nettles, 2006) and possibly place a cutout line over the cards. As they go through the sequence again, the students can place sequence words (first, next, then, etc.) on the line between the cards. A shared writing that summarizes the process can then be easily co-constructed.

Helping Children Deal With Problem-Solution Texts

Problem-solution is also a fairly easy structure for children to work with, as the process of solving problems and meeting people's needs has long been an aspect of their lives and a source of conversational anecdotes and stories. To build on this real life connection, a true personal narrative can be used as a "familiar frame" (Ukrainetz, 2006b). For example, one of authors of this chapter has dealt with raccoons in the garage; another had a family experience with a duck that waddled into a museum. By merging the personal experiences of encountering and solving problems with facts about the animals (e.g., problems that raccoons can cause in a garage or difficulties involved with catching an errant mallard), the teacher or SLP eases into problems and solutions in the context of the unit theme concerning animals.

A book can then be introduced that treats content related to the current unit in a problem-solution fashion. If structure is to be taught to preschool or early kindergarten children, a simple book like *Turtle Day* (Florian, 1989), described and diagramed above in Figure 9–4, demonstrates the structure neatly and directly.

For children in first grade (or some advanced groups of kindergartners), *Sturdy Turtles* (Martin-James, 2000) provides more of a challenge in finding problem-solution relationships. It treats several needs of turtles and explains how the animals are able to meet those needs in their habitats, but needs and solutions are not clearly marked as such. The teacher or SLP might introduce the structure by remarking that the title emphasizes *sturdy*, which might give the idea that turtles are good at holding up—at surviving. Perhaps the book will show why. Students can then be guided in using their inference skills to place the need (problem) beside the solution. Figure 9–6 is an example of how this sort of imposed structure might be represented visually.

The teacher or SLP would need to scaffold the co-creation according to the children's levels and needs. From this kind of visual a group of kindergarten or first grade children can give an oral report or create an illustrated "science journal."

	Problem	**Solution**
Avoiding trouble	Predators may want to eat the turtle.	The turtle pulls into its shell.
Surviving attack	Predators may want to turn the turtle over.	The turtle turns back over using its head and strong neck.
Keeping cool	Turtles spend a lot of time in the sun.	Turtles pull into their shells, find shade, or get in the water.

Figure 9–6. A graphic teacher and children can co-construct, drawing inferences of problem-solution relationships from information given in *Sturdy Turtles* (Martin-James, 2000). The book and the inferences are on late kindergarten to first grade level.

Another problem-solution topic frequently treated in children's expository texts is the challenges pet owners face in caring for their animals. The series *Keeping Minibeasts*, published by Franklin Watts (Henwood, 1988), starts many text sections by mentioning a problem, as in the example that opens this chapter ("As frogs are short and fat and very slippery, they are very difficult to handle")—and then giving a solution (how to pick up and handle frogs). Instructions for feeding and housing frogs are presented the same way (Henwood, 1988). To create an authentic project, children could prepare a pamphlet of instructions that a pet store could distribute to customers explaining the needs of the pet and how to meet them. Students can also create a brochure that might be distributed to patrons visiting a zoo; such a brochure could focus on problems animals have related to survival in the wild (what they have to do to keep safe), ways to prevent extinction, and steps taken to protect animals that were injured. (See Ukrainetz [2006b] for additional writing ideas).

Helping Children Recognize and Work with a Descriptive Text

The most common pattern in children's expository texts is description: the pattern in which a variety of facts are given about the topic in no particular discernible sequence. Many texts written on preschool-early kindergarten level (including Level 1 in some series of leveled texts such as *Time for Kids, Scholastic Readers,* or *Reading Discovery* by Scholastic) seem to give facts in miscellaneous groupings with no subtitles or headings for guidance. But some books that are written for children who are beginning to read on their own (e.g., Time's *Science Scoops* and *National Geographic Kids*) have rudimentary headings to indicate general information categories. Taken separately, each of the sections under these headings contributes descriptions of such topics as what frogs eat, what colors and sizes they may be, and what they look like as babies. As children become capable of handling greater amounts of detail, the sections become longer and the headings are more descriptive.

The descriptive structure can be represented visually by a simple diagram with the topic in the center and the various sections branching out from it. Young children can paste "rays" on a sun. When children are ready to prepare simple reports (possibly in second or third grade), they can construct this kind of visual organizer, assigning numbers to the rays in the order they want to discuss them.

Discerning and Working with Comparison-Contrast Patterns

Comparing and/or contrasting is another organizational pattern represented frequently in children's nonfiction books. Children can begin learning about this structure by experiencing the process without a text: perhaps comparing dogs they would choose as pets, activities they should play for recess, or snack items they enjoy. Dreher and Gray (2009) suggested adding the language of comparison and contrast by using word cards that picture two items and include one or two simple compare-contrast sentences which use signal words. The visual comparison of details is supported by a few descriptive phrases, and the relationship is expressed by the signal words. The visual comparison of details is supported by a few descriptive phrases, and the relationship is expressed by the signal words. Thus children come to understand the concepts of similar and different before dealing with them in a connected text.

Since comparison-contrast details presented in many expository texts for young children tend to be concrete, a graphic organizer for this structure can be especially helpful as it "supports high-level thinking and comprehension by providing a framework for focusing on important points, rather than getting lost in myriad unimportant, unrelated details" (Graves, Juel, & Graves, 2001, p. 296). A matrix highlights a particular dimension (e.g., size, color, habitat, body covering, food) and allows children to *see* similarities and differences. The main idea of the text represents the organizational pattern (Tompkins, 2002) in this particular text structure in a way that is obvious and easy for children to recognize as they examine the comparative details.

Frogs and Toads, by Kate Petty (1985), from the *Franklin Watts First Library* series, is a simple text that preschoolers as well as kindergartners and first graders are likely to understand. It begins with a comparison structure: Early pages facing each other represent a frog on one side and a toad on the other, with appealing pictures and corresponding facts in simple vocabulary and sentence structure. Because the text is simple and the illustrations reflect the contrast along two specific dimensions (i.e., their appearance and their eggs), a matrix like that represented in Table 9–4 could be easily co-constructed by teacher and children, perhaps displayed on large chart paper or scanned and showed with a computer projector.

Texts with Mixed Structures

Many factual books written for children do not have a clear, consistent pattern of organization, but have a mixed structure, with individual sections or even paragraphs being organized according to different patterns. Some appear to have no organizational pattern at all.

Teachers and SLPs can help children deal with these texts in a number of ways. They can impose a particular structure on a text in order to clarify content or meet curricular needs. For

Table 9–4. A Sample Graphic Comparison Based on Information from the Beginning Pages of *Frogs and Toads* by Kate Petty

	Frogs	*Toads*
What they look like	Shiny skin, often green	Rough, bumpy brown skin
What their eggs are like	Jelly with little dots	Ribbons wrapped around water plants

example, if the purpose of the lesson is to help children compare the characteristics of frogs and toads, and a book is not available that presents a specific comparison, the instructor can take facts from a less structured text and compile them into a matrix that will give children a visual pattern for understanding how frogs and toads are the same and how they are different. If one text does not have enough information, the matrix can be extended with information found in one or more additional texts or furnished by the teacher.

The book discussed above, *Frogs and Toads* by Kate Petty (1985), includes both mixed and non-apparent patterns. As mentioned, the first few pages are developed by a comparison-contrast pattern that is distinct enough that it can be used (even graphically represented) as an example of this form. But then the text structure changes. In one place there are three pages about what frogs look like and live like (a descriptive pattern), followed by five pages on how frogs and toads (both, not in contrast) eat, croak, and protect themselves from danger (a second and separate descriptive pattern). The book ends with a short picture-discussion of a flying frog, followed by a comparable treatment of an exotic toad, but none of the characteristics correspond, and no comparison is indicated. Such texts are commonly referred to "messy" or "inconsiderate" (Armbruster & Anderson, 1988; Hall-Kenyon & Black, 2010). Overall, Petty's book is a rather inconsiderate text, but it is unfortunately not atypical. At times teachers may avoid dealing with portions of a mixed (or messy) text in order to focus on sections that are more tightly structured or are most critical in terms of the ideas being taught.

Beginning with the frog-toad comparison introduced in the book by Petty (1985), the teacher or SLP could scaffold kindergarten or first grade students in extending the initial diagram by including information from elsewhere in the book where the same animals are discussed but not sequenced as a comparison. First or second grade children might join the teacher in co-constructing the matrix further by adding information learned from other books or class activities. Table 9–5 extends Table 9–4 with information from another text. Teachers should be well acquainted with the book(s) as well as the interests and skill levels of the children so that they can guide and scaffold such a process smoothly.

Table 9–5. A Sample Graphic Comparison That Adds to Table 9–4 by Giving Information Taken Both from the Text and Teacher Additions

	Pond Frogs	*Common Toads*
Where they sleep in winter	In damp mud	In damp mud
What they eat	Insects	Insects
How they protect themselves	Use strong back legs to jump high and escape predators	Puff selves up with air and become too big for small predators to swallow; may have skin that poisons predators
What they do and when	Hang out around pond or other habitat during the day, hunt for food, and eat	Hide and sleep during the day under logs or stones; hunt for food and eat at night
How they see	With bulging eyes that see in all directions	With bulging eyes that see in all directions

The comparison-contrast example was chosen to illustrate these processes because it is simple and easy to follow. But similar steps can be used in adapting messy texts with any of the patterns (e.g., problems and solutions to prevent extinction of certain animals, or sequence for a schedule for feeding and caring for pets). In this way the organizational pattern or structure provides a means for understanding the relationships among ideas so that children do not need to deal with expository information in a haphazard way.

Conclusion

Although many teachers in the past have hesitated to use expository texts with children before second or third grade level, and some still do, research is showing that young children can handle expository texts and some of the techniques and conceptual relationships involved with them, as described earlier in this chapter.

Although few may be ready for online encyclopedias, young children have a natural curiosity that makes them want to learn about topics that interest them—such as animals. Texts have been created to introduce young children to a wide array of interesting subjects. Fascinating pictures (often photographs by skilled subject-area photographers) draw the children in and give them images on which to build ideas.

Because of the variation in children's background, experiences, abilities, and needs, teachers and SLPs need to select texts, choose contexts, and plan discussions and activities carefully. If some of the children are not engaged, then lessons need to be adapted, with more hands-on activities and more relevant discussion. Vocabulary, sentence structure, and word choice can be easily adapted as the teacher reads, paraphrases, or leads a discussion. The SLP or teacher can gradually introduce some of the more complex language structures found in expository texts and choose words that need further explanation or development.

Along with aspects of content and language, teachers and SLPs may want to deal appropriately with organizational features of expository texts, preparing students for more complex texts that they will be using throughout their school experience. They can teach text features as well as basic organizational patterns, such as sequence, problem/solution, description, or comparison/contrast. Such texts and activities must be chosen and scaffolded carefully according to the children's interest, attention span, and ability to deal with patterns and reasoning. Preschool, kindergarten, and first grade children can learn about, learn from, and build skills to understand expository texts—and enjoy doing so.

References

Alvermann, D. E., & Moore, D. W. (1991). Secondary school reading. In R. Barr, M. L. Kamil, P. B. Mosenthal, & P. D. Pearson (Eds.), *Handbook of reading research* (Vol. 2, pp. 951–983). New York, NY: Longman.

Armbruster, B. B., & Anderson, T. H. (1988). On selecting "considerate content area textbooks." *Remedial and Special Education, 9*(1), 47–52.

Beck, I. L., McKeown, M. G., & Kucan, L. (2002). *Bringing words to life.* New York, NY: Guilford Press.

Blank, M., Rose, S. A., & Berlin, L. (1978). *The language of learning: The preschool years.* New York, NY: Grune & Stratton.

Bunce, B. H. (2008). *Early literacy in action: The language-focused curriculum for preschool.* Baltimore, MD: Paul H. Bookes.

Bunce, B. H., & Watkins, R. V. (1995). Language intervention in a preschool classroom: Implementing a language-focused curriculum. In M. L. Rice & K. A. Wilcox, *Building a language-focused curriculum for the preschool classroom: Vol. 1. A foundation for lifelong communication* (pp. 39–71). Baltimore, MD: Paul H. Brookes.

Calfee, R. C., & Patrick, C. L. (1995). *Teach our children well: Bringing K–12 education into the 21st century.* Stanford, CA: Stanford Alumni.

Catts, H. W. (1997). The early identification of language-based reading disabilities. *Language, Speech, and Hearing Services in Schools, 28,* 86–87.

Chall, J. S. (1983). *Stages of reading development.* New York, NY: McGraw-Hill.

Chall, J. S., Jacobs, V. A., & Baldwin, L. E. (1990). *The reading crisis: Why poor children fall behind.* Cambridge, MA: Harvard University Press.

Crosbie, S., Holm, A., & Dodd, B. (2009). Cognitive flexibility in children with and without speech disorder. *Child Language Teaching and Therapy, 25,* 250–270. doi:10.1177/0265659009102990

Culatta, B., Hall-Kenyon, K. M., & Black, S. (2010). Teaching expository comprehension skills in early childhood classrooms. *Topics in Language Disorders, 30*(4), 323–338.

Culatta, B., Horn, D., & Merritt, D. (1998). Expository text: Facilitating comprehension. In D. Merritt & B. Culatta (Eds.), *Language intervention in the classroom* (pp. 215–275). San Diego, CA: Singular.

Dreher, M. J., & Gray, J. L. (2009). Compare, contrast, comprehend: Using compare-contrast text structures with ELLs in K–3 classrooms. *Reading Teacher, 63*(2), 132.

Duke, N. K. (2000). 3.6 minutes per day: The scarcity of informational texts in the first grade. *Reading Research Quarterly, 35,* 202–224.

Duke, N. K., & Pearson, P. D. (2002). Effective practices for developing reading comprehension. In A. E. Farstrup & S. J. Samuels (Eds.), *What research has to say about reading instruction* (3rd ed.). Newark, DE: International Reading Association.

Duthie, C. (1994). Nonfiction: A genre study for the primary classroom. *Language Arts, 71*(8), 588–595.

Englert, C. S., & Thomas, C. C. (1987). Sensitivity to text structure in reading and writing: A comparison between learning disabled and non-learning disabled students. *Learning Disability Quarterly, 10,* 93–105.

Friend, M, Cook, L., Hurley-Chamberlain, D., & Shamberger, C. (2010). Co-teaching: An illustration of collaboration in special education. *Journal of Educational and Psychologiocal Consultation, 20*(9), 9–27. doi:10.1080/10474410903535380

Gajria, M., Jitendra, A. K., Sood, S., & Sacks, G. (2007). Improving comprehension of expository text in students with LD: A research synthesis. *Journal of Learning Disabilities, 40*(3), 210–226.

Gillam, S. L., Fargo J. D., & Robertson, K. S. (2009, February). Comprehension of expository text: Insights gained from think-aloud data. *American Journal of Speech-Language Pathology, 18*, 82–94. doi:10.1044/1058-0360(2008/07-0074)

Graves, M. F., Juel, C., & Graves, B. B. (2001). *Teaching reading in the 21st century* (2nd ed.). Boston, MA: Allyn & Bacon.

Gunning, T. G. (2000). *Creating literacy instruction for all children* (3rd ed.). Boston, MA: Allyn & Bacon.

Hall, K. M., Sabey, B. L., & McClellan, M. (2005). Expository text comprehension: Helping primary grade teachers use expository texts to their full advantage. *Reading Psychology, 26*(3), 211–234.

Hall-Kenyon, K. M., & Black, S. (2010). Learning from expository texts: Classroom-based strategies for promoting comprehension and content knowledge in the elementary grades. *Topics in Language Disorders, 30*(4), 339–349.

Justice, L. M., & Ezell, H. K. (2004, April). Print referencing: An emergent literacy enhancement strategy and its clinical applications. *Language, Speech, and Hearing Services in Schools, 35*, 185–193.

Justice, L. M., Kaderavek, J. N., Fan, X., Sofka, A., & Hunt, A. (2009, January). Accelerating preschoolers' early literacy development through classroom-based teacher-child storybook reading and explicit print referencing. *Language, Speech, and Hearing Services in Schools, 40*, 67–85.

Kindle, K. J. (2010). Vocabulary development during read-alouds: Examining the instructional sequence. *Literacy Teaching and Learning, 14*(1,2), 65–88.

Meyer, B. J. (1975). Identification of the structure of prose and its implications for the study of reading and memory. *Journal of Reading Behavior, 7*, 7–47.

Meyer, B. J. F., & Freedle, R. O. (1984). Effects of discoiurse type on recall. *American Eduational Research Journal, 21*, 121–143.

Meyer, B. J. F., & Poon, L. W. (2001). Effects of structure training and signaling on recall of text. *Journal of Educational Psychology, 83*, 141–159.

Meyer, B. J. F., & Rice, G. E. (1984). The structure of text. In R. Barr, M. L. Kamil, P. Mosenthal, & P. E. Pearson (Eds.). *Handbook of reading research* (Vol. 1, pp. 319–352). New York, NY: Longman.

Moore, D. W., & Readence, J. E. (1984). A quantitative and qualitative review of graphic organizer research. *Journal of Educational Research, 78*(1), 11–17.

Murawski, W. W., & Dieker, L. (2008). 50 ways to keep your co-teacher: Strategies for before, during, and after co-teaching. *Teaching Exceptional Children, 40*(4), 40–48.

Nelson, N. W., & Van Meter, A. M. (2006). Finding the words: Vocabulary development for young authors. In In T. A. Ukrainetz (Ed.), *Contextualized language intervention* (pp. 95–143). Greenville, SC: Thinking Publications.

Nettles, D. H. (2006). *Comprehensive literacy instruction in today's classrooms: The whole, the parts, and the heart.* Boston, MA: Pearson.

Neuman, S. B., & Dickinson, D. K. (2001). *Handbook of early literacy research.* New York:, NY: Guilford Press.

Neuman, S. B., & Dwyer, J. (2009). Missing in action: Vocabulary instruction in Pre–K. *Reading Teacher, 62*(5), 384–492.

Ninio, A., & Snow, C. E. (1996). *Pragmatic development.* Boulder, CO: Westview Press.

Ogle, D., & Blachowicz, C. L. Z. (2002). Beyond literature circles: Helping students comprehend informational texts. In C. C. Block & M. Pressley (Eds.), *Comprehension instruction: Research-based best practice* (pp. 259–274). New York, NY: Guilford.

Otto, W., & White, S. (1982). *Reading expository material.* New York, NY: Academic Press.

Pappas, C. C. (1991). Fostering full access to literacy by including information books. *Language Arts, 68,* 449–462.

Pappas, C. C. (1993). Is narrative "primary"? Some interesting insights from kindergartners' pretend readings of stories and information books. *Journal of Reading Behavior, 25,* 97.

Pearson, P. D., & Duke, N. K. (2002). Comprehension instruction in the primary grades. In C. C. Block & M. Pressley (Eds.), *Comprehension instruction: Research-based best practices* (pp. 247–258). New York, NY: Guilford Press.

Scruggs, T. E., Mastropieri, M. A., & McDuffie, K. A. (2007). Co-teaching in inclusive classrooms: A metasynthesis of qualitative research. *Exceptional Children, 73*(4), 392–416.

Sileo, J. R. (2011). Co-teaching: Getting to know your partner. *Teaching Exceptional Children, 43*(5), 32–38.

Silliman, E. R., Bahr, R., Beasman, J., & Wilkinson, L. C. (2000, July). Scaffolds for learning to read in an inclusion classroom. *Language, Speech, and Hearing Services in Schools, 31,* 265–279.

Snow, C. E., & Kurland, B. (1995). Sticking to the point: Talk about magnets as a preparation for literacy. In D. Hicks (Ed.), *Child discourse and social learning: An interdisciplinary perspective.* New York, NY: Cambridge University Press.

Tompkins, G. E. (2002). *Language arts: Content and teaching strategies.* Upper Saddle River, NJ: Merrill Prentice Hall.

Tompkins, G. E. (2012). *Teaching writing: Balancing process and product* (6th ed.). Boston, MA: Pearson.

Ukrainetz, T. A. (2006a). Assessment and intervention within a contextualized skill framework. In T. A. Ukrainetz (Ed.), *Contextualized language intervention* (pp. 9–58). Greenville, SC: Thinking Publications.

Ukrainetz, T. A. (2006b). The many ways of exposition: A focus on discourse structure. In T. A. Ukrainetz (Ed.), *Contextualized language intervention* (pp. 247–288). Greenville, SC: Thinking Publications.

Ukrainetz, T. A., & Ross, C. L. (2006). Text comprehension: Facilitating active and strategic engagement. In T. A. Ukrainetz (Ed.), *Contextualized language intervention* (pp. 503–563). Greenville, SC: Thinking Publications.

Vukelich, C., Evans, C., & Albertson, B. (2003). Organizing expository texts: A look at possibilities. In D. M. Barone & L. M. Morrow (Eds.), *Literacy and young children: Research-based practices* (pp. 261–288). New York, NY: Guilford Press.

Westby, C. E. (1985). Learning to talk—Talking to learn: Oral/literate language differences. In C. S. Simon (Ed.), *Communication skills and classroom success.* San Diego, CA: College-Hill Press.

Williams, J. P., Hall, K. M., & Lauer, K. D. (2004). Teaching expository text structure to young at-risk learners: Building the basics of comprehension instruction. *Exceptionality, 12*(3), 129–144.

Williams, J. P., Hall, K. M., Lauer, K. D., Stafford, K. B., DeSisto, L. A., & deCani, J. S. (2005). Expository text comprehension in the primary grade classroom. *Journal of Educational Psychology, 97*(4), 538–550.

Children's Books Cited

Carney, E. (2009). *Frogs.* National Geographic Readers (Level 1). Washington, DC: National Geographic Society.

Cutting, B., & Cutting, J. (1993). *Keeping warm! Keeping cool!* Applecross.

Florian, D. (1989). *Turtle day.* New York, NY: Thomas Y. Crowell.

Gibbons, G. (1991). *Whales.* New York, NY: Holiday House.

Henwood, C. (1988). *Frogs.* New York, NY: Franklin Watts.

Kalman, B., Smithyman, K., & Rouse, B. (2002). *The life cycle of a frog.* New York, NY: Crabtree.

Linley, M. (1986). *Discovering frogs and toads.* New York, NY: Bookwright Press.

MacLulich, C. (1996). *Frogs.* New York, NY: Scholastic.

Martin-James, K. (2000). *Sturdy turtles.* Minneapolis, MN: Lerner.

Petty, K. (1985). *Frogs and toads*. New York, NY: F. Watts.
Satterfield, K. H. ((2006). *Frogs*. New York, NY: HarperCollins.
Schultz, E. (1999). *Frogs and toads*. New York, NY: Scholastic.
Zoehfeld, K.W. (2011). *From d to frog*. New York, NY: Scholastic.

Chapter 10

Working with Parents: Ways to Involve Parents in Early Literacy at Home and at School

*Gary Eldon Bingham, Byran Korth,
and Esther Marshall*

Parents are powerful contributors to their children's literacy and language development. As children's first teachers, parents are critical in communicating the joy of reading and in building children's early literacy and language skills before they enter and once they are in formal schooling. Almost all parents, regardless of their cultural and social backgrounds, desire to provide positive support for their children. There are also a number of ways in which teachers can acknowledge and draw upon the role parents play, ranging from valuing parents' interactions at home to inviting parents to play a role in classroom instruction.

Over the last 50 years, researchers have used the terms *parental involvement, engagement,* and *collaboration* to characterize parents' participation in their child's education, either through home experiences or school involvement. Although these terms on the surface may appear to represent similar constructs, considerable differences exist in the way that each has been conceptualized. Traditionally, older models of school-parent "partnerships" or "parental involvement" emphasize the need for school personnel to work with parents as a means to increase children's learning in school (Epstein & Dauber, 1991; Hoover-Dempsey & Sandler, 1995). From this perspective, although parents are valued, it is often from the viewpoint that they are not involved or engaged "enough" and that schools and teachers must do more to encourage this involvement. This perspective has lead to many schools acting as one-way streets, with teachers' imparting knowledge or pushing traditional notions of literacy learning that do not value parents' and children's home experiences with digital literacies (e.g., media and televisual texts) or popular culture (Marsh, 2003). Hence, although parental involvement perspectives demonstrate that schools have long valued the contribution of parents to children's learning and school achievement, they are sometimes heavily teacher centered and controlled (Christianakis, 2011; McCarthey, 2000).

In contrast, models that are more collaborative and parent centered place particular value on parents' and children's diverse home experiences and recognize parents' significant role in their children's literacy and language development (Christianakis, 2011). As children's first teachers, parents may do a variety of activities in the home that develop children's literacy and language skills even before they begin formal schooling. Such activities build on the tenet that, regardless of their cultural and social backgrounds, parents desire to provide positive support for their children's future. However, given parents' varied cultural, educational, and life experiences, their view of literacy may not be the same as that of classroom teachers, principals, or speech language pathologists (SLPs), and they may place value on different experiences in preparing their children for school (Okagaki & Bingham, 2010). Thus educators need to understand and appreciate what parents do and what they value in order to create a context for sharing the responsibility of teaching language and literacy skills. Diverse home experiences contribute to children's varied language abilities when they enter school, which, in turn, impacts their navigation of school literacies (Heath, 1983; Au, 1998). Although the diversity of the public school population in the Unites States presents unique challenges for teachers and SLPs, it also represents a wide range of opportunities for school professionals to engage families in true school-home collaborations that value children's cultural, linguistic and social contexts and build upon the strengths and experiences that children bring to school.

This chapter examines how teachers can collaborate with parents to improve children's literacy development, while also ensuring that they value cultural and family traditions. In the first section, we consider how parents contribute to their children's literacy development and how opportunities in the home environment serve as a foundation for later learning. Next, we consider ways that teachers and SLPs can facilitate parent collaboration opportunities that build on parents' cultural models of literacy development and home literacy environments. In this section, we also examine how research on the nature of home literacy practices, such as parents' culturally situated beliefs, knowledge, and skills (i.e., funds of knowledge) can be incorporated and utilized to engage parents in family-school partnerships. Finally, we consider multiple models of parent-school collaboration that school personnel may utilize to create home, school and home/school learning opportunities for children and their families. We draw on research from both parental involvement and parental collaboration literatures in presenting best practices that have been shown to positively impact children's literacy development. Specifically, we consider how teachers and SLPs can value parental contributions in the home and how they utilize parental support in the classroom.

Recognizing Parenting Practices and Beliefs

The home is where children first encounter language and literacy (Hart & Risley, 1995; Reese, Sparks, & Leyva, 2010; Strickland, 1990). Children's literacy experiences at home matter to their literacy development before and after they begin school. Literacy-rich home environments support children's developing identity as readers regardless of other variables such as disabilities, language delays, and other differences that may positively or negatively impact children's literacy development. Literacy-rich environments also contribute to the development of children's language abilities (Crain-Thoreson & Dale, 1992; Dickinson & Tabors, 2001; Storch & Whitehurst, 2001) and early literacy skills (Bus, van Ijzendoorn, & Pellegrini, 1995; Klesius & Griffith, 1996), as well as to their motivation for and enjoyment of literacy experiences.

Children's home language and literacy experiences, however, are not alike. Considerable variation has been documented in the literature with regards to parents' own literacy experiences (e.g., how much parents read and write at home) and the opportunities they provide their children. Parents' literacy experiences in the home vary according to cultural traditions and the education opportunities of the parents (Hammer, Nimmo, Cohen, Draheim, & Johnson, 2005; Reese & Gallimore, 2000). Unfortunately, educators sometimes view variation in children's home literacy practices as a weakness or as a potential problem. When teachers fail to see traditional school-based notions of literacy learning occurring in the home, they may view children as lacking appropriate literacy experiences and parental support (Hogg, 2011). However, with raised awareness of how literacy-rich environments can vary from family to family, teachers will begin to value the role families play in helping children develop literacy skills.

Redefining Home Environments: Drawing Upon Funds of Knowledge

Although home literacy environments have traditionally been conceptualized and measured as children's access to and experiences with books and print (Bus, van Ijzendoorn, & Pellegrini, 1995; Griffin & Morrison, 1997; Sénéchal, LeFevre, Thomas, & Daley, 1998), more recent perspectives document the importance of multiple and diverse home language and literacy opportunities (see McCarthey, 2000; Purcell-Gates, Melzi, Najafi, & Orellana, 2011). For example, funds of knowledge theory and research suggest that children and their families possess knowledge, strengths, and skills that can enhance the educational process but often do not fit well within traditional notions of literacy experiences (Moll, 1992; Moll, Amanti, Neff, & Gonzales, 2005). Central to a funds of knowledge approach is the belief that homes contain multiple cultural, linguistic and cognitive resources and opportunities for children that could be used at school to increase the impact and effectiveness of classroom instruction (Moll et al., 2005). Unfortunately, for many ethnic minority children considerable discontinuity exists between cultural, home, and school contexts (Brown, Souto-Manning, & Laman, 2010). For example, although African American families may spend more time in home-based learning activities, such as conversations and interactions with their children, they may not be as likely to read storybooks with their children, a practice seen as a traditional part of a home literacy environment that is also highly valued in school (Barbarin, McCandies, Coleman, & Hill, 2005).

Researchers and practitioners have long agreed that parent-child book reading is important to children's early language abilities, although Scarborough & Dobrich (1994) demonstrate that its contribution to the variance of school literacy skills is actually relatively small. Hence, although book reading may (and we would suggest should) still be seen as a valuable home literacy skill for building oral language, other literacy activities (e.g., spending time in the home with children and engaging in mutual activities and conversations) should also be valued by teachers as a critical component of a family's funds of knowledge. This point is further illustrated in a longitudinal study of 71 families by Zimmerman and colleagues (2009) who found that children's exposure to adult language (i.e., total number of words directed at or in the vicinity of the child) in the home mattered to children's development. More important than the number of words, however, was the relation between children's participation in adult-child conversations and their language development. In other words, it was the give and take between adults and children that mattered to their language development, something that is not often measured or traditionally considered to contribute to school literacy skills. In particular, these findings may have importance for families with cultural models of literacy sharing that emphasize oral traditions of storytelling (Grace, 2004; Heath, 1989).

An additional reason to be cautious about narrow conceptualizations of home literacy activities resides in research documenting that some parents may feel uncomfortable sharing books with children or sharing books in a way prescribed by "reading professionals." For example, in their study about the implementation of a family literacy project with Latino parents, Janes and Kermani (2001) documented the challenges that Latino parents faced when trying to implement school literacy related practices that emphasized higher order thinking questions during parent-child book readings. Teaching a prescribed European-American school-based reading model to Latino parents constrained their natural reading styles with their children and, as a consequence, contributed to parents' views of reading as a punishment. Although parents' own histories with books may vary considerably, teachers can ease the pressures of school cultures on family literacy practices by encouraging parents to share literacy activities and books in relation to familiar family and community happenings, particularly in their home languages. Further, because research on Latino parents' book reading interactions reveals that parents often emphasize important moral messages and interactiveness (Perry, Kay, & Brown, 2007), teachers should seek for activities and books that emphasize these values. Understanding the interactive nature of parent-child book reading can help teachers think of ways to facilitate parents' and children's involvement with books in the home.

Recognizing the Value of Parent-Child Interactions in Book Reading

Although not all families may have cultural literacy models that value the sharing of traditional storybooks in ways consistent with school literacy practices, many families value opportunities to share books with their children. Because parent-child book reading is a socially created, interactive activity (Sulzby & Teale, 1991), the quality of joint book reading comes from the give and take that occurs between the adult and the child and support that parents or caregivers give children during interactive book reading encounters (Bingham, 2007). The importance of child participation in conversation interactions is supported by research suggesting that it is children's participation in language interactions, rather than just being talked at, that is important to their language development (see Ruston & Schwanenflugel, 2010; Zimmerman et al., 2009).

In addition to being important to children's reading skill in school (Sénéchal & LeFevere, 2002), reading together can provide the context for rich conversations between a child and parent, often going beyond the written text to create significant personal dialogue. For example, reading about all the funny, child-significant things that go wrong during Alexander's Terrible, Horrible, No Good, Very Bad Day (Viorst, 1972) can easily generate a discussion of things that upset the child and of ways to deal with them more effectively than moving to Australia (as Alexander plans). As a child becomes comfortable in these interactions, conversation is more spontaneous, and shared reading becomes a frequent, loving experience.

High quality parent-child early literacy interactions involve mutual enjoyment and emotional support (Bus & van IJzendoorn, 1997). Of no surprise to teachers and parents is that studies have found the affective quality of joint book reading interactions to have a strong influence on children's interest in books (Ortiz, Stowe, & Arnold, 2001; Sonnenschein & Munsterman, 2002), as well as on children's desire to continue in these activities (Baker, Mackler, Sonnenschein, & Serpell, 2001), with these effects being experienced by parents and children across racial/ethnic groups (Morrow & Young, 1997). Research highlights the importance of attending to the affective aspects of parent-child literacy interactions inherent in the underlying parent-child relationship. Parents ensure the quality of joint book reading by making the reading enjoyable and comprehensible to their children through help and support (Bus, 2001; Wasik & Bond, 2001). It is important that teachers and parents have conversations about things that each can do to build on the interactive nature of adult-child book reading.

Engaging and Collaborating with Parents Through Book Sharing

Whenever possible, teachers and SLPs can encourage parents to share books with their children. When considering how to encourage parents to share books with their children, teachers and SLPs should remember that parents should read to and with their children—not at them. Parents should be encouraged to point to and label pictures, ask questions, respond to children's verbalizations, and talk about the text by elaborating on ideas or connecting them to the child's personal experiences (Whitehurst et al., 1988, 1994; Neuman & Gallagher, 1994). In their research about promoting effective interactions between parents and children, Whitehurst and colleagues found that a dialogic book reading approach, in which parents are encouraged to engage in rich conversations when reading with their child, improved children's literacy skills, particularly for children from low-income households (Whitehurst et al., 1988, 1994).

In some cases, SLPs and teachers may need to provide support to parents to help them understand how both the quality and quantity of interactions during book reading are critical to a child's success. In such experiences, it is important that teachers and SLPs value parents' current approaches to sharing stories and texts with their children while providing ideas for child involvement and vocabulary learning during parent-child shared book reading experiences. Some of this information can be shared through classroom newsletters or occasional "literacy nights," where teachers and SLPs offer suggestions and/or demonstrations on some strategies that parents might use. In addition, teachers can encourage parents to model for each other and discuss ways that they share books or other texts in the home.

Because previous research demonstrates considerable variation in parents' sharing of home literacy experiences with their children within cultural groups and across different socioeconomic groups, parents' experiences should be valued and encouraged. Engaging parents in collaborative literacy interactions that value their cultural and home experiences can positively impact the quality of family-school partnerships and children's literacy development. For example, Rothstein-Fisch and colleagues (2009) found that having teachers find informal opportunities to connect with parents, such as during drop off or pick up, and redesigning curriculum to value family traditions of working together, demonstrates to parents that educators value them. In cultures where oral storytelling may be common practice, teachers can encourage parents to share stories with their children and have their children share stories at school (Goss & Barnes, 1989; Pewewardy, 2002).

One way that SLPs and teachers can be particularly encouraging of family book sharing is through providing materials to families and through valuing parental sharing of books and stories with their children. For example, in a study of low income, prekindergarten children (many of whom were dual language learners), Rowe (2011) demonstrated how sending backpacks home with children with culturally appropriate texts (see below for resources for selecting texts) and writing and coloring supplies (e.g., crayons, markers, stickers, paper, Post-its, and books) can encourage parental participation in culturally sensitive ways. Multicultural texts that were selected to go home were translated into the home language of parents who did not speak English. Parents were encouraged to share the texts with their child and to write or draw about the books in a family response journal. The results of this study show that providing parents with culturally appropriate materials helps facilitate the use of traditional school literacy activities in a way that also values the family's contributions and interests. Parents were seen drawing story elements, summarizing stories, making connections between the books and their family life, practicing writing, and creating multimodal responses. Children were co-participants in many reading and writing activities in which families demonstrated their child's comprehension and experiences with the books. As this study demonstrates, teachers and SLPs should provide multiple supports for parents' engagement in home literacy interactions that are open ended and encourage families to connect books to current funds of knowledge from family and community experience.

Creating cultural literacy backpacks is an excellent way to connect school and home literacy practices. Many resources exist for choosing appropriate multicultural texts. For example, the Web site http://papertigers.org/ contains lists of books that are culturally appropriate for children from the Pacific Rim as well as ideas of how to use such materials. Another useful Web site is the Worlds of Words at http://wowlit.org/. Because teachers may have little knowledge about all of the children's specific cultures and languages, these websites and their book lists provide a place to start. However, when teachers utilize these materials, they should encourage parent feedback on whether the books represent children's cultures in appropriate and meaningful ways.

Helping Parents Call Attention to Sounds and Print

During the last 30 years, most attention by researchers and policy makers has focused on the context of parent-child joint book reading as discussed above, a context within which parents or other caregivers read and interact with the child but likely do little explicit teaching of the alphabetic principle, phonological awareness, or writing. An increasing research base demonstrates that parents' home literacy practices that involve a focus on literacy skills (i.e., teaching children to print or read words) positively contribute to children's literacy learning above and beyond benefits of traditional book reading activities (Sénéchal et al., 1998; Sénéchal & LeFevre, 2002). However, it is likely that some parents will need teacher or SLP support in learning how to directly teach their children literacy skills. This is particularly true when these practices are not central to the parents' home literacy practices, such as using print referencing (i.e., pointing or talking about print and letters) during book reading interactions (for an example, see an intervention by Justice & Ezell, 2000).

Teachers and SLPs also need to acknowledge the myriad of other ways in which parents share and teach literacy to their children (Evans & Shaw, 2008; Gillanders & Jimenez, 2004). For example, in their qualitative study of the home literacy environments of low-income immigrants of Mexican descent, Gillanders and Jimenez (2004) found that both parents' formal (conceptualized by the authors as direct teaching activities such as letter work, writing, and reading activities) and informal literacy teaching (defined as everyday routines that may not have an explicit educational goal) contributed to kindergarten children's literacy learning and bilingual development. Informal literacy teaching occurred in these families when parents played school with their children, made lists of ingredients for a cake, and invented stories orally in Spanish before going to bed (Gillanders & Jimenez, 2004). It is important that teachers and SLPs appreciate both formal and informal literacy teaching that happens in many homes.

Research on features of books that draw children's attention to print is relevant for facilitating positive interactions that parents often have during shared book reading (Justice, Skibbe, Canning, & Lankford, 2005; Justice & Ezell, 2000, 2004). Teachers and SLPs can suggest or lend parents trade books that are designed to highlight print (e.g., books that place text in a large dialogue bubble or increase the font size). Parents are more likely to call children's attention to letters and words when the print stands out on the page. Similarly, trade books that exaggerate rhyme or alliteration patterns make it easier to focus on sound patterns. Such books should also be selected to depict a wide array of content and situations that fit within the family's cultural context and the child's specific interests, thus ensuring that book conversations can center on interesting topics and content.

Creating Home-School Connections

Teachers and SLPs should value parents and seek to create positive relationships. Efforts to develop positive relationships with parents of all students, which include consultation and support, should be the norm for teachers as well as SLPs. Although parents' participation in certain home literacy practices may relate to their social or cultural contexts, home literacy research consistently supports the belief that nurturing children's literacy is a responsibility to be shared by all who educate and care for children (Stooke, 2005). It is encouraging that preschool and early grade teachers generally value parents' contributions to their children's development and consider parent involvement "very important" in children's literacy development (Lynch, 2009a). Hence the school's efforts at promoting early literacy and preventing future problems should focus on "supporting parents in [providing] literacy-promoting activities, sensitive and responsive engagements, and age-appropriate materials that facilitate learning" (Tamis-LeMonda & Rodriguez, 2009, p. 4).

One way teachers and SLPs can support parents' efforts to engage children in appropriate and engaging literacy activities at home is to provide parents with ideas for highly engaging and interactive activities that have a range of options for participation rather than traditional worksheets. Much like the backpack book model described above, teachers and SLPs can share materials with families that encourage children to "play" together as they practice target letters, sounds, and words. For example, when working with the word family *-ag*, teachers might, as part of literacy centers, have children make a "rag bag" full of rags that they can tear, label with tags, and place in their rag bags. Children can label their rag bags and take them home to show their parents how they can drag or wag the rags to dust; tape or glue a rag to a popsicle stick or pencil to make a flag to wag; write the word *rag* on the rags with markers; or place tags on bags they find in the house. Parents can also encourage children to find or create other words that end with *-ag*. Although such opportunities may feel at times to be rather teacher focused, teachers can get parent feedback about which activities work best or give parents a range of choices to select from. Such interactions can encourage parents to be alert for opportunities to reinforce important oral and print-based skills in the home, with little planned or direct teaching (Nelson, 1998). Multiple examples of activities that can be sent home for parents of young children are available at http://education.byu.edu/seel/library.html.

Developing Relationships and Communicating

Because relationships with parents are key to helping parents feel valued in school environments, it is important that teachers and

SLPs seek for opportunities to communicate regularly with families. Unfortunately, some teachers may become frustrated when they feel that parents are not responding to their attempts to become "involved" in the children's literacy (e.g., ignoring materials sent home—even "book bags") in ways that are consistent with traditional models of parental involvement in U.S. schools (Lynch, 2009a). Teachers' perceptions of unresponsiveness may occur as a result of discontinuity between home and school literacies of ethnic minority youth and because some parents may feel isolated, ignored or unwelcome in schools (Christianakis, 2011). For example, research documents that African American parents may feel less welcomed in their child's school than European American parents (Chavkin & Williams, 1993). Although misunderstandings occasionally arise between individuals from different cultures, including teachers and parents from dissimilar backgrounds, teachers and SLPs can do a lot towards building collaboration by valuing parents' experiences and seeking opportunities for parents to share their knowledge about their child. Teachers and SLPs can also gain an understanding for and appreciation of parents and children's perceptions, beliefs, and traditions by observing children at school and encouraging them to talk about or draw pictures that depict their cultural origins.

School personnel should always be careful not to alienate parents by communicating to them (either intentionally or unintentionally) that their participation is no longer needed. Before their children enter school, many parents tend to view themselves as the child's first teacher, who can significantly influence the young child's emerging literacy. However, some have observed that when formal school starts, "literacy goes to school" (Weinberger, 1996 as quoted by Stooke, 2005, p. 4), which can lead parents to believe that their role is secondary and that the most important literacy lessons take place at school—without them. Consequently, even confident and actively involved parents may feel confused about their role in children's literacy development and thus in need of encouragement and even sometimes explicit directions from the classroom teacher, SLP, or other school professional (Stooke, 2005; Weinberger, 1996).

Disconnects and misunderstandings may be more complex and intense if (a) the family is of a cultural group other than the

American middle-class majority group and/or (b) the family does not share the SLP's and teacher's goals for the child. For example, White middle-class SLPs and teachers tend to focus on getting the child to speak freely, to initiate conversations, and to participate as equals in conversations with adults. However, some cultures do not value a talkative child and may not consider it desirable for a child to initiate conversations with adults or to assume communication equality (Owens, 1999). Rather, parents may have cultural models of education and learning that emphasize child behaviors that are not valued in the majority culture. Cultural models are widely shared views within a group about "how the world works, or ought to work" (Gallimore & Goldenberg, 2001, p. 47). To make the challenge of cultural sensitivity more complex, parents with similar ethnic, linguistic, and socioeconomic backgrounds often have diverse belief structures (Okagaki & Bingham, 2006). For example, Neuman, Hagedorn, Celano, and Daly (1995) suggested that a "continuum of perspectives" exists among parents about learning and literacy, including a desire in some cultures for more worksheets and other very structured methods that many European American teachers tend to avoid (Lynch, 2009b).

Although some families may not participate in formal school events, volunteer in the classroom, or communicate frequently with teachers and school staff, such behavior does not necessarily reflect lack of interest in their child's education (e.g., Delgado-Gaitan, 1992; Lareau, 1996; Ramirez, 2003). Teachers, SLPs, and administrators should be culturally sensitive as they build on parents' early feelings of confidence and natural desire to help by incorporating parents into the design of the literacy program. Many parents are directly engaged in their child's schooling in ways that meet the expectations of teachers and school administrators; other parents utilize indirect strategies (e.g., supporting their child in homework activities, having high educational expectations for their child, or socializing children to be well-behaved at school) to support their child's education. In order to best support parents, teachers must understand how cultural models along with individual characteristics may inform their chosen role in their child's education. They must recognize differences, find out as much as they can about families' cultural preferences, and treat all with understanding and respect.

Obtaining Information About Family Goals and Children's Experiences

As a result of their cultural models of education, parents may have different ideas about (a) what children should learn, (b) how children learn, (c) what it means to do well in school, (d) what children need to do to succeed in school, and (e) what parents and schools should do to support children's education. It is important that teachers and SLPs have conversations with parents about their expectations for their child, the teacher, and the school. It is essential that teachers and SLPS do not view themselves as the keepers of all literacy knowledge or literacy best practices. Rather, communication should value what parents have to say in ways that communicate that parents' perspectives, cultural experiences, and home language are important to helping their child succeed.

At the beginning of the school year, teachers should learn as much as they can about each of the children's families—including interests, cultural practices, parenting beliefs and values, and home literacy and language practices. Whenever possible, such conversations should happen in person with parents through home visiting or by inviting parents to come with their child to an individual appointment with the child's teacher before school begins. These visits should be about getting to know and appreciate the family and the child. Teachers can introduce themselves, explain how the particular classroom works, ask about the parents' expectations for the child at school and at home (e.g., "What responsibilities does your child have at home?" "What expectations do you have for your child at school?"), share the teachers' expectations, and get to know information about the child and the family that may be useful in planning culturally appropriate instruction.

Parents have valuable knowledge about their children's interests and ways of speaking and behaving in the home. However, because home visiting and school visits are not always possible, teachers may need to send home activities or an information sheet designed to gain information about children and their families. These "getting to know you" information sheets might involve a sample of the teacher telling the family about his or her background, with a photo of teacher doing something he or she enjoys (e.g., gardening, going to the movies, spending time at the park, etc.). Materials should be translated into the family's home language and should contain simple enough prompts to be easily read by parents with various literacy skill levels.

In addition to finding out information from home, teachers and SLPs should seek for ways to bring family experiences and environments into the classroom. This sharing of home to school can be as simple as sending pictures from home to school to be featured on an "All About Me" poster for each child or may involve sharing a favorite book, child- or parent-drawn picture, treat, toy, or story written by the child (and dictated to the parent or teacher). One formal way that this might occur is through activities that celebrate families, such as a special family week. Special family weeks allow parents or families to share information about their child and family that teachers may use in the classroom to increase children's knowledge and engagement with each other, thus creating a caring community of learners. During each week, teachers can brainstorm with parents about something special they might do to contribute some understanding about their child's life. These things may involve sending a poster to school with pictures or drawings of the family's and child's favorite activities. Because research documents that most parents believe that education provides access to opportunities—a means to attaining a better life (e.g., Goldenberg & Gallimore, 1995; Sue & Okazaki, 1990)—and want their children to do well in school, teachers should be creative in seeking opportunities for parents to team up with them to help ensure the children's success. In addition, having parents share information from their family life and culture as well as details about their child's interests, hobbies, and strengths will help teachers and SLPs ensure that the child's language and literacy experiences are meaningful (Tracey, 2000).

Involving and Collaborating with Parents at School

Because much of parents' participation in their children's education occurs through school-family communication, most research on parental involvement and collaboration has been studied within the contexts of home engagement and teacher communication. However, parental involvement and engagement in children's literacy activities at school should facilitate true parental collaboration where parents' experiences are valued and incorporated into classroom environments. If parents' circumstances permit them to come into the classroom or attend family enrichment nights, the circle of parental influence on children's language and literacy learning can be expanded. With the increasing pressure on classroom teachers to implement effective early literacy programs that meet the needs of a wide variety of children, it seems plausible that parents can provide valuable assistance by engaging in in-class activities as "agents of intervention" (National Early Literacy Panel [NELP], 2008; Shanahan & Lonigan, 2010). However, if such participation is to be successful, teachers and SLPs do need to consider how to utilize parents' knowledge and skills in the classroom (whenever possible), how to make parents comfortable in the school and classroom, what forms of participation will be appropriate for them, and what kind of support, preparation and/or training they might need.

For example, as mentioned earlier, parents and other family members (e.g., grandparents, siblings, aunts, godparents, etc.) can visit children's classrooms and share stories of their families and culture. Within some Native American communities, tribal elders have considerable cultural knowledge and serve in highly respected roles within the community. These elders can be invited to visit classrooms and show how some Native American cultural practices are done, such as making drums. They may also share stories, legends, or fables that are tied to their cultural knowledge (Pewewardy, 1994). Such experiences demonstrate valuing of children's cultures in the classroom and show that passing down cultural stories is an important and respected practice. Within this context children's own cultural identities can be strengthened and teachers can become aware of the learning characteristics of students in ways that may also strengthen their language and literacy learning.

Valuing Parents' Contributions

From the perspective of those in the majority school culture, so-called "little things" can affect minority parents' sense of exclusion/inclusion at their children's schools. For some families, a first step is getting them to feel comfortable coming into the school and classroom, or interacting with the teacher or SLP. Some parents may limit their participation in school activities because they do not perceive the school to be welcoming to them or may have difficulty understanding the culture or language of school. For some families, as articulated by Miller and Endo (2004), it is essential that schools reduce both the cultural and language load for linguistically diverse parents and children. Reducing the cultural load may include behaviors that teachers and SLPs can undertake to demonstrate that they value families' cultural experiences by treating them with respect, building personal relationships with parents and children, and making an effort to include aspects of the home culture in school on a regular basis. Learning something about a family's culture, including a few words, phrases, and greetings from their native language (Owens, 1999), can help the parents realize the teacher and SLP are sincerely interested in having them come to the school, regardless of differences in background or culture. Because teachers and SLPs use language that may be unfamiliar to English-language learning parents and children, they should reduce the school language load by providing summaries of or orally paraphrasing difficult texts and avoiding teacher or SLP jargon and acronyms (Miller & Endo, 2004). In addition, materials or school communications that are sent home should be available in the home languages of families. This translation can be done by school personnel or possibly through an advisory group of parents who speak the native languages of children attending the school. Involving parents in these sorts of tasks allows them to participate and contribute important language and cultural knowledge.

Socioeconomic level and other aspects of lifestyle may cause similar feelings of hesitation for entering a school. Some parents have had negative experiences during their own schooling that may have caused them to fear or resent educators. Some parents are embarrassed because they struggle with the English language, may have difficulty reading, and/or struggle to support their children with their homework. Making parents welcome and building rapport with them as the school year begins can establish some necessary contexts and foundations for continued communication and classroom involvement (Staples & Diliberto, 2010). Research conducted on the factors that influence parents' involvement in their children's learning and school experiences confirms that many do not participate because they feel their input is unwanted or irrelevant (Overstreet, Devine, Bevans, & Efreom, 2005; Patrikakou

& Weisberg, 2000). Even willingness to become involved in a child's homework may depend partly on the parents' perceptions of the degree to which their child or their child's teacher wants them to help (Hoover-Dempsey et al., 2001). Because of these factors, it is important that teachers find ways to involve and accept all forms of parental and family contributions.

Encouraging Parents' Classroom Support

As discussed earlier, families' diverse cultural and social experiences, expectations and resources impact their ability to participate in their child's schooling in traditional ways. Thus, teachers need to provide multiple ways and opportunities for families to participate in different capacities in their children's learning and school experience. As children's first teachers, parents are knowledgeable about children's learning and interest in ways that can greatly improve classroom instruction. Allowing parents to actively participate in their child's education at school is an excellent way to form strong collaborative relationships between home and school cultures. We acknowledge that there are a variety of ways to describe and promote parent involvement. However, for the purpose of this chapter we consider two ways to involve parents in the classroom: invite them to provide behind-the-scenes support and arrange for them to support in-class instruction as volunteers.

Permit Behind-the-Scenes Support

Parents may become active volunteers in their child's classroom without even setting foot in the door. Because many parents have heavy time commitments and limited financial reserves, parents may find an ideal fit as a behind-the-scenes contributor to classrooms activities. Although these parents may not be able to participate in classroom activities by coming into the classroom, they can still contribute a great service to their child and the teacher. For example, parents can furnish readily available, inexpensive household items that can be used during playful literacy activities (e.g., discarded socks, bottle caps, empty paper towel rolls, egg cartons, scraps of fabric, buttons). At school children can sort these materials into pre-labeled bins or bags for later use. As the teacher, SLP, or other classroom instructors design activities to promote various skill areas, a new materials list can be sent home each month, urging parents to save and contribute.

Parents who are able and willing can also join in the process of sorting and organizing lesson kits that will be sent home to all children, to small groups, or to individual children in the class. Each kit, designed by the classroom teacher or parent volunteer, comes with predetermined materials and instructions for how to play or work with the materials. Parents can do this sorting either once a week at their child's school (at lunch or before or after school) or at their home. Because sorting and assembling home literacy materials is not particularly time consuming, this volunteer work can take place at times convenient to the parent.

Arrange for Classroom Volunteers

Parent classroom volunteers are invaluable members of early childhood and elementary school classrooms. Although the majority of parents may not be able to volunteer in their child's classroom on a regular basis, teachers and SLPs should encourage parent and family involvement in classroom activities, on children's birthdays, during school events, and throughout the week whenever possible. Once teachers have built a strong relationship with parents by valuing their experiences and cultures, they should encourage parents to contribute to classrooms through actively participating in daily classroom life, attending school to read a child's favorite story or teach a few words in their child's home language, supplying information about their child (through sharing pictures or stories), or serving as a regular parent volunteer who takes on or shares a small instructional role each week. Parents often have areas of expertise, such as foreign language knowledge, a trade or craft skill, musical or artistic talents, or a job that is unusual or possibly relevant to a classroom theme that would be interesting to other children.

Depending on their level of comfort and expertise, parents who are classroom volunteers can eventually be actively and meaningfully involved in classroom instructional routines as well. Parent volunteers may assume such roles as reading or telling stories, taking dictation from young children, assisting with children's independent reading and writing, or supervising centers (Tracey, 2000). They may also supervise activities, lead discussions, or help prepare materials. Teachers and children benefit from parents' in-class involvement when it is feasible, well planned, and reliably carried through. The classroom teacher, SLP, or other school personnel can prepare and direct parents in implementing small group activities that provide children with beneficial practice with literacy targets. Parents with more experience (and confidence) may on occasion take the role of assistant teacher. Teachers and SLPs should be sensitive to parents' level of comfort with such activities and provide them with adequate support in learning how to manage large groups of children.

Recruiting Classroom Parental Support

In their review of parenting interventions targeting preschooler's language development and emergent literacy skills, Reese et al. (2010) suggested that parents are an underused resource. They recommend that parents can be "engines of change in early intervention programs" (p. 98) and that incorporating them into program models clearly influences the effectiveness of early literacy intervention. Teachers and SLPs should be prepared to make parents welcome, value their funds of knowledge, and provide various levels or types of classroom involvement. Even when parents are valued, however, it still may be challenging to recruit them to become involved in classroom instructional routines.

Invite Parents to Share Their Knowledge and Skills

Teachers should carefully and intentionally utilize a variety of approaches and strategies to communicate to parents their support of family literacies and their need for parent collaboration. Some teachers may simply make a general request during and after a back-to-school night or other general parent meeting, designating a place to meet or a form to fill out for parents who would be willing to volunteer in classroom literacy instruction. A general request may lead to parents volunteering, including some that the teachers might not have otherwise considered. Other teachers find opportunities (e.g., home visiting, letters to parents) to interact with parents near the beginning of the year and get to know about their values, personalities, dispositions, and skills. As teachers and parents come to know each other, both will feel more comfortable working together. Some teachers may use a combination of both general and personal invitations to invite parents to participate. One very effective approach implemented by a first grade teacher involved writing a brief note to the parents of each child that mentioned something that she particularly liked and appreciated about their child. Recognizing her personal interest and positive attitude toward their children, parents responded positively to her advice and her invitations for participation (Korth & Marshall, 2009).

In some classes the "room mothers" or Parent-Teacher Association (PTA) representatives, who are already acquainted with parents of class members, may volunteer to do some recruiting and even scheduling of volunteers. Some parents may feel more comfortable expressing enthusiasm, questions, and/or doubts about their own abilities and experience to a fellow parent than to their child's teacher, who may seem professionally distant during early contacts.

As parents accept invitations and become involved in the classroom, teachers must continue to help them feel welcome and perceive themselves as partners in the instructional process. Positive encouragement and an active valuing of home and cultural experiences are important to their continued willingness, confidence, and motivation.

Provide Opportunities for Participation in the School Curriculum

Once parents are recruited, encouraged, and ready to begin volunteering in classrooms, teachers and SLPs need to provide well planned and intentional training to ensure that parents implement instructional practices that lead to positive early literacy outcomes (Justice & Ezell, 2000; Lonigan & Whitehurst, 1998; Neuman & Gallagher, 1994; Neuman & Roskos, 1993; Nye, Turner, & Schwartz, 2006; Reese et al., 2010). Because parents' individual experiences with certain instructional practices may vary considerably, it is important that working with parents involves collaborative two-way communication that is supportive of parents' feedback and perspectives (McCarthey, 2000). Often relatively low levels of parents' involvement in classrooms may be due to teachers' and other school professionals' failure to acknowledge parents' broad range of experience and education and to fine tune interactions or training sessions accordingly. Training should be adjusted based on a parent's prior experience working with young children and their familiarity with teaching and intervention strategies. Teachers and SLPs should utilize modeling, practice, and feedback, including a gradual release of responsibility from teachers to parent volunteers. These strategies can help avoid future misunderstandings, increase the quality of instruction being offered to children, and increase parental participation in classroom contexts (Reese et al., 2010).

Conclusion

This chapter examined parent-school collaborations from the perspective of the home and school. We began by considering the importance of home experiences in building children's literacy knowledge and the myriad roles, including classroom roles, that parents may assume. Teachers need to recognize, value, and communicate with parents about their home literacy values, beliefs, and practices. When needed, teachers and SLPs should provide support and possibly training about the benefits of and suggestions for sharing literacy in the home through a literacy-rich environment and through positive and purposeful interactive experiences. Parents of children with language difficulties should be encouraged and supported in participating in implementing interventions.

Teachers and SLPs need to help parents realize that there is not just one home pattern that supports young children's literacy. Many differences are apparent in literacy-rich homes, including perspective, circumstances, and a wide range of variables: A "best approach" does not exist (Nelson, 1998). Parents should be encouraged to share what comes naturally in their personal love for literacy, considered in terms of their children's needs and circumstances. Parents and caregivers should also be encouraged to share their cultural values, stories, and language with their children. Teachers and SLP can make them aware of what can be done and support them in finding what works best in their family.

Teachers and SLPs should strive to establish warm and encouraging school-home partnerships, assuring all parents that their participation is valued and welcome, as well as engaging in a variety of communication strategies to help them understand ways that they can contribute. Strong communication between schools and parents is particularly crucial with parents of students with language disabilities or delays. Strong teacher-parent communication is also key to helping teachers and SLPs value parents' funds of knowledge and experiences in the home. Parents and SLPs should seek for opportunities to help families bring these language and literacy strengths into the classroom.

Although the majority of parents will not be able to participate by coming into the classroom, parents whose schedules and life contexts allow them to take part in classroom ativities should be encouraged to do so. If parents want to become involved but cannot come to the school, behind-the-scene roles such as gathering and/or organizing supplies or creating classroom props can be arranged. Actively involving parents in classrooms by encouraging, recognizing, and drawing upon their traditional family-based literacy routines will most likely require time and effort from teachers and SLPs. However, the benefit of these relationships to the children, parents, and eventually the teacher and SLP are significant. Parents are undervalued and underutilized in early childhood and early elementary grade programs, but as the research has demonstrated, they can become effective agents for change.

References

Au, K. H. (1980). Lesson with Hawaiian children: Analysis of a culturally appropriate instructional event. *Anthropology and Education Quarterly, 11*(2), 91–115.

Baker, L., Mackler, K., Sonnenschein, S., & Serpell, R. (2001). Parents' interactions with their first-grade children during storybook reading and relations with subsequent home reading activity and reading achievement. *Journal of School Psychology, 39*, 415–438.

Barone, D. (2011). Welcoming families: A parent literacy project in a linguistically rich, high-poverty school. *Early Childhood Education Journal, 38*, 377–384.

Bingham, G. E. (2007). Maternal literacy beliefs and the quality of mother-child book-reading interactions: Associations with children's early literacy development. *Early Education and Development, 18*, 23–50.

Bradley, R. H. (1999). The home environment. In S. L. Friedmand & T. D. Wachs (Eds.), *Measuring environment across the life span: Emerging methods and concepts* (pp. 31–58). Washington, DC: American Psychological Association.

Brown, S., Souto-Manning, M., & Laman, T. T. (2010). Seeing the strange in the familiar: Unpacking racialized practices in early childhood settings. *Race Ethnicity and Education, 13*(4), 513–532. doi:10.1080/136 13324.2010.519957

Bus, A.G. (2001). Early book reading in the family: A route to literacy. In S. Neuman & D. Dickinson (Eds.), *Handbook of research in early literacy* (pp.179–191). New York, NY: Guilford.

Bus, A. G. (2002). Joint caregiver-child storybook reading: A route to literacy development. In S. B. Neuman & D. K. Dickinson (Eds.), *Handbook of early literacy research* (Vol. 1, pp. 179–191). New York, NY: Guilford Press.

Bus, A. G., & van Ijzendoorn, M. H. (1988). Mother-child interactions, attachment, and emergent literacy: A cross-sectional study. *Child Development, 59*, 1262–1272.

Bus, A. G., & van Ijzendoorn, M. H. (1997). Affective dimension of mother-infant picturebook reading. *Journal of School Psychology, 35*, 47–60.

Bus, A. G., van Ijzendoorn, M. H., & Pellegrini, A. D. (1995). Joint book reading makes for success in learning to read: A meta-analysis on intergenerational transmission of literacy. *Review of Educational Research, 65*, 1–21.

Chavkin, N. F., & Williams, Jr., D. L. (1993). Minority parents and the elementary school: Attitudes and practices. In N. F. Chavkin (Ed.), *Families and schools in a pluralistic society* (pp. 73–84). Albany, NY: State University of New York Press.

Christianakis, M. (2011). Parents as "help labor": Inner-city teachers' narratives of parent involvement. *Teacher Education Quarterly, 38*(4), 157–178.

Cirrin, F. M., Schooling, T. L., Nelson, N. W., Diehl, S. F., Flynn, P. F., Stakowski, M., & Adamczyk, D. F. (2010). Evidence-based systematic review: Effects of different service delivery models on communication outcomes for elementary school-age children. *Language, Speech, and Hearing Services in Schools, 41*, 233–264. doi:10.1044/0161-146(2009/08-0128)

Crain-Thoreson, C., & Dale, P. S. (1992). Do early talkers become early readers? Linguistic precocity, preschool language, and emergent literacy. *Developmental Psychology, 28*, 421–429.

Delgado-Gaitan, C. (1992). School matters in the Mexican-American home: Socializing children to education. *American Educational Research Journal, 29,* 495–513.

DeTemple, J. M. (2001). Parents and children reading books together. In D. K. Dickinson & P. O. Tabors (Eds.), *Beginning literacy with language: Young children learning at home and school* (pp. 31–51). Baltimore, MD: Paul H. Brookes.

Dickinson, D. K., & Tabors, P. (2001). *Beginning literacy with language: Young children learning at home and school.* Baltimore, MD: Paul H. Brookes.

Drummond, K. V., & Stipek, D. (2004). Low-income parents' beliefs about their role in children's academic learning. *Elementary School Journal, 104,* 197–213.

Edwards, P. A., Pleasants, H. M., & Franklin, S. H. (1999). *A path to follow: Learning to listen to parents.* Portsmouth, NH: Heinemann.

Epstein, J. L., & Dauber, S. L. (1991). School programs and teacher practices of parent involvement in inner-city elementary and middle schools. *Elementary School Journal, 91,* 289–305.

Evans, M. A., & Shaw, D. (2008). Home grown for reading: Parental contributions to young children's emergent literacy and word recognition. *Canadian Psychology, 49,* 89–95.

Gallimore, R., & Goldenberg, C. (2001). Analyzing cultural models and settings to connect minority achievement and school improvement research. *Educational Psychologist, 36,* 45–56.

Gillanders, C., & Jimenez, R. T. (2004). Reaching for success: A close-up of Mexican immigrant parents in the USA who foster literacy success for their kindergarten children. *Journal of Early Childhood Literacy, 4,* 243–269.

González, N., Moll, L. C., & Amanti, C. (Eds.). (2009). *Funds of knowledge: Theorizing practice in households, communities, and classrooms.* New York, NY: Routledge.

Goss, L., & Barnes, M. (1989). *Talk that talk: An anthology of African-American storytelling.* New York, NY: Simon & Schuster.

Grace, C. M. (2004). Exploring the African American oral tradition: Instructional implications for literacy learning. *Language Arts, 81,* 481–490.

Griffin, E. A., & Morrison, F. J. (1997). The unique contribution of home literacy environment to differences in early literacy skills. *Early Child Development and Care, 127–128,* 233–243.

Hammer, C. S., Nimmo, D., Cohen, R., Clemons Draheim, H. C., & Johnson, A. A. (2005). Book reading interactions between African American and Puerto Rican Head Start children and their mothers. *Journal of Early Childhood Literacy, 5,* 195–223.

Hart, B., & Risley, T. R. (1995). *Meaningful differences in the everyday experience of young American children*. Baltimore, MD: Paul H. Brookes.

Heath, S. B. (1989). Oral and literate traditions among Black Americans living in poverty. *American Psychologist, 44,* 367–373.

Hogg, L. (2011). Funds of knowledge: An investigation of coherence within the literature. *Teaching and Teacher Education, 27*(3), 666–677.

Hoover-Dempsey, K. V., Battiato, A. C., Walker, J. M. T., Reed, R. P., & DeJong, J. M. (2001). Parental involvement in homework. *Educational Psychologist, 36,* 195–209.

Hoover-Dempsey, K. V., & Sandler, H. M. (1995). Parental involvement in children's education: Why does it make a difference? *Teachers College Record, 97,* 310–331.

Huang, G., & Dolms, B. (2007). Reading theatre, parents as actors: Movie production in a family literacy workshop. *Reading Improvement, 44*(2), 87–98.

Janes, H., & Kermani, H. (2001). Caregivers' story reading to young children in family literacy programs: Pleasure or punishment? *Journal of Adolescent and Adult Literacy, 44,* 458–466.

Justice, L. M., & Ezell, H. K. (2000). Enhancing children's print and word awareness through home-based parent intervention. *American Journal of Speech-Language Pathology, 9,* 257–269.

Justice, L. M., & Ezell, H. K. (2004). Print referencing: An emergent literacy enhancement strategy and its clinical applications. *Language, Speech, and Hearing Services in Schools, 35,* 185–193.

Justice, L. M., Skibbe, L., Canning, A., & Lankford, C. (2005). Preschoolers, print and storybooks: An observational study using eye movement analysis. *Journal of Research in Reading, 28,* 229–243.

Klesius, J. P., & Griffith, P. L. (1996). Interactive storybook reading for at-risk learners. *Reading Teacher, 49,* 552–560.

Korth, B. B., & Marshall, E. E. (2009). *Preparing early childhood teachers to involve parents: Involving parents in early literacy instruction and intervention in the classroom*. Presentation at the fall meeting of the National Association of Early Childhood Teacher Educators, Washington, DC.

Lareau, A. (1996). Assessing parent involvement in schooling: A critical analysis. In A. Booth & J. F. Dunn (Eds.), *Family-school links: How do they affect educational outcomes?* (pp. 57–64). Mahwah, NJ: Erlbaum Associates.

Lee, B. Y. (2010). Investigating toddlers' and parents' storybook reading during morning transition. *Early Childhood Education Journal, 38,* 213–221. doi:10.1007/s10643-010-0396-y

Lonigan, C. J., & Whitehurst, G. J. (1998). Relative efficacy of parent and teacher involvement in a shared-reading intervention for preschool children from low-income backgrounds. *Early Childhood Research Quarterly, 13*(2), 263–290.

Lynch, J. (2009a). Preschool teachers' beliefs about children's print literacy development. *Early Years, 29*(2), 191–203.

Lynch, J. (2009b). Print literacy engagement of parents from low-income backgrounds: Implications for adult and family literacy programs. *Journal of Adolescent and Adult Literacy, 52,* 509–521.

Marsh, J. (2003). One-way traffic? Connections between literacy practices at home and in the nursery. *British Educational Research Journal, 29,* 369–382.

McCarthey, S. J. (2000). Home-school connections: A review of the literature. *Journal of Educational Research, 93,* 145–153.

Miller, P. C., & Endo, H. (2004). Understanding and meeting the needs of ESL students. *Phi Delta Kappan, 85,* 786–791.

Moll, L., Amanti, C., Neff, D., & Gonzales, N. (2005). Funds of knowledge for teaching: Using a qualitative approach to connect homes and classrooms. In N. Gonzalez, L. C. Moll, & C. Amanti (Eds.), *Funds of knowledge* (pp. 71–87). Mahwah, NJ: Lawrence Erlbaum Associates.

Morrow, L. M., & Young, J. (1997). A family literacy program connecting school and home: Effects on attitude, motivation and literacy achievement. *Journal of Educational Psychology, 89,* 736–742.

Muller, C., & Kerbow, D. (1993). Parent involvement in the home, school, and community. In B. Schneider & J. S. Coleman (Eds.), *Parents, their children, and schools* (pp. 13–42). Boulder, CO: Westview Press.

National Early Literacy Panel. (2008). *Developing early literacy: Report of the National Early Literacy Panel.* Washington, DC: National Institute for Literacy.

Nelson, N.W. (1998). *Childhood language disorders in context: Infancy through adolescence* (2nd ed.). Boston, MA: Allyn & Bacon.

Neuman, S. (1996). Children engaging in storybook reading: The influence of access to print resources, opportunity, and parental interaction. *Early Childhood Research Quarterly, 11,* 495–513.

Neuman, S. B., & Gallagher, P. (1994). Joining together in literacy learning: Teenage mothers and children. *Reading Research Quarterly, 29*(4), 383–401.

Neuman, S. B., Hagedorn, T., Celano, D., & Daly, P. (1995). Toward a collaborative approach to parent involvement in early education: A study of teenage mothers in an African-American community. *American Educational Research Journal, 32*(4), 801–827.

Neuman, S. B., & Roskos, K. (1993). Access to print for children of poverty: Differential effects of adult's mediation and literacy-enriched play settings on environmental and functional print tasks. *American Education Research Journal, 30*(1), 95–122.

Nye, C., Turner, H. M., & Schwartz, J. B. (2006). *Approaches to parental involvement for improving the academic performance of elementary school children in grades K–6.* (Family Involvement Research Digest). Cambridge, MA: Harvard Family Research Project. Retrieved January 25, 2010 from http://www.hfrp.org/publications-resources/browse-our-publications/approaches-to-parental-involvement-for-improving-the-academic-performance-of-elementary-school-children-in-grades-k-6

Okagaki, L., & Bingham, G. E. (2006). Parents' social cognitions and their parenting behaviors. In T. Luster & L. Okagaki (Eds.), *Parenting: An ecological perspective* (2nd ed., pp. 3–34). Mahwah, NJ: Lawrence Erlbaum Associates.

Okagaki, L., & Bingham, G. E. (2010). Diversity in Families and Schools. In S. L. Christenson & A. L. Reschly (Eds.), *The handbook of school-family partnerships for promoting student competence* (pp. 80–100). New York, NY: Routledge/Taylor and Francis Group.

Ortiz, C., Stowe, R. M., & Arnold, D. H. (2001). Parental influence on child interest in shared picture book reading. *Early Research Quarterly, 16,* 263–281.

Overstreet, S., Devine, J., Bevans, K., & Efreom, Y. (2005). Predicting parental involvement in children's schooling within an economically disadvantaged African American sample. *Psychology in the Schools, 42,* 101–111.

Owens, R. E., Jr. (1999). *Language disorders: A functional approach to assessment and intervention* (3rd ed.). Boston, MA: Allyn & Bacon.

Patrikakou, E. N., & Weisberg, R. P. (2000). Parents' perceptions of teacher outreach and parent involvement in children's education. *Journal of Prevention and Intervention in the Community, 20*(1–2), 103–119.

Paul, R. (2007). *Language disorders from infancy through adolescence: Assessment and intervention* (3rd ed.). Canada: Mosby Elsevier.

Perry, N. J., Kay, S. M., & Brown, A. (2007). Continuity and change in home literacy practices of Hispanic families with preschool children. *Early Child Development and Care, 178,* 99–113.

Pewewardy, C. (1994). Culturally responsible pedagogy in action: An American Indian magnet school. In E. R. Hollins, J. E. King, & W. C. Haymon (Eds.), *Teaching diverse populations: Formulating a knowledge base.* Buffalo, NY: State University of New York Press.

Pewewardy, C. (2002). Learning styles of American Indian/Alaska Native students: A review of the literature and implications for practice. *Journal of American Indian Education, 41,* 22–56.

Pitcher, S. M. (2009). The great poetry race. *Reading Teacher, 62*(7), 613–616.

Ramirez, A. Y. F. (2003). Dismay and disappointment: Parental involvement of Latino immigrant parents. *Urban Review, 35,* 93–110.

Reese, E., Sparks, A., & Leyva, D. (2010). A review of parent interventions for preschool children's language and emergent literacy. *Journal of Early Childhood Literacy*, *10*(1), 97–117.

Roberts, M. Y., & Kaiser, A. P. (2011). The effectiveness of parent-implemented language interventions: A meta-analysis. *American Journal of Speech-Language Pathology*, *20*, 180–199. doi:10.1044/1058-0360(2011/10-0055

Rothstein-Fisch, C., Trumbull, E., & Garcia, S. G. (2009). Making the implicit explicit: Supporting teachers to bridge cultures. *Early Childhood Research Quarterly*, *24*, 474–486.

Rowe, D. (2011). *The family backpack project: Responding to dual-language texts through family journals.* Paper presented at the Annual Conference of the Literacy Research Association. Jacksonville, Florida.

Rudner, K., Bunce, B., & Rudner, C. (1984). Language intervention in a preschool classroom setting. In L. McCormick & R. Schieflebusch (Eds.), *Early language intervention: An introduction* (pp. 267–297). Columbus, OH: Merrill.

Ruston, H. P., & Schwanenflugel, P. J. (2010). Effects of a conversation intervention on the expressive vocabulary development of prekindergarten children. *Language, Speech, and Hearing Services in Schools*, *41*, 303–313.

Scarborough, H. H., & Dobrich, W. (1994). On the efficacy of reading to preschoolers. *Developmental Review*, *14*, 245–302.

Sénéchal, M., & LeFevre, J. (2002). Parental involvement in the development of children's reading skill: A five-year longitudinal study. *Child Development*, *73*, 445–460.

Sénéchal, M., LeFevre, J., Thomas, E. M., & Daley, K. E. (1998). Differential effects of home literacy experiences on the development of oral and written language. *Reading Research Quarterly*, *33*, 96–116.

Shanahan, T., & Lonigan, C. J. (2010). The National Early Literacy Panel: A summary of process and the report. *Educational Researcher*, *39*, 279–285.

Smith, J. D. (1998). *Inclusion: Schools for all students.* Belmont, CA: Wadsworth.

Sonnenschein, S., & Munsterman, K. (2002). The influence of home-based reading interactions on 5-year-olds' reading motivations and early literacy development. *Early Childhood Research Quarterly*, *31*, 8–337.

Staples, K. E., & Diliberto, J. A. (2010). Guidelines for successful parent involvement: Working with parents of students with disabilities. *Teaching Exceptional Children*, *42*(6), 58–63.

Stooke, R. (2005). "Many hands make light work" but "too many cooks spoil the broth": Representing literacy teaching as a "job for experts" undermines efforts to involve parents. *Journal of Curriculum Studies*, *37*(1), 3–10.

Storch, S. A., & Whitehurst, G. J. (2001). The role of family and home in the literacy development of children from low-income backgrounds. *New Directions for Child and Adolescent Research, 92*, 53–71.

Strickland, D. S. (1990). Emergent literacy: How young children learn to read and write. *Educational Leadership, 47*(6), 18–23.

Sue, S., & Okazaki, S. (1990). Asian-American educational achievement: A phenomenon in search of an explanation. *American Psychologist, 45*, 913–920.

Sulzby, E., & Teale, W. H. (1991). Emergent literacy. In R. Barr, M. L. Kamil, P. Mosenthal, & P. D. Pearson (Eds.), *Handbook of reading research*, (Vol. 2, pp. 727–757). New York, NY: Longman.

Tamis-LeMonda, C. S., & Rodriguez, E. T. (2009). Parents' role in fostering young children's learning and language development. In R. E. Tremblay, R. G. Barr, R. Peters, & M. Boivin (Eds.), *Encyclopedia of early childhood development* (pp. 1–9). Retrieved from http://www.child-encyclopedia .com/documents/Tamis-LeMonda-RodriquezANGex_re-Language.pdf

Tracey, D. H. (2000). Enhancing literacy growth through home-school connections. In D. S. Strickland & L. M. Morrow (Eds.), *Beginning reading and writing*. New York, NY: Teachers College, Columbia University.

Wasik, B. A., & Bond, M. A. (2001). Beyond the pages of a book: Interactive book reading and language development in preschool classrooms. *Journal of Educational Psychology, 93*, 243–250.

Weinberger, J. (1996). *Literacy goes to school: The parents' role in young children's literacy learning*. London, UK: Paul Chapman.

Whitehurst, G. J., Arnold, D. S., Epstein, J. N., Angell, A. L., Smith, M., & Fischel, J. E. (1994). A picture book reading intervention in day care and home for children from low-income families. *Developmental Psychology, 30*, 679–689.

Whitehurst, G. J., Falco, F. L., Lonigan, C. J., Fischel, J. E., DeBaryshe, B. D., Valdez-Menchaca, M. C., & Caulfield, M. (1988). Accelerating language development through picture book reading. *Developmental Psychology, 24*(4), 552–559.

Zimmerman, F. J., Gilkerson, J., Richards, J. A., Christakis, D. A., Xu, D., Gray, S., & Yapanel, U. (2009). Teaching by listening: The importance of adult-child conversations to language development. *Pediatrics, 124*, 342–349.

Chapter 11

Enriching Language and Literacy: Integrating Visual Arts, Music, Dance, and Drama

Sharon Black

A group of first graders are gathered around their teacher, who is enthusiastically introducing a new book. *Spot A Dog*—she reads the title (Micklethwait, 1995). The teacher turns to a page of a classic painting that includes a dog, but not prominently. "Can you spot a dog?" She points to the words as she reads them. The children repeat the text and eventually find the dog. The next painting, *Madame Charpentier and Her Children* by August Renoir, includes a dog as part of the family. One of the children points to the dog as the teacher reads and points to the words: "I can see a big dog." The children read together, "I can see a big dog." The following pages each show a classic painting accompanied by a simple text challenging the children to find a certain type of dog: big, little, dappled, fluffy, shy, hungry, black, white, and flat.

The vocabulary may remind one of a basal reader, and the children are having some experiences often associated with this kind of text (Figure 11–1). As they follow the teacher's reading,

Figure 11–1. A teacher uses *Spot a Dog* to promote literacy skills through visual art.

her selectively emphatic voice helps them to notice phonemes and experience blending of sounds (Morrow, 2001; Savage, 2007)— awareness and skills that are important in learning to read. Reading the text back, of course, strengthens word and sound recognition and promotes engagement. But the children are also having some experiences less commonly prescribed.

Some of the dogs in the paintings are easy to "spot"; some aren't. Children look hard at the details of the paintings and the rendering of the dogs, thus sharpening their observational skills and learning to consider details. As they look at a variety of paintings, they notice how different the dogs look and how many contexts are natural (or in some of the abstract paintings unnatural) for dogs. This gives the teacher an opportunity to ask which is the "right way" to draw or paint a dog and allows the children to respond that in drawing there is no "right" or "wrong." The teacher asks each child what kind of dog he or she might like to draw. After each child has had a turn to share, the teacher leads the group in discussing how each person draws his or her own "mind picture," and mind pictures are not right or wrong (Cecil & Lauritzen, 1994, p. 38).

After a break for recess, the children will draw their dogs and share these pictures. On the following day the children may experience interactive writing with their teacher, SLP, or other classroom helpers to prepare brief descriptions or statements about their pictures.

Some students find it easier to engage and learn when they can work with mind pictures rather than language alone. Some engage and recall better when they can sing the sounds or clap the rhythms, others when they can participate with movement/dance or with dramatization. And all students benefit from the variety and engagement that these alternate modalities involve.

The arts stand alone as important experiences for children, but they can also be integrated into other instructional areas, such as literacy, social studies, science, or mathematics. This chapter will focus on integration of the arts with literacy experiences, including both obvious connections (such as reading *Spot a Dog* aloud to experience sounds and print) and more intangible, cognitive connections (including observation, reasoning, and expressive skills/ perspectives). The chapter begins with reasons for incorporating the arts with preschool and early grade literacy instruction and then offers practical age-appropriate suggestions for doing so. Visual arts, music, dance, and drama are discussed in that sequence, with both strategies and benefits.

Arts Integration: Bridges Into Literacy

Linguistic lessons and activities are not the easiest or most natural ways of learning for many children, and teachers can easily underestimate the abilities of a child whose natural gifts are in areas other than language. Today teachers are recognizing that there are many ways that children can be smart and capable (Merrefield, 1997). The arts are among instructional modalities that can provide bridges between a child's preferred learning style and the literacy knowledge and skills that the child must master to be successful in school. Merrefield (1997), a special education teacher, uses these bridges with her students to "celebrate and capitalize on alternative forms of smartness" (p. 61), thus including all students in the invitation to enjoy and progress in literacy. Arts integration invites and enhances engagement of all students—cognitively as well as emotionally and socially.

Symbol Systems

All of the arts, including language, are systems of symbols that people use to give concrete form to ideas, feelings, impressions, emotions, dreams, knowledge, and understanding: the inner person, whether 3 or 93 (Figures 11–2A and 11–2B). Table 11–1 lists some symbols associated with the arts and ways they can be used in classrooms.

These lists are not intended to be all inclusive—only suggestive of ways that various symbols are involved in different systems of expression. Language, the dominant form of expression in classrooms, involves complex and difficult symbol systems. Some children find the symbols of language to be their "native language"; others think, learn, and express themselves more easily with pictures or movement and thus require the multimodal bridges to cross into literacy skills. Involving and associating language with

A   B

Figure 11–2. Welcome to literacy! We come to it from different places, and teachers and parents create different bridges by which we can enter it. Once inside, we all enjoy it together.

Table 11–1. Symbol Systems as Children May Experience Them

System	Some Symbols	Activities
Language	Sounds, letters, words, sentences, paragraphs, punctuation; rhythm, tone, vocal variety and expression; nonverbal reinforcement such as facial expressions, gestures, etc.	Reading, writing, speaking, listening: (1) print forms including books, signs, posters, letters, notes, news items, etc. (2) activities including student-made books, shared and interactive reading and writing, reports and speeches, (3) literacy games and activities
Visual arts	Dots, lines, direction, color, light, texture, dimension, implied motion (Pomona, 1998)	Drawing, painting, sculpting, creating collages, constructing dioramas, making puppets, sketching to explore ideas and organize writing
Music	Rhythm, melody, harmony, tone, pitch, volume, tempo, timbre, intonation	Clapping rhythms, singing well-known songs, singing from posted lyrics, making up songs, creating mental pictures from music, describing and discussing music
Dance	Shape, locomotion, patterns, space, speed, energy, collaboration	Moving in response to sounds and words, portraying a pattern or process, dancing a picture or a story
Drama	Character, setting, background, conflict, climax and resolution; actor's voice movement, interaction with other characters	Improvising role play, presenting skits, telling and retelling stories, enacting stories, creating process drama, speaking through puppets, engaging in reader's theatre

symbol systems more natural for many of the children increases engagement, meaning, learning, and retention, particularly through engaging and interactive experiences.

As in the opening example, sounds and simple words grouped around a theme like dogs can be taught in association with visual symbols, enriching literary symbols that occur in stories. The student who is particularly sensitive to visual images may be the first to spot the dogs. The words in the book can mean more to him when they relate to and help him be successful with something he is "good at." With this association he may focus harder on the words and sounds and be more likely to learn and retain them.

Literacy can also be taught by using music to help children discriminate sounds and become aware of rhythms that exist in both music and language. In addition, singing simple songs may reinforce literacy targets: sounds and letters or alliteration and rhyme. Dance and drama are also powerfully associated with literacy capabilities and skills. As each child recognizes her strengths as part of a lesson, each crosses a personal bridge into the literacy experience. Children whose dominant style is verbal do not suffer; they are enriched by discovering new ways of experiencing and thinking about what they learn.

Once children are engaged in the experiences, cognitive skills highly relevant to literacy can be honed by practicing with different sets of symbols. Various symbol systems provide varied ways of making meaning (O'Neill, 2006), and all children benefit.

Thinking in Multiple Systems

Arts/literacy writers Cowan and Albers have pointed out that literacy in its complexity "necessarily involves thinking across and within multiple sign systems" (2006, p. 135). Classroom teacher and author Karen Gallas (1994) put the same perspective on a more concrete level with the comment that "drawing, painting, movement and dance, drama, poetry, music, and creative writing . . . enable children to think about new knowledge in more complex and meaningful ways by transforming their understanding of difficult concepts into metaphoric language and acts" (pp. 111–112). As they utilize a variety of symbol systems, students become actively involved with what they are learning, whether they are reading it, writing it, drawing it, singing it, dancing it, or acting it out. Learning is retained when students "actively participate in the experience and secure insight from that experience" (Intrator, 2001, p. 26). Reeves (2007) extended this concept, commenting that active participation in the arts creates "powerful visual, auditory, and kinesthetic associations that help students learn essential content and concepts" (p. 80).

Using Multiple Systems to Clarify Language Functions

To help students understand the concept of using different media to communicate what they think, feel, and know, a teacher or SLP might begin by teaching a full-class lesson comparing words to other symbol systems (though probably not using that terminology). Simplified face drawings might be used to help children realize that varied lines can represent different ideas and feelings (e.g., upward curved line, happiness, downward curved line sadness). Next drawings of scenes or objects (perhaps some of the children's own drawings) can show that different shapes, lines, and colors are used together to share what someone sees. Brief clips of music portraying different moods and feelings could then be used to demonstrate how rhythms, melodies, and sounds of instruments convey feelings and general impressions, though they do not fill in details. (Instruments and themes that represent various characters in Prokofiev's Peter and the Wolf do this very well; narrative versions provide child-friendly explanations.) Movements from dance and pantomime showing various feelings and emotions can also be demonstrated and discussed as time allows. For example, the teacher and/or SLP can demonstrate how walking differently can communicate different things about what people are feeling. Children can do a little creative walking as well.

The SLP or teacher can then explain how spoken and written words come together to express meaning just as lines and colors come together to draw a face or musical sounds come together to make a tune. Letters tell us which sounds are being used. A big book that the children have enjoyed in the past, a poem on a poster, or one of the children's shared writings recorded on chart paper can be used to complete the comparison.

After this kind of introduction and some modeling and guided practice, children can be engaged some multisymbol experiences. For example, they may combine visual arts with language by drawing and then dictating a story. Music and language blend in the fun of singing the words of a favorite song printed on chart paper and feeling the way the melody and the words both contribute to the meaning and the feeling expressed. Including pictures, shapes, or motions with the words of the song adds another symbol system to enhance the experience. Children whose more dominant strengths are musical, kinesthetic, and/or visual have been able to use their preferred systems, and more verbal children are practicing expression and communication in new blended contexts and finding new ways of thinking as well as representing themselves.

Personal Involvement

As Hoyt (1992) has noted, "Learning occurs when one creates a personal interpretation." She explained that when children receive opportunities to engage in different communication systems, imagination stirs, understanding deepens, and language learning improves. Providing options for self-expression allows children to "create a tighter link between themselves and the new learning . . . [engaging] the learner's affective as well as cognitive self through a wide variety of interactions" (p. 581).

Gallas (1994) wrote about her student Juan, whose family had immigrated to the US from South America. Juan was not learning English quickly. But he could draw. He was constantly drawing, and he drew well. Juan was particularly fascinated by science, and he would often slip over to the science table to reproduce in detail what he learned with his eyes. Gallas recalled,

> His visual representations became a catalogue of science information and science questions, and that information began to provide material for his involvement in reading and writing and learning a new language. As Juan drew, we built a reading and speaking vocabulary from his pictures, and that vocabulary, together with his interest in representing science, also became the subject matter of his writing.

For Juan, visual art created a link between his personal experiences/interests and his language use. His art form became his medium for communication and ultimately his motivation for learning language. The source of Juan's language difficulty was inexperience with English, but the relationship of the art as a link or bridge can be generalized to other language struggles. An important role of the SLP is to help the teacher recognize such opportunities, whether the student has a disability, is attempting to connect his personal experience to the English language, or has any other form of language-related problem needing help.

Some children sort and extend their thoughts by drawing, others by dancing, others by making music, still others by acting things out. By including experiences with these media in early literacy instruction, SLPs and teachers can individualize/personalize for their students and students can individualize/personalize for themselves.

In their book on the integrated classroom, Cecil and Lauritzen (1994) concluded, "A curriculum based on the integration of art, music, dance, and drama and a creative literacy program has the potential to make school and learning an exciting, fulfilling experience for all children" (p. 5). Elliot Eisner explained why this is true: "The arts—literature, visual art, music, drama, and dance—are our culture's most powerful means for making life in its particulars vivid. In this way the arts escalate consciousness" (1983, p.155). Children's awareness of the sounds and images of sensory language turns to personalized skills when they have heard, seen, felt, and created with the "language" (symbol system) of each sense. To maximize such potential, teachers and SLPs need to work together to utilize the broader, more general arts coverage with which teachers have been prepared in addition to the deeper and more specialized linguistic knowledge/experience of the SLP.

Each of the following sections considers one of the art forms used often in early childhood and early elementary classrooms: visual arts, music, dance, and drama. Benefits, uses, and applications relevant to literacy are suggested.

Visual Arts

Teacher/researcher/author Lucy Calkins told of a young child who, when asked what she was going to write about in her story, replied, "How should I know? I haven't drawed it yet" (Calkins, 1983). By drawing her story ideas before putting them into words, this child was learning to use her mind in both nonverbal and verbal ways as she worked to communicate her ideas in different forms (Longley,

Figure 11–3. Many children explore their ideas or feelings by drawing.

1999), beginning with the modality that was, for her age and disposition, the easiest. Hoyt (1992) extended this concept: Combining visual arts with literacy enables children "to look back to the images and feelings that precede the words" (p. 583) (Figure 11–3).

In learning, practicing, and reviewing literacy skills within contexts of visual arts activities, those images and feelings become connected in the students' minds with words and sounds that have been involved with the experience. Such connections are valuable for any child—invaluable for a child struggling with language. Ritter (n.d.) called attention to researchers' affirmation of the efficacy of visual strategies in improving reading comprehension for children with language learning difficulties.

Senses and Sounds

Both visual and related tactile and kinesthetic sensations that are experienced with visual arts produce strong, memorable associations when experienced in connection with other learning situations. Children experience the vividness of language, increasing their engagement in and memory for sounds and words that may be embedded in the visual arts experience. Table 11–2 demonstrates

Table 11–2. Sensory Experiences Related with Letters and Sounds

Impression	Potential Benefit	Specific Activity
Color	Creates vivid, memorable sensations associated with sounds and letters.	Make projects with "purple and pink paint, paper, and play dough" (Morrow, 2001)—possibly adding pasta, polka dots, and popsicle sticks.
Texture	Explore the media and some words that describe impressions; associate words and sounds with the experiences.	Compare sensations of poster paints, water colors, finger paints, varied fabric scraps, yarn, pipe cleaners, play dough (see Morrow, 2001): S-words including *sloppy, slimy, slippery, squishy, squiggly*.
Motion	"Clay is something that is nothing, but which can become anything and everything" (Tonucci, n.d., p. 77).	Practice motions and sounds with *P*: pushing, pulling, patting, pounding, punching.
	Painting with just the tip of the brush allows a different range of motion and new sensations.	Make an *-ip* painting which has children *dip* the *tip* of the brush in the paint and *drip* and *flip* paint onto the paper, using motions that *zip* and *whip* as they do so—even making the brush *skip* across the paper.

some ways that sensory experiences can be used to teach, practice, and reinforce some letters with sounds.

As they get their hands in visual arts media, children can become engaged with sounds that express their sensory experience, whether the /p/ of pounding, the /s/ of sliding, or the /-ip/ of flipping. The teacher or SLP can emphasize the sounds by conversing playfully with the children during the experience:

> Let's pound the purple playdough! *Pound, purple,* and *playdough* all start with *P*. Robbie is punching his purple playdough. Punch

is another good *P* word. Brooke is pushing and pulling—*push* and *pull* both begin with /*p*/. Chris is doing a good job—he's *poking* the playdough. I'm going to pinch my playdough? Does *pinch* start with /*p*/?

Images and Words

Taking the learning to a more abstract level, students are able to explore the power of sounds and words in relation to more complex images that they carry in their minds. These "mind pictures" (Cecil & Lauritzen, 1994), which often generate drawings, portray what children experience on a more abstract level with more extensive application than manipulation of collages or clay. Such visual images can provide an intermediate context (another bridge, perhaps) as children are becoming accustomed to decontextualized language use.

Because both drawing and using language are "ways of thinking, knowing, and making meaning" (Norton, 2004, p. 287, see also Cornett, 2003)—alternative systems for children to explore and express what they know (Hoyt, 1992)—students can use them interactively to strengthen interest, spontaneity, and comprehension. Visualizing and using language are generally symbiotic: "Ability or practice in one tends to reinforce the other, culminating in enhanced learning" (Cecil & Lauritzen, 1994, p. 38).

Experimenting with Descriptive Language

To utilize pictures in helping children learn to use vivid language, Claudia Cornet (2003) suggested having students list descriptive words in response to a picture. Lucy Micklethwait's *A Child's Book of Play in Art* (1996) includes details from and full reproductions of a wide variety of paintings and art objects that portray themes of imagination and play—great art made motivating. The art titles alone suggest uses: in addition to *The Little Blue Horses* and *The Yellow Cow* (Franz Marc, 1911), children could find words for *Tiger by a Torrent* (Kishi Ganku, c.1795) and list descriptives as they snicker at *Gorgon's Head*, painted on a Greek vase about 490 BC.

Children learn to read visual art by paying careful attention to details; through the specific details meaning is conveyed (Cornett, 2003). They need time to look carefully at a piece of artwork (Cornett, 2003) and opportunities to share and compare their ideas and impressions; conversations with their peers and their teacher bring out words that convey the details of the images. These words can be repeated, discussed, manipulated into different contexts, and eventually written out on chart paper to be placed on a word wall. To make the picture-language experience more personal, several pictures drawn or painted by the students could be added.

Relating to Everyday Life

Through creating and sharing daily life images, children share their thoughts, feelings and experiences; Hertzog (2001) referred to sharing images as "mak[ing] the learning experience 'visible'" (p. 4). Karen Gallas (1994) emphasized how "through the arts, teachers and children build an understanding together of how school concepts relate to the child's personal reality" (p. 118). This relationship is especially important for children with language disabilities, who may have a particular need to connect lesson content with what they already know in order "to form a durable representation that can inform future behavior and learning" (Catts, 2009, p. 180). Thus if an art-language experience (a school concept activity) portrays, describes, or relates to something in students' everyday lives, letters and sounds take on personal meaning. Through their visual art, they construct ways to understand the world and their experiences in it (Althouse, Johnson, & Michell, 2003), and associated language experiences take on real-world application.

For example, children in preschool, kindergarten, and early grades are accustomed to picture books that portray fairly common activities with vivid pictures and only a little text on each page. Teachers and SLPs can help children similarly blend visual and written composition on daily life topics by creating group or class books in which each child contributes an illustration and creates a sentence or two of text describing it. Depending on the writing level of the students, this may be done through dictation, shared writing, or interactive writing. Table 11–3 offers some possibilities.

An activity focused on daily life allows teachers and SLPs to stress that students' lives, experiences and ideas are similar in some ways and different in others. Thus a play *mat* for *M*-day's activities may be made of vinyl, canvas, patchwork quilting, straw, tapa cloth, tree bark, or woven banana leaves; and mangos and melons may be added to meat and milk on the day's menu. Children's drawings often portray such differences more vividly and more accurately than the words some of them may struggle to produce. If children are to risk exploring and sharing their ideas and experiences, in visual arts and/or in language, they must feel nurtured and secure in classroom contexts (Althouse et al., 2003). Children feel unconditionally accepted when their differences are celebrated (Purnell, Parveen, Begum, & Carter, 2007), regardless of the symbols in which they are represented or the difficulty some children may have in expressing them.

As drawing, painting, using clay, and making collages are naturally attractive activities in which many young children engage by choice, relating them with a literacy component brings meaning and engagement into the literacy experience, allows for increased exposure to the targets, and offers a variety of opportunities for teacher-student and student-student interaction.

Music

In a classroom on Hawaii's North Shore, the predominantly Polynesian preschool children sang enthusiastically as their teacher pointed to words on a "song chart" enhanced by a picture of a snowman:

> Once there was a snowman,
> Snowman, snowman.
> Once there was a snowman
> Tall, tall, tall.

Table 11–3. Group or Class Books That Blend Visual Art, Phonics, and Written Text

Book	Group Activity	Child Participation
"Mighty M Monday"	Children brainstorm all the things they can do on Monday that start with M.	Each child selects an item or action and creates a page by drawing it and then writing and/or dictating text to an adult "editor."
Class Cooks	Children discuss what they like to cook and how they do it. They list items they can cook that start with C.	Each child selects a food item starting with C, draws it, and writes and/or dictates how he or she thinks it is made.
Student Shopping	Children discuss things they may shop for that start with S.	Each child chooses an item, draws him or herself shopping for it, and writes and/or dictates text.
Book of Colors	The group chooses a color and brainstorms things that start with the same sound that could be that color: e.g., red things that start with R.	Each child chooses a color, then draws and labels on his or her page, and labels things that could be that color that start with the same sound: e.g., red roses, radishes, robots, rockets.
Halloween Haunting	The group chooses spooky sounds and matches them to creatures: "greedy, grabby, grubby green gremlins"; "knobby, snobby, gobby, goblins"; "sneaky, creaky, leaky, freaky, beaky freaks," etc.	The SLP or teacher may need to start (and/or extend) some of the lists, particularly if the students have language difficulties. Students draw their creature, write the word list, and may write brief descriptions or stories as well. Writing should be scaffolded as much as needed by individual students.
Book of Feelings	Children brainstorm H-things that make them happy, S-things that make them sad, F-things that make them fearful, etc.	Each child creates his or her page by drawing and labeling the items. Brief comments can be added if desired.

Having stretched as high as they could reach, the children melted gradually to the floor as they continued:

> In the sun he melted,
> Melted, melted
> In the sun he melted,
> Small, small, small.

These Hawaiian children loved that song. Few if any of them had ever seen or felt snow, and their experiences with melting were limited to ice cubes and ice cream. But the rhythm was strong, the tune was "catchy," and stretching and melting to the floor in time to the music was irresistible.

The teacher reinforced past rhyming instruction by drawing attention to the stressed words *tall* and *small*, as the children briefly practiced "standing tall" and "becoming small." The teacher continued, "Our snowman loves to rhyme," and she led the group in pantomiming words with the rime *-all* that he might enjoy: standing by a *wall*, and being careful not to *fall*, playing with a *ball*. With a song like this as an introduction, a variety of possible rhyme experiences might be incorporated.

Music is another art form that brings engagement and meaning into the literacy experience, making repeated exposure to letters, sounds, and words enjoyable for children and their teachers. Jalongo and Riblett (1997) explained that by participating in sing-aloud experiences accompanied by words and pictures, children "are involved in authentic, holistic literacy experiences" (p. 16). During the snowman song-activity the children were feeling in their bodies and minds the rhythm and flow of the English language (native to some, not so to others). They were following the words in print, listening to the rhyme that was inseparable from the music, and noticing how it could be carried out in other words as well. And their perception of language was stretched as they learned about the common word *melt* in a new geographic and cultural perspective—an unusual but effective celebration of diversity, which is an important byproduct of multicultural musical experiences (see Wiggins, 2007). All of these benefits were enhanced by the "total body movement" of the song's melody and the reaching-melting action (see Fisher & McDonald, 2001, p. 107), which enhanced both focus and enjoyment.

Like the visual arts, music can be used as a context to practice and reinforce literacy targets or on a deeper level to develop sensitivities, skills, and dispositions that enhance literacy, often at the same time. The many similarities between music and language enable some very significant applications.

Music-Language Relationships

Music and language have much in common: Both are engaging and personal, both consist of sounds coming together in meaningful patterns, and both have rhythm that gives continuity and an underlying sense of organization. In addition, both convey meaning, and music can include words—bringing the more explicit expressive capabilities of the language experience into unity with the more abstract emotive appeal of the music.

Cognitive skill development results from the overlap of modalities. From their work with music-literacy connections, Hansen and Bernstorf (2002, p. 18) have concluded, "In a practical sense, then, instruction in music can be a particularly rich source of support for achieving reading literacy" (see also Jalongo & Ribblett, 1997; Wiggins, 2007). At kindergarten/early elementary school age, children are experiencing rapid progress in abilities and skills that are important to both reading and musical development, and musical experiences are particularly appealing to them (Anvari, Trainor, Woodside, & Levy, 2002). Teachers who are developing systematic programs and methods for early literacy can make purposeful use of the developmental connectivity as well as similarities in the processes involved.

As children develop sound awareness and auditory processing skills, they are also enjoying engagement and expression, developing a sense of language rhythm, and participating in forms of interaction and predictable repetition that promote receptive vocabulary (Jalongo & Ribblett, 1997).

Developing Sound Awareness and Auditory Processing Skills

Phonological awareness, phonemic awareness, and orthographic awareness have been referred to as "parallel skills" (Register, 2000, p. 3) to those gained in school music experiences. Music perception has been correlated significantly to phonological awareness through the auditory processing necessary for both (Anvari et al., 2002; Hansen & Bernstorf, 2002; Wiggins, 2007). Such awareness, of course, is critical in decoding words as well as participating in music experiences (Wiggins, 2007). Phonemic awareness is also developed as the rhythm of songs requires separation of some syllables and stretching of others (Cornett, 2003). Structure and progression of chords gives an automatic emphasis to rhymed endings as part of the rhythm of the song. In addition, auditory memory is a part of the relationship (Anvari et al., 2002).

Experiencing Rhythm

Rhythm is an important commonality between music and language. The popular activity of clapping syllables or beating them on drums develops many skills that benefit the emergent reader. On an obvious plane, the sense of the rhythm common to music and language eventually enhances fluency as the child begins to read aloud (Cornet, 2003). Although the students may not think the word *rhythm* as they read, they sense it and respond to it. Though less obvious, this activity can also develop and refine phonological awareness as it helps students become aware not only of differences in rhythmic patterns but of differences in syllable sounds and patterns as well. And the relationship of the two is established in students' memories.

Most children enjoy hearing their own names, and having the entire class chant and clap the rhythm pattern of the name gives each child a moment as the center of everybody's learning experience. The exaggerated sound contrasts that come from the chant/clap routine make distinctions clear and obvious. Advancing to clap the rhythm of random sentences, dialogue, and even poetry extends the practice along with the fun. Imitative clapping and response clapping can be used to vary the experience.

As children with language problems may have difficulty with segmenting and blending and they can benefit from segmentation practice (Catts & Kamhi, 1986; Schuele & Boudreau, 2008), SLPs may want to conduct specialized small group word and phrase clapping activities to build children's ability to recognize and listen for varying numbers of syllables. The SLP can add the element of oral/written language connectivity (Ritter, n.d.) by having children read syllables from chart paper or overheads as they clap.

Noticing Variations

Learning to recognize the distinctive sounds of musical instruments further develops students' ability to notice characteristics of sounds and distinguish among them. For example, a kindergarten lesson which the teacher titled "Tubas and Tambourines" began by introducing orchestral instruments with part of the book *Meet the Orchestra* by Ann Hayes, then focused on instruments that begin with the sound /t/: tuba, tambourine, trumpet, and trombone.

This group of instruments doesn't represent the orchestra with much balance or accuracy, but it does provide some sound awareness and processing along with intensive reminders of /t/ and /tr/). Having real instruments brought to class and played for the children is, of course, ideal if the school happens to have a band program or a number of musical parents/siblings; if not, clips available on YouTube can be easily selected, shared, and discussed. The teacher can make discrimination a more deliberate process by discussing the sounds with the children: talking about what makes the sounds different from each other, how the various sounds make them feel, and what pictures the sounds bring to their minds (Cecil & Lauritzen, 1994). The book provides descriptions of instrument sounds that can stimulate discussion.

As part of "Tubas and Tambourines," the class learned the traditional children's song "I Am A Fine Musician" (adapted from the German folk song "Ich bin ein Musikante"), which is available on the Internet in a version from Sesame Street and also in a Disney version with read-along lyrics. Each time a verse is sung representing an instrument, children imitate the instrument sound, which can be adapted easily for practice with /t/. Tubas and tambourines both begin with /t/, but *tuba* has a deep, heavy sound like the instrument itself.

My tuba, my tuba
I love to play my tuba
toompa, tompa, toompa, toompa, toompa

The tambourine, also a /t/ word, has a brighter, percussive sound—again easy to compare with the instrument: *tam, tam, tam, tam, tam*.

Trumpets and trombones have brassier names and sounds, so they use the /tr/ blend. If the SLP or teacher wants to stress the /t/ sound as part of the blend, he can make the transition by softly repeating the /t/ sound at the beginning of *trumpet*—tttttrumpet as he introduces the section for that instrument. Once the group is into the song, the refrain goes like this:

> My trumpet, my trumpet
> I love to play my trumpet.
> Trut, trut, trut, trut, trut, trut,

Trombone is represented by *tremba, tremba, tremba, tremba, tremba*. Imitating the sound, of course, increases awareness of it, even though the imitations do not involve real words. Many schools have tambourines available for students to play as well as imitate. By the time children finish this activity, a lot of /t/ and /tr/ variations have been chanted, some vivid sound experiences have taken place, and the children have enjoyed some verbal and musical fun.

With its emphasis on language/sound, this lesson might be especially effective if conducted by SLPs, whose sense of language sounds and rhythms is well developed along with their knowledge in these areas. As with the clapping activity, students who need more intensive practice with sounds can do the same or closely related activities in small groups. Those children with language disorders who have trouble with alliteration (Crosbie, Holm, & Dodd, 2009) will benefit from the emphasis on /t/ and /tr/ instruments with corresponding sounds. Chanting and singing these sounds can be incorporated into brief transitional activities to provide extra practice without taking up class instructional or guided practice time.

Engagement and Imagination

Making music—whether clapping, singing, imitating instrument sounds, or playing simple rhythm instruments—engages children physically. Listening with appropriate introduction and follow-through can engage them personally and imaginatively, making meaning as well as practicing skills. Angela Salmon (2010) quotes a six-year-old: "When I hear music, I create stories in my mind" (p. 937). Both imagery and story structure can be experienced through music.

Experiencing Images in Music and Language

Mind pictures can be produced and developed by musical sound, often more vividly though less specifically than those generated by words. Because musical sounds are related to sounds in children's daily experiences, music "facilitate[s] mental imagery" (Salmon, 2008, p. 937). Many composers have deliberately imitated nature and human activity through their music. For example, Vivaldi's *The Seasons* includes birds and waterfalls in "Spring," a barking dog and a sudden storm in "Summer," and a blizzard during "Winter." (Since Vivaldi taught and conducted children and youth in a boarding school, he was accustomed to composing for young audiences.) Discussion of how the musical passages portray natural events can strengthen awareness of sounds as well as provide imaginative ideas that children can represent in pictures, descriptions, or stories. Table 11–4 suggests some additional music composed to represent particularly vivid images.

Experiencing Story Elements Through Music

Music composed to represent stories can be used to reinforce story sense, sequence and elements (Fisher & McDonald, 2001; Jalongo & Ribblett, 1997) that are being taught in literacy lessons. Particularly around the time of Halloween, Mussorgsky's "Night on Bald Mountain" can be appealing, as it combines vivid musical imagery with the outline of story. The composer wrote that accurately representing the Russian folk fantasy was important to him, and literary elements such as plot structure, setting, and even character can be perceived in the music. The witches gather to, as the composer himself expressed it, "gossip, play tricks and await their chief" (letter from composer to Vladimir Nikolsk, as cited in Night on Bald

Table 11–4. Music for Visualizing and Generating Descriptive Language

Title	Composer	Imagery
"Flight of the Bumblebee"	Rimsky-Korsakov	Ferocious energy of bee: fast, fluttery, frenetic
"The Bee" (L-Abeille)	Francois (not Franz) Schubert	Bee movement: fast, frenetic
"The Moldau"	Smetana	River that flows, gathers speed, passes active people, goes through storm; tranquil flowing theme
"Summer" and "Winter" from *The Seasons*	Vivaldi	"Summer" includes a fast-moving thunderstorm "Winter" includes an intense cold storm
"Sabre Dance"	Khachaturian	Swinging, swishing, swooping sabres
"In the Hall of the Mountain King"	Grieg (from *Peer Gynt*)	Trolls dancing furiously (angry, vindictive)
"Baba Yaga"	Mussorgsky (from *Pictures at an Exhibition*)	Legend of a very strange and picturesque witch whose movements are portrayed in the music
Quintet Op. 114 (Trout) Fourth movement	Schubert	A mid-sized swimming fish (very easy to identify)
Carnival of the Animals	Saint-Saens	Musical portrayal of several animals. "The Swan" depicts graceful, dignified movement.
The Nutcracker	Tschaikovsky	Story of a Christmas dream. "The March of the Toy Soldiers" and "The Waltz of the Flowers" are particularly descriptive.
Peter and the Wolf	Prokoviev	Musical portrayal of the classic story. The scene with the hunters and the triumphal march at the end might be especially effective.

Mountain, 2010). From this beginning the music becomes more intense as their leader appears, building to a frenzy as participants engage in a witches' sabbath. Mussorgsky himself called it "hot and chaotic "(as quoted. in Oldani, n.p.). As common in folklore, the story comes to an abrupt end as the cock crows and the threatening creatures are dispersed with the rising sun.

From the portrayal of the music, children can visualize the setting and describe the characters and/or draw them, noticing how the composer helps listeners know what the witches look like and how they dance. This enables practice with story elements as well as an opportunity to experience the blending of literary and musical symbol systems. Students who struggle with language difficulties benefit from extra practice with narrative structure (Catts, 2009), particularly in understanding ways in which story elements come together (Cirrin & Gillam, 2008), and the exciting music makes the elements vivid and less dependent on words to comprehend. Thus the SLP might want to give her special small group the privilege of a little extra time with witchery.

Songs with Text

Music is by nature vivid, inviting active involvement. As children are active in musical experiences that include written text, progress in areas like print knowledge, vocabulary, and vivid word use can develop.

Increasing Print Knowledge

By providing song lyrics on posters, big books, or overheads, teachers help students "make the speech to print match essential for reading success" (Cornett 2003, p. 340; see also Cecil & Lauritzen, 1994; Towell, 2000). A teacher or SLP can point to and discuss features of the lyrics with the students, including directionality, functions and relationships of particular words, use of punctuation, etc. (Fisher & McDonald, 2001). Such a focus on print functions and conventions is particularly valuable for students with oral language difficulties, building a "concrete anchor for children's metalinguistic exploration and for the timely success of important emergent literacy fundamentals" that are slow to develop in children with language delays (Justice & Ezell, 2004, p. 286).

Increasing Vocabulary

Students learn new words as they encounter them in songs (Morrow, 2001), which generally provide vivid and memorable contexts. As students sing together, lyrics bend with melody and are reinforced by association. For example, children enjoy (and some can identify with) the plaintive song sung by the popular Muppet Kermit the Frog, "It's Not Easy Being Green." The song was written for children, but some of the words might not be in the spontaneous speaking vocabulary of many them:

> It seems you *blend* in with so many other *ordinary* things.
> And people tend to *pass you over*
> 'cause you're not standing out like *flashy sparkles* in the water
> or stars in the sky.
>
> [From: http://www.elyrics.net/read/m/muppets-lyrics/
> it_s-not-easy-being-green-lyrics.html (emphasis added)]

These words are not difficult — just not spontaneous in the expression of young children. Reading text including such words from chart paper while singing them, pausing momentarily on them, and talking about them briefly (particularly in the context of Kermit the Frog), helps children increase their options for expressing themselves.

Children can share and teach classmates some of their own favorite words as they make up new lyrics to familiar songs. "Down by the Bay" by Raffi (1987) is a popular choice, as the context and refrain of the song allow a very wide variety of words/meanings; also the rhythm and rhyme patterns require students to practice their rhyming skills (Towell, 2000).

The vocabulary demonstrated in song lyrics is emphasized and reinforced when the teacher relates the words of the song to the students' own experiences (Cecil & Lauritzen, 1994). Songs connected with seasons, holidays, popular activities, or themes from classroom units are particularly useful for getting students engaged personally with song lyrics and eager to remember interesting related words.

Music for its own sake is enriching and invaluable at any age. In addition, teachers have found that "music is a powerful way to teach sound to word correspondence" (Towell, 1999, p. 284). Sound awareness and processing, engagement and imagination, and awareness of words and word relationships are only a few of many important benefits. With their in-depth training in language sounds and rhythm, SLPs may want to take the lead in developing and teaching many of the music activities to the entire class as well as in small groups of children with specific language needs.

Dance

"Remember, witches are sharp pointy people," cautioned Mr. R. as his students devised ways they could use movement to portray a witch who is determined to get a huge, stubborn pumpkin off the vine so she can make Halloween pies. When a ghost arrived to help her, Mr. R. reminded the children that ghosts are different from witches: They are light and soft; they *fllloat* and *fllllutter* rather than *jerk!* and *jab!* A vampire came next; he was dressed up fancy, and he was *sssstiff* but *sssssneaky*. The children's movement went from pointy to floaty to sneaky, in response to the meanings and the sounds of the words their teacher used. This class was dancing *The Big Pumpkin* by Erica Silverman, one of their favorite Halloween stories. Yes, dancing, but the boys were as enthusiastic as the girls, and Mr. R. was the most enthusiastic of all.

In addition to the widely noted physical and social benefits of group physical activity, dance makes important contributions to children's literacy. It has been labeled as a "strong interface between motor and cognitive activities" (Cecil & Lauritzen, 1994, p. 109). When dance is integrated with a literacy program, the multimodal learning experiences (Isbell & Raines, 2003) enable children to integrate physical movement with visual and auditory processing. This integration generates more lasting impressions for all children (Isbell & Raines, 2003). Dance is "an active problem-solving" activity (Isbell & Raines, 2003, p. 175): Finding just the right positions and movements to represent a pointy witch requires critical consideration and creative thinking, which are basic to literacy.

Dance develops a set of prereading skills including language rhythm, symbolic processing, and story structure and development. In addition, specific literacy targets can be related to and practiced within energetic and appealing dance activities, making them more memorable and thus of particular benefit for the children who struggle most with language symbols and sounds.

Dance as Symbolic Experience

The dance medium has particular benefits for children who are English language learners, have language impairments, or have a "primary orientation [which] is physical rather than mental" (Cecil & Lauitzen, 1994, pp. 109–110). Movement can be a free, universal language. Dance movements function as symbols (like words do). They can be simple and realistic, portraying everyday activities or representing action in a story sequence; or they can be individual-istic and abstract, exploring complex situations and inner feelings (Cecil & Lauritzen, 1994). Some dance symbols seem to have meanings that are shared almost universally: "jumping for joy, cowering in fear, withdrawing in sorrow, approaching, fleeing, or attacking" (Cecil & Lauretzen, 1994, p. 108). Others are generated by personal feelings, sounds, or pictures. Dance movements, like mind pictures, cannot be "wrong."

First grade teacher/author Karen Gallas (1994) concluded, "Providing opportunities for creative [movement such as dance] gives children who are less facile with dominant language forms a chance to communicate about themselves and their most important concerns" (p. 50). Children may express abstract feelings, reactions, even character representations from a story through dance, then find words that express what their bodies are feeling as they move. Thus children are able to experience success in literacy-relevant activities as they process learning and express themselves with a modality that is more natural and comfortable for some of them than language.

Dance and Language Rhythm

Music, dance, and language are all rhythmic experiences. There is rhythm in sound, rhythm in movement, rhythm in the flow of words and in the development of meaning. Children make and express meaning through all these rhythmic media, but they do so through movement long before language develops (Cecil & Lauritzen, 1994). This "natural" form of expression need not end when the others begin to develop. Dance can be easily blended in as an element of literacy experiences.

Listening and Tapping

Rap a Tap Tap: Here's Bojangles — Think of That!, a picture book by Leo and Diane Dillon (2002), initiates children into sounds and rhythms of dance and language, takes them into dance as an expressive medium, and introduces them to a fascinating individual who has been called "the greatest tap dancer of all time" (Dillon & Dillon, 2002, n.p.). Bojangles (Bill Robinson) "made art with his feet" (Dillon & Dillon 2002, n.p.), and the book shows him tapping among the rich and the poor — from the showplaces, to the fish market, to "the skids" — doing just that. The refrain, "Rap a tap tap — think of that," follows each example, all of which are portrayed in language that is rhythmic and rhymed. Children can and should tap to it, reciting the refrain as the instructor supplies the rest of the text and experiencing the rhythm with their feet as well as their voices. Clips of Robinson dancing can be found on YouTube, and students can experiment with their own tapping to some of the melodies that he made famous.

Creating with Rhythm and Sound

Few children's books are as specifically dance oriented as *Bojangles*, but many emphasize rhythm and sound in appealing ways that can be easily blended into movement-literacy experiences. For example, *Hand, Hand, Fingers, Thumb* by Al Perkins (1969) uses rhythms and sounds that imitate drum beats, with the refrain "dum ditty, dum ditty, dum, dum, dum." Children can engage in creative movements suggested by drum beats, chanting the refrain as the teacher reads the book. Both the sound of *ŭ* and some -*um* family words can be practiced in this context.

Many of the books by Dr. Seuss and Seuss imitators—for example, *The Nose Book* (Seuss, 1996), *The Foot Book* (Perkins, 1970)—can be used in similar ways. All of these books have creative and amusing illustrations that contribute a visual dimension to the multimodal experience. Once they get a feel for the rhythm and rhyme of these books, children can dance their interpretation as the teacher reads the text. To practice rhythm, rhyme, vocabulary, and movement, children can make up their own stanzas and add illustrative movements as well. Such books include alliteration, rhyme, and many repeated sounds, any of which can be pulled out for target practice.

Experiencing Dance, Music, and Initial F

Students in one preschool classroom loved a lesson their teacher titled "Fuzz Frenzy: Frenzy Freeze." She began by reading *The Great Fuzz Frenzy*, a zany story by Janet Stevens and Susan Stevens Crummel in which a group of prairie dogs find a fuzzy green tennis ball, adorn themselves with the fuzz, and have a "frenzy" with it. After the story, each student was given a piece of *fuzzy fabric* (i.e., *fur, fleece* or *flannel*). Since *F* was the letter of the day, the children began by *feeling the fuzz,* letting it *fall, folding* it, *fitting it into their fists, flipping* it, *floating* it, and *freezing* with it. They enjoyed *feeling* the *fuzz* in their *fingers* and *fists* and on their *faces.* Since the children were young and were just learning initial sounds, the /*f*/ sound was emphasized and the blends were not introduced as combined sounds (which would come later with more instruction and experience).

After feeling the fuzz, the children were ready to dance with it (Figure 11–4). The frenzy dance alternated musical segments that were *fast* and *frenzied* with those that were *floating* and *flowing.* When the music suggested a *frenzy,* the students moved with *fast feet*—*freaky* and *frightening*; when the music was *flowing,* they

Figure 11–4. Children dance the fuzz frenzy, with pieces of fuzzy fleece.

could *float, fly, flit* and *flutter.* A group doing this routine can rotate through as many frenzied and flowing segments as the children's energy and the instructor's nerves can handle.

Not everyone may comprehend or generate English words quickly, but everyone CAN feel the music and dance, and the intense movement drives the sounds and words into short-term (and eventually long-term) memory. If teachers and SLPs will consider the potential benefits of dance and recognize that *The Great Fuzz Frenzy* is not *Swan Lake*, they can be successful in using dance in their classroom literacy.

Drama

The second graders were excited about their "play": working out their script together, practicing their lines, painting scenery, rehearsing over and over until everything was just right. The newest student in the class, a boy who had recently immigrated with his parents from Ecuador, hung back with a look of disgust on his face. The teacher described the experience and its unexpected results:

> He actually told me that I was "wasting his education" because in Ecuador they work and in America we play! After the play [in which he reluctantly participated], he told the entire class that he thought at first our class was silly and not hard working. Then he told them that he has learned more here than ever before and that he had more importantly made friends. His mom told me . . . he was more confident in his writing and language skills and was participating in activities that helped him enjoy school. (Laurie Benson, email communication, 2008)

Some teachers have had to defend their use of drama in the classroom, but rarely to the students. Like dance, drama brings literacy to life (ideas, language, and stories), but with more specificity and detail. As the Ecuadorian student did not realize, when children improvise dialogue they develop oral communication skills; as they write out the scripts (often with a teacher, SLP, or parent scribe), they have the experience of seeing how conversation is related to and can be portrayed in written words. Making up songs allows them to practice alliteration and rhyme, and reading from song charts and cue cards gives them the experience of reading and rereading familiar text. And the social context and performance opportunity increase motivation by providing reasons for these literacy activities and, as the boy from Ecuador experienced, coming to like school (and literacy).

Not all drama used in classrooms will be this complex. Drama is flexible; teachers and SLPs may view drama almost as a philosophy rather than a set of "curriculum models" for teaching (Sun, 2003). Aspects or portions of it or adaptations of general processes can be used in varying circumstances for a wide variety of purposes: from something as simple as pantomime or spontaneous role play to a rehearsed production that will be presented to outside audiences. Grasp of story structure, along with use of a number of cognitive language skills, can be part of the drama experience.

Story Structure From Inside the Story

As children become characters, they explore how people (or personified animals or creatures) think, behave, speak, and respond to circumstances involving experiences, frustrations, problems, and other people. Portraying behavior and emotions directly (as actors) or indirectly (through puppets or other caricatures) brings both pleasurable and challenging situations into more concrete form so that children can relate, identify, and get their minds around them. They have explored these aspects of human experience in reading or listening to stories; with the addition of some forms of drama, they are able to experience some of the story elements from inside the story.

In describing her own child's experience of acting out stories, Rowe (2000) referred to the activity as "experiencing the book in the multisensory medium of dramatic play" (p. 12), noting that language and movement were enhanced by sensory stimulation of sets, props and costumes. Rowe concluded that children "redimensionalize the imagined worlds offered by books so they can feel it with their whole bodies" (p. 20).

Story structure can be easily explored through *process drama*, which focuses on imaginative use of dramatic formats in exploring texts as aspects of curricular and literacy learning (Crumpler, Rogers, & Schneider, 2003). For example, drama education professor Karla Huntsman (n.d.) uses several simple techniques of process drama to take first- through third-grade students inside the story *Goin' Someplace Special* by Patricia McKissack and Jerry Pinkney (2001). She reads the story, stopping frequently and directing the children in simple mini-dramas and asking them to share how they (as characters) feel. Table 11–5 shows a few of the highlights of Huntsman's sequence to illustrate how the story structure can be handled. In consideration of space, not all incidents have been included.

Table 11–5. Process Drama Segments Used in Teaching *Goin' Someplace Special*

Setting	1950s southern states Racial tension—Jim Crow laws	Teacher makes explanation and introduces African American characters.
Initiating event	Tricia Ann obtains her mother's reluctant permission for a bus trip.	Teacher reads from the book and shows pictures.
Goal	Tricia Ann wants a fun adventure.	Teacher reads from the book and shows the pictures, calling attention to worried look on the mother's face.
Attempt	Tricia Ann gets on the bus and finds no seat in "Colored" section.	A bus is set up (with chairs) having a distinct front and back section. Teacher assigns some students to be "Whites," who think they are better and don't want "Blacks" in their section. She assigns "Blacks" who want seats and justice but have to conform. Tricia Ann walks down the row, tries to sit in an empty seat.
Consequence	Tricia Ann is roughly pushed to the back of the bus and told to stand.	Children portray the action; Whites speak rudely, Blacks are sad but accepting. The teacher asks Tricia Ann, some of the Whites and some of the Blacks to tell what they are feeling.
Attempt	Tricia Ann tries to play in the park near the Peace Fountain.	Teacher reads the transition. Some children stand as the fountain, others pantomime playing around it.
Consequence	Tricia Ann is forced away.	She is asked to explain how she is feeling.
Attempt	Tricia joins a crowd of people going into a party in a hotel lobby.	The class portrays people standing around talking and having drinks. They seem to be enjoying themselves.

Table 11–5. *continued*

Consequence	People verbally attack Tricia Ann, and she is forced to leave.	Children point fingers and make disparaging remarks. The hotel manager calls a policeman who drags Tricia Ann out of the hotel. Crowd members, hotel manager, and Tricia Ann tell how they feel.
Attempt	Other people try to get Tricia to give up and go home.	Students form two lines facing each other. Tricia walks between them. Students on one side tell her the reasons she should go home; those on the other tell her why she should keep trying.
Solution	Tricia finally finds her "someplace special," where all are welcome.	Students write about their own feelings and impressions.

Individual Expression

In using drama to enhance literacy, teachers and SLPs should focus on creating a classroom environment that nurtures individual development and expression (Isbell & Raines, 2003) and emphasizes individual strengths (Jalongo, 2000)—both crucial to literacy development. As most drama involves multiple roles and applications, students should choose their own roles and forms of participation so that they can work at levels where they can be comfortable and can anticipate success (Isbell & Raines, 2003). Dramatic expression, like visualization and dance, is not "right" or "wrong"; it's individual, and everyone is invited to contribute. Children's ideas should be welcome and accepted.

For example, when a first grade class was creating and performing a play of the traditional folk story *Stone Soup*, several of the little girls wanted to be princesses; however, the story takes place in a small village with impoverished citizens and no castles or kings. So the girls (with the consent of their somewhat surprised teacher) decided that there would be a princess academy on the edge of town, and the princesses would all come out to watch the villagers make the soup; thus all the girls who wanted to be princesses could have that opportunity. The group even wrote a song for the princesses to sing. If children can work a princess academy into *Stone Soup*, there's no limit to what they can do with a little dramatic license. Ping-Yun Sun comments that drama offers students "a free and flexible space in which to grow and to learn" (p. 4) (Figure 11–5).

Language Laboratory

One of the most important requirements for developing language is having opportunities to use language (Morrow 2001). Creative drama has been referred to as "a form of verbal and nonverbal language laboratory for the elementary classroom" (Cecil & Lauritzen, 1994, p. 71). This may be at least partially because of the "expressive and imaginative uses of language" (Jalongo, 2000) that are continually involved (e.g., convincing a crowd to make soup from a stone). Additionally, the processes involved in negotiating drama (perhaps adding princesses) immerse children in vocabulary and verbal structures that may be new to many of them.

Giving Life to Vocabulary

Words become more meaningful (and thus more memorable) for students when they are used dramatically. One teacher was dis-

Figure 11–5. Children explore stories creatively through classroom drama, including the joy of being a princess.

tressed when her early-elementary students' weekly vocabulary test scores were continually below 50%. Desperate to motivate her students to study the words, she decided to let them "act out" the words with pantomimes and brief skits. Vocabulary scores went up dramatically, and the children begged for more. Within a few weeks MOST scores were either 100% or in the high 90s. Movement, imagination, and humor literally brought the words to life.

Blending Through Language

The strength of drama in such applications goes beyond motivation. The power of drama to promote language development for children is partially due to the way it can enable "action and visual elements [to] support verbal language, creating multiple connections in the brain" (Isbell & Raines, 2003, p. 197). Hoyt (1992) explained that during creative drama children draw information from their reading and blend it with their prior knowledge and experience to form ideas and insights, then express these ideas through dialogue ("verbal interpretation") as well as action (p. 581).

For example, *beneath* is on the national vocabulary list for first grade. A mini-drama using this word might involve a treasure hunt with the clue "beneath" sending children (wearing pirate hats) helter skelter to look beneath everything in one area of the classroom—chattering about what they should look beneath, why they should look beneath it, and how they're going to move things to get *beneath* it.

Individual Needs

Children struggle with language and reading skills for a variety of reasons, ranging from severe disabilities to a home situation with limited literacy experience. Drama offers ways in which SLPs and teachers can individualize literacy participation to meet specific needs.

Experiencing Language Holistically

The process of finding information, forming ideas, and expressing ideas through action and dialogue (Hoyt, 1992) was exemplified by an experience of Donna Adomat (2009), a reading specialist who worked with struggling first graders. Adomat used process drama techniques (e.g. role play, interview, "hot seat") to develop the children's reading comprehension and language use. In a journal article she described Nathan, who disliked reading because his need to slowly sound out each word prevented him from enjoying either the content or the language of the stories. Being an outgoing, creative, and actually very verbal child, Nathan participated eagerly in the dramatic activities. "He enjoyed playing with the language of the story," his teacher wrote (Adomat, 2009, p. 630), noting how he savored and manipulated specific words. Nathan quickly became a leader in his class as his "dramatic play became a creative mixture of story and personal elements" (Adomat, pp. 630–631). "He used stories and drama to express his own personal purposes and intentions. He wanted to play with the ideas in the story, savor the language, and create his own scenarios and dialogue" (Adomat, p. 651).

As he both created dialogue and negotiated its use, Nathan's expressive language was strong and fluent. Nathan also did well at "hot-seating," a form of process drama in which children put one of the characters in the hot seat: asking him questions that make him explain and defend his position.

> Drama helped Nathan to realize that all literacy experiences would not be difficult and excruciatingly slow; literacy's broader meaning and practices enfolded his strengths and interests and connected him in multifaceted ways to making meaning and the expression of that meaning. (Adomat, 2009, p. 632)

The carefully structured drama experiences were effective for this particular child, as observed by his teacher, who purposefully planned, implemented, and observed the needs and development of her students. By the end of the year Nathan was able to leave the remedial group.

Developing Fluency

Though Nathan struggled with the processes of sounding out words in both reading and writing contexts, he was strong in oral fluency; he understood the rhythms and patterns of English and was able to use them smoothly and easily in oral expression. Many children do not have this advantage, particularly those who are English language learners or have not had rich language experiences in their home. Fluency skills can be improved by repeatedly rereading texts that are a slight challenge at the students' reading level (Leahy & Justice, 2006). But repeated rereading of most texts is not motivating for most students.

Reader's theatre, a dramatic format in which all lines are read aloud from a hand-held script, gives children this rereading experience in the guise of motivating social interactions and performance opportunities (Leahy & Justice, 2006). Students experience and become accustomed to language rhythm and flow as they read (not having to create or remember) rhythmic sentences with the participation and support of the rest of the class. Some lines are read by individuals, others by pairs or small groups of students. Still others are read in unison by the entire group. As readers speak together, they "see and hear words simultaneously," joining in "correct pronunciation, intonation, and expression" (Flynn, 2005, p. 148). Thus, as they rehearse they participate repeatedly in correct, fluent reading (which might, perhaps, be considered a form of ultimate scaffolding). Students who struggle with reading can be successful with readers' theatre because all of the reading is rehearsed repeatedly with plenty of peer coaching, and with teacher help available if needed (McGee & Richgels, 2008).

If the teacher and SLP are aware of potential advantages, they can organize the experience to maximize certain areas. Rosalind Flynn (2005), an educational drama specialist, noted that in her experience students who are going to perform for an audience may practice the same script 15 to 20 times (which they would never do in reading a passage by themselves), and students are strongly motivated by group loyalty to focus and do their best. Thus, the rhythm of sentences and the meaning of new vocabulary become more strongly engrained, and fluency (including rhythm, rate, prosody and accuracy) is enhanced (Leahy & Justice, 2006). Opportunities can be easily arranged for students to perform before other classes and/or at parent participation events.

Since one hand holds the script, the other is free for gestures such as pointing fingers, raising fists, cupping a hand over an ear, snapping fingers, beckoning, calling etc. (Flynn, 2005). Students typically sit on stools but may stand (McGee & Richgels, 2008) and may engage in appropriate movement and/or act on simple props (Isbell & Raines, 2003). Any form of movement increases retention

(Flynn, 2005) as well as motivation. Additionally, young children enjoy wearing simple items representing their characters, such as hats, ties, or scarves—further increasing motivation and interest.

Adapting A Variety of Forms

As with many strategies and techniques, classroom drama is beneficial for all students, and additional or repeated drama is particularly helpful for students who struggle with speech or language, especially if guided by an experienced SLP. Table 11–6 mentions some simple, non-threatening drama forms that can be easily adapted for or repeated with students needing extra language support.

Regardless of the chosen form of creative drama, students should participate as much as possible in the creation and performance. The teacher must function as a guiding and supporting leader: setting goals, introducing various phases of the experience, and assisting in all aspects of the project (Isbell & Raines, 2003).

Conclusion

Literacy programs for preschool to second grade students can help children become more confident, develop emergent reading knowledge and skills and, in the process, enjoy school. During kindergarten and early grades, a critical time for establishing both preliminary skills and positive attitudes toward literacy, teachers need to consider the query and response of Longley (1999):

> And what are young people learning when they learn the arts? To use their minds in verbal and nonverbal ways. To communicate complex ideas in a variety of forms. To understand what someone else is trying to tell them in words, sounds, or images. (p. 71)

Children naturally learn and express themselves in a variety of ways, some favoring language as a medium of communication, some preferring pictures, others enjoying music or working most effectively through various types of drama. When the arts are integrated with literacy, they serve as bridges into literacy for

Table 11–6. Additional Classroom Drama Forms

Drama Form	Need/Benefit	Possible Applications
Pantomime	Motions without words allow practice of organization and content skills needed by LD children[a] without having to struggle with words.	Begin with simple daily activities and routines (shopping at a store, eating at a restaurant), gradually progressing to more complex actions (Isbell & Raines, 2003). Eventually the adult may read or tell a story as the students pantomime with simple props and costumes.
Narrative theater	Individually scaffolded dialogue allows students to produce language at their own skill level. Informal nature of dialogue removes grammar threat.	Adult reads or tells the story, but stops intermittently to let the children portraying the various characters create dialogue; any refrain is recited in unison by all (Jalongo, 2000).
Puppet drama	Puppet allows self-conscious children to speak as someone else. Puppets are expected to say silly or illogical things or to use unusual speech patterns, and repetitious vocabulary.	Puppets may interact with each other to portray a story or role play a situation; a child may engage in dialogue with the puppet—conversation, interview, or even hot seat. Puppet characters may step out of the story and talk with a child (or adult) standing to the side of the stage.
Interview or "hot seat"	Adult or more advanced peer can guide the course of conversation and scaffold the LD student's participation.	A character, bystander, or outsider interviews one of the story characters: e.g. asking how she felt or why she did what she did. How "hot" the seat is can be controlled by the adult either asking or guiding composition of the questions.

[a]See Fey, Catts, Proctor-Williams, Tomblin, & Zhang, 2004.

diverse learners and as significant enrichment experiences for those who acquire language easily. All are ways of providing for children's needs and preferences while working at language and literacy development. All offer opportunities for variety, imagination, language development, personal application, and emotional involvement through "many kinds of literacies" (Hoyt, 1992, p. 581). All have important roles in children's early literacy development

References

Adomat, D. S. (2009, May). Actively engaging with stories through drama: Portraits of two young readers. *Reading Teacher, 62*(8), 628–636.

Althouse, R., Johnson, M. H., & Mitchell, S. T. (2003). *The colors of learning: Integrating the visual arts into the early childhood curriculum.* New York, NY: Teacher College Press.

Anvari, S. H., Trainor, L. J., Woodside, J., & Levy, B. A. (2002). Relations among musical skills, phonological processing, and early reading ability in preschool children. *Journal of Experimental Child Psychology, 83*(2), 111–130.

Calkins, L. M. (1983). *Lessons from a child: On the teaching and learning of writing.* Exeter, NH: Heinemann.

Catts, H. W. (2009, April). The narrow view of reading promotes a broad view of comprehension. *Language, Speech, and Hearing Services in Schools, 40,* 178–183. doi:10.1044/0161-1461(2008/08-0035)

Catts, H. W., & Kamhi, A. G. (1986, October). The linguistic basis of reading disorders: Implications for the speech-language pathologist. *Language, Speech, and Hearing Services in Schools, 17,* 329–341.

Cecil, N. L., & Lauritzen, P. (1994). *Literacy and the arts for the integrated classroom: Alternative ways of knowing.* White Plains, NY: Longman.

Cirrin, F. M., & Gillam, R. B. (2008, January). Language intervention practices for school-age children with spoken language disorders: A systematic review. *Language, Speech, and Hearing Services in Schools, 39,* 110–137. doi:10.1044/0161-1461(2008/012)

Cornett, C. E. (2003). *Creating meaning through literature and the arts* (2nd ed.). Upper Saddle River, NJ: Merrill Prentice-Hall.

Cowan, K., & Albers, P. (2006). Semiotic representations: Building complex literacy practices through the arts. *Reading Teacher, 60*(2), 124–137.

Crosbie, S., Holm, A., & Dodd, B. (2009). Cognitive flexibility in children with and without speech disorder. *Child Language Teaching and Therapy*, *25*(2), 250–270.

Crumpler, T. P., Rogers, T., & Schneider, J. J. (2003). Introduction. In J. J. Schneider, T. P. Crumpler, & T. Rogers (Eds.), *Process drama and multiple literacies: Addressing social, cultural, and ethical issues* (pp. xiii–xx). Portsmouth, NH: Heinemann.

Eisner, E. (1983). *Beyond creating*. Los Angeles, CA: Getty Center for Education in Art.

Fisher, D., & McDonald, N. (2001). The intersection between music and early literacy instruction: Listening to literacy. *Reading Improvement*, *38*(3), 106–115.

Flynn, R. M. (2004-05). Curriculum-based readers theatre: Setting the stage for reading and retention. *Reading Teacher*, *58*(4), 360–365.

Gallas, K. (1994). *The languages of learning*. New York, NY: Teachers College Press.

Hansen, D., & Bernstorf, E. (2002). Linking music learning to reading instruction. *Music Educators Journal*, *88*(5), 17–21.

Hertzog, N. (2001, Spring). Reflections and impressions from Reggio Emilia: "It's not about art!" *Early Childhood Research and Practice*, *3*(1) [Online version].

Hoyt, L. (1992). Many ways of knowing: Using drama, oral interactions, and the visual arts to enhance reading comprehension. *Reading Teacher*, *45*(8), 580–584.

Huntsman, K. (n.d.). *Lesson plan for* Goin' Someplace Special. Retrieved from http://education.byu.edu/arts/lessonplans/grade36.html

Intrator, S. (2001). Teaching the media child in the digital swarm. *Arts Education Policy Review*, *102*(6), 25–27.

Isbell, R. T., & Raines, S. C. (2003). *Creativity and the arts with young children*. Clifton Park, NY: Delmar Learning.

Jalongo, M. R. (2000). *Early childhood language arts* (2nd ed.). Boston, MA: Allyn & Bacon.

Jalongo, M. R., & Ribblett, D. M. (1997). Using song picture books to support emergent literacy. *Childhood Education*, *74*(1), 15–22.

Justice, L. M., & Ezell, H. K. (2004, April). Print referencing: An emergent literacy enhancement strategy and its clinical applications. *Language, Speech and Hearing Services in Schools*, *35*, 185–193.

Leahy, S. B., & Justice, L. M. (2006). Promoting reading fluency and motivation through readers theatre. In T. A. Ukrainetz (Ed.), *Contextualized language intervention: Scaffolding PreK–12 literacy achievement* (pp. 469–502). Greenville, SC: Thinking Publications.

Longley, L. (1999, October). Gaining the arts literacy advantage. *Educational Leadership*, *57*(2), 71–74.

McGee, L. M., & Richgels, D. J. (2003). *Designing early literacy programs: Strategies for at-risk preschool and kindergarten children.* New York, NY: Guilford Press.

McGee, L. M., & Richgels, D. J. (2008). *Literacy's beginnings* (5th ed.). Boston, MA: Pearson.

Merrefield, G. E. (1997). Theee billy goats and Gardner. *Educational Leadership, 55*(1), 58–61.

Morrow, L. M. (2001). *Literacy development in the early years* (4th ed.). Boston, MA: Allyn & Bacon.

Night on Bald Mountain. (2010). *Wikipedia.* Retrieved from http://en.wikipedia.org/wiki/Night_on_Bald_Mountain#Composition_history

Norton, D. E. (2004). *The effective teaching of language arts* (6th ed.). Upper Saddle River, NJ: Pearson, Merrill, Prentice-Hall.

Oldani. R. W. (n.d.) Musorgsky, Modest Petrovich. In *Grove Music Online. Oxford Music Online.* Retrieved from http://www.oxfordmusiconline.com/subscriber/article/grove/music/19468

O'Neill, C. (2006). Foreward. In J. J. Schneider, T. P. Crumpler, & T. Rogers (Eds.), *Process drama and multiple literacies: Addressing social, cultural, and ethical issues* (pp. ix–xii). Portsmouth, NH: Heinemann.

Paquette, K. R., & Rieg, S. A. (2008). Using music to support the literacy development of young English language learners. *Early Childhood Education Journal, 36,* 227–232.

Pomona College. (1998). *What is visual literacy?* Retrieved from http://www.pomona,edu/Academics/courserelated/classprojects/visual

Purnell, P. G., Parveen, A., Begum, N., & Carter, M. (2007). Windows, bridges and mirrors: Building culturally responsive early childhood classrooms through the integration of literacy and the arts. *Early Childhood Education Journal, 34*(6), 419–424.

Reeves, D. (2007, February). Academics and the arts. *Educational Leadership, 64*(5), 80–81.

Register, D. (2004). The effects of live music groups versus an educational children's television program on the emergent literacy of young children. *Journal of Music Therapy, 41*(1), 2–27.

Ritter, M. (n.d.). The speech-language pathologist and reading: Opportunities to extend services for the children we serve. *Perspectives on School-Based Issues.* Retrieved from http://journals.asha.org/perspectives

Rowe, D. W. (2000). Bringing books to life: The role of book-related dramatic play in young children's literacy learning. In K. A. Roskos & J. F. Christie, *Play and literacy in early childhood* (pp. 3–25). Mahwah, NJ: Lawrence Erlbaum Associates.

Salmon, A. (2010). Using music to promote children's thinking and enhance their literacy development. *Early Child Development and Care, 180*(7), 937–945.

Savage, J. F. (2007). *Sound it out.* New York, NY: McGraw-Hill.

Schuele, C. M., & Boudreau, D. (2008, January). Phonological awareness intervention: Beyond the basics. *Language, Speech, and Hearing Services in Schools, 39,* 3–20. doi:10.1044/0161-1461(2008/002)

Sun, P. Y. (2003). *Using drama and theatre to promote literacy development: Some basic classroom applications.* ERIC Clearinghouse on Reading, English and Communication. Retrieved from http://www.indiana .edu/-reading/ieo/digests/d187.html

Tonucci, F. (n.d.). Wonderful games. In L. Malaguzzi, S. Spaggiari, & C. Rinaldi (Eds.), *The hundred languages of children: Catalogue of the exhibit* (pp.74–77). Reggio Emilia, Italy: Reggio Children.

Towell, J. H. (2000). Teaching reading: Motivating students through music and literature. *Reading Teacher, 53*(4), 284–287.

Wiggins, D. W. (2007). Pre–K music and the emergent reader: Promoting literacy in a music-enhanced environment. *Early Childhood Education Journal, 35*(1), 55–64. doi:10.1007/s10643-007-0167-6

Children's Books Cited

Dillon, L., & Dillon, D. (2002). *Rap a tap tap: Here's Bojangles—think of that!* New York, NY: Blue Sky Press (Scholastic).

Hayes, A. (1991). *Meet the orchestra.* Singapore: Harcourt.

McKissack, P., & Pinkney, J. (2001). *Goin' someplace special.* New York, NY: Simon & Schuster.

Micklethwait, L. (1995). *Spot a dog.* New York, NY: Dorling Kindersley.

Micklethwait, L. (1996). *A child's book of play in art.* New York, NY: Dorling Kindersley.

Perkins, A. (1969). *Hand, hand, fingers, thumb.* New York, NY: Random House.

Perkins, A. (1970). *The nose book.* New York, NY: Random House.

Raffi. (1987). *Down by the bay.* New York, NY: Crown.

Seuss, T. G. (1996). *The Foot Book.* New York, NY: Random House.

Silverman, E. (1992). *Big pumpkin.* New York, NY: Simon & Schuster Children's Publishing.

Stevens, J., & Crummel, S. S. (2005). *The Great Fuzz Frenzy.* China: Harcourt.

SEEL Lessons Cited

Aspects of the following lessons from the Systematic and Engaging Early Literacy Web site have been mentioned in the chapter; full lesson plans can be found at http://education.byu.edu/projectseel/resources/db.html.

Fuzz Frenzy: Frenzy Freeze

Tubas and Tambourines

Chapter 12

Assessing Students' Needs and Progress: Use of Data to Adjust Instruction

Barbara Culatta and Kendra M. Hall-Kenyon

Effective early literacy instruction must be based on relevant assessment information concerning children's performance on the various literacy components. Specific methodologies and procedures have been developed to provide reliable data. This chapter discusses some of the important considerations involved with administering early literacy assessments and explains specific procedures for gaining information about children's performance in a variety of ways.

Considerations for Selecting and Conducting Assessments

If assessments are to be the foundation for making instructional decisions, they must be based on practices that are appropriate for young children. This section deals with some general considerations that should be kept in mind when selecting and administering early literacy tools.

Purpose of the Assessment

The purpose for collecting assessment data should focus and guide both collection and use of the information. All assessment data should lead to setting goals, making instructional decisions, and modifying and tailoring instruction to fit children's needs. Table 12–1 designates important purposes of assessment, which

Table 12–1. Purpose of Assessment and Sources of Assessment Information

Purposes of Assessment	Specific Instructional or Programmatic Uses	Types of Tools and Procedures
Screening	Determine which students are at risk for literacy difficulties; identify children in need of supplemental or differentiated instruction; set goals	Formal or standardized screening measure; probes tied to the curriculum (tasks or skills that are indicators of literacy performance)
Identifying specific needs	Identify specific learning needs; determine skills children have and don't have; gain in-depth understanding of abilities and needs; make instructional decisions; set goals	Standardized measures that explore performance within targeted areas; performance probes, observations
Monitoring progress (benchmarking)	Evaluate progress in attaining literacy targets; identify gains made on specific curricular tasks; individualize instruction; periodically adjust goals	Probes; behavior samples; responses to curricular tasks
Determining outcomes, evaluating the effectiveness of intervention	Determine level of performance as compared to a normative standard; evaluate effectiveness of instruction	Beginning and end of year comparisons on formal measures and curricular tasks

include screening children for delays, identifying specific needs and abilities, monitoring progress, and determining the effectiveness of instruction. It also lists some methods and data sources that are typically used to achieve those purposes. Addressing these assessment purposes affects intervention decisions that will be made, along with ways they will be monitored and revised.

Nature of the Assessment Measures

Despite the significant purposes for assessing young children's early literacy skills, SLPs and teachers must be careful to select tools and tasks that are appropriate for young children (Salinger, 2001). In assuring that assessments are relevant, the examiner should balance the use of formal and informal procedures and know the advantages of each.

Formal

Formal assessments provide structured ways to observe children's performance, and many also offer normative data by which an individual's performance can be judged relative to the performance of other children. SLPs and teachers, however, must be cautious not to overassess young children using formal procedures that are highly structured, since many formal tools are not consonant with the types of activities children encounter in their typical classroom or curricular instruction (Salinger, 2001, 2006) and do not provide information that directly impacts instructional practices. Educators need to be aware of how difficult it is to collect valid information about young children (Epstein, Shweinhart, & DeBruin-Parecki, 2004; Salinger, 2006) regardless of the tool they are using.

In addition, teachers and SLPs need to ensure that any assessment tools selected are developmentally appropriate for young children. If children are not able to understand or perform the task, the examiner does not know whether they lack knowledge of the skill, are unfamiliar with the nature of the particular task, or misunderstood the task completely. Even simple instructions can be misunderstood by young children. For example, when responding to "what is the name of this letter?" as a prompt on the Letter Naming subtest from the PALS-K, one kindergartner looked carefully at the first letter and said, "Not in my name." Thus, those who administer assessments to young children must be careful to monitor children's understanding of the assessment task, even with tasks that are developmentally appropriate.

Formal measures should not be used solely to obtain a score relative to a normative group. Children's performance on particular items on formal measures can and should be more closely inspected to provide specific information about what they are or are not able to do on the measure. For example, a report specifying the kinds of errors in decoding, spelling, or phonological awareness that children make or indicating their level of confidence in responding to tasks can provide important information regarding areas in which they need extra attention. In addition, SLPs and teachers should discontinue testing if children exhibit signs of discomfort. In sum, formal assessments can be helpful to teachers and SLPs as they determine children's relative abilities, but many are not very helpful in making specific instructional decisions and may contain tasks that are not appropriate for young children.

Informal

Unlike formal procedures, informal procedures can fit well into regular classroom contexts, as they tend to be consonant with the types of activities children encounter in instruction. In fact, some suggest that assessment procedures and practices should actually mirror the types of instructional activities young children are accustomed to (Salinger, 2006). Thus they can be implemented during regular classroom instruction and "disguised" as typical or familiar instructional activities. Many are presented in a playful manner, making them more child friendly. Thus many children feel more comfortable with and even enjoy these types of tasks and are more likely to produce responses that accurately represent their abilities (Kieff & Casbergue, 2000). Two common informal procedures are observations of children's performance and probes.

Observation, a common informal assessment, includes noting children's behavior during instruction and paying attention to their responsiveness when provided with typical supports. During instruction the examiner can note variability in performance, conditions under which children's performance improves or deteriorates, and types of supports provided in regular instruction that facilitate performance.

Probes, another common informal assessment, consist of tasks designed to target a specific concept or skill. They are typically structured or semi-structured tasks that are easy to administer and quickly elicit a behavior reflecting some emergent or early literacy ability (Pence, 2007). Probes can address a wide variety of literacy components. Examples include asking a child to think of a word that starts with a particular sound, blend phonemes to create a word, generate a rhyme, give a sound to a particular letter, read a sight word or small core of phonetically regular words, identify which object in a line is last, find the one object out of three or four that does not rhyme, and recall a story event.

Probes also have the advantage of giving teachers and SLPs a mechanism to monitor children's progress. Probes can be incorporated into a center activity or be presented at the end of a lesson or during transition times. If probes are presented as part of transition, children are given a task to respond to as their "ticket" or opportunity to move to the next activity, and the adult notes how the child responds. Each child can be given a turn to respond to a question or task before moving from one station or activity to another. For example, when focusing on rhyming with preschool children, the SLP can follow up a small group rhyming activity with -*eep* by asking each child to think of a word that rhymes with *beep* or to tell if *sheep* and *sleep* rhyme before moving to another area. The task is a quick notation of whether the child can generate or recognize a rhyme with a particular targeted ending. The information gained from probes should then be considered when determining which literacy skills to address in instruction.

Task Demands Relative to Children's Abilities

In using either formal or informal measures, educators must ensure that task demands are appropriate. They need to determine that children understand the instructional task and its various components, and they must anticipate which aspects of the task may influence performance. If children performing a rhyming task do not have the capacity to hold a pair of words in memory to reflect on whether they are the same or different, then the task of evoking a response is interfering with the child's performance of the skill being tapped.

A task analysis can also help members of an educational team determine if prerequisite skills need to be further assessed or taught. For example, if a child has difficulty decoding words, the adult will want to analyze the student's knowledge of letter-sound associations as well as his or her capacity to engage in auditory blending, segmenting, and manipulating sounds in words.

Additionally, vocabulary and comprehension demands are part of children's initial knowledge of language. Selecting tasks that fit the children's current linguistic level is particularly important when assessing children from different language backgrounds as well as children with language-learning disabilities, as students from either group may lack prerequisite language skills to handle a particular task. The examiner needs to consider whether the children have had experience with and are able to use the content and vocabulary involved in the task. The following questions may need to be considered:

- ◆ Are the children familiar and comfortable with the context and task demands?
- ◆ Do children feel confident with the skills or tasks requested?
- ◆ How much prior experience have they had with the same sorts of tasks?
- ◆ Is the skill one that is common or that they have encountered?
- ◆ Have children had experience with the content in the task?
- ◆ Do they know the language used?
- ◆ Are there any memory or cognitive demands that may influence performance?

Examiners can determine if children understand or can handle a task either by teaching its steps/process or by presenting it with content or skills that are simple and familiar before applying it to assess literacy-related skills. If tasks involved in an assessment do not align with those the children encounter in instruction, the examiner must consider whether the information gained from them is applicable or appropriate (Salinger, 2001).

Contrasts in Performance With and Without Supports

Observations of student performance in instructional settings with and without supports can provide very useful information about children's language and literacy learning. As part of the assessment process, the teacher or other team member observes the child's performance without support to modify behavior and then contrasts the performance level with what the child is able to do with support. This process of contrasting performance with and without supports, part of a framework referred to as *dynamic assessment*, permits educators to know not only what children are currently able to do, but which instructional manipulations are needed to achieve certain behaviors (Gutiérrez-Clellen & Peña, 2001; Lidz, 1991,1996).

Typically the framework for dynamic assessment includes the four following steps: (1) identify the literacy skill, (2) analyze the task, (3) determine the zone of actual development (ZAD), and (4) explore the zone of proximal development (ZPD). SLPs and teachers first identify the target skill they will assess, based on the developmental sequence of the curriculum, the child's displayed strengths and weaknesses, and/or information from traditional assessments. After the skill has been identified, the teacher or SLP selects and analyzes the task in order to determine the skills, both linguistic and metalinguistic, that are necessary to complete the task. As the child then engages in the assessment task, the SLP or teacher determines the zone of actual development by examining the child's performance without support. This performance is then contrasted with the child's performance on the same task with support. Identifying the gap between supported and unsupported performance provides relevant diagnostic information, and determining supports that positively impact performance provides a starting point for interventions (Merritt & Culatta, 1998).

The process of comparing performance with and without supports can be seen in the following example of a sorting task used to assess sound awareness. The child might be asked to go to a "sss-store" and put things that begin with /s/ in a sack: things like sandwich, sucker, soup, syrup. The teacher would first model a number of /s/ words while exaggerating the /s/ sound, giving the child opportunities to respond with the assistance of gestures or prompts (e.g., a head nod indicating *yes* when asked about putting soda in the sack and a head shake indicating *no* when asked about putting bread in the sack). After the child has been provided with many positive examples and been given high levels of support in rejecting negative ones, cues are gradually withdrawn, and the child is given a chance to respond independently. The teacher or SLP gives particular attention to whether the child correctly discards items that don't begin with /s/, such as pizza and bananas. Also the examiner notices the degree to which the child responds impulsively, watches for cues, or lacks confidence in his responses—particularly when negative examples are involved (Culatta & Hall, 2006).

Integration of Information from Multiple Sources

Although assessments must be administered sparingly, early childhood team members realize that information will be more accurate if they draw upon multiple sources (Jones, 2003; Maxwell & Clifford, 2004). By sharing and synthesizing information, the team can obtain a more accurate view of children's needs and can share instructional goals and strategies. Recognizing that structured or standardized assessments may not be culturally or linguistically appropriate for a particular group of children or may be inaccurate in assessing those with language differences or delays, they balance use of structured tasks with naturalistic ways to gain information. They know that the context and task variables (e.g., task demands, supports provided, children's familiarity with the experience, and level of engagement) influence children's performance, and thus informal and observational processes can help them understand why children perform as they do during instruction and on formal assessment measures (Epstein, Schweinhart, & DeBruin-Parecki, 2004; Salinger, 2001). Thus, a multiple-source assessment gives a more complete picture.

In addition to integrating information from multiple sources, teachers and SLPs should take into account assessments that address both skill and meaning components of literacy. While it is often easier to measure the skills, such as letter naming and phonological awareness, assessing children's comprehension abilities in addition to skills provides a clearer picture of what children can do. The following sections suggest a number of assessment procedures that can be used to assess the full spectrum of literacy skills.

Assessments for Skill Components

Early literacy researchers emphasize skills related to acquiring the *alphabetic principle*: the understanding that letters and combinations of letters represent speech sounds in words. Children must realize that there is a predictable relationship between sounds and letters and between sound combinations and letter patterns (or "chunks" of words) if they are to understand how reading works. Skills involved in the alphabetic principle and in the processes of decoding and writing words include letter knowledge, phonological awareness, decoding/word analysis, and spelling. Table 12–2 provides examples of a number of literacy assessments in each of the component areas. Some of these are discussed in greater detail in the sections below.

Letter Naming and Letter-Sound Association

Children's recognition of letters is an important part of early literacy assessment. Their interest in and awareness of letters should be observed and assessed in preschool and kindergarten (Justice, Invernizzi, & Meier, 2002; Snow, Burns, & Griffin, 1998).

Assessment Tasks

Letter knowledge is easily assessed by asking children to choose a named letter from an assortment or to give the names of letters they are shown (in random sequence). Most early literacy assessments include such letter naming tasks (see Table 12–2). In addition to accuracy in naming or identifying letters, evaluators must pay attention to the speed and automaticity of children's responses.

In addition to knowing letter names, kindergarten children begin to learn the sounds that letters make. The ability to associate letters with their sounds is essential for early reading (reading. uoregon.edu). This ability can be assessed by asking children to identify the letter that goes with a sound or produce the sound that typically goes with a letter (e.g., *T, P, Z*) or digraph (e.g., *sh, ch*). Letter-sound assessments are particularly important for kindergarten children, who learn the most common sounds that letters make,

Table 12–2. Measures for Assessing Skill- and Meaning-Based Early Literacy Components

Component	Measures
Letter Naming and Letter- Sound Association	DIBELS (Good & Kaminski, 2002)
	ERDA-2 (The Psychological Corporation, 2003)
	An Observational Survey of Early Literacy Achievement (Clay, 2006)
	PALS-PreK (Invernizzi, Sullivan, Meier, & Swank, 2004)
	PALS-K (Invernizzi, Juel, Swank, & Meier, 2005)
	TERA-3 (Reid et al., 2001)
	WJ-III Tests of Achievement (Woodcock, McGrew, & Mather, 2001).
	TOPEL (Lonigan, Wagner, Torgesen, & Rashotte, 2007)
Phonological Awareness	Test of Auditory Analysis Skills (Rosner, 1993)
	Roswell-Chall Auditory Blending Task (1997)
	TOPEL (Lonigan et al., 2007)
	TOPA -2+ (Torgesen & Bryant, 2004)
	PALS-PreK (Invernizzi et al., 2004)
	PALS-K (Invernizzi et al., 2005)
	PALS-1-3 (Invernizzi et al., 2011)
	PAT (Robertson & Salter, 1997)
	IGDI (Early Childhood Research Institute on Measuring Growth and Development, 1998)
	WJ-III Diagnostic Reading Battery (Woodcock, Mather, & Schrank, 2004)
	TOPAS (Newcomer & Barenbaum, 2003)
Decoding, Phonics	Basic Reading Inventory (Johns, 2008)
	QRI-5 (Leslie & Caldwell, 2010)
	DRA-2-K-3 (Beaver, 2011)
	TWRE-2 (Torgesen, Wagner, & Rashotte, 2011)
	PALS-K (Invernizzi et al., 2005)
	PALS-1-3 (Invernizzi et al., 2011)
	WRMT-III (Woodcock, 2011)
	WJ-III Diagnostic Reading Battery (Woodcock et al., 2004)

Table 12–2. *continued*

Component	Measures
Fluency	Oral Reading Fluency Assessment (Deno, 1985)
	Multidimensional Fluency Scale (Zuttell & Rasinsky, 1991)
	DIBELS (Good & Kaminski, 2002)
	GORT-4 (Wiederholt & Bryant, 2001)
Spelling	Words Their Way (Bear, Invernizzi, Templeton, & Johnson, 2012)
	SPELL-2 (Masterson, Apel, & Wasowicz, 2006)
	TWS-4 (Larsen, Hammil, & Moats, 1999)
	PALS-K (Invernizzi et al., 2005)
	WJ-III Diagnostic Reading Battery (Woodcock et al., 2004)
Vocabulary and Semantic Knowledge	BBCS-R (Bracken, 1998).
	Boehm Test of Basic Concepts (Boehm, 2000).
	TOPEL Definitions (Lonigan, Wagner, Torgesen, & Rashotte, 2007)
	TOLD-P:4 (Newcomer & Hammill, 2008)
	CREVT-2 (Wallace & Hammill, 2002)
	WRMT-III (Woodcock, 2011)
	EOWPVT-4 (Martin & Brownell, 2011)
	LPT-3 (Richard & Hanner, 2005)
	IGDI (Early Childhood Research Institute on Measuring Growth and Development, 1998)
Comprehension	Basic Reading Inventory (Johns, 2008)
	WRMT-III (Woodcock, 2011)
	QRI-5 (Leslie & Caldwell, 2010)
	CELF-4 (Semel, Wiig, & Secord, 2003)
	GORT-4 (Wiederholt & Bryant, 2001)
	Assessing Narrative Comprehension in Young Children (Paris & Paris, 2003)
	WJ-III Diagnostic Reading Battery (Woodcock et al., 2004)
	DRA-2-K-3 (Beaver, 2011)

and for first- and second-grade children, who learn to associate letters with less common sounds and to represent sounds with multiple spellings (e.g., contexts in which the long *e* sound can be spelled with *ee*, *ea*, or *y*). The educational team should track which letter-sound correspondences children know by periodic use of benchmarking or progress-monitoring letter-sound association tasks. Benchmarking and progress monitoring are particularly important with letter-sound associations, as SLPs or teachers must specifically teach any letter sounds that children haven't acquired. See Table 12–2 for examples of assessments for letter naming and letter-sound association.

Reading/Writing Contexts

Information about letter-sound associations can also be observed in the context of reading and writing. For example, if the children just packed a sack with *-ack* words, the teacher or SLP can write words (e.g., *pack, sack, tack, jack, rack, back*) or phrases (e.g., "a sack that lacks a back," "a rack to hang a backpack") on chart paper and involve children in using initial letter-sound information to attach meaning to the print with shared reading supports. As the teacher or SLP encounters a particular word, she can stop, point to the letter, and say, "Look at this letter; let's see what sound it makes so we know what *-ack* word this is." Similarly, if the teacher and children are doing an interactive writing experience in which they share the marker as they write about their walk out back with a snack in a sack, the teacher or SLP observes which initial sounds or letter patterns the child can write on the chart independently and which he can supply only with support.

Phonological Awareness

Phonological awareness, understanding that words are made up of sounds that can be blended and segmented, includes a number of skills at different developmental levels (see Chapter 5 in this book). Phonological awareness may be assessed through tasks that reflect specific developmental stages: casual play with sounds, recognition of sounds and sound patterns, and identification and manipulation of individual phonemes in words (Gillon, 2004; Hester & Hodson, 2007; Schuele, Skibbe, & Rao, 2007).

Sound Pattern Sensitivity

Preschool children's early phonological awareness includes sensitivity to sound patterns that can be reflected in sound play. At the awareness level children may participate in playing with sounds (e.g., rhyming and alliteration) without explicitly talking about or labeling the sound pattern or generating the pattern when asked (Bradley & Bryant, 1983; Brady & Shankweiler, 1991; Goswami & Bryant, 1990; Muter, Hulme, Snowling, & Stevenson, 2004). Teachers and SLPs can assess children's early sound awareness by observing spontaneous behaviors such as making up nonsense words, generating or imitating rhymed words, repeating familiar nursery rhymes, and either repeating alliteration phrases or making up words that start with the same sound (Dowker, 1989; MacLean, Bryant, & Bradley, 1987; Snow, Burns, & Griffin, 1998).

In addition to observing sound play, adults can attempt to elicit behaviors that reflect early sensitivity to speech sound patterns. The adult can prime sound play with modeling to see if children join in. For example, researchers have had children complete a familiar nursery rhyme in order to monitor their rhyme ability and thus to predict later literacy development (Bryant, MacLean, Bradley, & Crossland, 1990; Goswami & Bryant, 1990; MacLean et al., 1987; Fernandez-Fein & Baker, 1997). A similar way to elicit early sound play is through cloze tasks (Christie, Enz, & Vukelich, 2010; Dorsey, 1972; Gillon, 2004). A cloze (sentence completion) rhyme task consists of presenting a rhymed verse that exemplifies the pattern and then pausing before the last word to have the child(ren) complete the verse with a word that carries out the same rhyme pattern: for example, "Sam didn't get his way. He can't come out to play. He is having a very bad _____" (Condie, 2009).

Sound and Sound Pattern Recognition

As phonological awareness develops, older preschoolers should be able to recognize and generate rhyme and alliteration, segment sentences into words, blend and segment words at the syllable level, and blend onset + rime (initial consonant or cluster + ending vowel and consonant) into words. Explicit alliteration or rhyme knowledge is reflected when children demonstrate that several words have the same initial sound or the same rime ending and that words may be sorted into categories of sounds (Goswami, 2001; Goswami & Bryant, 1992). A common way to assess this ability is to present a categorization task by which children identify words in a series that begin or end with the same sound or sound combination (e.g., PALS [Phonological Awareness Literacy Screening], IGDI [Individual Growth and Development Indicators]). See Table 12–2 for more examples. Children may be given a series of pictures and asked to identify words or sound patterns that are similar to other words pictured in the series: for example, to tell which word rhymes with *cat—ship, bat, jeep,* or *box.* Or they may be asked to identify the word that doesn't belong (oddity task): for example, from the set of words *cat, dog, mat,* and *hat* they are asked to tell which word does not belong.

Before children can detect and identify individual phonemes in words, they need to be able to blend and segment sentences into words, compound words into their word parts, words into syllables, and words into their initial consonant or cluster (onset) and word ending (rime or vowel + final consonant chunk). Thus assessment tasks for late preschool (age 4) and early kindergarten require children to blend and segment units larger than the phoneme.

Early blending and segmenting tasks include clapping out or counting the number of words in a sentence, breaking words into syllables, combining syllables to make words (e.g., clapping and saying the syllables heard in the word *table* to produce *ta-ble* or blending those syllables to make the word), and blending onsets and rimes to make words (*f-ast, l-ast, p-ast, c-ast*) (Gillon, 2004). Several literacy tools have been developed to assess early blending and segmenting (Lonigan, Wagner, Torgesen, & Rashotte, 2007; Roswell & Chall, 1997). For example, a subtest of The Test of Preschool Early Literacy (TOPEL; Lonigan et al., 2007) assesses children's ability to break sentences into words, split compound words into their word parts, and segment words into their onset and rime.

Phoneme Identification and Manipulation

A developmental shift generally begins to appear about the time children enter kindergarten as they learn to recognize and identify the smallest sound units in words—phonemes (Charles-Luce & Luce, 1990, 1995; Storkel, 2002; Walley, 1993). This ability, known as *phonemic awareness,* is a higher level skill under the larger umbrella of *phonological awareness* (Cunningham, Cunningham, Hoffman, & Yopp, 1998; Snow et al., 1998). With phonemic awareness children have the ability to manipulate phonemes to create and take apart words, with specific skills to blend individual phonemes to make words, segment and identify individual phonemes in words, and manipulate phonemes into new words.

Blending at the phoneme level refers to children's ability to combine individual sounds to create words: for example, *d-o-g* = *dog* (Goswami, 1986, 1988; Goswami & Bryant, 1992). The Rosewell-Chall Auditory Blending assessment (Rosewell-Chall, 1997) assesses the ability to blend words at the onset and rime level (*/b/-oat* = *boat*) as well as the phoneme level (*b-a-t* = *bat*). It also includes some blending of words with blends (*pl-ay*).

Segmenting at the phonemic awareness level refers to children's ability to divide words into their individual speech sounds (Goswami, 1986, 1988; Goswami & Bryant, 1992). Segmenting at the level of this smallest unit includes stating what sounds are heard in a word (e.g., *cup* contains the sounds *c-u-p*) and isolating individual phonemes in words (e.g., the initial, medial, or final sound heard). Phoneme segmentation tasks require the child to identify what sound a word starts with (e.g., "Think of a word that starts with the /s/ sound" or "Tell me the first sound in *mouse*"). The child must also tell how many sounds he or she hears in a word. Closely related to segmenting is the ability to tell how letters attach to sounds in words so that children can recognize when one letter stands for two sounds (*x* = /ks/, for example) or when two letters stand for one sound (e.g., *sh* and *ch*). Children who can adequately segment know there is not always a one-to-one correspondence between letters and sounds, and they are able to count a number of letters different from the number of sounds in the same word (e.g., *knife* has five letters and three sounds).

Phoneme manipulation is a high level metalinguistic skill that includes the ability to delete a phoneme from a word, add a sound to a word, or change a phoneme to make a new word (and state the word). Students change sounds in order to change words. In the Test of Auditory Analysis (Rosner, 1993), for example, the child is asked to say a word and then to say the word without a particular phoneme (e.g., say the word *slip*, then say it without saying the /l/). Other early manipulation tasks appear on the Test of Preschool Early Literacy (TOPEL; Lonigan et al., 2007).

Decoding

Decoding is the process of attaching sounds to letter combinations in order to pronounce and attach meaning to written words. When children decode, they either quickly recognize words or analyze them into their individual sounds and parts such as prefixes, suffixes, or common letter patterns (e.g., *-ain* or *-ake*). Decoding is assessed at the word and text levels.

Word Level

At the word level, decoding is assessed by asking children to read a list of single words that are easy at the beginning but become progressively more difficult. Such word lists typically follow a developmental continuum corresponding to a curricular sequence. Early words are simple and phonetically regular, and they have short vowels (e.g., consonant-vowel-consonant words such as *dog, bat, top*). As the assessment progresses, words become more difficult: for example, those with the silent *e* pattern (e.g., *ride*) or with different vowel combinations (e.g., the different vowels in *book* and *moon*). Eventually children are given words that are compound (e.g., *hotdog*), sounds with multiple spelling patterns (e.g., long *e* sound in *feed* and *bead*), and words with more than one syllable (e.g., *television*). Word recognition assessments also deal with children's ability to read high frequency sight words that don't follow a regular phonic pattern (e.g., *was, is, put, me, I*). Word-level decoding tasks can be found as separate tests, like the Test of Word Reading Efficiency-2 (Torgesen, Wagner, & Rashotte, 2011). Sometimes they are found as subtests of other measures: for example, PALS-K (Invernezzi, Juel, Swank, & Meier, 2004); PALS 1-3 (Invernezzi, Meier, & Juel, 2003); and DRA (Beaver, 2011).

Speed and confidence in recognizing words can be observed and assessed as well as accuracy of word identification. Some children quickly recognize written words, and others segment and blend the individual sounds to read words (e.g., "*fff-aaa-nnn, fan*"). The more experience children have decoding particular words, the more automatically they are able to recognize the word without having to sound it out first (Ehri, 2002). Of interest also is whether a child quickly recognizes sight words or attempts to sound out words that don't follow a regular pattern.

Some measures have subtests that look at children's ability to decode nonsense words that follow regular phonic patterns: for example, the Test of Word Reading Efficiency-2 (Torgesen et al., 2011) and the Word Attack subtest of the Woodcock Reading Mastery Test (WRMT-III; Woodcock, 2011). While children can't attach meaning to these "words," their ability to decode regularly spelled letter patterns reflects knowledge of orthographic sound patterns and the ability to attack or sound out words. The nonsense words contain letter combinations that approximate the process involved in reading real words.

Text Level

Assessing children's decoding skills also includes noting the extent to which children can recognize words that appear in larger printed passages. The adult monitors the degree to which children quickly and effortlessly pronounce written words versus the extent to which they sound out words, hesitate as they read words, read slowly, or make errors in substitution or deletion. Some children guess at words, using only partial cues, such as the initial letter, to approximate the word. Informal reading inventories provide a system for keeping track of the errors children make in decoding at the text level: For example, the Basic Reading Inventory (Johns, 2008) and the Qualitative Reading Inventory-5 (Leslie & Caldwell, 2010) do this. They also provide opportunities to observe children engaged in oral reading of passages that gradually increase in complexity of phonic patterns.

A system for noting and recording decoding errors can be used to assess reading independent of administering an informal reading inventory. Referred to as *miscue analysis* or *running records*, this notation system provides a record of how children engage in oral reading of a text (Clay, 2006). When using this system, the SLP, teacher, or other examiner notes such things as phonological substitutions, omissions, and repetitions. Types of reading miscues (errors) reflect a child's mastery of letter-sound associations and understanding of decoding or word attack strategies. A miscue analysis is a particularly useful assessment tool for children who are in kindergarten or beyond, as it allows the examiner to look for patterns of performance in children's oral reading. Children may exhibit a tendency to substitute words, guess a word based on the initial consonant or context, or struggle in attempting to decode words with a particular pattern (e.g., words with a long vowel and silent *e* pattern). Identifying patterns in children's reading behaviors can permit teachers to target particular skills during instruction. Important sources of information concerning analysis of reading miscues include the work of Laing (2002) and Valencia, Rhodes, & Shanklin (1999).

Fluency

Closely related to decoding assessment at the text level is *fluency*, the ability to read text in appropriate phrase units at a reasonable rate and level of expression. A child who has difficulty decoding will have trouble reading fluently. The more quickly and automatically the child recognizes words, the more expressive and fluent his or her reading can be. However, teachers and SLPs should be cautious in using only rate (words per minute) calculations to determine fluency. Rubrics constructed for measuring fluency, such as the Multidimensional Fluency Scale (Zuttell & Rasinsky, 1991), permit the examiner to judge pace, expression, smoothness, and phrasing. Such rubrics can be more useful in judging students' reading fluency, as they often allow these judgments to be based on more than one dimension, typically a combination of expression, rate, and accuracy. Additional examples of fluency assessments can be found in Table 12–2.

Spelling

Spelling can be assessed by reviewing samples of children's writing and by asking children to write words from dictation. Early childhood educators are interested in children's use of both invented and early conventional spelling patterns.

Invented Spelling

In early stages of writing, children create spellings by using their knowledge of letter names and letter sounds (Ahmed & Lombardino, 2000). This invented spelling, which represents a child's idiosyncratic mapping of speech sounds onto print, reveals much about children's understanding of letter-sound associations (Apel, Masterson, & Niessen, 2004; Bear & Templeton, 1998; Gentry, 2000).

Invented spelling patterns can be analyzed from samples of students' writing and from word dictations (Clay, 2006; Cunningham, 2005; Edmiaston, 1988). Although most spelling assessments focus on types of errors relative to a standard form of the word (omissions, substitutions, or confusion between similar sounding phonemes), focusing on whether children represent only sounds heard at the beginning of words, include also some sounds from the end of words, or represent most sounds heard in words reveals a good deal about their basic knowledge and skills. Typically these analyses also compare children's spellings to what is known about the developmental progression of spelling (Bear, Invernizzi, Templeton, & Johnston, 2000). For example, invented spelling often begins with the child using the letter name to represent its sound (e.g., spelling *way* as *wa* or *tie* as *ti*). Based on error patterns and developmental progression, profiles can be developed that show where children are on a developmental continuum (Ahmed & Lombardino, 2000). (See Chapter 7 in this book for a description of levels of spelling development.)

Early Conventional Spelling Patterns

There is no specific demarcation between invented and conventional spelling. Conventional spelling is assessed by observing presence of the various patterns or "rules" in representing sounds with letters and letter combinations. As with invented spelling, children's written products can be evaluated as they (1) show understanding of how letters and letter combinations are associated with their sounds and (2) demonstrate that children can recognize some spelling patterns (Masterson & Apel, 2000; Temple, Nathan, & Burris, 1982). Stage theory and spelling inventories identify what sound patterns children can and cannot spell.

Developmental spelling inventories (Bear, Invernizzi, Templeton, & Johnston, 2011) are used to determine children's stage of spelling ability and then to plan and organize appropriate instruction. These inventories, which can be used as early as kindergarten, consist of lists of words that represent spelling features that increase in difficulty based on a developmental progression so that patterns in errors can be detected. Teachers or SLPs evaluate children's spelling based on their use of such features as initial and final consonants, short vowels, digraphs, blends, and long vowels. Children's understanding of spelling patterns can also be reflected in their spontaneous writings. A 5½ year old's made up "chicken" joke reflected common spelling miscues: "Wi did the chicin cros the rowd it wonted to git ranovr" (Why did the chicken cross the road? It wanted to get run over). His writing revealed the common, logical errors of missing a double consonant (e.g., *c* for *ck* and *s* for *ss*), confusing short vowels (*i* for *e*), using the vowel-like glide of /*r*/ as a vowel (*ovr* for *over*), and representing a long vowel with a different spelling pattern (*rowd* for *road*). By classifying a student's use of spelling features along with his errors, the teacher or SLP can more accurately identify areas of need and thus focus instruction.

In addition to looking at developmental spelling errors, a multiple linguistic repertoire analysis inspects a child's spelling patterns to identify linguistic deficits that may be interfering with spelling and reading (Apel & Masterson, 2001; Apel, Masterson, & Hart, 2004; Apel, Masterson, & Niessen, 2004; Masterson, Apel, & Wasowicz, 2002, 2006). This type of analysis is useful in determining how limits in word and morphology knowledge can interfere with spelling and what kind of instruction is useful.

Assessments for Comprehension Components

As children are acquiring basic skills such as phonological awareness, phonics, and spelling, they must also understand the purposes of reading and writing and be able to receive and convey meaning. Assessment of these meaning-based literacy components, however, is challenging because children's performance is influenced by such factors as prior knowledge, the communicative context, and size of the linguistic unit. This section addresses assessment practices in the meaning-based areas of vocabulary and comprehension, along with generation of both oral stories and written texts.

Vocabulary Knowledge

Vocabulary knowledge is an important part of early literacy assessment. Children must understand key words they encounter in an oral or written text in order to be able to comprehend it.

Limited vocabulary thus impacts children's ability to follow directions, obtain information, and understand explanations related to instruction.

Several types of vocabulary measures have been developed (Pence, Bojczyk, & Williams, 2007). Standardized measures of word recognition, in which the child identifies a picture that best represents a given word, enable an educator to obtain a rough idea of a child's level of receptive vocabulary. Such a broad-based vocabulary measure is not as instructionally relevant as other measurement types, such as inventories of curricular words that children learn as part of instructional units or themes. More useful measures might ask a child to identify an example of a curriculum-specific word without contextual support, create an example, demonstrate the meaning, use the word correctly, talk about the word, or answer questions about it.

Some vocabulary measures assess children's knowledge of a particular list of words: For example, a test may isolate knowledge of specific relational words, such as those that stand for temporal, spatial and number concepts (Boehm, 2000; Bracken, 1998). These words can be taught and practiced in the contexts of multiple content areas, but educators should probe children's understanding prior to and after instruction. For example, to assess the word *cause* (or *because*), the teacher might tell about a situation or problem she encountered and ask the children to guess a possible cause, choose from a series of plausible causes, or explain the cause, realizing that some children will come up with a logical cause but will have difficulty producing a well-formed explanation.

More in-depth vocabulary measures, to be used with children who are in kindergarten or in higher grades, address understanding of how words can be defined and related to other words. Such measures of word knowledge are designed to show children's ability to explain the meaning of words, give synonyms and antonyms, make word associations, state examples of category words, state how two items are similar or different, or give the function of objects. They address children's ability to reflect on and talk about how words are constructed and used. These measures reflect deep word knowledge. For example, the Language Processing Test-3 (LPT-3; Richard & Hanner, 2005) contains subtests relating to synonyms and antonyms, relationships between words, and meanings that are similar or different.

Listening and Reading Comprehension Skills

Comprehension is a dynamic process that is influenced by variables; vocabulary is just one. Others include the nature of the text (oral or written) and text complexity (e.g., content, inferencing requirements, sentence structure, organization, presence or absence of contextual support). Thus an important part of the assessment process is examining children's abilities using both listening and reading comprehension tasks with a variety of texts. This variety is particularly important when assessing comprehension with young children who are just learning or have not yet acquired basic decoding skills. The examiner should ensure that a child has sufficient oral language ability to support or serve as a basis for the comprehension task. Texts that refer to information that is remote from children's experience or include abstract ideas will be more difficult to comprehend. If such texts are used, examiners should remember that comprehension is influenced by children's knowledge and interest in a subject.

The response requirements should be varied and manipulated to observe children's performance under different conditions. Two very common comprehension assessment tasks that enable the necessary flexibility are engaging in interactive conversation and retelling the text that has been read.

Observations and Responses to Questions During Interactions

Valuable information about children's comprehension can be discerned by asking questions about passages. Questions can be asked after the children have read or listened to a passage, the approach used in formal assessments and informal reading inventories, and also during interactions with children as they read. During discussions, the adult can periodically ask the child(ren) to answer questions, make predictions, relate ideas in the text, or connect the text to prior knowledge or experiences.

The SLP or teacher may ask students to explain certain parts of the story, talk about what they like about it, relate the story or part of it to their own lives, identify with a character, or contrast experiences or perspectives of different characters—including how characters' actions can be interpreted in relation to their feelings or goals. During a discussion, teachers and SLPs often use questions to probe more deeply into a child's understanding of a text in order to reveal specific information about the child's comprehension level. Types of questions vary, but they often include identifying main ideas, supplying facts, and drawing inferences. A child's responses, of course, will not depend exclusively on the demands of the questions asked. Responses will also be influenced by his prior knowledge and interest in the content as well as by the linguistic and structural complexity of the text. Since spontaneous answers to questions offer little opportunity to explain or elaborate understanding, questions/answers alone cannot reveal much about children's ability to integrate information or to build a mental representation of the story as it is read. And questions may not encourage children to explain their personal responses.

Fluency and Expression

Observing the fluency and expression with which a child reads orally can also indicate comprehension ability. Children who read laboriously are struggling to decode at the phonological level and are using up cognitive resources that are needed for comprehension (Perfetti, 1985; Bashir & Hook, 2009). Thus if a child reads words inaccurately and is unable to maintain appropriate pace, expression and phrasing, the assessor may suspect comprehension difficulty. However, the reverse is not true: A child may be able to fluently decode words without accurately understanding the meaning of the text.

Text Retelling

Retelling requires the child to understand the story and to be able to highlight, connect, and organize events in a way that reflects plot structure. To process a story, children must listen carefully so that they can progressively build and update a mental representation of it, organizing the events and retrieving the language necessary to convey that representation (Ehri & Snowling, 2004). While the retell may appear to be primarily an assessment of a child's organization of a story and recall of details, it also adds significant expressive language demands to the comprehension task. Thus the examiner must attempt to separate out a child's comprehension from his expressive oral language ability.

Story retelling tasks appear on some measures of language comprehension: for example, the Test of Early Language Development-3 (TELD-3; Hresko, Reid, & Hammill, 1999). Paris and Paris (2003) also used story retelling to assess comprehension in young children. Oral retelling tasks are included in many informal reading inventories (Johns, 2008; Leslie & Caldwell, 2010) or may be incorporated with stories children read from informal reading inventories. For example, the Qualitative Reading Inventory-II (QRI-II; Leslie & Caldwell, 1995) and the Basic Reading Inventory (Johns, 2008) solicit retelling of graded reading passages from children who are kindergarten level and higher.

Story retelling demands can be manipulated by the examiner, as the nature of the task does influence performance. The examiner can control the task, selecting the stimuli and task demands to glean useful information concerning conditions that influence a child's retelling (Hedberg & Westby, 1993; Hughes, McGillivray, & Schmidek, 1997) or to increase the likelihood that the child will experience success. Or the examiner can provide a supported context, guiding the retelling with questions or Cloze prompts when necessary. The supported retell task keeps children motivated, because many can succeed with support who would have been unable to do so without it. For additional support the adult can supply props that allow the child to act out the story or provide cutout figures or toy miniatures for the child to portray the story actions; thus the story can be represented with concrete objects and actions in addition to language.

Once recordings of retold stories are collected and transcribed, they must be analyzed—parsed into story grammar or plot elements (Paris & Paris, 2003; Rhodes, 1993; Stein & Glenn, 1979). After these elements are identified and listed, the examiner checks off those the child included in the retelling. The examiner can rely on frameworks or guidelines for analysis, including rubrics, checklists, and holistic scoring systems (Hedberg & Westby, 1993; Hughes, McGillivray, & Schmidek, 1997). For example, checklists created for specific stories keep track of which story ideas or details the student included. Rubrics can provide descriptions of behavior that reflect or represent particular levels of skill attainment or performance quality, useful for determining whether performance exceeds, meets, or ranks below expectation.

Oral Text Generation

Educators should also examine young children's oral text generation to ensure that their expressive language abilities are sufficient to provide the raw material for expressing connected ideas and for developing their use of written language. Before children can be expected to write connected sentences or create coherent stories, the teacher or SLP will want to know if they have sufficient oral language for generating such texts.

Creative Storytelling

Creating stories orally can show much about children's language abilities. Since making up a story doesn't require comprehending a text, as does retelling, creative storytelling demonstrates a child's expressive language skills, which include conveying story events in a logical sequence, retrieving vocabulary, signaling causal connections, and conveying content. Expectations and assessments for children's stories depend on the nature of the task.

Teachers can initiate stories in a variety of ways: an open-ended prompt, picture(s), props, or a specific story starter (a brief scenario that provides a context for a story). Wordless picture books have been used to involve students in telling stories (Strong, 1998). Other structured tools with picture stimuli have been developed as well (Gillam & Pearson, 2004). Once children's stories are collected and recorded, various rubrics, checklists and scoring systems are available for analysis and/or scoring (Hedberg & Westby, 1993; Hughes, McGillivray, & Schmidek, 1997), although like all scoring of children's creative work, they must be used with care.

Co-construction

SLPs and teachers can provide different levels of support for student storytelling. In story co-construction tasks, an adult guides the process and children participate in creating a story. When story co-construction is used for assessment, the adult varies the level of support and notices the type and amount of support the child needs. After initiating the story, the adult listens carefully and may provide connective or signaling devices (such as key words) to support children in filling in the details. She could even use a Cloze or sentence completion technique to signal the important elements such as causal connections (e.g., "She was angry because . . . ," or "So she wanted to . . ."). For young children, co-constructed stories may function like planned play, with a running narration of a story as the child[ren] are developing a play sequence (Paley, 1992; Pelligrini & Galda, 1990); thus story co-construction can be used with preschoolers.

Co-construction tasks yield information about children's understanding of story structure as well as their oral language abilities. In story co-construction, children are assessed in terms of elements they generate themselves, so the examiner must distinguish the child's role from her own, which will be different according to each child's needs. Comparable final products do not necessarily indicate comparable levels of child skill or competence.

Written Expression

In addition to evaluating what children can generate orally, examiners will want to know the extent to which children can represent in writing what they can say. Young children's written language will be much less complicated than their oral expression, as writing adds to the challenge of choosing language the necessity of spelling the words and writing them. Thus to assess children's literacy the teacher or SLP will find it beneficial to contrast children's ability to convey ideas and experiences through writing with their ability to generate language orally.

This section emphasizes informal and formative strategies for assessing young children's writing. Formative procedures are recommended because they guide instruction and make it easy to document improvement in writing, also because it is inappropriate to "test" children who are in initial stages of learning to write. Writing is typically assessed at three levels: emergent level, contextualized word and sentence level, and text level.

Emergent (Prephonetic) Writing

Donald Graves (1983) wrote that most young children do not come to kindergarten thinking that they can read (unless they really can), but most do think that they can write. Children engage in emergent writing that develops to reflect their understanding of the conventions of writing as they pretend to write, make scribbles or letter-like forms on paper, and differentiate between drawing and writing. In the early stages children may produce letter strings, but the letters don't represent sounds.

These children do, however, demonstrate their emerging awareness of the appearance and functions of print. Lucy Calkins (1994) wrote of a boy who assigned a word to each of the seemingly random letters on his page as he "read" his story to her. As an assessor Calkins would not dismiss or ignore students' emergent efforts:

> I give these hieroglyphics the same respect I give to the baby's "dada-dada." I say to the babbling baby, "Daddy? You want your daddy?" I say to Tiziana when she shows me her [page of random markings], "Will you read it to me?" (p. 67)

As the child "reads" the story, Calkins can actually assess a good deal about the child's concept of story structure in addition to her ability to use language and to think and express herself with sentence-like forms. The ways in which children dictate their ideas to be written by an adult also give information about their understanding of how writing works. While writing down children's stories, an assessment-conscious teacher or SLP can also notice matters such as story components, vocabulary, and sentence structure.

Contextualized Word and Sentence Level Writing

At an early writing level, children often combine words with pictures to convey ideas. Some children like to draw a picture of the thought or experience and compose the written piece by describing the picture (Graves, 1983). Many teachers both support and assess by conferencing with their students, asking questions and engaging them in conversation to draw out their ideas, allowing them to think and express themselves with words they may be afraid to try to spell (but can ask during their personal conference time). At this stage children are able to write a message that conveys meaning with invented or scaffolded conventional spelling (Rhodes, 1993).

Early writing assessment involves determining what children understand about the writing process and how well they are able to use letter-sound associations to symbolize words they want to use in expressing themselves. In an assessment situation, children are asked to write about something they drew or experienced so that the product does not have to stand alone. Calkins (1994) noted that assessment of the product isn't part of the way young children naturally view writing:

> Kindergartners and first graders rarely . . . fret about whether their stories will be good enough . . . first graders often write as they play blocks: for the sheer fun of the activity rather than for an eventual product, for themselves rather than for an audience. (p. 118)

Assessors need to recognize and celebrate this absence of assessment fear. (Fortunately, the children can't read the teacher's observation notes if they happen to find them.)

Text Level Writing

Obviously writing connected sentences is more complicated than conveying meaning with words and sentences amplified by contextual supports such as pictures or oral dialogue. There is also more to address when assessing a written product at the story or passage level. For prekindergarten groups, "text level" may not be a possibility. For kindergartners and first graders, text level assessment should be handled with extreme care.

Informal Process Assessment. Informal assessment is particularly important for young children's writing. Children's "authentic literacy behavior" is the "most valid assessment" of literacy progress as it is more personal and "better matched to classroom needs" (Cramer, 2004, p. 99) than standardized formalized assessments that are available.

Any assessment of young children's writing should reveal information about their ability to engage in the writing process, not just to produce a written product (Chalfee & Miller, 2007). Such assessment should involve observation that is carefully focused, including anecdotal notes that are detailed and specific (Tompkins, 2012). Donald Graves (1994) recommended that the teacher sit next to or across from each individual student for a short time, explaining to the child that he or she is doing this to learn how to help the student become an even better writer. Gail Tompkins (2004) suggested that each child should be observed about once a month. She advised (2004, 2012) that an experienced teacher can learn what she needs to know about the progress of a child in a few minutes. Tompkins concluded that such observing is "one of the richest sources of information" (2004, p.154) that teachers can use in learning about students' writing, including how children feel about writing, how they make decisions, which strategies they use as they write, and what they discuss as they interact with their classmates (2004, 2012).

In most classes only a small percentage of children's pieces will go through all the steps of the writing process, and assessment should be involved with which steps children go through and how--not necessary the quality or skill with which they do so. For example, if revision and publication are going to be included in a writing project, an observer should be concerned with whether the child has a concept of revision as reconsideration and change rather than counting the number of changes that are made (particularly if most of them are concerned with neatness and spelling). Caring teachers go below the surface to understand the reasons behind the writing behavior they observe (Cramer, 2004), including misconceptions and insecurities.

More Formal Product Assessment. When young children's writing *must* be assessed by product characteristics, this has to be done very thoughtfully. The SLP or teacher must tell the children in advance what the criteria will be, and ensure that each point has been taught, modeled, and practiced. Shared and interactive writing give children opportunities to experience various processes involved in writing, from applying the alphabetic system to considering purpose and audience (Gunning, 2005). Additionally, they *experience* the criteria for assessing an assignment when they assess as a group what they have written as a group: for example, "Details make writing more interesting. Do we have enough details here?" In "Tying Assessment to Instruction," Nelson, Kalmes, and Hatfield-Walsh (1999) explained that the "positive social learning environment" with its opportunities to "recognize and support children's strengths" created by such activities is particularly reassuring to children who struggle with writing (1999, p. 109) and may dread having their work looked at critically. If a rubric is desired for kindergarten children, a few brief statements concerning original ideas, interesting details, personal voice, and capitals/periods on sentences would probably be sufficient.

Over time a variety of the children's writing projects should be collected and retained for comparison in individual writing folders (Graves, 1983; Tompkins, 2012, 2004). As children progress through kindergarten and first grade, purpose and audience become clear and meaningful, support and feedback should be available, and the final product should have value to the student (Chalfee & Miller, 2007). As children practice writing for different purposes and audiences (e.g., writing a thank you note, an invitation to a party, or three reasons why the class should receive a new soccer ball), specific criteria related to these projects could be added to a checklist or rubric which the child might participate in filling out (Tompkins, 2004).

For older children analytic or trait rubrics can be designed around specific facets such as ideas, organization, word choice, sentence fluency, connectedness, grammatical conventions, mechanics (spelling, grammar, punctuation), and coherence (Spandel, 2005), gradually adding these as students receive instruction, modeling, and experience in these areas. But a kindergarten child given such a rubric might decide to abandon writing altogether.

Summary

In assessing young children's literacy skills, the teacher or SLP must take into consideration factors that influence performance. The assessment process should address both skill and meaning components of literacy and should include formal tools as well as informal procedures that consider how instructional supports influence children's performance in literacy-learning contexts. With an understanding of how children perform with and without supports, initial goals can be set that lead to specific instruction. The assessment and goal setting process should be iterative, with continued observations of how children perform in instruction leading to modifications in goals and raising criteria or expectations for performance. Learning opportunities created from or based on assessment information, which are periodically subject to informal probes or formal assessments, are compared with revisited goals and adapted, adjusted, or completely revised according to what the assessments show (Suskie, 2004). Information obtained from all assessments of skills can help SLPs and teachers set new goals, design new instruction, evaluate its effectiveness, and again modify goals and instruction.

References

Ahmed, S., & Lombardino, L. (2000). Invented spelling: An assessment and intervention protocol for kindergarten children. *Communication Disorders Quarterly, 22,* 19–28.

Apel, K., & Masterson, J. J. (2001). Theory-guided spelling assessment and intervention. *Language, Speech, and Hearing Services in Schools, 32,* 182–195.

Apel, K., Masterson, J. J., & Hart, P. (2004). Integration of language components in spelling: Instruction that maximizes students' learning. In E. R. Silliman & L. C. Wilkinson (Eds.), *Language and literacy learning in schools* (pp. 292–315). New York, NY: Guilford Press.

Apel, K., Masterson, J. J., & Niessen, N. L. (2004). Spelling assessment frameworks. In A. Stone, E. R. Silliman, B. Ehren, & K. Apel (Eds.), *Handbook of language and literacy: Development and disorder* (pp. 644–660). New York, NY: Guilford Press.

Bashir, A., & Hook, P. (2009). Fluency: A key link between word identification and comprehension. *Language, Speech and Hearing Services in Schools, 40,* 196–200.

Bear, D., Invernizzi, M., Templeton, S., & Johnston, F. (2012). *Words their way: Word study for phonics, vocabulary, and spelling instruction* (5th ed). New York, NY: Pearson.

Bear D. R., & Templeton, S. (1998). Explorations in developmental spelling: Foundations for learning and teaching phonics, spelling, and vocabulary. *Reading Teacher, 52*(3), 222–242.

Beaver, J. (2011). *Developmental Reading Assessment-2 K–3.* New York, NY: Pearson.

Big ideas in beginning reading: Alphabetic principle. University of Oregon, Center on Teaching and Learning. Retrieved from reading.uoregon.edu

Boehm, A, (2000). *Boehm Test of Basic Concept, Third Edition (Boehm-3).* New York, NY: Pearson.

Bracken, B. (1998). *Bracken Basic Concept Scale-Revised (BBCS-R).* New York, NY: Pearson.

Bradley, L., & Bryant, P. E. (1983). Categorizing sounds and learning to read: A causal connection. *Nature, 30,* 419–421.

Brady, S. & Shankweiler, D. (1991). *Phonological processes in literacy: A tribute to Isabelle Y. Liberman.* Hillsdale, NJ: Lawrence Earlbaum Associates.

Bryant, P. E., MacLean, M., Bradley, L. L. & Crossland, J. (1990). Rhyme and alliteration, phoneme detection, and learning to read. *Developmental Psychology, 26,* 429–438.

Calkins, L. M. (1994). *The art of teaching writing* (2nd ed.). Portsmouth, NH: Heinemann.

Chalfee, R., & Miller, R. (2007). Best practices in writing assessment. In S. Graham, C. MacArthur, & J. Fitzerald (Eds.), *Best practices in writing instruction* (pp. 265–286). New York, NY: Guilford.

Charles-Luce, J., & Luce, P. A. (1990). Similarity neighbourhoods of words in young children's lexicons. *Journal of Child Language, 17*(1), 205–215.

Charles-Luce, J., & Luce, P. A. (1995). An examination of similarity neighbourhoods in young children's receptive vocabularies. *Journal of Child Language, 22,* 727–735.

Christie, J. F., Enz, B. H. M., & Vukelich, C. (2010). *Teaching language and literacy: Preschool through the elementary grades* (4th ed). Boston, MA: Allyn & Bacon.

Clay, M. M. (2006). *An observation survey of early literacy achievement* (2nd ed). Portsmouth, NH: Heinemann.

Condie, K (2009). *Finish-a-rhyme-story: A rhyme cloze assessment for pre-school children.* Unpublished master's thesis, Brigham Young University, Provo, Utah.

Cramer, R. L. (2004). *The language arts: A balanced approach to teaching reading, writing, listening, talking, and thinking.* Boston, MA: Pearson.

Culatta, B., & Hall, K. M. (2006). Phonological awareness instruction in early childhood settings. In L. M. Justice (Ed.), *Clinical approaches to emergent literacy intervention* (pp. 179–221). San Diego, CA: Plural.

Cunningham, J. W., Cunningham, P. M., Hoffman, J. V., & Yopp, H. K. (1998). *Phonemic awareness and the teaching of reading: A position statement from the board of directors of the International Reading Association.* Newark, DE: International Reading Association.

Cunningham, P. M. (2005). *Phonics they use: Words for reading and writing* (4th ed.). Boston, MA: Allyn & Bacon.

Deno, S. L. (1985). Curriculum-based measurement: The emerging alternative. *Exceptional Children, 52,* 219–232.

Dorsey, M. E. (1972). *Reading games and activities.* Belmont, CA: Fearon.

Dowker, A. (1989). Rhyme and alliteration in poems elicited from young children. *Journal of Child Language, 16*(1),181–202.

Early Childhood Research Institute on Measuring Growth and Development. (1998). *Research and development of individual growth and development indicators for children between birth and age eight* (Tech.

Rep. No. 4), Minneapolis, MN: Center for Early Education and Development, University of Minnesota.

Edmiaston, R. K. (1988). Preschool literacy assessment. *Seminars in Speech and Language, 9*(1), 27–35.

Ehri, L. C. (2002). Phases of acquisition in learning to read words and implications for teaching. In R. Stainthorp & P. Tomlinson (Eds.), *Learning and teaching reading* (pp. 7–28). London, UK: British Journal of Educational Psychology Monograph Series II.

Ehri, L. C., & Snowling, M. J. (2004) Developmental variation in word recognition. In A. Stone, E. R. Silliman, B. J. Ehren, & K. Apel (Eds.), *Handbook of language and literacy: Development and disorders* (pp. 433–460). New York, NY: Guilford Press.

Epstein, A. S., Schweinhart, L. J., & DeBruin-Parecki, A. (2004) Assessing children's development: Strategies that complement testing. In D. Koralek (Ed.), *Spotlight on young children and assessment* (pp. 45–53). Washington, DC: National Association for the Education of Young Children.

Fernandez-Fein, S., & Baker, L. (1997). Rhyme sensitivity and relevant experiences in preschoolers from diverse backgrounds. *Journal of Literacy Research, 29*, 433–459.

Gentry, J. R. (2000). A retrospective on invented spelling and a look forward. *Reading Teacher, 54*(3), 318–332.

Gillam, R. B., & Pearson, N. (2004). *Test of Narrative Language.* Austin, TX: Pro-Ed.

Gillon, G. T. (2004). *Phonological awareness: From research to practice.* New York, NY: Guilford Press.

Good, R. H., & Kaminski, R. A. (2002). *Dynamic indicators of basic early literacy skills* (6th ed.). Eugene, OR: Institute for the Development of Educational Achievement. Retrieved from http://dibels.uoregon.edu/

Goswami, U. (1986). Children's use of analogy in learning to read: A developmental study. *Journal of Experimental Child Psychology, 42*, 73–83.

Goswami, U. (1988). Orthographic analogies and reading development. *Quarterly Journal of Experimental Psychology, 40A*, 239–268.

Goswami, U. (2001). Early phonological development and the acquisition of literacy. In S. B. Neuman & D. K. Dickinson (Eds.), *Handbook of early literacy research* (pp. 111–125). New York, NY: Guilford Press.

Goswami, U., & Bryant, P. E. (1990). *Phonological skills and learning to read.* Hillsdale, NJ: Lawrence Erlbaum Associates.

Goswami, U., & Bryant, P. (1992). Rhyme, analogy, and children's reading. In P. Gough, L. Ehri, & R. Treiman (Eds.), *Reading acquisition* (pp. 49–63). Hillsdale, NJ: Lawrence Erlbaum Associates.

Graves, D. S. (1983). *Writing: Teachers and children at work.* Portsmouth, NH: Heinemann.

Graves, D. S. (1994). *A fresh look at writing.* Portsmouth, NH: Heinemann.

Gunning, T. G. (2005) *Assessing and correcting reading and writing difficulties* (3rd ed.). Boston, MA: Allyn & Bacon.

Gutiérrez-Clellen, V., & Peña, E. (2001). Dynamic assessment of diverse children: A tutorial. *Language, Speech, and Hearing Services in Schools, 32,* 212–224.

Hedberg, N. L., & Westby, C. E. (1993). *Analyzing storytelling skills: Theory to practice.* San Antonio, TX: Communication Skill Builders.

Hester, E., & Hodson, B. (2007). Metaphonological awareness skills: Enhancing literacy skills. In P. Rhyner (Ed.), *Emergent literacy and language development: Promoting learning in early childhood* (pp. 78–103). New York, NY: Guilford Press.

Hresko, W., Reid, D. K., & Hammil, D. (1999). *Test of early language development* (3rd ed.). New York, NY: Psychological Corporation.

Hughes, D., McGillivray, L. & Schmidek, M. (1997). *Guide to narrative language: Procedures for assessment.* Austin, TX: Pro-Ed.

Invernizzi, M., Juel, C., Swank, L., & Meier, J. (2005). *Phonological Assessment Literacy Screening-Kindergarten* (PALS-K). Charlottesville, VA: University of Virginia.

Invernizzi, M., Meier, J., Juel, C. (2003). *Phonological Awareness Literacy Screening-1-3 (PALS 1–3).* Charlottesville, VA: University of Virginia.

Invernizzi, M. Sullivan, A., Meier, J., & Swank, L. (2004). *Phonological Awareness Literacy Screening-Prekindergarten (PALS-PreK).* Charlottesville, VA: University of Virginia.

Johns, J. (2008). *Basic reading inventory* (10th ed.). Dubuque, IA: Kendall Hunt.

Jones, J. (2003). *Early literacy assessment systems: Essential elements.* Princeton, NJ: Educational Testing Service.

Justice, L. M., Invernizzi, M. A., & Meier, J. D. (2002). Designing and implementing an early literacy screening protocol: Suggestions for the speech-language pathologist. *Language, Speech, and Hearing Services in Schools, 33,* 84–101.

Kieff, J. E., & Casbergue, R. M. (2000). *Playful learning and teaching: Integrating play into preschool and primary programs.* Boston, MA: Allyn & Bacon.

Laing, S. P. (2002). Miscue analysis in school-age children. *American Journal of Speech Language Pathology, 11*(4), 407–416.

Leslie, L., & Caldwell, J. (2010). *Qualitative Reading Inventory, 5th Edition.* Cranbury, NJ: Pearson Education.

Lidz, C. S. (1991). *Practitioner's guide to dynamic assessment.* New York, NY: Guilford Press.

Lidz, C. S. (1996). *Dynamic assessment: Theory, application and research.* Paper presented at the annual convention of the American Speech-Language-Hearing Association, Seattle, WA.

Lonigan, C., Wagner, R., Torgesen, J., & Rashotte, C. (2007). *The Test of Preschool Early Literacy (TOPEL)*. Austin, TX: Pro-Ed.

MacLean, M., Bryant, P., & Bradley, L. (1987). Rhymes, nursery rhymes and reading in early childhood. *Merrill-Palmer Quarterly, 33*, 255–281.

Martin, N., & Brownell, R. (2011). *Expressive One-Word Picture Vocabulary Test-4 (EOWPVT-4)*. Austin, TX: Pro-Ed.

Masterson, J. J., & Apel, K. (2000). Spelling assessment: Charting a path to optimal intervention. *Topics in Language Disorders, 20*(3), 50–65.

Masterson, J. J., Apel, K., & Wasowicz, J. (2002). *SPELL Spelling Performance Evaluation for Language and Literacy* [Computer software]. Evanston, IL: Learning By Design. Retrieved from http://www.learning bydesign.com

Masterson, J. J., Apel, K., & Wasowicz, J. (2006). *SPELL-2 Spelling Performance Evaluation for Language and Literacy* (2nd ed.) [Computer software]. Evanston, IL: Learning By Design. Retrieved from http://www.learningbydesign.com

Maxwell, K. L., & Clifford, R. M. (2004) School readiness assessment. In D. Koralek (Ed.), *Spotlight on young children and assessment* (pp. 29–37). Washington, DC: National Association for the Education of Young Children.

Merritt, D. D., & Culatta, B. (1998). Dynamic Assessment, Language Processes, and Curricular Content. In D. D. Merritt & B. Culatta (Eds.), *Language intervention in the classroom* (pp. 277–330). San Diego, CA: Singular.

Muter, V, Hulme, C, Snowling, M. J., & Stevenson, J (2004). Phonemes, rimes and language skills as foundations of early reading development: Evidence from a longitudinal study. *Developmental Psychology, 40*, 663–681.

Nelson, O. G., Kalmes, P. A. C., & Hatfield-Walsk, E. (1999). Tying assessment to instruction. In. O. G. Nelson & W. M. Linek (Eds.), *Practical classroom applications of language experience: Looking back, looking forward* (pp. 109–122). Boston, MA: Allyn & Bacon.

Newcomer, P., & Barenbaum, E. (2003). *Test of Phonological Awareness Skills* (TOPAS). Austin, TX: Pro-Ed.

Newcomer, P., & Hammill, D. (2008). TOLD-P:4: *Test of Language Development-Primary* (4th ed.). Austin, TX: Pro-Ed.

Paley, V. (1992). *You can't say you can't play.* Cambridge, MA: Harvard University Press.

Paris, A. H., & Paris, S. G. (2003). Assessing narrative comprehension in young children. *Reading Research Quarterly, 38*(1), 36–76.

Pellegrini, A. D., & Galda, L. (1990). The joint construction of stories by preschool children and an experimenter. In B. Britton & A. D. Pellegrini (Eds.), *Narrative thought and narrative language* (pp. 113–129). Hillsdale,NJ: Lawrence Erlbaum.

Pence, K. L. (2007). Introduction: Measuring contexts of learning and development and children's early literacy growth. In K. Pence (Ed.), *Assessment in emergent literacy* (pp. xiii–xxi). San Diego, CA: Plural.

Pence, K., Bojczk, K., & Williams, R. (2007). Assessing vocabulary development. In K. Pence (Ed.), *Assessment in emergent literacy* (pp. 433–480). San Diego, CA: Plural.

Perfetti, C. (1985). *Reading ability*. New York, NY: Oxford University Press.

Psychological Corporation. (2003). *The Early Reading Diagnostic Assessment* (2nd ed.). San Antonio, TX: Author.

Reid, D. K., Hresko, W., & Hammill, D. (2001). *Test of Early Reading Ability-3*. Austin, TX: Pro-Ed

Rhodes, L. K. (1993). *Literacy assessment: A handbook of instruments*. Portsmouth, NH: Heinemann.

Richard, G., & Hanner, M. A., (2005). *Language Processing Test-3 (LPT-3)*. East Moline, IL: LinguiSystems.

Robertson, C., & Salter, W. (1997). *The Phonological Awareness Test*. East Moline, IL: LinguiSystems.

Rosner, J. (1993). *Test of Auditory Analysis Skills* (TAAS). Novato, CA: Academic Therapy Publications.

Roswell, F., & Chall, J. (1997). *Roswell-Chall Auditory Blending Test*. New York, NY: Essay Press.

Salinger, T. (2001). Assessing the literacy of young children: The case for multiple forms of evidence. In S. B. Neuman & D. K. Dickinson (Eds.), *Handbook of early literacy research* (pp. 390–418). New York, NY: Guilford Press.

Salinger, T. (2006). Policy decisions in early literacy assessment. In D. Dickinson & S. Neuman (Eds.), *Handbook of early literacy research* (Vol 2, pp. 427–444). New York, NY: Guilford Press.

Schuele, M., Skibbe, L., & Rao, P. (2007). Assessing phonological awareness. In K. Pence (Ed), *Assessment in emergent literacy* (pp. 275–325). San Diego, CA: Plural.

Semel, E., Wiig, E. H., & Secord, W. A. (2003). *Clinical Evaluation of Language Fundamentals, Fourth Edition (CELF-4)*. Toronto, Canada: Psychological Corporation/A Harcourt Assessment Company.

Snow, C., Burns, S., & Griffin, P. (1998). *Preventing reading difficulties in young children*. Washington, DC: National Academy Press.

Spandel, V. (2005). *Creating writers: Through 6-trait writing assessment and instruction*. Boston, MA: Allyn & Bacon.

Stein, N. L., & Glenn, C. G. (1979). An analysis of story comprehension in elementary school children. In R. Freedle (Ed.), *New directions in discourse processing* (pp. 53–120). Norwood, NJ: Ablex

Storkel, H. L. (2002). Restructuring of similarity neighborhoods in the developing mental lexicon. *Journal of Child Language, 29*(2), 251–274.

Strong, C. (1998). SNAP: *Strong narrative assessment procedure*. Austin, TX: Pro-Ed.

Suskie, L. (2004). *Assessing student learning: A common sense guide*. Bolton, MA: Anker.

Temple, C. A., Nathan, R. G., & Burris, N. A. (1993). *The beginnings of writing* (3rd ed.). Boston, MA: Allyn & Bacon.

Tompkins, G. E. (2004). *Teaching writing: Balancing process and product* (4th ed.). Upper Saddle River, NJ: Pearson.

Tompkins, G. E. (2012). *Teaching writing: Balancing process and product* (6th ed.). Upper Saddle River, NJ: Pearson.

Torgesen, J., & Bryant, B. (2004). *Test of Phonological Awarness-2 plus (TOPA-2+)*. Austin, TX: Pro-Ed.

Torgesen, J., Wagner, R., & Rashotte, C. (2011). *Test of Word Reading Efficiency-2*. Torrance, CA: Western Psychological Services.

Valencia, S. W., Rhodes, L. K., & Shanklin, N. L. (1999). Miscue analysis in the classroom. In S. J. Barrentine (Ed.), *Reading assessment: Principles and practices for elementary teachers* (pp. 160–163). Newark, DE: International Reading Association.

Wallace, G., & Hammill, D. D. (2002). *Comprehensive Receptive and Expressive Vocabulary Test* (2nd ed.). Austin, TX: Pro-Ed.

Walley, A. C. (1993). The role of vocabulary development in children's spoken word recognition and segmentation ability. *Developmental Review, 13*(3), 286–350.

Wiederholt, J., & Bryant, B. (2001). *Gray Test of Oral Reading (GORT-4)*. Cranbury, NJ: Pearson Education.

Woodcock, R. (2011). *Woodcock Reading Mastery Tests* (WRMT-III) (3rd ed.). San Antonio, TX: Pearson.

Woodcock, R., Mather, N., & Schrank, F. (2004). *Woodcock-Johnson III Diagnostic Reading Battery (WJ-III DRB)*. Rolling Meadows, IL: Riverside.

Woodcock, R. W., McGrew, K. S., & Mather, N. (2001). *Woodcock-Johnson III Tests of Achievement*. Itasca, IL: Riverside.

Zuttell, J., & Rasinski, T. (1991). Training teachers to attend to their students' oral reading fluency. *Theory into Practice, 30*, 211–217.

Chapter 13

Learning and Improving Together: Collaborative Professional Development

John Wilkinson and Barbara Culatta

To be successful "every teacher has to learn virtually every day" (Fullan, 2007, p. 36). Finding, planning, and implementing effective interventions for helping each student achieve competence in literacy can be complex, even daunting. However, these complexities can be managed when the work is shared among members of a team consisting of teachers and speech-language pathologists, along with other school personnel such as school psychologists, classroom aides, etc. "The willingness of individuals to cooperate with other members of an organization is one of the major determinants of organizational effectiveness and efficiency" (Pfeffer & Sutton, 2000, p. 197).

Learning and growing through combining knowledge and skills is made possible in a culture that values sharing and cooperation. Such a collaborative, systemic process for improving professional practice was recommended in the review of research on professional development by the National Staff Development Council (Wei et al., 2009). This report described how an open and positive interchange among teachers can inform decisions about assessment of student performance and plans for instruction. This is in direct contrast to the traditional workshop approach to improving instruction in which most of the suggested practices are not discussed among colleagues or tried out in classrooms with results shared (Easton, 2008; Fullan, 2007; Stein, Smith, & Silver, 1999). The authors of this chapter participated in professional development with two grade-level teams of kindergarten teachers implementing Systematic and Engaging Early Literacy (SEEL) instruction and found that teachers' performance improved and their expectations were higher when they cooperatively planned, tried, and measured instruction in an environment that fostered collaborative relationships. The SEEL experience is used to illustrate teacher improvement practices throughout this chapter. Enabling teachers to learn and apply SEEL was a shared endeavor between the SEEL project team, consisting of university professors and a staff member with experience in elementary education, and two school-based kindergarten teams. The SEEL project team supported the kindergarten teachers in adopting the SEEL pedagogy and in implementing four practices that underlie improvement in instructional practice:

1. Collaborating in a professional learning community (PLC)
2. Creating positive learning environments for teachers and students
3. Adjusting and monitoring instruction to prevent failure
4. Refining teaching practices to ensure learning

Figure 13–1 indicates the relationship among these elements. The sections below contain a description of each of these practices along with an example of how they were implemented in the SEEL project.

Collaborating in a Professional Learning Community

Teachers need a place to share, discuss, and practice alternative approaches with their colleagues in an ongoing cycle of continuous improvement (Easton, 2008; Fullan, 2007; Stein, Smith, & Silver, 1999). Professional learning communities (PLCs), one way of organizing continuous professional learning in collaborative teams, can provide a framework for teachers to actively collaborate with

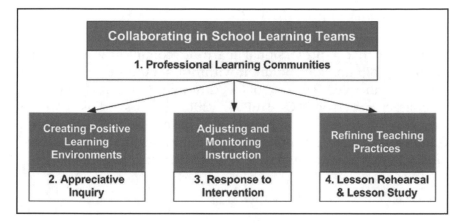

Figure 13–1. Collaborating in school learning teams.

peers to improve their practice. The Systematic and Engaging Early Literacy (SEEL) group was a small professional learning community of five kindergarten teachers from two schools with leadership support from both principals: not exactly a typical school PLC, but effective because of shared needs, common goals, and a commitment to support each other.

Meeting needs and achieving goals should be seen more as a process than as an event. Deep, lasting improvement takes time. Educators who invest their time to assess student performance, reflect on what is needed, learn more about evidence-based methods, and put those methods into practice can improve student learning and build their capacity as professionals in their classrooms and schools (Speck & Knipe, 2001, p. xi). Speck and Knipe warned that professional learning and development is not just another item on a menu of opportunities that teachers may dabble in. Fullan (2006) suggested that teachers see their investment in collaboration as long term and continuous. "Professional learning communities," he explained, "are in fact about establishing lasting new collaborative cultures. They are meant to be enduring capacities, not just another program innovation" (p. 37). Sustained professional learning to produce continuous improvement is not a fad, and PLCs should be adopted only if the team is committing to a rigorous road toward increasing learning with ongoing improvement.

Characteristics of Effective PLCs

To ensure that a professional learning community is "not just another program," collaboration within it should be structured by guiding principles (Fullan, 2006). Although there are several lists of characteristics of PLCs, DuFour (2004, p. 6) synthesized them into three "big ideas" or principles that can serve as a guiding framework: create a "culture of collaboration," "focus on results," and "ensure . . . students learn" (DuFour, 2004, pp. 8–10).

Create a Culture of Collaboration

Teachers in a culture of collaboration commit to work together to achieve collective goals and purposes. Collaborating with a focus on goals motivates the teachers to create a highly effective teaching team. "We must shift from a culture of teacher isolation," explained Eaker, DuFour, and Burnette (2002), "to a culture of deep and meaningful collaboration" (p. 10). All members of the team must acknowledge that they are much more effective together than separately and that they commit to learning for every student, no matter what. They are aware of and value their interdependence.

Educational team members in PLCs structure their collaboration to help each other move away from the traditional isolation of educators. The work of professional educators is more effective when each has a safe place to take concerns, questions, ideas, and successes. When everyone belongs to a team and the team focuses on student learning, the vision and goal for each child can more easily be realized.

Focus on Data to Make Decisions

Along with shared goals and commitment to student learning, team members in a PLC focus on data-based decision making. DuFour et al. (2006) expressed the belief that members of a PLC must realize that all of their efforts must be assessed by results — not intentions. The PLC creates learning goals and common assessments to measure achievement or areas of difficulty to be addressed. "Frequent common formative assessments represent one of the most powerful tools" of the PLC, a tool which enables it to retain an ongoing orientation to results (DuFour et al., 2006, p. 5). Focusing on results begins by collecting assessment evidence, which guides the team in planning and implementing instruction, monitoring results, and applying the resulting data to planning new instruction. The focus on student results helps teams avoid the trap of focusing on the strategy or the curriculum: on finishing the lesson or "covering" the unit.

Following the implementation of an intervention, PLC members reflect, ask questions, examine progress-monitoring data, and analyze results. With this new information teachers decide how instruction should be changed: for example, increasing the intensity of instruction/experience by organizing smaller groups. This process is expressed in the phrase "continuous improvement," which characterizes the commitment of the PLC.

Ensure That Students Learn

Part of ensuring that students learn is for teachers to focus on their own practice. "A persistent discomfort with the status quo and a constant search for a better way [is at] the heart of a professional learning community" (DuFour & Eaker, 1998, p. 28). In ensuring student learning, team members consider the ways they are implementing instruction, analyze what worked and did not work, and apply what they learned to a new cycle of improved instruction. As their capacity for supporting students increases, they begin to experience continuous progress in their instruction and in their students' learning (DuFour, DuFour, Eaker, & Many, 2006).

PLC members also engage in collective inquiry by which they identify the status of students' knowledge and skills and inspect instructional practices in terms of the learning that has been purposefully assessed (Eaker, DuFour, & Burnette, 2002). They then collaboratively seek evidence-based practices to replace methodologies and practices that are insufficient in supporting students' learning. This kind of collaboration results in a collective commitment to ensure that all children learn.

SEEL as an Example of Professional Development in a PLC

The SEEL project presented opportunities for the SEEL team to look qualitatively at effective ways to implement early literacy practices. The SEEL project team and the kindergarten teachers from the two schools were organized according to findings on effective professional development from the National Staff Development Council (NDSC): Thus the effort was to be on site, job embedded, and continuous (Wei, Darling-Hammond, Andree, Richardson, & Orphanos, 2009).

The school-based kindergarten teams drew on the teachers, support staff, and principals of the elementary schools; advocated processes that define the core value and work of PLCs; and grounded their work in a collaborative culture focused on results, with an emphasis on student learning. The SEEL project team, consisting of university faculty/staff with backgrounds in early childhood education or speech-language pathology, carried out professional development activities and facilitated the work of the PLC.

Both the SEEL project and kindergarten teams found that reflecting on practice and results and following the guiding framework recommended for PLCs positively impacted instruction and student performance. For example, while reflecting on her ability to engage her students, prompted by her team's feedback, one of the kindergarten teachers said, "I think [what] I was teaching at the beginning of the year maybe wasn't engaging enough. I don't think I have enough experiences with playful practice." The teacher's reflection on her practice caused her to engage her associates on the team in a discussion of how to make her future learning activities more engaging and meaningful. Their ideas and suggestions helped her in making plans to improve her future instruction.

During another interaction, a kindergarten teacher shared with her colleagues what she had learned about focusing on learning instead of on covering curriculum, an area of discomfort the others understood. She observed the value of assessment and intervention when she said, "And then we monitor the kids who don't know [and we can] go back and re-teach instead of [introducing] different letters, different endings . . . it makes it a little more even and more organized." Her personal experience with change gave others the courage to make changes in their own outlook and practice.

Another kindergarten teacher summed up her endorsement of the learning community experience:

> The best part about it, as far as collaboration goes, you can sit down and say "I taught this. This is what happened." And then we all give our ideas of maybe why it didn't work out and how we could modify it to make it a stronger lesson.

Thus teachers who collaborated found that when they discussed their experiences and shared ideas they could better understand their practice and find ways of improving it. Through the SEEL professional learning experience, the teachers committed to collaborative professional improvement and felt that they benefited significantly from it.

Prior to the establishment of the PLC, the support personnel assumed that the teacher knew who needed instructional interventions and what interventions to employ. As the PLC became more cohesive, opportunities to make suggestions about student needs, co-plan instruction, try out instruction, and evaluate student progress against jointly set goals created a sense of purpose and achievement not before experienced. This led to even greater collaboration and benefit. One of the kindergarten teachers said, "It just made us so much more cohesive in our working. And in fact, our principal would like us to share what we are doing with other people on our staff."

The natural willingness to review student progress and plan interventions blossomed into a high-energy collaboration focused not only on individual children but on the success of each member of the team. This mutual interest in each other's success created an enjoyment of teaching that some had lost.

Creating Positive Learning Environments

A collaborative PLC can develop best within a positive environment where good working relationships energize the members. DuFour (1998) emphasized, "A school does not become a professional learning community simply by advancing through the steps on a checklist, but rather by touching the wellspring of emotions that lie within the people of that school" (p. 57). Emotional involvement that is controlled and constructive can contribute to developing the positive climate of collaboration that characterizes the PLC.

Every day teachers face a diverse population of students who have a full range of needs and issues. It is natural for teachers to quickly see the deficits—and thus the children who have them—as problems. "I wonder what will go wrong today?" "How did I lose control of my class so quickly?" "Why won't Marcus pay attention when I'm teaching?" (adapted from examples by Whitney, Cooperider,

Trosten-Bloom, & Kaplin, 2005). Research by Cooperider and others has demonstrated that, ironically, focusing on problems may not be the most effective way to solve them.

Vitalizing the school environment by maintaining a learning community that sees teachers and students as people with strengths to build on is a more effective way to develop the "culture of collaboration" and affirm it as an important component of a PLC (Fredrickson, 2003). The model of appreciative inquiry is one way to frame positive professional learning because it builds from strength. Examples of this practice from the SEEL project are used to show it in action.

Contribution of Appreciative Inquiry to Positive Environments

The collaborative culture specified for PLCs is enabled when teachers create an appreciative environment that emphasizes building on strengths by recognizing and valuing the capacities of each participant in a group. Cooperrider and Whitney (n.d.) defined *appreciative* as "recognizing the best in people or the world around us, affirming past and present strengths, successes, and potentials." Then they defined inquiry as "the act of exploration and discovery," including the disposition "to ask questions [,] to be open to seeing new potentials and possibilities" (Cooperrider & Whitney, p. 2).

"What would happen," asked Cooperrider and Whitney (n.d.), "if we began all of our work with the positive presumption—that organizations, as centers of human relatedness, are 'alive' with infinite constructive capacity?" (p. 2). Such a question, an invitation to appreciative inquiry, may inspire a productive reflection on the collective capacity of the PLC. When each teacher in the PLC is valued by the group and the group identifies and magnifies the strengths of its members, the full potential can be focused on facilitating the highest literacy achievement of the students.

Appreciative inquiry maintains that "organizations change fastest and best when their members are excited about where they are going, have a clear plan for moving forward and feel confident about the ability to reach their destination" (Ludema, Whitney, Mohr, & Griffin, 2003, p. 13). Appreciative inquiry motivates individuals through focusing on ways each individual is good and productive instead of on a problem. Problems are not ignored, but they are approached through collective inquiry that seeks strengths to build on as needs are discussed.

Continuous improvement of teaching and learning is a rigorous endeavor that demands openness and communication in the relationships among teachers on the team. A culture of appreciation is the glue that holds the collaboration together. Appreciative inquiry and recognition of the positive aspects of differences are dispositions that guide team members to do the things that contribute to that culture of collaboration.

Appreciative Inquiry in SEEL Collaboration

Within the PLC that was developing from a collaboration between the SEEL and kindergarten teams, appreciative inquiry served to focus team members on positive appreciation for the successes already experienced that provided evidence of strengths to be drawn on. This focus on strengths within the team enabled the team members to take risks such as permitting observations and sharing data from common assessments.

The initial professional development activity requested that teachers respond to this prompt:

> Please think about a time in your teaching career when you felt most alive as a teacher. It could be a time when you put it all together — your strengths, purpose, values, knowledge, and tools — and you achieved exciting results in your classroom. Perhaps it was a time when you found yourself inspired by a student's involvement; or when you felt empowered and skilled to be your most creative self; or when you just knew that your investment of effort was yielding great returns! Please tell me a story about that time. (Jody Jacobsen, personal communication, 2007)

Each participant responded with a story of an influence that drew him or her toward a profession in teaching or of a peak teaching experience. This initiation of a positive "collaborative culture" (DuFour et al., 2006, p. 3) brought the group members together, resolved to engage in professional learning and excited about the possibilities the investment would yield. The goal was to create an environment of mutual respect, sharing, and positive communication where the effort to continuously improve would be enjoyable, hence more likely to continue. The work of the professional educator is difficult but can significantly benefit from sharing successes and building on strengths.

As the SEEL project progressed, specific appreciative processes became regular components of the professional learning community operation. One important process was setting aside planning time for team members to reflect on appreciative questions. Following are some questions that prompted effective discussion:

◆ Think back over the span of your teaching experience and describe a time when you provided the greatest number of opportunities to respond in an intervention with a small group. How could this successful experience inform your current efforts?

◆ Describe a time when you clearly identified the specific strengths of your students and aligned your instruction to those strengths. Tell how planning instruction around strengths increased student engagement and achievement.

◆ As you reflect on your experiences in a highly effective grade level PLC, what were the key elements of success and how could we repeat those today?

◆ As we think back on our collective experience and the information we have on our students' needs, what successes have we achieved that may help with our current student learning needs?

The responses to appreciative questions result in a vision of what could result, a dream outcome as some put it, for student learning as facilitated by teachers energized by the desire to achieve their vision.

Appreciative inquiry helps a group maintain enthusiasm for the shared goal of improving learning for all. As the SEEL team members collaborated to find and solve learning problems, they built on team member and student strengths. For example, three kindergarten students had been underperforming with early reading tasks that had been targeted in instruction. The teachers and other staff had identified methods and time for instruction to resolve the students' learning shortfall and were meeting to discuss the progress of the three children. To create an appreciative environment, the SEEL project director began the session with a comment affirming results achieved by a teacher who had been struggling with how to proceed:

> I am amazed at the difference in those three children from the beginning until now. Isn't it wonderful to see all of the effort you put into small group instruction, reviews during transition time in the classroom, getting parents to help, and involving Title I paraeducators finally pay off? How do you feel about their progress?

The meeting began by celebrating success in solving a problem; group members needed to recognize that success as they moved on to focus on solving additional problems—perhaps involving similar efforts and applications. An appreciative environment is the context for the most effective problem solving. It will help ensure that the work of the team will be more highly engaging and team oriented.

Adjusting and Monitoring Instruction

Another process embedded within and central to the concept of the PLC is joint data-based decision making to strengthen instruction. In addition to drawing up AI processes to strengthen teachers' commitment to engage in joint goal setting and data analysis, PLC members need to monitor instruction and adjust it to provide effective interventions based on assessed needs.

This section describes a process for preventing student failure to learn by conducting classroom screening and monitoring performance. Initial instruction is optimized for all students, and follow-up interventions are designed and implemented to support students with learning needs. The response to intervention (RTI) framework was used by the team members to maintain attention on student results and adjust instruction as required.

The Response to Intervention Framework

RTI suggests that adjusting instruction based on assessment data will ensure that the team implements the requisite nature and intensity of instruction deemed necessary for every student's success. Today's teachers are becoming more aware of the need to continuously monitor student performance data in order to differentiate instruction to solve learning problems and meet individual students' needs (Stanovich & Stanovich, 2003).

RTI is a process for focusing on student results in order to ensure that students who need more personalized or specialized instruction are identified by student assessment and progress monitoring (Walker & Shinn, 2010). Using a tiered system of support, instruction is fit to students' needs, enabling them to be successful. Many effective teachers use the RTI approach to prevent failure to learn by implementing strong classroom instruction (Tier 1 instruction), strengthening interventions designed to meet the needs of individuals (Tier 2 instruction), and providing intense supplemental and personalized intervention for the students with the greatest needs (Tier 3 instruction).

Generally, approximately 80% of students are able to learn from strong evidence-based methods that are taught to all students (Tier 1) (Roth & Troia, 2009). However, most assessment data will show that some students are not progressing as desired (approximately 15%) and could benefit from increased specialization and intensity of instruction along with practice adapted to focus on their individual needs (Tier 2) (Roth & Troia, 2009). When observation and testing reveal that some of these students are *still* unable to achieve learning goals, a highly specialized and individualized intervention is applied, often requiring one-on-one work with the SLP, special education teacher, or other resource personnel (Tier 3) (Roth & Troia, 2009).

In RTI, teachers and SLPs set objectives, design instruction focused on desired results, monitor student progress with curriculum-aligned assessments, and employ effective instructional practices, which include modifying instruction based on student responses to previous instruction (IDEIA, 2004). Research has found RTI to be accessible by teachers for literacy needs: This accessibility means that "early childhood educators can implement it with high fidelity" (Justice, McGinty, Guo, & Moore, 2009, p. 62).

The PLC team collaborates in analyses and solutions on all three levels. A high quality RTI implementation is characterized by selecting students for adjusted instruction based on appropriate and accurate data, implementing effective instruction on all tiers, monitoring student performance consistently to follow progress of all students, altering applications or increasing/decreasing intensity of supports as needed, and making data-based decisions on regrouping students or removing interventions.

Often finding the true cause of a student's learning deficit or unresponsiveness to instruction, as emphasized by Cooper, McWilliams, Boschken, & Pistochini (2000), requires detecting a practice gap between need and intervention. The process of fitting instruction to the specific deficit draws on the multiple perspectives and experiences of team members. The PLC collects and shares observations and data regarding student performance in order to evaluate progress in the quality and effectiveness of instructional interventions.

Implementation of RTI in the SEEL Project

The SEEL project applied the problem-solving process model of RTI to differentiate instruction based on student needs. The PLC meetings focused on student performance reported in teacher observations and assessment data. Students on a Tier 2 level participated in additional small group intervention. Those who were assessed as Tier 3 also received individual instruction from a Title I paraeducator and frequently intervention from a special education teacher. Additional means of increasing intensity involved embedding opportunities to practice targeted skills during non-instructional contexts (snack time, transitions, class routines).

On many occasions the team engaged in an extensive discussion about a student or group of students who had particular needs, considering available instructional resources and determining from their collective knowledge and experience the intervention best suited to the problem. On one occasion the kindergarten teachers, Title I paraeducators, and two SEEL team members came together at one of the two schools to revisit the implementation of the SEEL instruction and its impact on three kindergarten students who were having difficulty making specific letter-sound associations and reading short vowel CVC words. The team reviewed assessment data, identified factors interfering with the students' performance, and shared observations about their interests. They made a plan that embedded additional opportunities to practice targeted skills during transition time, class routines, and centers. Since the students involved had demonstrated particular interest in creative dramatics, the team members arranged for them to practice target skills by engaging in representational play scripts, enacting stories, and participating in theme-based routines that highlighted or focused on a core of targeted CVC words.

The team then carried out the interventions and collected evidence on the effectiveness of their instructional practices. At the end of each set of activities based on classroom themes, the girls demonstrated the ability to read and write words exemplifying the targeted phonic pattern without support in non-instructional contexts and were confident in their responses. The classroom teachers and Title I paraeducators on the team recognized the value of using a variety of practice methods to increase intensity with the literacy targets and basing the types of activities on the students' interests and personalities; all experienced a sense of accomplishment.

While realizing improvement in students' skills, the PLC continued to monitor student performance and adjust the problem identification and problem solving processes. Teachers remained alert to new opportunities to understand problems and to collaborate in solving them. When teachers monitor and measure the results of their instruction (i.e., the ways students are responding to it), they have the data they need to engage in a collaborative discussion of its meaning, to identify problems, and to design solutions to try out (Gamse, Jacob, Horst, Boulay, & Unlu, 2008, p. xiii). Figure 13–2 is a sample form for recording PLC data.

Explaining the benefits of recording the performance data collected by the PLC, one of the teachers reported the following:

> To me the major benefit is about student learning. We really do know what our students know. We know what they are supposed to learn, and we know if they learned it or not. And so I like that change of focus from saying "I taught the lesson" to "What did the children learn?"

While addressing the major benefit of collaborating, this description also reveals the value of adapting intervention based on ongoing assessment, a primary feature of an RTI framework. Without data and without the culture of collaboration to plan differentiated

PLC Agenda	Assessment Data for Instructional Decisions
Team: Date: Facilitator: Recorder:	Team Norms: (reviewed regularly) Be on time Bring student achievement data No texting/email Bring completed assignments

Purpose and Goals for Meeting:
Review progress monitoring data to ensure all students are learning.
Review effectiveness of interventions
Other

Meeting Topics: Examine commons assessment data Examine strengths and weaknesses Review progress of individual students Identify next steps	Desired Outcomes: Understand student strengths and weaknesses Identify student opportunities for improvement Define evidence-based strategies for intervention

Meeting Record (Summary of discussions and decisions)

Actions:	Person(s) Responsible:

Agenda Items for Next Meeting:	Attached Documents:

Date of next meeting:	Date documents to be submitted:

Figure 13–2. PLC agenda form sample.

instruction, there is little hope of effective intervention. One teacher explained:

> A lot of times we'd be scrambling before a report was due. We'd hurry and do all these assessments because we don't really know [where the students were]. I hate to admit to you that we did that. So now we know. I think . . . the greatest benefit is to the student.

The SEEL team observed another benefit that is hinted at in these comments. The teacher says, "I hate to admit to you that we did that," when talking about doing a quick assessment only when scrambling to get a report out. This admission points to a change in culture from compliance, even surface-level compliance, to true professional decision making based on data in a safe and collaborative environment.

Refining Teaching Practices

In addition to collectively making program decisions for individual students, teachers can work together to improve effectiveness of lessons. Collaboration to refine instructional strategies by engaging in collective inquiry improves practice and results in instruction focused on student needs (Dieker & Murawski, 2003). Teachers share ideas and measure the impact of ideas for possible improvements. This section defines two collaborative practices that effectively support mutual sharing of information and feedback for the purpose of improving practice: lesson rehearsal and lesson study. These practices are described and then illustrated by experiences from the SEEL project.

Processes for Practicing and Refining Lessons

Merely describing teaching principles and processes is usually insufficient for teachers to apply them in instruction. Even when a more complete description and a model of application are provided, the gap between the description and the effective implementation can be significant. An athlete, such as a gymnast, must practice in order to develop "muscle memory" to master a sport; similarly a teacher benefits from teaching a planned lesson until what might be called "methods memory" is well established. A teacher with methods memory is competent enough with the lesson to apply it with the flexibility required to meet needs in the "heat" of the teaching moment. She is able to engage in rich and interactive exchanges that demonstrate and provide opportunities to practice using the literacy target. She is also able to generalize and customize the instruction to the responses students are supplying during the lesson. The precision with which a teacher applies the planned intervention is also positively affected by "methods memory." After multiple approximations, teachers acquire confidence in their ability to apply new instructional processes as designed.

Lesson Rehearsal

An effective process for developing "methods memory" for instruction, called lesson rehearsal, includes modeling and role-playing in a workshop or coaching experience in which teachers observe and then practice applying research-based instructional methodologies. Teachers can benefit significantly from rehearsing individual lesson components, according to Grossman and McDonald (2008), using an approach they call "approximations of practice" (p. 190). This method is somewhat comparable to the way other professionals, including physicians, musicians, or attorneys, develop their skills. This process has often been used to set a particular course with preservice teachers, but it can also be effective in collaborations such as this one. The apprentice (practicing professional) rehearses specifics of expected performance in a controlled environment shaped by expert modeling and feedback, a process referred to by Scott and Benko (2010, p. 4) as a "coached rehearsal": "a role play in which the . . . teacher is enacting a lesson that is being watched by peers and the course instructor; the focus of the role play is on rehearsing a lesson and tuning performance so that the lesson is of high quality and well-aligned with the principles of teaching and learning that have been introduced in the course." Similarly, Lewis (2008) mentioned that the purpose of rehearsal is "to test or improve the interaction among several participating people, or to allow technical adjustments to be done" (p. 2). Other benefits have been identified by Scott and Benko (2010): Lesson coached rehearsal helps the teacher put aside traditional modes and challenges her with new approaches and ideas about teaching.

The lesson rehearsal process provides repeated opportunities to practice with feedback, which is just as important in preparing to teach as in learning something new as a student. Lesson rehearsal within a PLC involves inviting an expert in an instructional method to discuss, model, and guide rehearsal of the methods for teachers. Sufficient rehearsal opportunities are given to enable each teacher to develop the methods memory for the new instructional practice. For most PLCs, lesson rehearsal generally involves an experienced teacher presenting a lesson, with participating teachers working together in role plays to approximate the lesson methods.

Lesson Study

Lesson study provides an established framework for collaboration that structures the examination of lesson development and lesson delivery in an authentic instructional context (Fernandez, 2002). It involves two or more teachers planning, trying, observing, recommending improvements, and retrying instruction, emphasizing the effectiveness of the lesson on student learning.

The original lesson study approach was developed in Japan to guide teacher collaboration to improve instruction. This approach has proven to be very useful for perfecting not merely lesson plans, the static representation teachers create before they teach, but instruction, the actions they take as they actually engage the students in the lesson. Teachers work together to plan a "study lesson"—a lesson intended to be improved. Once the professional learning team has refined the plan, one teacher implements the lesson while the others observe ("study") it (Fernandez, 2002). Teachers who observe are looking for the responses of students as they make notes on lesson effectiveness. The lesson plan itself can be more effectively evaluated if the copy given to observers includes a summary of what the teacher is doing, along with anticipated student responses. The more detailed this plan is, the more effectively the impact of the lesson on student learning can be measured.

Lesson study works because it focuses on the response of students. The teacher's specific actions are not being evaluated as much as the quality of the lesson plan she presents. As teachers on the team reflect on the students' responses, they identify ways the plan can be improved and refined to produce higher quality of student responses and learning (Fernandez, 2002).

One of the most significant outcomes of lesson study is the way it increases teachers' understanding and application of differentiated instruction (Hurd & Licciardo-Musson, 2005). An intervention focused on the needs of the students revealed by assessment data needs to be varied and adapted (differentiated) according to needs of groups and individual students. Once the lesson and its methods and strategies are "classroom ready," the PLC members continue to collaboratively plan, observe, and improve lessons in a continuous process.

Experience with Lesson Rehearsal and Lesson Study in the SEEL Project

Lesson rehearsal was used by the SEEL team in their collaborative professional development. The SEEL project team conducted several lesson rehearsals during which they presented new methods and provided feedback for teachers as they practiced or "rehearsed" applications of what they had learned. Practicing instruction in a role playing environment gave the SEEL project team the opportunity to identify improvement and point this out through feedback.

The SEEL project team identified and made visible significant improvements in the application of pedagogical processes outlined in Chapters 1 and 2 (e.g., create playful and varied opportunities to practice, embed instruction into theme-based contexts, acknowledge and elaborate children's contributions to meaning construction). These observations added instances of strengths to draw on in maintaining an appreciative and collaborative professional learning community. Teachers' strengths were identified as they participated in the lesson rehearsal process: stated the purpose of an activity, modeled a lesson, discussed what worked well in the modeled lesson, planned and rehearsed a similar lesson, presented the lesson, and solicited feedback.

In the SEEL project, lesson study was conducted and carried out by the practitioners functioning as equal voices. Building on what the teachers had learned during lesson rehearsal, lesson study processes gave practitioners the chance to "talk shop" as they implemented, observed, and critiqued their own co-created lessons in their own classrooms with their own students (Table 13–1).

Table 13–1. A Description of a Lesson Study Sequence

Step	Example from the SEEL-kindergarten PLC
Plan: Make decisions with input from teaching partners.	Members jointly brainstormed lesson ideas: • Learning expectations: read and write -*at* words; blend words at the onset-rime and phoneme levels • Introduction: tell a memory about a hat; read *Aunt Flossie's Hats* (Howard, 1991); ask about a special hat or about something that children might have experience while wearing one • Opportunities to engage and practice: read and write signs, labels, and sentence strips during and after making paper hats; set up a hat store; try hats on bats, cats, and rats; enact a story about a bat, cat and rat who sat on a witch's hat; read and write about the witch's hat story and the hat store routine
Teach: Obtain information from the first implementation.	One member taught the lesson while the others observed and noted the students' responses and reactions.
Discuss: Identify how the students responded, and revise the lesson.	Team members (a) observed children's success in reading and blending -*at* words and their opportunities to respond and need for support; (b) created a follow-up target text based on acting out the witch's hat script: "A fat black bat landed on a hat. Then came a fat black cat. He jumped up on the black hat, next to the bat. A big rat jumped up. He sat by the cat and the bat on the hat. "SCAT!" said the witch to the rat, the cat, and the bat. "Get off my hat! SPLAT! "Oh, Drat!," said the witch. "Look at that!" My big, black hat is flat!"
Teach again: Observe students' responses and reactions to the revised lesson.	Another teacher presented the revised lesson with team members observing (e.g., increased support for specific child; all children given a chance to read cue cards; children engaged while making name cards for the bat, rat and cat, along with sentence strips to read while enacting the witch's hat story).
Implement subsequent iterations: Further develop the lesson.	The team further revised and tested the lesson, identifying additional reasons for having the children write and blend words at the phoneme level, and deciding to follow up by combining -*ap* with -*at* as children could make and sell caps and hats, and finding ways to arrange for children to create new -*ap* and -*at* words by changing initial and final consonants.

The example in Table 13–1 illustrates basic steps the SEEL kindergarten practitioners used to employ lesson study. The group was planning and studying a lesson on -*ip* family words, based on *Sheep on a Ship* by Nancy Shaw (1989).

Although analysis and perfection of lessons following the process depicted in the table could go on almost indefinitely, teachers encounter a continuous flow of student needs and thus must adopt a standard of "good enough" that allows them to go on to develop additional lessons based on data they are collecting. "Good enough" can mean two things. First, the lesson studied by the PLC should produce learning sufficient to achieve its goal, overcoming the assessed learning deficits. Second, the lesson as taught enables the group to discover or rediscover methods for improving "first instruction" for the whole class in the future. Even though further perfection of the lesson is still possible, it is generally advisable to apply the process to improvement of additional lessons. While lesson study is most often thought of as a process for use by traditional classroom teachers, it can also be applied to the work of other staff as they study instruction for small groups.

Figure 13–3 summarizes the Lesson Study framework. The lesson is planned by the team, taught by an individual, analyzed/critiqued and revised by the team, then made ready for implementation by the whole team. Lesson rehearsal and lesson study each bring a structure for collaborating to learn instructional methods and improve the effectiveness of instruction. One of the teachers described lesson study in this way:

> [Lesson study] is about our learning. So [the children] are learning; we're learning. And we're learning how, you know, how to do this better. I've never done anything like this in all the time that I've taught. I've been, in fact we were talking today at our collaboration, observed by other teachers. [The principal] has given us released time; I've gone and watched other teachers, but we've never had a thing where we watched someone critique the lesson, turned around and taught it immediately.

The teacher went on to say that this is very different from professional development efforts in the past. "I think that is very profound in that what we usually would say [in our past experiences] would be, 'Well that didn't go very well, so we'll do better the next time.' And then so when's the next time? The next time is the next year!"

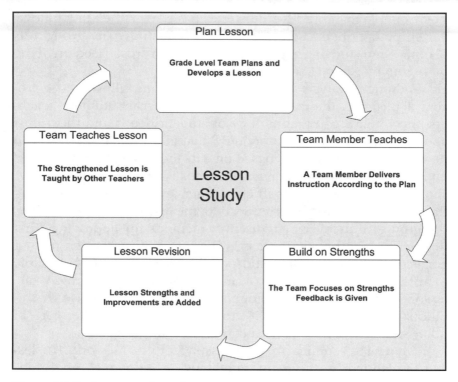

Figure 13–3. Lesson study cycle.

Analyzing student progress data and making decisions about interventions is at the core of the work of a PLC. Once an intervention is indicated by the data, the school-based kindergarten team is committed to ensure that the children learn. But the learning can be ensured only when evidence-based teaching practices are employed and measured. This is the very work of lesson study: to study and improve the teaching practices with the goal of continuous improvement of student learning success.

Conclusion

The experience of the SEEL project demonstrated to the authors that the guiding principles of a PLC—supported by careful application of the processes of appreciative inquiry, response to intervention, and lesson rehearsal/lesson study—can result in a culture of professional collaboration in which the needs of students are identified and met. These processes interact within the framework of the professional learning community, supplying its necessary substance and development (Figure 13–4).

"Billions of dollars have been spent on education reform in the past decade and a half with results in literacy and math, at best, inching forward" (Fullan, Hill, & Crévola, 2006, p. 15). The purpose of this chapter has been to provide an overview of ways educators can engage with each other in professional development practices that have the potential to move literacy, math, and other important curricular areas forward more effectively than an inch at a time.

In the spirit of appreciative inquiry, the authors conclude with a question: "What have you done as a teacher that was successful

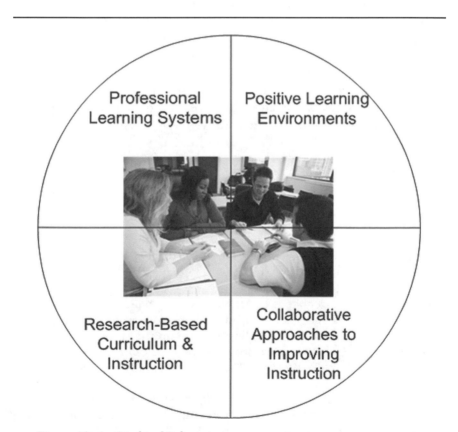

Figure 13–4. Circle of Balance.

enough that you could give yourself an *A*?" Benjamin Zander, in *The Art of Possibility*, suggests that we should give ourselves an *A* before the end of the "course" and then write out a narrative for how we earned our *A* (Zander & Zander, 2000). The narrative becomes a prediction, and the prediction is a vision. We end this chapter with the first step: a vision with a goal. Giving yourself an *A* and then defining how you earned it may include applying some of the principles in this chapter. Those who read this chapter thoughtfully and consider these principles deserve an *A*.

Synthesizing research on collaboration into an operating combination of tools means personalizing and applying through discussing, trying out, and evaluating. The principles have been implemented effectively by researchers and practitioners, and teachers can trust the research and experience on which they are based.

We invite early childhood teachers and SLPs to discover for themselves how the work life of a teacher can be much more enjoyable and effective when everyone works well together under the research-based practices defined here. This chapter does not intend to prescribe the use of these resources in detail, nor does it provide training in their implementation. The intent is to invite collaborating team members to consider these resources and to incorporate the principles if, when, and how they may choose.

References

Bauer, K. L., Iyer, S. N., Boon, R. T., & Fore, C., III. (2010). 20 Ways for classroom teachers to collaborate with speech-language pathologists. *Intervention in School and Clinic*, *45*(5), 333–337. doi:10.1177/1053451208328833 http://www.teacherdrivenchange.org/teacherdrivenchange/positive _deviance_pd_/

Cooper, David J., Boschken, I., McWilliams, J., & Pistochini, L. (2000). A study of the effectiveness of an intervention program designed to accelerated reading for struggling readers in the upper grades. In T. Shanahan & F. V. Rodriquez-Brown (Eds.), *National reading conference yearbook, 2000*, *49* (pp. 477–486). Chicago, IL: National Reading Conference.

Cooperrider, D. L., & Whitney, D. A. (n.d.). *Positive revolution in change: Appreciative inquiry*. Retrieved from http://appreciativeinquiry.case .edu/practice/toolsPackDetail.cfm?coid=2159

Culatta, B., & Kovarsky, D. (2004). U.S. Office of Education, Model Demonstration Grant Final Progress Report. *Project call: Contextualized approach to language and literacy instruction.* Grant Award Number: H32M990066.

Danielson, L. M. (2009). Fostering reflection. *Educational Leadership, 66*(5). Retrieved from http://www.ascd.org/publications/educational-leadership/feb09/vol66/num05/Fostering-Reflection.aspx

DuFour, R. (1998, Spring). Learning communities: You won't find this on any checklist. *Journal of Staff Development, 19*(2), 57–58.

DuFour, R. (2004). What is a "professional learning community"? *Educational Leadership, 61*(8), 6–11.

DuFour, R., DuFour, R., Eaker, R., & Many, T. (2006) *Learning by doing: A handbook for professional learning communities at work.* Bloomington, IN: Solution Tree.

DuFour, R., & Eaker, R. (1998). *Professional learning communities at work.* Bloomington, IN: Solution Tree.

Dieker, L. A., & Murawski, W. W. (2003). Co-teaching at the secondary level: Unique issues, current trends, and suggestions for success. *High School Journal, 86*(4), 1–13.

Eaker, R., DuFour, R., & Burnette, R. (2002). *Getting started: Recruiting schools to become professional learning communities.* Bloomington, IN: National Education Service.

Easton, L. B. (2008). From professional development to professional learning. *Phi Delta Kappan, 89*(10), 755–759.

Fernandez, C. (2002, November-December). Learning from Japanese approaches to professional development. *Journal of Teacher Education, 53*(5), 393–405.

Fredrickson, B. L. (2003). Positive emotions and upward spirals in organizations. In K. Cameron, J. Dutton, & R. Quinn (Eds.), *Positive organizational scholarship: Foundations of a new discipline* (pp. 163–175). San Francisco, CA: Berrett-Kohler.

Fullan, M. (2006). Leading professional learning. *School Administrator, 10*(63). Retrieved from http://www.aasa.org/SchoolAdministrator Article.aspx?id=7620

Fullan, M. (2007). Change the terms for teacher learning. *Journal of Staff Development, 28*(3), 35–36.

Fullan, M., Hill, P., & Crévola, C. (2006). *Breakthrough.* Thousand Oaks, CA: Corwin Press.

Gamse, B. C., Jacob, R. T., Horst, M., Boulay, B., & Unlu, F. (2008). *Reading First Impact Study final report* (NCEE 2009-4038). Washington, DC: U.S. Department of Education, Institute of Education Sciences, National Center for Education Evaluation and Regional Assistance.

Grossman, P., & McDonald, M. (2008, March). Back to the future: Directions for research in teaching and teacher education. *American Educational Research Journal, 45*(1), 184–205.

Hurd, J., & Licciardo-Musson, L. (2005). Lesson study: Teacher-led professional development in literacy instruction. *Language Arts, 82*(5), 388–395.

Jacobsen, J. (2007). Appreciative activity provided in a personal communication.

Justice, L. M., McGinty, A., Guo, Y., & Moore, D. (2009). Implementation of responsiveness to intervention in early education settings. *Seminars in Speech and Language, 30*(2), 59–74.

Lewis, J. M. (2009, April). *Lesson study and the test of practice.* Paper presented at the annual conference of the American Educational Research Association, San Diego, CA.

Ludema, J. D., Whitney, D., Mohr, B. J., & Griffin, T. J. (2003). *The appreciative inquiry summit.* San Francisco, CA: Berrett-Koehler.

Pfeffer, J., & Sutton, R. I. (2000). *The knowing-doing gap: How smart companies turn knowledge into action.* Cambridge, MA Harvard Business School Press.

Roth, F. P., & Troia, G. A. (2009). Applications of responsiveness to intervention and the speech-language pathologist in elementary school settings. *Seminars in Speech and Language, 30*(2), 75–89. doi:10.1055/s-0029-1215716

Scott, S. E. (2008). *Rehearsing for ambitious instruction in the university classroom: A case study of a literacy methods course.* Paper presented at American Educational Research Association Annual Meeting, March 24–28, 2008, New York, NY. Presented in symposium: The role of rehearsal in learning to do ambitious practice.

Scott, S. E., & Benko, S. (2010). *Coached rehearsals in preservice teacher education: What's coachable?* Paper presented at the annual meeting of the American Educational Research Association, Denver, CO.

Shaw, N. (1989). *Sheep on a ship.* New York, NY: Houghton Mifflin.

Snow, C. E., Burns, M. S., & Griffin, P. (Eds.). (1998). *Preventing reading difficulties in young children.* Washington, DC: National Academy Press.

Speck, M., & Knipe, C. (2001). *Professional development in our schools: Why can't we get it right?* Thousand Oaks, CA: Corwin Press.

Stanovich, P. J., & Stanovich, K. E. (2003). *Using research and reason in education: How teachers can use scientifically based research to make curricular and instructional decisions.* U.S. Department of Education, National Institute of Child Health and Human Development, National Institute for Literacy. Retrieved from http://www.nifl.gov/partnershipforreading/publications/html/stanovich/

Stein, M. K., Smith, M. S., & Silver, E. A. (1999, Fall). The development of professional developers: Learning to assist teachers in new settings in new ways. *Harvard Educational Review, 69*(3), 237–270.

Walker, H. M., & Shinn, M. R. (2010). Systemic, evidence-based approaches for promoting positive student outcomes within a multitier framework: Moving from efficacy to effectiveness. In H. M. Shinn & M. R. Walker (Eds.), *Interventions for achievement and behavior problems in a three-tier model including RTI* (pp. 1–26). Bethesda, MD: National Association of School Psychologists.

Wei, R. C., Darling-Hammond, L., Andree, A., Richardson, N., & Orphanos, S. (2009). *Professional learning in the learning profession: A status report on teacher development in the United States and abroad.* Dallas, TX: National Staff Development Council.

Zander, R. S., & Zander, B. (2000). *The art of possibility.* Boston, MA: Harvard Business School Press.

Chapter 14

Applying Systematic and Engaging Practices: Planning Units and Lesson Activities

Kendra M. Hall-Kenyon and Barbara Culatta

This chapter brings many of the literacy components in this book together to illustrate how teachers and SLPs can plan systematic and engaging early literacy activities as units and lessons to be implemented in multiple contexts throughout the day. It will include a brief discussion of key considerations in planning instruction for young children, illustrated by a sample unit plan, a lesson plan, and additional ideas for implementing instruction in different contexts (large group, small group, transitions, snack, etc.). As the considerations are described, they will be applied to the specific unit, lesson, and activities. The considerations are consistent with the underlying principles and practices of the Systematic and Engaging Early Literacy program (SEEL), and the plans are among those applied in this program. Thus additional resources and can be found on the SEEL website: www.education.byu.edu/seel.

Unit Planning

When planning a unit, teachers and SLPs must choose the skills to be taught, decide on relevant unit themes and texts to create meaningful experiences, and select the classroom contexts to be used throughout the day to ensure that children receive adequate exposure and practice with the target skills. Developing a unit is a fluid and complex process that involves a number of considerations and decision-making steps. The process of development works best when teachers, SLPs, and other members of the grade-level team collaboratively plan units as they consider the unique needs of the children in their classrooms. The following sections represent some of the major decisions that the instructor(s) must make, even though sequences will vary and not all decisions can be represented. A sample of the *Taking a Trip* unit, partially described in the sections below, is included in chart form at the end of the chapter, along with a sample lesson plan from the unit.

Identify Scope and Sequence of Skills

When planning a unit, teachers and SLPs must select the skills to be taught, based on the children's needs and developmental levels. Instruction that systematically builds in a developmental progression from simpler foundational skills to more complex skills is often thought to be the most effective way to teach early literacy (Justice, Mashburn, Hamre, & Piante, 2008; National Reading Panel, 2000).

Several early literacy curricula provide teachers with methods for systematically teaching both code-based and meaning-based components, including the Systematic and Engaging Early Literacy (SEEL) project curriculum, which can be found on the SEEL website. Teachers and SLPs might begin with these curricula and adjust them as necessary to meet children's individual needs and/or to fit district and program specifications. Using established curricula as guidelines can prevent haphazard sequencing and enhance purposeful and intentional decisions regarding which skills to teach and when to teach them.

When making decisions about what skills to teach and when to teach them, the teacher and SLP should also carefully consider how the skills build upon one another and can be combined in meaningful ways around a particular theme. For example, near the end of the year, a SEEL kindergarten teacher may choose to introduce the digraph *sh*. Introducing the short i (/ĭ/) is another aspect of the curriculum typically targeted at the same time of year, and taking these at the same time would enable her to include the *-ish* rime ending, increasing the number of words the students would be able to read and write. Adding the *-ip* rime ending would also reinforce the /ĭ/ and add even more words to the repertoire she could use for the unit. The teacher may then decide, based on these targets, that she will conduct this unit under the engaging theme of taking a trip. This theme will allow her to emphasize words like *ship*, *trip*, *flip*, *dip*, and *rip*, as well as words with the *-ish* rime ending (e.g., *wish* and *fish*). This teacher and her collaborating SLP may also want to consider initial sounds and rime endings that need to be reviewed. Table 14–1 lists additional objectives and target words that might be selected as part of the unit plan.

No matter how the curriculum is devised, teachers and SLPs must work together and include special educators, paraprofessionals, and other school personnel to ensure that a child receives consistent support and feedback across service delivery contexts (e.g., regular classroom instruction, supplemental instruction, pull-out interventions, tutoring). Thus, all members of the instructional team need to communicate with one another to ensure that they understand how each member of the team is addressing the student's needs, and when possible make sure that similar concepts and content are being taught and reviewed. This consistency does not require that all members of the team do the exact same thing or address the same target skills. Instead, all members of the team should combine their strengths and perceptions to collaboratively select basic objectives to introduce and review. In this way the team can ensure that students are receiving sufficient opportunities to review targets that have not yet been mastered as well as appropriate exposure to and repeated practice with new targets. These objectives should allow each member of the instructional team to work within his or her area of expertise and responsibility but with consistency in the overall support of class and individual student needs.

For example, the teacher who was planning the unit on taking a trip might meet with her instructional team to discuss goals for the students. She would explain that she wanted to attach the sound to the letter digraph *sh*, identify the /*sh*/ sound at the beginning and

Table 14–1. The Ship Trip Unit Sample Goals and Targets

Goals	Example Targets
Read, write, and spell simple CVC -ip words	Tip, dip, sip, rip, ship
Identify and read -ip in words with blends and less common onsets	Trip (noun and verb), skip, drip, flip, strip, zip, slip, grip, lip
	(adult reads onsets and the children read the rime ending (e.g., -ip)
Read and write simple -ish words	Dish, fish
Identify and read the ending in other -ish words	Wish, squish, swish
Blend onset + rime into words and then blend the individual phonemes into words	-ip words: tip, dip, sip, rip, ship; and -ish words dish, fish, wish
Segment CVC words into onset and rime and into phonemes	tip, dip, sip, rip, ship (tip = t-ip or t-i-p); ship, fish, dish (fish = f-ish or f-i-s-h)
Attach sound to the letter digraph sh	sh
Review words that end in -ack	pack, back, pack, backpack, snack, shack, black, tack, track, clack, rack, sack, smack, stack, crack
Read previously introduced -ap words in new contexts (e.g., incorporate -ap with -ack)	map, nap, cap (put on a cap and a backpack; follow a map; get to a shack and take a nap)
Identify sh sound in beginning and ending of words	shack, ship, sheep, hush, shush (be quiet noise), wish, dish, fish
Identify or state the vowel heard in CVC words	Tap vs. tip; trip vs. trap; zip vs. zap; slip vs. slap; click vs. clack
Sort words according to the vowel	pick vs. pack; stick vs. stack; sick vs. sack; quick vs. quack; tick vs. tack; click vs. clack
Analyze words	*Slip* without /l/ is *sip*; *slip* without /s/ is *lip*

ending of words, and read and write simple -*ish* words. The SLP might then comment on the teacher's ideas and offer suggestions for extending the instruction in small group sessions with children needing extra support. She might also share her observation that some of the students were still uncertain with the -*ack* and -*ap* endings, which had been taught earlier. The teacher would then note that revisiting these endings would increase the number of words that could be read in conjunction with the unit (e.g., *track, sack, pack, map*). The paraeducator might mention that she had noticed hesitation over the letter-sound associations for the letters *b, s, t,* and *m* while playing a review game with children at one of the stations. Together they would probably agree that the paraeducator could combine these letters with the -*ack* and -*ap* endings to form *back, sack, map,* and *tap*—words that would be useful in reading and writing about trips. In this way, the three members of the instructional team can work collaboratively to meet the varied needs of the students. Chapter 13, which focuses on professional development, suggests some specific structures and procedures involved with such collaboration.

Select Meaningful Themes and Texts

When systematic and explicit instruction has been planned, teachers and SLPs must find texts and contexts that are engaging for the students. Lesson content and objectives are learned more effectively if embedded into "relevant and engaging content or themes related to children's prior knowledge" (Culatta & Hall, 2006, p. 187). Themes should also connect to core curricular content from social studies, science, art, health, and/or math. Common themes include taking care of animals, going places, dressing to go outside, doing things in summertime, and using and playing in water (Blank & White, 1992; Dickinson, McCabe, & Clark-Chiarelli, 2004; Neuman, Copple, & Bredekamp, 2000; Rand, 1993).

    Within unit themes, teachers and SLPs should purposefully select texts that involve children in reading and writing experiences during their unit of study. For example, during the *Taking a Trip* unit, teachers may choose to incorporate Nancy Shaw's book *Sheep on a Ship* (1989). This book offers some vivid images, with particular emphasis on two *sh*-words, and it can be dramatically told and enacted to support children's comprehension.

The story of *Sheep on a Ship* (Shaw, 1989) is about sheep on a ship taking a trip. During their trip, they run into a terrible storm. The "winds whip" and the "sails rip." The storm gets so bad that the sheep "abandon ship" and use a raft to get to land. The story is written in rhyme, although the teacher can dramatically tell the story either in or out of rhyme using simple props (e.g., a ship made from a cardboard box with a fabric sail made from scraps, a small chest to represent the treasure, a map, a spray bottle to lightly spray as rain during the storm, a small handheld fan to create wind.). The teacher tells the story emphasizing the main events of the story, which are the problems that the sheep have while on their ship trip.

The teacher or SLP can also teach vocabulary words while telling the story. For example, during the dramatic telling of the ship trip, the teacher can use the props to show the children what a *sail* is or use actions to differentiate the meaning between *trip* and *slip*. (The sheep slip and trip when the ship is tossed around in the storm.) The teacher may also choose to explain a word such as *abandon*, as the sheep abandon the ship to a raft when the storm gets too strong. A quick child-friendly definition would be sufficient: "*Abandon* means to leave something. The sheep got off the ship and left it in the middle of the sea because they were in danger."

After the children have experienced the story in a large group, the props that are appropriate for children to play with independently are made available for children during small group center time. As the children manipulate the props, they have opportunities to tell and retell the story. The teacher and SLP continue to support children's comprehension as they engage in smaller group enactments with children. As the children become more and more familiar with the story, the teacher or SLP lessens her involvement and releases more control to the students. At the beginning of the week the adult may perform the role of *storyteller* (Saracho, 2002), retelling the main events of the story as the children act them out. By the middle to end of the week, the children use the props to act out the story independently, with little or no adult participation. Some stories can be told, retold, and enacted multiple times throughout an entire week, but others are only revisited for a few days. Children's comprehension is enhanced as they listen to the story and then tell and retell the story events through their enactments. The teacher and SLP can support comprehension by revisiting story events or by slipping important vocabulary words in with the children's explanations of the story events. See Chapter 8, which focuses on narrative comprehension, for more information and examples of enactments and story co-construction.

Additional books can also be blended into the unit for a variety of purposes. For example, in the *Taking a Trip* unit, books about fish are included as part of what the sheep experience on their ship trip (e.g., the sheep see shiny, shimmery fish in the ocean or the sheep count the fish that they see on their trip). *Rainbow Fish* (Pfister, 1992), with its emphasis on glittering fish scales, is included in the unit to generate art projects emphasizing *shine, sheen, shake, shower* and possibly even *shimmer* (for initial sound emphasis). The shared visual-creative experience might be extended into an interactive writing activity in which children co-create a text with the teacher or SLP. As the teacher or SLP writes their words, she can emphasize the target *sh* digraph. Another book, *Fish Eyes: A Book You Can Count On* (Ehlert, 1990) also furnishes interesting images and adds a counting theme that can generate some games in which children's knowledge of numbers is involved with the sounds they are learning. After reading this book the children engage in an activity where they wish for a particular number of fish and see if the fish will fit in their dish ("How many fish do you wish to put in your dish? [Cups cut from an egg carton can be used as 'dishes.'] Will those fish all fit in your dish? How many fish will fit in your dish? Can you squish one more in? So now how many fish do you have in your dish?") These additions allow the teacher to teach another short *i* word ending (-*ish*), revisit the *sh* digraph, as well as introduce new content as part of the unit.

The examples in this section are given only to illustrate decision factors. All choices must support the needs of the children and the purposes of the adults. These decisions are critical in helping the planners determine how skills can be used together in meaningful ways. Once the unit is conceived and materials are selected and sequenced, planning of individual lessons is the next concern.

Lesson Planning

When planning individual lessons the teacher and SLP must determine the lesson objective, ensure that instruction is explicit, and provide for playful practice of the target skill. This process requires attention to many of the same decisions described above in the unit planning section. However, when planning individual lessons these things are done on a tighter, more specific level.

Determine Lesson Objective

Planning a lesson, like planning the overall unit, begins with the objective or instructional goal. If the lesson is part of a unit, the objective will make a contribution within the unit scope and sequence. However, the objective can come directly from the curriculum if a unit is not involved. Lesson objectives can be written in a number of ways, but each needs to express a result that is measurable. Typically instructors want to avoid using general terms such as *know* or *understand*, as children have innumerable and unidentifiable ways of knowing and understanding. In contrast, words such as *identify, recall, generate, sort,* or *describe* are more specific, as they are things an instructor can watch children do.

For example, lesson activities for the SEEL unit on taking a trip may include objectives such as "Students will name and write upper- and lowercase *t* and associate the letter with its sound" or "Students will read and write words that end in *-ack* and read a prepared text focused on *-ack* words." Such statements of objectives keep the instructor(s) focused while working out the plan; and announcement of the objective keeps the students focused while the lesson is being carried out.

Ensure That Instruction Is Explicit

Research suggests that children of all ages benefit greatly from explicit instruction, but it is particularly important for those who struggle with early literacy skills (Ehri, Nunes, Willows, Schuster, Yaghoub-Zadeh, & Shannahan, 2001; Elbro & Peterson, 2004). Explicit instruction typically has a predictable sequence that clearly describes and models the target skill, with high levels of exposure to it to ensure student learning. Three specific steps are often identified (Adams, 1990, 2001; Torgesen, Al Otaiba, & Grek, 2005). First, the target goal or objective is clearly stated. Second, the teacher models the target skill and gives children opportunities to practice. Finally, the skill is reviewed or extended to other contexts for additional practice. Explicit instruction is intense as well as predictable; children encounter the target skill multiple times and in a variety of ways as the teacher or SLP emphasizes and repeats it throughout the activity.

Goal or Objective

In a lesson designed to review the *-ack* rime ending, the teacher or SLP might catch the children's attention by reading the book *I Saw an Ant on the Railroad Track* by Joshua Prince (2006), then introduce the skill and objective something like this:

> We are going to pack for our trip. We are going to pack things that end in *-ack* in our black backpack. The letters *a-c-k* make *ă-k*; the *c* makes the /*k*/ sound and the *k* makes the /*k*/ sound so *ck* together make one /*k*/ sound. You can hear *-ack* in *pack* and *snack* and *track*. Only things that end with the ack sound can go in our backpack.

Thus, the children know what they are going to learn and how they are going to learn it. There is no uncertainty with explicit instruction.

Modeling and Practice

As the teacher has announced, the class packs a black backpack with things that end with *-ack*. The students take turns selecting a picture or object from a container and pronouncing its name carefully; then the teacher or SLP asks the class, "Does _____ go in our backpack?" Items that end with *-ack* are put in the pack, and items that do not are put in a bin. So correct responses and the process for making them are modeled over many examples in the guise of a game. The children then pack their backpack with a snack, a track, something black, a tack, etc., with the teacher making comments to reinforce the sound: "Jenni, did you pack a snack in your backpack?" "Should we pack something black in our pack?" "We can write the letters *a-c-k* on our pack because everything in our pack ends with *-ack*."

Many suggest that repeated practice is helpful for students when learning early literacy skills. We agree, but would add that teachers and SLPs should consider "playful practice" as critical to any lesson (Bingham, Hall-Kenyon, & Culatta, 2010). This notion of playful practice is intended to help those planning lessons consider the importance of engagement. Often practicing and re-practicing skills can be boring and mundane. *Engagement* has been referred to as the active component of positive learning, which "includes attention, persistence, flexibility, self-regulation" (Hyson, 2008; see also Ponitz, Rimm-Kaufman, Grimm, & Curby, 2009). Active engagement allows children to associate literacy with success and fun (Neuman, 2006); Verhoeven and Snow (2001) assert that engagement occurs "only if joy is part of the experience" (p. 4). Teachers need to remember to make practice playful and interesting through the use of engaging children's literature, hands-on activities, playful use of language, representational play and high levels of energy.

Children become engaged when playfulness and enjoyment can be emphasized. For example, if the teacher cuts the back off the snack pack so that the snack pack lacks a back, the snacks will fall out of the pack, and the children can rush to gather them up. Or the SLP may play with words and sounds: perhaps sharing a snack that goes crack (e.g., a pretzel) or introducing a puppet named Jack who snacks on *-ack* words. Fortunately an infinite number of ways can be found to make practice playful, because playfulness may be one of the most critical components of a successful lesson.

Review and Extension

Students recall a lesson more specifically if it is concluded with a brief review that ties all loose ends together. After packing the backpack, the class can go back through the items, renaming each so the teacher and children can create a list on the board or on chart paper by a shared writing or interactive writing process. As the group reads the list together, students can take turns underlining the *-ack* rime ending in each word. Depending on the age and skill level of the students, the teacher or SLP can either highlight the *-ack* rime ending as a chunk or have the students read and write the word with emphasis on each individual phoneme. If further review is needed, students can label a blackline drawing of a backpack with each of the *-ack* objects they included, using the list on the board to "spell" the words.

An additional sample lesson plan, Get the Fish Into the Dish, which further illustrates these lesson planning strategies, is shown in Figure 14–1.

Lesson Plan: Get the Fish Into the Dish

Goal: Students will read and write words that end in *-ish* (e.g., *fish*) and texts that focus on *-ish* words.

Target Words: fish, dish, wish, swish, squish

Statement of Objective:
Do any of you have a fish? I have a fish (show students a toy fish or a fish cracker), and I also have a dish (show students a dish). I am going to put the fish in the dish. We are going to play a game called, "Get the Fish in the Dish." The words *fish* and *dish* rhyme. They both end with *-ish*. While we play our game we are going to read and write words that rhyme with *fish*.

Modeling and Playful Practice
- Teach students the chant: "Wish! Wish! I wish I could get a fish in the dish!"
- Have students take turns tossing a toy or cardstock fish into a dish. At the beginning of each turn, the child reads the sentence, "I wish for a fish" before they try to get their fish in the dish.
- If students get the fish in the dish, they say, "The fish is in the dish!"
- Hand out goldfish crackers in small plastic bowls; let the students swish and squish the fish in the dish.

Figure 14–1. Sample lesson plan. *continues*

Ways to Emphasize and Repeat the Target Throughout the Activity:

Comment on Actions and Objects
  "You got the fish into the dish!"
  "Here's a fish to swish in your dish"

Offer Choices and Turns
  "It's your turn to toss the fish into the dish."
  "Are you going to swish or squish the fish in your dish?"

Ask Questions
  "Do you wish for the fish to go into the dish?"
  "Did you take the fish cracker out of the dish and squish it in your mouth?"

Make Playful Statements
  "Make a wish! Get the fish into the dish!"
  "Watch out! The fish will be squished if it gets out of the dish!"

Acknowledge Students' Responses
  "Yes! Fish do like to swish!"
  "That's right! We don't squish real fish. We only squish pretend fish."

Request Actions
  "Toss the fish into the dish."
  "Show me how you swish the fish in the dish."

Read and/or Write About the Playful Experience:

- Have a student say a word ending with *-ish*. Write the word on the board and then ask another student to change the first letter(s) to make a new word. Write the new word below the first word. Continue this pattern until a number of *-ish* words have been created.

- Using the word blending cards, hold up a beginning consonant with the *-ish* ending. Ask students to read the word.

- Read the *Wish for a Dish* target text with the students.

  Wish for a Dish
  Wish for a dish,
  "I wish I had a dish."
  Wish for a fish,
  "I wish I had a fish."
  Here is a dish, and here is a fish.
  Swish your fish in the dish.
  Squish your fish in the dish.
  Swish and squish the fish in the dish.

- Read the target text again and have students clap every time they see or hear an *-ish* word.

- Have students write instructions for how to play the game.

Figure 14–1. *continued*

Planning within Multiple Instructional Contexts

With the unit outlined and specific lessons taking shape, teachers and SLPs should strategically plan to implement instruction in a variety of contexts throughout the day so children will have frequent opportunities to practice skills they are learning. In addition to activities conducted in large- and small-group instructional sessions, targets can be reinforced and practiced during free play, centers, classroom routines, and transitions (Gillon, 2004; McGee & Richgels, 2000).

Large Group

During large-group sessions, the teacher or SLP "introduces themes, provides motivational experiences, and introduces and teaches skills. Typically, the teacher introduces books tied to the curricular theme and comments on the story, demonstrates story elements, manipulates materials, and provides children with occasional turns" (Culatta & Hall, 2006, p. 188).

For example, in the unit on taking a trip the class as a group enjoyed listening to *Sheep on a Ship*, discussing what went wrong on the trip. The next whole group meeting used movement to introduce, model, and practice reading target words: "Skip to the ship; don't trip; don't slip. The ship can tip, flip, and go zip when it goes fast." Following the movement activity, a teacher-made decodable text based on this shared experience was read by the children with the necessary support.

Let's go on a ship trip.

Skip to the ship

Don't slip.

Don't trip.

The ship zips.

Zip, ship!

The ship tips.

The ship tips and flips.

The ship dips.

Dips down.

The ship drips.

Drip, drip, drip!

Additional large group activities can be found in Table 14–2, which gives the activities planned for all contexts during the first week of the unit.

Small Group

In contrast, the small group context, being more intense and individualized than large group situations, permits SLPs or teachers to differentiate instruction and to provide supplemental opportunities for children with language delays, differences, or deficits to acquire literacy skills (Foorman & Torgesen, 2001; Justice & Kaderavek, 2004; Kaderavek & Justice, 2004). Small group activities provide opportunities for all children to practice or revisit skills and for children who are struggling with a particular skill or concept to relearn and practice with additional SLP or teacher instruction/support (Foorman & Torgesen, 2001; Kaderavek & Rabidoux, 2004; Kaderavek & Justice, 2004).

Hands-on experiences provide effective reinforcement for children. During the ship trip unit, a small group of children needing more practice reading words with the *-ip* rime ending made paper ships and created signs that could be used to tell the ships to *tip, dip, zip, skip,* and *flip*. As the children created and read their signs, the SLP placed emphasis on the *-ip* rime ending. She also had the children listen carefully for each phoneme (*t-i-p*) in order to stress phonemic awareness, but she could have stressed the ending as a chunk (*-ip*) if the rime ending had been her objective. The students then took turns holding up their signs to signal the other children on how to move their paper ships. Additional small group activities are included in Table 14–2.

Table 14–2. Going on a Ship Trip: Weekly Plan Targeting *-ip*, *-ish*, and *sh*

	Monday	Tuesday	Wednesday	Thursday
Begin or end of day	Ask if any of the children came to school on a ship. Talk about different ways to travel. Tell the children about taking a pretend ship trip.	Introduce the sign "Ship Trip" (where a pretend ship trip will start) and announce that the children will take a ship trip. Read an announcement: Today we will take a ship trip. The ship will tip, dip, and zip.	Have a stuffed sheep be asleep on a rug with a big *sh* sign. Explain that the sheep is sleeping so the sign makes the *sh* sound to tell us to shush and be quiet.	Pass out a dish for each child to take home and a paper fish; tell them they can let the fish go swish in the dish.
Whole group	Read and dramatize *Sheep on a Ship*; talk about what really happens on a ship trip; ask what went wrong on the sheep's trip; ask if sheep can really take a ship trip by themselves.	Take a ship trip using movement and chants. ("Skip to the ship, tip toe, don't trip, and don't slip getting on the ship, tip toe; the ship can tip and flip and go zip.") Dictate an account about the ship trip.	Explain that if you were on a ship trip you might wish you would see some fish. Tell or read the book *Rainbow Fish*.	Explain that a ship trip isn't the only way to get from place to place; you can take a train. (Pretend to take a train to a *sh* shack and find things that start with the *sh* sound along the way.)

Note: Some activities are repeated across contexts with variation.

continues

457

Table 14–2. *continued*

	Monday	*Tuesday*	*Wednesday*	*Thursday*
Whole group	Read about getting ready for a ship trip: Get map, pack snack, get hat, pack back pack.	Read text: Go on a ship trip. Skip to the ship. Don't slip. Zip, ship! The ship zips. The ship tips. The ship tips and flips. The ship dips. Dips down. The ship drips. Drip. Drip. Drip!	Read about the tip and drip activities (making -ip art or ways to drink using -ip words: grip a strip of paper; clip the end to make a tip or rip a tip; clip the tip with a paper clip; dip and drip	Students sit in a circle and pretend to be fish that squish into a small space inside the fish bowl (circle). "One fish, two fish, three fish, four fish. Five fish, six fish, Try to squish, fish. Too many fish in my dish!" Children then read the text.
Small group	Enact *Sheep on a Ship* with props (e.g., spray bottle to make rain, box for the ship, map).	Pack *sh* things the sheep can take on the ship (shovel, shoe, shirt, shaver, shake [milk shake]).	Make paper ships; make the ships do things; read signs—tip, dip, zip, skip, and slip—and let the ship or children carry out the actions.	Children prepare the *sh* store where they label items with the *sh* (e.g., shoes, shells, shirt, shaving cream, paper ship, etc.); continue to associate the sound with the digraph.
Centers	Make dip and drip art. (Snip the tip of a straw, dip the tip, drip the paint or water to make a picture.)	Put props for *Sheep on a Ship* in dramatic play corner; guide the enactment of the sheep's ship trip.	Make a paper ship to tip, dip, drip, go on a trip; what did the ship do? It got to tip, dip, drip, go zip, and flip.	Drip drops of water in a cup with a straw, tip and drip, dip and drip, sip a drip; tip and sip; dip and drip water on paper lips.

	Monday	Tuesday	Wednesday	Thursday
Snack	Show various *-ip* ways to drink; clip a tip of a straw; snip a straw to make it smaller, tip a cup, drip water from a pitcher to a cup, etc.	Go to the table with the *sh*; highlight the words *shed* and *shack*; pretend to have snack in a shack or shed; pretend to eat on a ship or in a shed or shack; put out a sign that says *ship*, *shack*, or *shed*.	Wish for a fish in a dish (fish cracker); let the fish swish in the dish; squish the fish (cracker) to eat it.	Serve chips in paper ships. Drip water in a cup using a straw; highlight and "read" the words *sip*, *tip* and *drip*.
Transitions & routines	Hold up words that say *skip*, *slip*, *trip*. Children can skip, but not trip or slip. Pretend to slip, trip, or skip from place to place. (Read the words to know how to move.)	Let each child read the word *tip* in a sign saying "tip, tip, tip toe" so they can tip toe from one center to another; read *slip*, *skip*, *trip* to let the child decide which way to move.	Make paper drips of water for the ship to follow, blending words as the children walk. (Say "dr" with left foot on drip and "ip" on right foot drip.)	Blend words to decide how to move (tr-i-p or sk-i-p).
Art	Drip water on watercolors and salt; shake on salt; drip on paint, drip on water; dip paper in water, drip on paint.	What might the sheep eat when they go on their ship trip? Or when they get back from the ship trip? (Make an "*ip*" pizza with strips of pepper or cheese [paper or real]; rip strips of cheese and pepper [paper]).	Make ship (small paper ships or large ship out of a box); make a ship out of cardboard (group project); make small ship by folding paper and decorating.	

Nontraditional Instruction Opportunities

An SLP or teacher can integrate practice opportunities that most classroom personnel do not recognize: classroom routines that are typically considered "noninstructional" (Culatta & Hall, 2006) because they involve taking care of necessities rather than presenting developed lessons. During snack time a little imagination and some construction paper or newsprint can create a "snack shack," a shed, or even a ship (of sorts). Fish crackers can swish in a dish before being squished or eaten by the children (as they wish).

Transitions are going to require movement, so the children can enjoy responding to *-ip* movement signs—*skip, slip, dip,* or *trip* as they cross the floor to a new instructional site or move toward the doorway to line up for lunch (one table at a time, of course). If there is a center with a bowl or basin, students can experiment with various ways of dipping, tipping, and dripping water, with some teacher-composed decodable texts to describe what they are doing (exemplified in Figure 14–2). At the beginning of the day, a "Ship Trip" sign over the classroom doorway or a large plush sleeping *sheep* with a "Shhhh" sign can make a good phonetic conversation starter. (See Table 14–2 for additional activities for noninstructional times.)

Once a number of activities have been selected or brainstormed, the team decides which to use and where in the schedule to place them. Although most activities throughout the week fit the theme, not every activity has to do so. Table 14–2 provides a sample week schedule for the unit on taking a trip. It should also be noted that the nature and complexity of the skills increase as the week progresses. For example, at the beginning of the week children encounter rime endings as chunks; by the end of the week they blend and analyze words into phonemes, identify different vowels heard in short *a* and short *i* word endings (e.g., *-ack* and *-ip* words), and spell and write words at the phoneme level.

Conclusion

Planning, at both the unit and lesson levels, is a complex process that requires a number of important decisions and considerations.

Tip, Drip, and Sip

Experiment with drips and drops (drip and drop from tip of pen, from tip of straw, from eye dropper; count the drops—explore different ways to drip drops.

Engage in shared reading about tipping, dipping, dripping, and sipping:

Tip and drip.
Drip and drop.
Sip.
Drip and drop.
Tip and drip.

Tip, Drip, and Drop

Let paint or water drip in drops into a bowl or onto paper; dip paper clip into paint while holding string.

Clip a strip of paper.
Rip the tip off the strip.
Dip the tip in paint.
Let the paint drip off the strip.
Now dip your finger tip in paint.
Let the paint drip off the tip.

Drip Water From a Straw

Take a straw and snip.
Snip the tip.
Snip. Snip.
Tip a cup of water.
Tip. Tip.
Dip the straw in water.
Dip. Dip.

Figure 14–2. Teacher-created texts to use at a center where water or other liquid is used to experiment with drips and drops.

However, in every case the goal is to provide children with frequent opportunities for exposure to target skills in many varied, engaging, and noticeable ways. In order to meet this goal, teachers and SLPs must begin with a systematic curriculum (scope and sequence of skills) and then make plans to teach each target skill within engaging themes in varied contexts throughout the day. Teachers and SLPs must also carefully construct individual lesson plans that incorporate both explicit teaching strategies and opportunities for playful practice. All children benefit from the kind of instruction that results from this thoughtful planning process, but it is perhaps most important for those children who typically struggle. In sum, teachers who carefully plan each unit and lesson find unique opportunities to make connections among target skills and to systematically visit and revisit goals and objectives in multiple contexts to ensure success for all children.

References

Adams, M. (2001). Alphabetic anxiety and explicit, systematic phonics instruction: A cognitive science perspective. In S. B. Neuman & D. K. Dickinson (Eds.), *Handbook of early literacy research* (pp. 66–80). New York, NY: Guilford Press.

Adams, M. J. (1990). *Beginning to read: Thinking and learning about print*. Cambridge, MA: MIT Press.

Bingham, G. E., Hall-Kenyon, K. M., & Culatta, B. (2010). Systematic and engaging early literacy: Examining the effects of paraeducator implemented early literacy instruction. *Communication Disorders Quarterly*, *32*(1), 38–49.

Blank, M., & White, S. (1992). A model for effective classroom discourse: Predicated topics with reduced verbal memory demands. *Australian Journal of Special Education, 16,* 23–39.

Culatta, B., & Hall, K. M. (2006). Phonological awareness instruction in early childhood settings. In L. M. Justice (Ed.), *Clinical approaches to emergent literacy intervention* (pp. 170–224). San Diego, CA: Plural.

Dickinson, D. K., McCabe, A., & Clark-Chiarelli, N. (2004). Preschool-based prevention of reading disability. In C. A. Stone, E. R. Silliman, B. J. Ehren, & K. Apel (Eds.), *Handbook of language and literacy: Development and disorders* (pp. 209–227). New York, NY: Guilford Press.

Ehri, L. C., Nunes, S. R., Willows, D. M., Schuster, B. V., Yaghoub-Zadeh, Z., & Shanahan, T. (2001). Phonemic awareness instruction helps children learn to read: Evidence from the National Reading Panel's meta-analysis. *Reading Research Quarterly, 36,* 250–287.

Ehlert, L. (1990). *Fish eyes: A book you can count on.* New York, NY: Voyager Books.

Elbro, C., & Petersen, D. (2004). Long-term effects of phoneme awareness and letter sound training: An intervention study with children at risk for dyslexia. *Journal of Educational Psychology, 96*(4), 660–670.

Foorman, B. R., & Torgesen, J. K. (2001). Critical elements of classroom and small-group instruction promote reading success in all children. *Learning Disabilities Research and Practice, 16*(4), 203–212.

Gillon, G. T. (2004). *Phonological awareness: From research to practice.* New York, NY: Guilford Press.

Hyson, M. (2008). *Enthusiastic and engaged learners: Approaches to learning in the early childhood classroom.* New York, NY: Teachers College Press.

Justice, L. M., & Kaderavek, J. N. (2004). Embedded-explicit emergent literacy intervention I: Background and description of approach. *Language, Speech, and Hearing Services in Schools, 35,* 201–211.

Justice, L., Mashburn, A. J., Hamre, B. K., & Piante, R. C. (2008). Quality of language and literacy instruction in preschool classrooms serving at-risk pupils. *Early Childhood Research Quarterly, 23,* 51–86.

Kaderavek, J., & Rabidoux, P. (2004). Interactive to independent literacy: A model for designing literacy goals for children with atypical communication. *Reading and Writing Quarterly, 20*(3), 237–260.

Kaderavek, J. N., & Justice, L. M. (2004). Embedded-explicit emergent literacy Intervention II: Goal selection and implementation in the early childhood classroom. *Language, Speech, and Hearing Services in Schools, 35,* 212–228.

McGee, L. M., & Richgels, D. J. (2000). *Literacy's beginnings: Supporting young readers and writers* (3rd ed.). Needham Heights, MA: Allyn & Bacon.

National Reading Panel. (2000). *Put reading first: Kindergarten through Grade 3.* Retrieved from www.nichd.nih.gov/publications/nrp/upload/report.pdf

Neuman, S., Copple, C., & Bredekamp, S. (2000). *Learning to read and write.* Washington, DC: National Association for Education of Young Children.

Neuman, S. B. (2006). N is for nonsensical. *Educational Leadership, 64*(2), 28–32.

Pfister, M. (1992). *Rainbow fish.* New York, NY: North-South Books.

Ponitz, C. C., Rimm-Kaufman, S. E., Grimm, K. J., & Curby, T. W. (2009). Kindergarten classroom quality, behavioral engagement, and reading achievement. *School Psychology Review, 38*(1), 102–120.

Prince, J. (2006). *I saw an ant on the railroad track.* New York, NY: Sterling.

Rand, M. (1993). Using thematic instruction to organize an integrated language arts classroom. In L. M. Morrow, J. K. Smith, & L. C. Wilkinson (Eds.), *Integrated language arts: Controversy to consensus* (pp. 177–192). Boston, MA: Allyn & Bacon.

Saracho, O. N. (2002). Teachers' roles in promoting literacy in the context of play, *Early Child Development and Care, 172*(1), 23–34.

Shaw, N. (1989). *Sheep on a ship.* Boston, MA: Houghton Mifflin.

Torgesen, J. K., Al Otaiba, S. A., & Grek, M. L. (2005). Assessment and instruction for phonemic awareness and word recognition skills. In H. W. Catts & A. G. Kamhi (Eds.), *Language and reading disabilities* (pp. 127–156). Boston, MA: Pearson Education.

Verhoeven, L., & Snow, C. E. (2001). Literacy and motivation: Bridging cognitive and sociocultural viewpoints. In L. Verhoeven & C. E. Snow (Eds.), *Literacy and motivation: Reading engagement in individuals and groups* (pp. 1–20). Mahwah, NJ: Lawrence Erlbaum Associates.

Index

Note: Page numbers in **bold** reference non-text material.